THIRD EDITION

The Tiger Guide to Writing

Chattanooga State Community College

Richard Bullock
WRIGHT STATE UNIVERSITY

Michal Brody
SAN FRANCISCO STATE UNIVERSITY

Francine Weinberg

WRITE

RESEARCH

EDIT

NORTON
CUSTOM

THIS HANDBOOK has been published for students at
Chattanooga State Community College. It's a custom
version of *The Little Seagull Handbook.*

Chattanooga State Community College

The Tiger Guide to Writing

As student writers at Chattanooga State, resources are available to assist you in developing your critical thinking and writing skills. These resources are student-centered and are designed to allow maximum flexibility in your ability to access them. Many of these resources are listed below.

Humanities and Fine Arts Division

Mission Statement. The mission of the Chattanooga State Humanities and Fine Arts Division is to guide students in expanding their knowledge and understanding of the world around them and in developing the oral, written, and performance skills necessary to articulate that expanded world view, thereby equipping them to function as better students in an academic community and as better citizens in the global community.

Donald F. Andrews College Reading and Writing Center

Whether you are having trouble getting started on an assignment or have a complete draft ready for review, the professionals at the Andrews Reading and Writing Center are happy to help with ANY written assignment for ANY class.

Though we can't wave a magic wand over your essay to make it perfect, consistent writing feedback *can* have pretty magical effects. We encourage writers to visit the center early (do not wait until the day a paper is due) and often (to build writing skills and confidence over time). We are happy to help with grammar and punctuation; however, to encourage long-term skills-building and student independence, we do not edit assignments.

Appointments made in advance are strongly encouraged. You may reserve a 30-minute session by calling **423-697-2410** during business hours, or stop in **IMC 215**. We would love to meet you!

We WILL . . .

- create and maintain a supportive, constructive environment
- help you at any stage of the writing process: planning, drafting, or revising
- discuss assignment requirements and any concerns you have about them
- help you focus on the most important aspects of an assignment
- help you identify and resolve major sentence-level errors
- provide strategies for long-term reading and writing success

We WON'T . . .

- criticize your work or writing skills
- correct sentence-level errors for you
- compose sentences or drafts
- choose your topics or subject matter
- discuss or predict grades

Course Connections

The writing courses at Chattanooga State follow a learning path designed to develop each writer in both his or her ability to analyze other written works and to compose his or her own written work in a variety of genres. Students enter the writing program at various levels of preparedness; thus, the courses are designed to allow students to engage at the level at which they are most comfortable while enabling them to develop skills toward the next level.

Literature Survey Courses

These courses explore literary works within their historical and cultural contexts while examining trends in writing and thinking as well as the continuing influence of these literary works on contemporary society.

ENGL 1020 (Composition II)

This intermediate composition course focuses on close reading of literary texts and on writing literary analyses (the application of writing to the interpretation of literary texts.)

ENGL 1010 (Composition I)

This beginning composition course teaches students the logical organization of essays using supporting evidence in language that reflects the students' professional rather than personal voices.

ENGL 0810 Lab

For students who need extra practice, the Writing Lab course focuses on writing process and teaching students to formulate essays based on personal experience.

CHATT-1 Outlining

OUTLINING is a tool. When outlining only the body of an essay instead of writing every word, it is easier to find and fix problems in the flow and support of ideas. Even though the reader never sees the outline, it serves as the framework for an essay and helps the writer organize his or her thoughts with the essay's AUDIENCE in mind.

In outlining, we use symbols to delineate one idea from another:

- Roman numerals (I, II, III, IV) – indicate the main points of the essay
- Upper case letters (A, B, C, D) – indicate ideas that support the main point by dividing the main point into "pieces" and include evidence that will be used to support that point
- Arabic numerals (1, 2, 3, 4) – indicate sub-points of each main point that are crucial to audience understanding (if necessary)

More information about outlines can be found on pages 56–7.

The way we use these symbols "outlines" the relationship of ideas. Because these symbols subdivide ideas, if you have a "I," you must have a "II." If you have an "A," you must have a "B," etc. The Roman numerals, letters, and numbers used are dependent upon the organization of each essay. Note the sample of the general outline structure of an essay below:

Introduction
    Thesis statement:

Body
    I.
        A.
        B.
    II.
        A.
        B.
            1.
            2.

III.

    A.

        1.

        2.

Conclusion

    Summary

Following is an outline sample from an actual student essay:

Introduction

    Thesis: Values and ethics are declining in America due to Americans' increased acceptance of ethical relativism, and this acceptance causes a lack of respect for authority, a lack of regard for others, and a lack of adherence to a moral code.

Body

I.   A lack of respect for authority through the acceptance of ethical relativism is lowering our ethical standard.

    A. A lack of respect is being seen in the classroom, in the workplace, and throughout society.

    B. As noted by author Mary Arguelles in her essay, "Money for Morality," "[a]s a society, we seem to be losing a grip on our internal control—the ethical thermostat that guides our actions and feelings toward ourselves, others and the world around us" (51).

II.   There has been a decline in regard for others since our nation left its intimate rural roots and has moved toward a depersonalized urban society.

    A. Authors and researchers John M. Darley and Bibb Latane in their essay, "Why People Don't Help in a Crisis," share that "[t]he megalopolis in which we live makes closeness difficult and leads to the alienation of the individual from the group" (45).

    B. A lack of regard for others is being seen throughout our society.

1. This disregard is illustrated when people rationalize that it is not their ethical responsibility to help someone in a crisis.
2. Due to ethical relativism, people have moved away from their former values.

III. Ethical relativism has changed people's desire to adhere to a moral code.
   A. With more people steering their moral guidance ships with ethical relativism, we are drifting away from any standard of right and wrong.
   B. People are determining their own moral codes individually instead of adhering to a moral code that benefits all of society.

Conclusion

Summary: Children and adults are susceptible to this acute epidemic of ethical relativism, and sadly, it is causing a decline of ethics in this nation.

CHATT-2 Library Resources

Thinking about Research. As the internet expands, so does the information it provides. This makes research increasingly complicated and complex. We live in a digital age where people can view and share information with the click of a button, in fractions of a second, but have you ever thought about where that information comes from and how it gets shared? Do you check to see if the information you find is true, relevant, current, real, accurate, reliable, valid, biased, or informed? Do you know how to do that? When you do research, are you really getting the information you want, and maybe more importantly, are you getting the information you need?

It is all too easy to find information that is outdated, misuses facts, lacks an author, quotes out of context, contains extreme bias, or turns out to be advertising or satire. Additionally worrisome is how this kind of misinformation can get shared millions of times and even become accepted by the general public as "fact." We should all be concerned with how to find and use information and whether the information available to us is accurate. You need information literacy skills to help find sources and to determine if your research is reliable.

Developing Information Literacy. Information literacy is the ability to know when there is a need for information, and to identify, locate, evaluate, and effectively and responsibly use and share that information for the problem at hand. These are essential skills for students when doing research for academic purposes and in their daily lives. Our ability to conduct research effectively directly relates to how information literate we are.

Kolwyck Library & Information Commons. The Kolwyck Library & Information Commons (KLIC) is one of the best places on campus to hone your information literacy skills. The library is your greatest resource for research and technology help. The services and spaces provided by KLIC are offered to help you succeed at Chattanooga State.

On Campus. KLIC is located in IMC-126. This recently renovated space is a great place to collaborate, study on your own, use technology, or even hang out between classes. You will find many resources to assist you:

- Librarians available to help you with research during all hours the library is open. You can even schedule a research consultation for help: http://libguides.chattanoogastate.edu/rad

- Multimedia study rooms that can be reserved for group collaboration.

- More than 110 computers, including both Macs and PCs.

- Options for printing, copying, scanning, and faxing.

- WiFi access, comfortable seating, and plenty of outlets for using laptops and tablets.

- A wide variety of books and DVDs available for students to check out using their Chattanooga State student IDs.

- Textbooks on reserve that can be used in the library.

Online. Library resources and assistance are accessible from anywhere, at any time, through the library's website: http://library .chattanoogastate.edu

On the library's website, you will discover additional resources:

- Research help through library chat and Frequently Asked Questions.

- 24/7 access to more than one hundred library databases containing articles, ebooks, images, audio clips, and videos. Use your TigerID and password to access online resources off campus.

- Research guides and tutorials to help you navigate the research process and find information.

Please use the "Research" section of The Tiger Guide to Writing to further assist you as you develop your information literacy skills here at Chattanooga State. More information about academic research can be found on pages 90–105.

CHATT-3 Integrating Sources

Many instructors teach students to use SIGNAL PHRASES as a method of introducing sources. In fact, some instructors require a specific set up for any QUOTE, PARAPHRASE, or SUMMARY that you write.

Some of the requirements for the use of sources may be:

- Using "active verbs" in your signal phrases like those listed in the "Signal Verbs" section on page 113
- Preventing the use of passive verbs like *is, are, were,* etc.
- Establishing author's credibility the first time you reference him/her

Additional suggestions to consider:

- Some instructors refer to the signal phrase as the "context" for your source or may use other terminology, so make note of those changes.
- Keep in mind you do not have to continue to use the author's name in your writing; in fact, sometimes your writing is more sophisticated without a signal phrase.
- When writing about literature, make sure you differentiate between the author and speaker/narrator of the literary piece.
- Some professors will encourage you to avoid paraphrasing because the length is often prohibitive in essay writing. Most often, summary is better suited to the PURPOSE and AUDIENCE of your assignments.
- Use quoted material to support the points you make within your essay; however, do not quote excessively as this can weaken the overall voice of the essay.

More information about quoting sources can be found on pages 108–110.

Some sample signal phrases. *For English 1010 from Benjamin Barber's work, "America Skips School":*

Example 1:

Political scientist Benjamin Barber argues American schools are failing because people "pretend [they] care" about education reform (114).

Example 2:

Some critics remember that the purpose of an education is to "teach men to be free" (Barber 120).

Example 3:

Barber* claims today's students are not stupid or incapable of learning, but are instead culturally literate which society values over true literacy (115-116).

*The reason Barber's full name is not given here is that it is an example of a second reference to Barber and the assumption is that he has already been introduced in a previous signal phrase. Some instructors will have a writer use the full signal phrase each time the source is named.

For English 1020 from Nathaniel Hawthorne's work, "Young Goodman Brown":

Example 1:

Hawthorne's narrator explains, "Whether Faith obeyed, he knew not" (255).

Example 2:

"Lo! There ye stand, my children" (Hawthorne 254).

Example 3:

Hawthorne calls Brown's wife "Faith" with particular intent (245).

CHATT-4 Understanding Plagiarism

Plagiarism means using another person's words or ideas without giving proper credit; it is a form of stealing and intellectual dishonesty. Whether intentional or accidental, plagiarism is a serious academic and professional offense, with equally serious consequences. Students must practice distinguishing between their own ideas and those they have found from other sources.

More information about avoiding plagiarism can be found on pages 107–8.

Examples of Plagiarism

Even if you choose to paraphrase a source but include your own words alongside those of the original author, without giving credit to the author it is still plagiarism. Review the example below:

Original: Shakespeare's enduring relevance to modern audiences is in part due to his writing about life as he knew it. He tackled big subjects such as the morality of Elizabethan England, the constant threat of plague, the balance of power and mercy, political unrest, and the heartache of death. While we may not think we have much in common with late sixteenth-century England, the universal themes of human experience, loss, jealousy, fear, love, joy, and many more, irrefutably connect us across both time and place. Shakespeare's plays still give rise to a multitude of insights into our modern lives.

Plagiarism: Shakespeare's enduring relevance to those who live 400 years after his death is because he tackled big issues that still means something to us today. We can all readily understand political unrest and the heartache of death, which is why his works will continue to give rise to a multitude of insights for generations to come.

Further, when using the ideas of source's work but completely changing the language of the original text, you still must give proper credit to that author in order to avoid plagiarism:

Original: During a summer holiday in Geneva, Switzerland, Mary Shelley was inspired to write her famous novel *Frankenstein*. In such literary company as her husband Percy Bysshe Shelley and Lord Byron, it is no wonder that the small group of traveling companions challenged each other to a contest of writing ghost stories. Drawing from the dreary weather, the stark and lonely landscape, and more than a little inspiration from the nightly readings of German horror stories and other works, Shelley crafted an iconic and haunting tale of man's desire for power that must be balanced with love and understanding.

Plagiarism: Mary Shelley's *Frankenstein* is a well-known novel that has made its way into American pop culture through movie adaptations and as inspiration to other works. While the work is purely of Shelley's creation, it would likely not have come into being if it were not for the influence of her husband, Percy Bysshe Shelley, and good friend Lord Byron.

When is it not plagiarism?

Some information can be used in your writing without citing its source. There are two types of such information:

Common expressions: Well-known sayings, including clichés and proverbs, that have no identifiable, original source. Examples such as "absence makes the heart grow fonder," and "think outside the box" are common expressions that don't require source citations.

Common Knowledge: Information that is widely known or can be found in a variety of sources. Facts, such as kangaroos are marsupials, and that George Washington was America's first president, are so well known that there is no need to find a source that provides that information.

In any case, if you are concerned that you may plagiarize information, always utilize the Turnitin plagiarism detector *before* submitting your work. You may also check with your professor or a Writing Center tutor for further help as well.

CHATT-5 Turnitin

Overview. Turnitin.com (or "Turnitin") is a web-based company known primarily for its plagiarism detection software. In fact, Turnitin provides users with three distinct services: (1) it enables teachers to grade student work online, (2) it facilitates peer review between students, and (3) it helps both teachers and students identify where writing assignments contain borrowed language from other sources.

Since most instructors who use Turnitin do so in order to scan papers for plagiarism, the focus of this section is to acquaint students with how teachers use the "originality report" software and with how students can use it themselves to avoid or correct plagiarism in their own writing. Students who are interested in learning more about peer review and online grading with Turnitin can visit http://turnitin.com/en_us/features/overview or consult with their professor.

Plagiarism Detection. At Chattanooga State, Turnitin is used in conjunction with the eLearn dropbox. Since many instructors who use Turnitin do so in order to scan papers for plagiarism, it is important for students to be familiar with how teachers use the software. Furthermore, students can also learn to use Turnitin themselves to avoid or correct plagiarism in their own writing.

The most popular service Turnitin provides to teachers and students is often referred to as "plagiarism detection." In fact, the "Match Overview" part of Turnitin helps users *identify* plagiarism, but it does not provide any explicit judgment as to whether a piece of writing is or is not plagiarized. While the software highlights portions of the written document that match other sources in the Turnitin database, it is up to the instructor (or the individual) to assess whether those highlighted passages are properly documented (quoted and cited) or not.

When Turnitin is enabled through the dropbox in eLearn, one of the first images users will encounter is a small, color-coded rectangular box which includes a numerical percentage (see Figure 1). Students can find this box by clicking on the "view" icon associated with their assignment feedback in eLearn. The percentage listed in the box reflects the amount of writing in the document that is an identical match with outside sources catalogued in the Turnitin

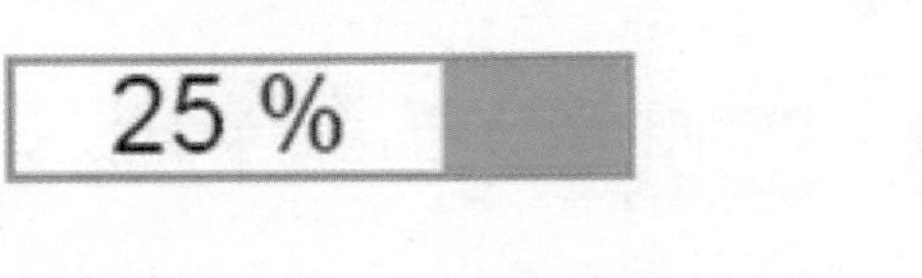

Turnitin Similarity

25 %

Figure 1: The similarity index generated by Turnitin.

database. (These sources include online sources, print books, and other student papers.) In other words, a result of 25%, for example, indicates that twenty-five percent of the content in the paper is not the student's own words.

Instructors may provide individual guidelines as to what percentage of borrowed language is within acceptable range for any given assignment, but Turnitin also automatically color codes the scores according to its own standard (as seen in Figure 1). A paper with a 99% originality index, for example, is coded red. If students are in doubt as to whether their similarity index is too high (or too low), they should ask for their instructor's guidance.

In order to access the full match breakdown, users simply click inside the colored portion of the rectangle and are redirected to the Turnitin website. Students will be able to review their own highlighted writing assignments, if the instructor enables this option in eLearn. Once the full report is opened, users see a match overview on the right-hand side (see Figure 2), which corresponds to the highlighted portions of text in the document.

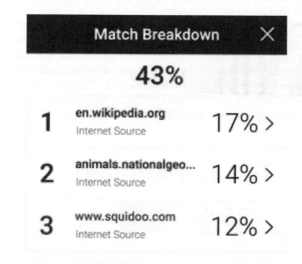

Figure 2: A color-coded list of sources that contain content matching the submitted paper.

By consulting the highlighted passages users can see where in the essay content overlaps with each of the listed sources in the match overview, and by reviewing the percentage provided, users can see how much content has been borrowed. Additionally, clicking on the number above the highlighted passage in the assignment itself reveals a pop-up box with the matching content as it appears in the outside source. The outside source can be accessed by clicking on the "full source view" icon in the pop-up or by following the link provided in the match overview.

Using Turnitin to Avoid Plagiarism. To help students use the Turnitin software for their own benefit, the following recommendations are offered:

Consult the instructor. As soon as possible, become familiar with his or her policies and expectations regarding Turnitin. Will all written assignments be scanned by Turnitin software? Has the student view been enabled? Are multiple submissions of the same assignment accepted? What is the desired percentage range on the originality report? Additionally, if the student has questions or concerns at any stage in the revision process, the student and the instructor can consult the Turnitin report together.

Submit early. If the instructor does allow multiple submissions, complete and submit the assignment before the deadline. Take time to review the originality report and check that all highlighted passages in the assignment are enclosed in quotation marks and attributed to their original sources. If paraphrases (ideas from outside sources rephrased in the student's own words) contain highlighting, they may need to be revised so that they are not too close to the original author's wording. Finally, ensure that the originality index percentage is within the instructor's recommended range.

Revise and Resubmit. If the assignment requires revision based on the preceding criteria, do not hesitate to resubmit it—multiple times if necessary. If the originality index is too high, cut down or omit some of the borrowed language and consult the originality index again on the resubmitted document. If passages matching outside sources need quotation marks or if paraphrases need rewording to avoid plagiarism after revising and resubmitting, use the highlighting in the originality report to ensure all necessary changes have been made.

CHATT-6 Peer Review

Peer review is the process of reading and offering feedback on another's written work. Professional writers, academics, and researchers all engage in peer review before their work is published. Peer reviewers serve as crucial partners in producing thoughtful and credible texts, whether in a college course or one's professional field.

Sharing one's work with others can be vulnerable and uncomfortable at times. However, the role of the peer reviewer is not to evaluate or judge, but rather to help ensure a writer's ideas are clearly expressed and strongly supported.

Peer review helps writers

- Develop an awareness of audience.
- Thoughtfully engage the work of peers.
- Identify potential problem areas in others' work as well as their own.
- Practice close, careful reading.
- Accept and evaluate constructive criticism.

In order to best participate in peer review, students should come to class with fully developed drafts, or fully developed portions of a draft (such as an introduction, or a body paragraph), depending on the assignment and instructor specifications. During peer review, readers are often asked to distinguish between higher order concerns and lower order concerns.

Higher order concerns are "big picture" issues that relate to the essay's ideas and contribute to the logic, strength, and organization of an argument.

Lower order concerns are often considered the "details," supporting the clarity of ideas through grammar, sentence structure, and vocabulary.

During the peer review process, priority is typically placed on higher order concerns. Clear grammar and mechanics are important, but their primary purpose is to support strong content.

Questions about higher order concerns:

- Does the essay fulfill the basic requirements of the assignment prompt?
- Can the writer's claim be summarized in a single sentence? Look for a clear THESIS statement.
- Do ideas flow logically into one another?
- Does each body paragraph include adequate EVIDENCE and support, or are more details needed?
- If sources are used, are these quotations smoothly integrated into the writer's sentences? Are they relevant?

Questions about lower order concerns:

- Are there repeated and distracting proofreading errors? Common and jolting issues include sentence fragments, run-on sentences, and comma splices.
- Does the vocabulary reflect an academic, professional tone?
- Are TRANSITION words and phrases used appropriately?

The Rules of Peer Review

Instructors have many ways to engage students in Peer Review. The one guiding principle is that the reader should focus on using critical thinking skills and providing strong critique that goes beyond basic descriptors of "good" or "bad."

The Tools of Peer Review

With this in mind, here are some helpful tools for students to use while doing a formal (in-class) or informal (out-of-class) peer review.

- **Close Reading** – One should never review a peer's writing without reading the piece in its entirety first. After one's initial viewing, the writing should be read more closely with a focus on the higher order or lower order concerns of the peer review.

- **Comments** – Whether comments are placed directly in the essay using Track Changes or the comment feature in Microsoft Word's Review tab, or on a worksheet provided by the instructor, there are certain guidelines they should follow:

  - **Comments should always guide the writer in ways that he or she can strengthen the essay**. Never offer a comment without suggestions for revision.

  - **Strengths should be pointed out as much as weaknesses**. Showing the writer where he or she engaged the reader or where the organization of the essay is strong will give him or her a guide to revise the rest of the work.

  - **Comments should never rely on a verbal discussion**. Always remember that the reader might not be around when the writer moves into revision. A discussion of the work is helpful, but strong comments are needed for the writer to make connections between written and verbal critique.

- **Highlighting** – Many times using multiple colors to break up the paper under review can be helpful for the reader and the writer. This can be done on the computer with the Highlight tool in most word processor programs or on a hard copy with colored pens.

The key is to make sure both the reader and the writer understand what each color represents. This can be set by an instructor or by mutual consent.

- **Higher order highlights** – When reading an essay for higher order concerns, one might highlight what he or she believes is the thesis of the work in one color, the claims (or topic sentences) of a work in another, the source incorporation (signal phrases, quotes, paraphrases, and citations) in a third, and so on to show the writer how the organization of his or her essay is interpreted by the reader.

- **Lower order highlights** – When reading an essay for lower order concerns, one might highlight certain grammar problems, sentence structure concerns, and misplaced vocabulary in different colors to alert the writer to the presence of these errors.

- **When using commenting tools** that are built into word processor programs, be sure to save your final document as a PDF. Students use many different programs, and many of the systems are not compatible with documents saved in Microsoft Word.

- **Reading out loud** – Strong peer review can be achieved by the writer listening to a reviewer reading his or her essay out loud and following along with his or her own copy. Here are things to listen for in this reading:

  - **Pauses** in sentences or places in the essay where the writing should flow from one idea to the next are indications of the reader dealing with a higher or lower order concern.

  - **Tricky vocabulary** can be revealed when the reader stumbles over a sentence or phrase.

  - **Structure problems** can be heard in the way that readers start and end paragraphs. Listening for the repetition of key words within the reading and taking note of where they fall in the structure can alert the writer to problems in organization.

Technology can be employed in the process of peer review to enhance both the reader's and the writer's experience. Reading the essay out loud into a cell phone and sending the mp3 file to the writer can provide him or her with a revision tool that he or she can listen to on multiple occasions. Recording a computer-based peer review in a screen and voice capture website or program can provide a walk-through of a writer's text that offers him or her distinct insight into the process of close reading and the reviewer's thought process as he or she progresses through the steps of review.

Sample Peer Review

Elizabeth Lavenza has been asked to write an essay about the benefits of her future career for her Composition class. Below is the **introduction** and first **body** paragraph of that essay. The peer review that her instructor has asked for guides the reviewer to focus primarily on **higher order concerns** and uses highlights to mark certain sections:

- The thesis should be marked in blue.
- The claims should be marked in green.
- Evidence should be marked in purple.
- Any sentence-level or grammar problem (lower order concern) should be marked in yellow.

Sample Peer Review:

Lavenza 1

Elizabeth Lavenza

Dr. Pretorius

ENGL 1010

21 Oct. 2014

The "Write" Job

All you ever hear about nowadays is the lack of jobs and the likelihood of college graduates starting a career or even simply getting a good, stable job. With unemployment so high, and with it constantly rising, one must be sure and certain with how they decide what job to pursue. When thinking about one's future and what to do for the rest of their life, one should seriously consider editing as a profession. Out of the numerous reason to get into the editing field, a few important ones are that it will always be relevant, there is a freedom of creativity and power, it is on the cutting edge of things, and the salary and special perks are very enticing.

One of the more alluring advantages of being an editor is the freedom of creativity and/or power one would have. In John Macfarlane's article from the Toronto Life, he compares editing to conduction an orchestra. He writes, "You're the big shot waving the baton. You take the bows. But you don't make the music" (par. 15). Ultimately, the point Macfarlane was getting at is that as an editor, everything is under one's control and power. Editors do not write the pieces, they are responsible for how well the pieces turn out. "As an editor, one has the author's writing, and confidence, in hand" (Anthony 3). The writing is under the editor's rule and that is a *whole* lot of power and responsibility. If one decides to be an editor of a magazine, they basically would have freedom over the

Margin annotations:

Avoid second person pronouns like "you," which can confuse a reader who has not had the experience.

You have an interesting thesis here, but your sections are out of order. Revise to show the structure of the essay. These sections could be combined.

Comma splice

Your essay would be stronger with a more focused hook. What about a short anecdote or statistic?

You have a strong signal phrase, quote, and citation here. You should change the one below to be more like this one.

Lavenza 2

whole publication, such as the format of the pages, the articles put
in, etc. If one decides to be an editor of books such as a literary ●········
editor one would have the responsibility and in the end, the
freedom, of copy-editing the piece itself and suggesting literary
criticism (which in itself is just as important as proofreading
because as an editor, one must know story flow, what will sell, and
what won't sell). ●··

This phrase should be set off with commas

You should add a conclusion sentence that ties up your ideas from this paragraph. Connect it back to the Topic Sentence.

CHATT-7 Self-Revision

More information about revision can be found on page 13.

The following checklist is often useful in revising your own work.

Checklist for Revision

Introduction:

- Is it interesting and does the audience want to read on?
- Is a clear thesis statement included?
- Can the audience determine my purpose for writing from the introduction?
- Structure:
  Hook (attention-getting opening sentence)
  Two to four support sentences (expand on the idea that the hook presents and lead to the thesis statement)
  Thesis (specifically lists what the main points will be)

Main Body:

- Is there sufficient background for my reader to understand my topic?
- Are my main points easy to pick out?
- Does each paragraph develop logically from the previous one?
- Are there transition words or phrases that connect the paragraphs?
- Do the paragraphs align with and support the thesis statement?
- Does each paragraph have a topic sentence?
- Is each paragraph well-developed (source voice and writer voice)?
- Is comma placement appropriate in each paragraph?
- Are the sentences clear and direct? Can they be understood at first reading?

Structure:

- Topic sentence (what is this paragraph about?)
- Supporting sentence(s) (expand on topic sentence)
- Introduce source (what does someone else say about the topic) (signal phrase)
- Add your voice to the source (how does the source information support the topic sentence?)
- Concluding sentence (summarizes main point and leads to the next main point)

Conclusion:

- Does the conclusion summarize my main points?
- Do I avoid beginning a new idea in the conclusion?
- Does my conclusion end memorably?
- Structure
    Summary of thesis (main points)
    Supporting sentences (what do you want the reader to learn from your essay?)
    Memorable close (leave your reader thinking)

Additional Elements to Consider

Citations:

- Are my in-text (parenthetical) citations correct?
- Is my Works Cited page formatted correctly?
- Do I have the correct number of sources as outlined in the assignment?
- Have I made and supported a strong argument for my position?
- Should I reorder my main points?
- Are there obvious questions within the text that need to be answered?
- Are there irrelevant sections or sentences I should cut?
- Have I used one or more rhetorical modes (Cause/Effect, Exemplification, Narration, Description, Definition, Classification/Division, Process) in my body paragraphs?
- Have any words been unnecessarily repeated?
- Is the writing interesting?
- Are my hook and my concluding sentence memorable?

CHATT-8 Grading Criteria for Writing Assignments

Use the following criteria as you put the finishing touches on your essay.

AN A PAPER

- Demonstrates a discernible pattern of organization derived from the assignment
- Expresses ideas clearly, utilizing a vocabulary appropriate to the assignment
- Develops points thoroughly and without digression
- Provides a sophisticated variety in sentence structure
- Supports assertions with explanation or illustration
- Includes appropriate transitions
- Is free of errors in grammar, punctuation, and spelling

A B PAPER

- Demonstrates a discernible pattern of organization derived from the assignment
- Expresses ideas clearly, utilizing a vocabulary appropriate to the assignment
- Develops points thoroughly and without digression
- Lacks consistency in its degree of sophistication in sentence structure
- Supports assertions with explanation or illustration
- Includes appropriate transitions
- Is free of serious errors in grammar, punctuation, and spelling

A C PAPER

- Demonstrates a discernible pattern of organization derived from the assignment

- Expresses ideas clearly, utilizing a vocabulary appropriate to the assignment
- Develops points thoroughly, although some digression may be evident
- Lacks consistency in its degree of sophistication in sentence structure
- Lacks consistency in supporting assertions with explanation or illustration
- Includes appropriate transitions
- Includes few errors in grammar, punctuation, and spelling

A D PAPER

- Demonstrates a weak, yet discernible, pattern of organization derived from the assignment
- Digresses from the topic
- Lacks thorough development of points, providing little or no support, explanation, or illustration
- Does not express ideas clearly
- Lacks sophistication in sentence structure
- Lacks appropriate transitions
- Uses a weak vocabulary
- Includes recurrent grammatical errors
- Includes punctuation errors which obscure sentence clarity
- Includes errors in spelling of common words

AN F PAPER

- Lacks a discernible pattern of organization derived from the assignment
- Digresses from the topic
- Lacks thorough development of points, providing little or no support, explanation, or illustration

- Does not express ideas clearly
- Lacks sophistication in sentence structure
- Lacks appropriate transitions
- Uses a weak vocabulary
- Includes recurrent grammatical errors
- Includes punctuation errors which obscure sentence clarity
- Includes errors in spelling of common words

CHATT-9 Elements to be Noted and Marked in Writing Assignments

Grammar and Format
Major Errors

Number/agreement of subject and verb

Number/agreement of pronoun and antecedent

Run-on sentence (Fused sentence)

Comma splice including punctuation of compound sentence with conjunctive adverb

Fragment

Minor Errors

Vague or remote pronoun reference

Incorrect use of semicolon

Ambiguous or misplaced modifier

Indiscriminate or incorrect capitalization

Dangling modifier

Failure to use quotation marks correctly

Incorrect parallelism

Missing end punctuation

Failure to use comma properly

Stray punctuation marks

Failure to use apostrophe to indicate possession

Spelling Format

Improper paragraphing/indenting

Wrong margin (one inch for all four sides for typewritten documents)

Page numbers missing or incorrectly placed

Sloppy or illegible text

Style (Structure)
Introduction

Lacks sufficient lead to establish topic/focus

No clearly stated topic/focus

Missing thesis, weakly stated or incoherent

Paragraph Structure

Weak or missing transitions

Weak paragraph development

Clutter, unnecessary words

Lacks concrete supporting details

Too general

Insufficient support

Illogical/inadequate support

Conclusion

Lacks closure, introduces new subject

Fails to conclude entire essay (may be only a summation of a single section)

THIRD EDITION

The Tiger Guide to Writing

Chattanooga State Community College

WRITE

Richard Bullock
WRIGHT STATE UNIVERSITY

Michal Brody
SAN FRANCISCO STATE UNIVERSITY

Francine Weinberg

RESEARCH

EDIT

NORTON
CUSTOM

THIS HANDBOOK has been published for students at
Chattanooga State Community College. It's a custom
version of *The Little Seagull Handbook*.

W. W. Norton & Company has been independent since its founding in 1923, when William Warder Norton and Mary D. Herter Norton first published lectures delivered at the People's Institute, the adult education division of New York City's Cooper Union. The firm soon expanded its program beyond the Institute, publishing books by celebrated academics from America and abroad. By mid-century, the two major pillars of our publishing program—trade books and college texts—were firmly established. In the 1950s, the Norton family transferred control of the company to its employees, and today—with a staff of 400 and a comparable number of trade, college, and professional titles published each year—W. W. Norton stands as the largest and oldest publishing house owned wholly by its employees.

Editor: Marilyn Moller
Associate editor: Tenyia Lee
Assistant editor: Claire Wallace
Project editor: Christine D'Antonio
Manuscript editors: Beth Burke, Rebecca Caine, and Connie Parks
Managing editor, College: Marian Johnson
Managing editor, College Digital Media: Kim Yi
Production manager: Ashley Horna
Media editor: Erica Wnek
Media project editor: Cooper Wilhelm
Media editorial assistant: Ava Bramson
Marketing manager, Composition: Megan DeBono Zwilling
Design director: Rubina Yeh
Text design: Lisa Buckley / Anna Palchik
Photo editor: Nelson Colón
Photo research: Dena Digilio Betz
Page layout: Carole Desnoes
Composition: Jouve
Manufacturing: TransContinental

ISBN: 978-0-393-65792-0

W. W. Norton & Company, Inc., 500 Fifth Avenue, New York, N.Y. 10110
www.wwnorton.com

W. W. Norton & Company Ltd., 15 Carlisle Street, London W1D 3BS

1 2 3 4 5 6 7 8 9 0

Preface

This book began as an attempt to create a small handbook that would provide help with the specific kinds of writing college students are assigned to do, and to make it as user-friendly as possible. It's been more successful than we ever imagined possible, and much to our surprise, it's been adopted by many instructors who had been using much larger handbooks. These teachers tell us they like it because it's got "just enough detail," it's easy to use, and it costs less than half what their former books cost.

From our own experience as teachers, we've seen how much students prefer smaller books, and so, to paraphrase Elmore Leonard, we've tried to give the information college writers need—and to leave out the details they skip. We've also seen how important it is that a handbook be easy to use. To that end, the book is organized around the familiar categories of *writing*, *researching*, and *editing*, and it includes menus, directories, a glossary / index, and more to help students find the help they need.

We're pleased now to offer a third edition, with a new section on "Editing the Errors That Matter," an updated MLA chapter that covers the new style introduced in 2016, two new genre chapters, and new coverage of the use of "singular *they*."

Highlights

Help with the kinds of writing students are assigned—arguments, analyses, reports, narratives, and more. Brief chapters cover nine common genres, with models demonstrating each genre on the companion website.

Easy to use. Menus, directories, a glossary / index, and color-coded parts help students find the information they need. And a simple three-part organization—Write, Research, Edit—makes it easy for them to know where to look. Even the cover flaps are useful, with an Index of guidelines for Editing the Errors That Matter on the front flap and a Checklist for Revising and Editing on the back.

Just enough detail, but with color-coded links that refer students to the glossary / index for more information if they need it.

User-friendly documentation guidelines for MLA, APA, *Chicago*, and CSE styles. Documentation directories lead students to the examples they need, color-coded templates show what information to include, and documentation maps show where to find the required detail. Model papers demonstrate each style, with a complete MLA paper and brief examples of the other three styles in the book and complete papers on the companion website.

A full chapter on paragraphs, a subject that other pocket handbooks cover in much less detail. But students write in paragraphs— and they'll find the help they need in this handbook. [W-4]

Customizable. We've created templates to make it easy for you to add your own materials to the book—course outcomes statements, syllabi, school policies, student writing, and so on. And you can even customize the title and cover to replace our little seagull with your school mascot. We've already published a *Little Duck Handbook,* a *Little Bobcat, Little Eagle, Little Aztec,* and three *Little Tigers*—and we'll be happy to do one for your school.

A full chapter on Englishes, from standard edited English to the varieties spoken in specific regions, communities, and academic contexts. [L-10]

Uniquely helpful guidance for students whose first language isn't English, including chapters on idioms [L-3] and prepositions [L-5] and additional detail on articles, phrasal verbs, and modal verbs. The companion website and mobile version include links to glossaries of idioms and phrasal verbs, and the Coursepack includes exercises and handouts.

What's New?

A new section on "Editing the Errors That Matter." Covering 14 errors that teachers identified as ones that undermine a writer's authority and weaken an argument, these chapters explain why each of these errors matters, describe how to spot them in a draft, and walk students through some ways of editing them out [E-1 to E-6].

New MLA style. The MLA chapter has been updated to explain the new core principles introduced in 2016 and to provide color-coded templates and models for documenting the kinds of sources college students most often cite [MLA-a to MLA-d].

Two new genre chapters. We've added new chapters on "Proposals" and "Reflections," two genres that students are often assigned or expected to write [W-12 and W-13].

New guidance on the use of "singular *they*." We've tried to help students navigate the use of pronouns in academic writing in light of evolving conventions and notions of gender. You'll find this new material in the chapter on "Pronouns" [S-6], of course, as well as in the chapters on "Words That Build Common Ground" [L-9] and "Editing Pronouns" [E-2].

What's Online?

The entire handbook is available as as ebook—and is free when packaged with the print book (and comes with four years of access). Allows students to highlight, bookmark, and take notes—and includes exercises and links to full glossaries of idioms and phrasal verbs. Access it at **digital.wwnorton.com/littleseagull3**.

A companion website includes model papers, exercises and quizzes, links to glossaries of idioms and phrasal verbs, and more. Access the site at **digital.wwnorton.com/littleseagull3**.

InQuizitive for Writers, an adaptive learning tool that provides students with personalized practice editing out common errors—comma splices, pronoun reference, mixed constructions, and more, including all the topics found in the new handbook chapters on "Editing the Errors That Matter." Personalized feedback and links to the *Little Seagull* ebook help students learn to edit what they write, and gamelike elements even make working with grammar fun. *InQuizitive* can be used to diagnose issues students need to practice or assigned to provide practice with particular issues you identify in your students' writing.

A Norton Coursepack is available for most learning management systems, including *Blackboard, Canvas, Moodle, Sakai*, and *D2L*, providing diagnostic quizzes; exercises; handouts for students whose primary language isn't English; documentation guidelines; and more. Because it all works within your existing LMS, there's no new system to learn. And it's yours to customize and edit—you choose the content you want to use, for your course. No extra costs, no registration codes. Access the coursepack at **wwnorton.com/instructors**.

norton/write. A free-and-open site with plagiarism tutorials, writing tips, model student writing, documentation guidelines, exercises—and more. Access the site at **digital.wwnorton.com/littleseagull3**.

Acknowledgments

It takes a big team to publish even a small handbook. We have benefitted from the astute comments and suggestions by a number of reviewers: Gillian Andersen, Eastern New Mexico University; Evan Balkan, Community College of Baltimore County–Catonsville; Jason Barr, Blue Ridge Community College; Josh M. Beach, University of Texas at San Antonio; Carole Chapman, Ivy Tech Community College–Southwest; Thomas Chester, Ivy Tech Community College–Marion; Jesseca Cornelson, Alabama State University; Michael Cripps, University of New England; Syble Davis, Houston Community College; Laura Ann Dearing, Jefferson Community and Technical College; Darren DeFrain, Wichita State University; Joann K. Deiudicibus, State University of New York at New Paltz; Christie Diep, Cypress College; Allison Dieppa, Florida Gulf Coast University; Clark Draney, College of Southern Idaho; Brenna Dugan, Owens Community College; Megan Egbert, Utah State University; Megan Fulwiler, The College of Saint

Rose; Jonathan C. Glance, Mercer University; Carey Goyette, Clinton Community College; Opal Greer, Eastern New Mexico University; Kendra Griffin, Aims Community College; Clinton Hale, Blinn College; Ann C. Hall, Ohio Dominican University; Joel B. Henderson, Chattanooga State Community College; Robert Hurd, Anne Arundel Community College; Geri (Geraldine) Jacobs, Jackson College; Anne Marie Johnson, Utah State University; Jo Johnson, Ivy Tech Community College–Fort Wayne; Debra S. Knutson, Shawnee State University; Brian Leingang, Edison State Community College; Joseph Lemak, Elmira College; Matthew Masucci, State College of Florida–Venice; L. Adam Mekler, Morgan State University; Lora Meredith, Western Wyoming Community College; Tracy Ann Morse, East Carolina University; Amy Nawrocki, University of Bridgeport; Eden Pearson, Des Moines Area Community College; Heather Pristash, Western Wyoming Community College; Glenda Pritchett, Quinnipiac University; Jonathan Purkiss, Pulaski Technical College; Paula Rash, Caldwell Community College; Louis Riggs, Hannibal-LaGrange University; Tony Russell, Central Oregon Community College; David Salomon, The Sage Colleges; Anthony Sams, Ivy Tech Community College; Karen Schwarze, Utah State University; Dixie A Shaw-Tillmon, The University of Texas at San Antonio; Carol Singletary, Eastern New Mexico University; Linda Strahan, University of California, Riverside; Hannah Sykes, Rockingham Community College; Jarrod Waetjen, Northern Virginia Community College—Alexandria; Christy Wenger, Shepherd University; Jenny Williams, Spartanburg Community College.

We are especially grateful to the following reviewers for their very helpful feedback on the new materials on "Editing the Errors That Matter": Jason Barr, Blue Ridge Community College; Jesseca Cornelson, Alabama State University; Michael Cripps, University of New England; Syble Davis, Houston Community College; Laura Ann Dearing, Jefferson Community and Technical College; Darren DeFrain, Wichita State University; Allison Dieppa, Florida Gulf Coast University; Brenna Dugan, Owens Community College; Shonette Grant, Northern Virginia Community College; Kendra Griffin, Aims Community College; Anne Marie Johnson, Utah State University; Brian

Leingang, Edison State Community College; Matthew Masucci, State College of Florida–Venice; L. Adam Mekler, Morgan State University; Lora Meredith, Western Wyoming Community College; Eden Pearson, Des Moines Area Community College; Glenda Pritchett, Quinnipiac University; Jonathan Purkiss, Pulaski Technical College; Paula Rash, Caldwell Community College; Tony Russell, Central Oregon Community College; Dixie A. Shaw-Tillmon, The University of Texas at San Antonio; Hannah Sykes, Rockingham Community College; Jarrod Waetjen, Northern Virginia Community College–Alexandria.

We owe a big thank you to all our friends at Norton, starting with Claire Wallace for her excellent editorial work on both the new chapters in the book and the editing exercises in *InQuizitive for Writers*. We are grateful as well to Tenyia Lee for her incredibly detailed work on all the documentation chapters. A deep bow goes to Erica Wnek for all her work on *InQuizitive*, the companion website, the coursepack, and the ebook—and to Ava Bramson as well. We are once again grateful to Carin Berger and Debra Morton Hoyt for yet another charming cover design. And we thank Megan DeBono Zwilling and Maureen Connelly for their work getting the word out about this book.

Little books are always more complex than they look, and we are especially grateful to Christine D'Antonio and Ashley Horna for their expertise managing and producing *The Little Seagull Handbook*. Finally, we thank Marilyn Moller, the guiding intelligence behind all our textbooks.

Rich thanks his students and colleagues at Wright State for all they've taught him about teaching and writing over the years, and the many writing teachers using the *Little Seagull* who have offered suggestions or invited him to campus: Kelly Ritter, Kristi McDuffie, and their graduate teaching assistants at the University of Illinois, Urbana–Champaign; Collie Fulford, Kathryn Wymer, and their students in ENG 3040 at North Carolina Central University; Kevin Moore at SUNY Cobleskill; and Mary S. Tuley at Fayetteville Technical Community College. Finally, he thanks his wife, Barb, for her unwavering and good-humored support. Michal thanks her families and students in the United States and Mexico for always keeping her thinking. Fran thanks Marilyn for trading places with her so many years ago and her husband, Larry Strauss, for his confidence in her at all times.

Hats off to you all.

Richard Bullock
Michal Brody
Francine Weinberg

How to Use This Book

Write. Research. Edit. Perhaps you've been assigned to write a paper that makes a case for why parking on campus should be free. Maybe you need to find sources for a report on organic farming in your state. Or you may just want to make sure that the punctuation in your cover letter is perfect before you apply for a new job. Whether you need to write, research, edit—or all three—this little handbook can help.

Ways of Using the Book

Menus. If you are looking for a specific chapter, start with the Brief Menu on the inside front cover; if you are looking for a specific section in a chapter, start with the Detailed Menu on the inside back cover.

Glossary / index. If you're looking for definitions of key terms and concepts, turn to the combined glossary and index at the back of the book. Be aware also that words highlighted in **TAN** throughout the book are defined in the glossary/index. Check the glossary/index when you aren't sure which chapter covers a topic you're looking for—for instance, guidance on when to use *a* and when to use *the*.

Color-coded organization. The parts of this book are color-coded for easy reference: red for **WRITE**, blue for **RESEARCH**, and yellow for **EDITING**.

Guidelines for common writing assignments. Chapters W-7 to W-15, cover nine kinds of writing you'll likely be expected to do in many college classes. And you'll find model papers demonstrating each of these kinds of writing on the companion website: **digital .wwnorton.com/littleseagull3**.

Checklist for revising and editing. On the back flap is a list of prompts to guide you as you revise and edit a draft—and that lead you to pages in the book where you'll find help.

Help editing common errors that matter. We all make mistakes and need to learn how to edit them out. The front flap lists some of the ones that really matter and leads you to places in the book where you'll find help spotting them in your writing and strategies for editing them out.

MLA, APA, *Chicago,* and CSE guidelines. Color-coded chapters cover each style, with directories in the back of the book that lead to the specific examples you need. Color-coded templates show what information to include, and documentation maps show you where to find the information required. You'll find a full MLA paper on pages 161–69 and model papers demonstrating each of the other styles on the companion website: **digital.wwnorton.com/littleseagull3**.

Scanning for information. Sometimes you may simply turn to a part of the book where you know that information you're looking for is located. You could scan the red headings to find where the topic is explained. Or if you just want to find an example showing you what to do, you'll find that examples are all marked by little red pointers (▶) to make them easy to spot.

Write

I think I did pretty well, considering
I started out with nothing but a bunch
of blank paper.

—STEVE MARTIN

W-1   Writing Contexts

Whenever we write, whether it's an email to a friend, a toast at a wedding, or an essay, we do so within some kind of context—a rhetorical situation that helps shape our choices as writers. Whatever our topic, we have a purpose, a certain audience, a particular stance, a genre, and a medium to consider—and often as not, a design. This chapter discusses each of these elements and provides some questions that can help you think about some of the choices you have to make as you write.

W-1a Purpose

All writing has a purpose. We write to explore our thoughts, express ourselves, and entertain; to record words and events; to communicate with others; to persuade others to think or behave in certain ways. Here are some questions to help you think about your purpose(s) as you write:

- What is the primary purpose of the writing task—to entertain? inform? persuade? demonstrate knowledge? something else?

- What are your own goals?

- What do you want your **AUDIENCE** to do, think, or feel? How will they use what you tell them?

- What does this writing task call on you to do? Do you have an assignment that specifies a certain **GENRE** or strategy—to argue a position? report on an event? compare two texts?

- What are the best ways to achieve your purpose? Should you take a particular **STANCE**? write in a particular **MEDIUM**? use certain **DESIGN** elements?

W-1b Audience

What you write, how much you write, and how you phrase it are all influenced by the audience you envision. For example, as a student writing an essay for an instructor, you will be expected to produce a text with few or no errors, something you may worry less about in an email to a friend.

- What audience do you want to reach? What expectations do they have from you? What's your relationship with them, and how does it affect your TONE?

- What is your audience's background — their education and life experiences?

- What are their interests? What motivates them? Do they have any political attitudes or interests that may affect the way they read your piece?

- Is there any demographic information that you should keep in mind, such as race, gender, sexual orientation, religious beliefs, or economic status?

- What does your audience already know — or believe--about your topic? What do you need to tell them?

- What kind of response do you want from your audience? Do you want them to do or believe something? accept what you say? Something else?

- How can you best appeal to your audience? What kind of information will they find interesting or persuasive? Are there any design elements that will appeal to them?

W-1c Genre

Genres are kinds of writing. Reports, position papers, poems, letters, instructions—even jokes—are genres. Each one has certain features and follows particular conventions of style and presentation. Academic assignments generally specify the genre, but if it isn't clear, ask your instructor. Then consider these issues:

- What are the key elements and conventions of your genre? How do they affect the type of content you should include?

- Does your genre require a certain organization or **MEDIUM**? Does it have any **DESIGN** requirements?
- How does your genre affect your **TONE**, if at all?
- Does the genre require formal (or informal) language?

W-1d Topic

An important part of any writing context is the topic—what you are writing about. As you choose a topic, keep in mind your rhetorical situation and any requirements specified by your assignments.

- If your topic is assigned, what do the verbs in the assignment ask you to do: **ANALYZE**? **COMPARE**? **SUMMARIZE**? Something else?
- Does the assignment offer a broad subject area (such as the environment) that allows you to choose a limited topic within it (such as a particular environmental issue)?
- What do you need to do to complete the assignment? Do you need to do research? find illustrations?
- If you can choose a topic, think about what you are interested in. What do you want to learn more about? What topics from your courses have you found intriguing? What local, national, or global issues do you care about?
- Do you need to limit your topic to fit a specified time or length?

W-1e Stance and Tone

Whenever you write, you have a certain stance, an attitude toward your topic. For example, you might be objective, critical, passionate, or indifferent. You express (or downplay) that stance through your tone—the words you use and the other ways your text conveys an attitude toward your subject and audience. Just as you likely alter what you say depending on whether you're speaking to a boss or a good friend, so you need to make similar adjustments as a writer. Ask yourself these questions:

- What is your stance, and how can you best present it to achieve your purpose?

- How should your stance be reflected in your tone? Do you want to be seen as reasonable? angry? thoughtful? ironic? Something else? Be sure that your language—and even your font—convey that tone.

- How is your stance likely to be received by your **AUDIENCE**? Should you openly reveal it, or would it be better to tone it down?

W-1f Media / Design

We communicate through many media, both verbal and nonverbal: our bodies (we wave), our voices (we shout), and various technologies (we write with a pencil, send email, tweet). No matter what the medium, a text's design affects the way it is received and understood. Consider these questions:

- Does your assignment call for a certain medium or media—a printed essay? an oral report with visual aids? a blog?

- How does your medium affect the way you write and organize your text? For example, long paragraphs may be fine on paper, but bulleted phrases work better on slides.

- How does your medium affect your language? Do you need to be more **FORMAL** or **INFORMAL**?

- What's the appropriate look for your writing situation? Should it look serious? whimsical? personal? Something else?

- What fonts and other design elements suit your writing context? Is there anything you should highlight by putting it in a box or italics?

- Would headings help you organize your material and help readers follow the text? Does your genre or medium require them?

- Will your audience expect or need any illustrations? Is there any information that would be easier to understand as a chart?

W-2   Academic Contexts

An **ARGUMENT** on a psychology exam debating whether genes or environment do more to determine people's intelligence, a **REPORT** for a science course on the environmental effects of electricity-generating windmills on wildlife, a **PROPOSAL** for a multimedia sales campaign in a marketing course—all of these are kinds of writing that you might be assigned to do in college classes. This chapter describes some of the elements expected in academic writing.

W-2a Key Elements of Academic Writing

Evidence that you've carefully considered the subject. You can use a variety of ways to show that you've thought seriously about the subject and done any necessary research, from citing authoritative sources to incorporating information you learned in class to pointing out connections among ideas.

A clear, appropriately qualified thesis. In academic writing, you're expected to state your main point explicitly, often in a **THESIS** statement, as MIT student Joanna MacKay does in an essay about selling human organs: "Governments should not ban the sale of human organs; they should regulate it."

Often you'll need to qualify your thesis statement to acknowledge exceptions or other perspectives. Here's a qualified thesis from an essay by Michaela Cullington, a student at Marywood University: "Although some believe that texting has either a positive or negative effect on writing, it in fact seems likely that texting has no significant effect on student writing." By adding **QUALIFYING WORDS** like *seems likely* and *significant*, the writer indicates that she's not making a definitive claim about texting's influence on student writing.

A response to what others have said. Whatever your topic, it's likely that others have written or spoken about it. It's almost always best to present your ideas as a response to what others have said— QUOTING , PARAPHRASING , or SUMMARIZING their ideas and then agreeing, disagreeing, or both.

For example, in an essay arguing that the American Dream is alive and well, University of Cincinnati student Brandon King presents the views of two economists who say that because wealth is concentrated in the hands "of a rich minority," "the American Dream is no longer possible for most Americans." He then responds by disagreeing, argu- ing that "the American Dream . . . is based on perception, on the way someone *imagines* how to be successful."

Good reasons supported by evidence. You need to provide good REASONS for your thesis and EVIDENCE to support those reasons. Joanna MacKay offers several reasons that sales of human kidneys should be legalized: a surplus exists; the risk to the donor is not great; and legalization would enable the trade in kidneys to be regulated, thereby helping many patients and donors. For that third reason, her evidence includes statistics about death from renal failure.

Acknowledgment of multiple perspectives. In any academic writing, you need to investigate and represent fairly the range of perspectives on your topic—to avoid considering issues in an overly simple "pro/con" way and, instead, to explore multiple positions as you research and write. Brandon King, for instance, looks at the American Dream from several angles: the ways it is defined, the effects of government policies on achieving it, the role of education, and so on.

Carefully documented sources. Clearly acknowledging sources and DOCUMENTING them correctly both in your text and in a WORKS CITED or REFERENCES list at the end is a basic requirement of aca- demic writing. If your text will appear online, you can direct readers to online sources by using hyperlinks, but your instructor may want you to document them formally as well.

A confident and authoritative STANCE. Your TONE should convey confidence and establish your authority to write about your topic.

To do so, use active verbs ("X claims," "Y and Z have found"), avoid such phrases as "I think," and write in a direct style. Michaela Cullington establishes an authoritative stance in her essay on texting this way: "On the basis of my own research, expert research, and personal observations, I can confidently state that texting is not interfering with students' use of standard written English and has no effect on their writing abilities in general." Her simple, declarative sentences and strong, unequivocal language ("I can confidently state," "has no effect") send the message that she knows what she's talking about.

An indication of why your topic matters. Help your readers understand why your topic is worth exploring—and why your writing is worth reading. In an essay called "Throwing Like a Girl," James Fallows explains why that topic matters, noting that his title reflects attitudes about gender that have potentially serious consequences.

Careful attention to correctness. You should almost always write in complete sentences, use appropriate capitalization and punctuation, check that your spelling is correct—and avoid any abbreviations used in texting.

W-2b Thinking about the Writing Context

- What GENRE does the assignment suggest—or require?
- What is your instructor's PURPOSE for this assignment? What is your purpose, apart from fulfilling those expectations?
- Who is your AUDIENCE?
- How can you convey a confident, authoritative STANCE?
- What MEDIA are available, permitted, and appropriate? Are any required?
- What DESIGN issues need to be considered?

》 To read the student essays cited in this chapter, go to **digital.wwnorton.com/littleseagull3**.

W-3 Writing Processes

To create anything, we generally break the work down into a series of steps. We follow a recipe (or the directions on a box) to bake a cake; we divide a piece of music into various singing parts to arrange it for a choir. So it is when we write. We rely on various processes to get from a blank page to a finished product. This chapter offers advice on some of these processes—from generating ideas to drafting to revising and editing.

W-3a Generating Ideas

The activities that follow can help you explore a topic—what you already know about it or how you might look at it in new ways.

- *Brainstorming.* Jot down everything that comes to mind about your topic, working either alone or with others. Look over your list, and try to identify connections or patterns.

- *Freewriting.* Write as quickly as you can without stopping for 5 to 10 minutes. Then underline interesting passages. Write more, using an underlined passage as your new topic.

- *Looping.* Write for 5 to 10 minutes, jotting down whatever you know about your subject. Then write a one-sentence summary of the most important idea. Use this summary to start another loop. Keep looping until you have a tentative focus.

- *Clustering.* Clustering is a way of connecting ideas visually. Write your topic in the middle of a page, and write subtopics and other ideas around it. Circle each item, and draw lines to connect related ideas.

- *Questioning.* You might start by asking *What? Who? When? Where? How?* and *Why?* You could also ask questions as if the topic were a play: What happens? Who are the participants? When does the action take place? How? Where? Why does this happen?

- *Keeping a journal.* Jotting down ideas, feelings, or the events of your day in a journal is a good way to generate ideas—and a journal is a good place to explore why you think as you do.

- *Starting some research.* Depending on your topic and purpose, you might do a little preliminary research to get basic information and help you discover paths you might follow.

W-3b Developing a Tentative Thesis

A **THESIS** is a statement that indicates your main point, identifying your topic and the **CLAIM** you are making about it. Here are some steps for developing a tentative thesis statement:

1. *State your topic as a question.* You may have a topic, such as "gasoline prices." But that doesn't make a statement. To move from a topic to a thesis statement, start by turning your topic into a question: *What causes fluctuations in gasoline prices?*

2. *Then turn your question into a position.* A thesis statement is an assertion—it takes a stand or makes a claim. One way to establish a thesis is to answer your own question: *Gasoline prices fluctuate for several reasons.*

3. *Narrow your thesis.* A good thesis is specific, telling your audience exactly what your essay will cover: *Gasoline prices fluctuate because of production procedures, consumer demand, international politics, and oil companies' policies.* A good way to narrow a thesis is to ask and answer questions about it: *Why do gasoline prices fluctuate?* The answer will help you craft a narrow, focused thesis.

4. *Qualify your thesis.* Though you may sometimes want to state your thesis strongly and bluntly, often you need to acknowledge that your assertion may not be unconditionally true. In such cases, consider adding **QUALIFYING WORDS** such as *may*, *very likely*, and *often* to qualify your statement: *Gasoline prices <u>very likely</u> fluctuate because of production procedures, consumer demand, international politics, and oil companies' policies.*

Whatever tentative thesis you start with, keep in mind that you may want to modify it as you proceed.

W-3c Organizing and Drafting

Organizing. You may want to use an outline to help organize your ideas before you begin to draft. You can create an informal outline by simply listing your ideas in the order in which you want to write about them.

Thesis statement

First main idea
    Supporting evidence or detail
    Supporting evidence or detail

Second main idea
    Supporting evidence or detail
    Supporting evidence or detail

An outline can help you organize your thoughts and see where more research is needed. As you draft and revise, though, stay flexible—and be ready to change direction as your topic develops.

Drafting. At some point, you need to write out a draft. As you draft, you may need to get more information, rethink your thesis, or explore some new ideas. But first, you just need to get started.

- *Write quickly in spurts.* Try to write a complete draft, or a complete section of a longer draft, in one sitting. If you need to stop in the middle, jot down some notes about where you're headed so that you can pick up your train of thought when you begin again.

- *Expect surprises.* Writing is a form of thinking; you may end up somewhere you didn't anticipate. That can be a good thing—but if not, it's okay to double back or follow a new path.

- *Expect to write more than one draft.* Parts of your first draft may not achieve your goals. That's okay—as you revise, you can fill in gaps and improve your writing.

- *Don't worry about correctness.* You can check words, dates, and spelling at a later stage. For now, just write.

W-3d Getting Response

As writers, we need to be able to look at our work with a critical eye, to see if our writing is doing what we want it to do. We also need to get feedback from other readers. Here is a list of questions for reading a draft closely and considering how it should or could be revised:

- Will the OPENING paragraph grab readers' attention? If so, how does it do so? If not, how else might the piece begin?

- What is the THESIS? Is it stated directly? If not, should it be?

- Are there good REASONS and sufficient EVIDENCE to support the thesis? Is there anywhere you'd like to have more detail?

- Are all QUOTATIONS introduced with a SIGNAL PHRASE and documented? Are they accurately quoted, and have any changes and omissions been indicated with brackets and ellipses?

- Is there a clear pattern of organization? Does each part relate to the thesis? Are there appropriate TRANSITIONS to help readers follow your train of thought? Are there headings that make the structure of the text clear—and if not, should there be?

- Are there any VISUALS—tables, charts, photos? If so, are they clearly labeled with captions? If you did not create them yourself, have you cited your sources?

- Will the text meet the needs and expectations of its AUDIENCE? Where might they need more information or guidance?

- Is your STANCE on the topic clear and consistent throughout? Is the TONE appropriate for your audience and purpose?

- Is the CONCLUSION satisfying? What does it leave readers thinking? How else might the text end?

- Is the title one that will attract interest? Does it announce your topic and give some sense of what you have to say?

W-3e Revising

Once you've studied your draft with a critical eye and gotten response from other readers, it's time to revise. Start with global (whole-text) issues, and gradually move to smaller, sentence-level details.

- *Give yourself time to revise.* Set deadlines that will give you plenty of time to work on your **REVISION**. Try to get some distance. If you can, step away from your writing for a while and think about something else.

- *Revise to sharpen your focus.* Examine your **THESIS** to make sure it matches your purpose and clearly articulates your main point. Does each paragraph contribute to your main point? Does your beginning introduce your topic and provide any necessary contextual information? Does your ending provide a satisfying conclusion?

- *Revise to strengthen the argument.* Make sure that all your key ideas are fully explained. If readers find some of your **CLAIMS** unconvincing, you may need to qualify them—or provide more **REASONS** or **EVIDENCE**. If you add evidence, make sure that it all supports your point and includes any needed documentation.

- *Revise to improve the organization.* You may find it helpful to outline your draft to see all the parts readily. If anything seems out of place, move it—or if need be, cut it completely. Check to see if you've included appropriate **TRANSITIONS** or headings.

- *Revise to be sure readers will understand what you're saying.* Make sure that you've defined any terms they may not know. If you don't state a thesis directly, consider whether you should. Look closely at your title to be sure it gives a sense of what your text is about.

W-3f Editing and Proofreading

Your ability to produce clear, error-free writing shows something about your ability as a writer, so you should be sure to edit and proofread your work carefully. Editing is the stage when you work on the details of your paragraphs, sentences, language, and punctuation to make your writing as clear, precise, and correct as possible. The following guidelines can help you check the paragraphs, sentences, and words in your drafts.

Editing paragraphs

- Does each paragraph focus on one point and have a **TOPIC SENTENCE** that announces that point? Does every sentence in the paragraph relate to that point?

- Where is the most important information in each paragraph—at the beginning? the end? in the middle?

- Check to see how your paragraphs fit together. Does each one follow smoothly from the one before it? Do you need to add **TRANSITIONS**?

- How does the **OPENING** paragraph catch readers' attention? How else might you begin?

- Does the **CONCLUSION** provide a satisfactory ending? How else might you conclude?

For more help with paragraphs, see **W-4**.

Editing sentences

- Check to see that each sentence is complete, with a **SUBJECT** and a **VERB**, and that it begins with a capital letter and ends with a period, question mark, or exclamation point.

- Are your sentences varied? If they all start with the subject or are all the same length, try varying them by adding **TRANSITIONS** or introductory phrases—or by combining some sentences.

- Be sure that lists or series are **PARALLEL** in form—all nouns (*lions, tigers, bears*), all verbs (*hop, skip, jump*), and so on.

- Do many of your sentences begin with *It* or *There*? Sometimes these words help introduce a topic, but often they make a text vague.

For more help with sentences, see **S-1** through **S-9**.

Editing language

- Are you sure of the meaning of every word?

- Do your words all convey the appropriate TONE?

- Is any of your language too general? For example, do you need to replace verbs like *be* or *do* with more specific verbs?

- Check all PRONOUNS to see that they have clear ANTECEDENTS.

- Have you used any CLICHÉS? Your writing will almost always be better without such predictable expressions.

- Be careful with language that refers to other people. Edit out language that might be considered SEXIST or would otherwise stereotype any individual or group.

- Check for *it's* and *its*. Use *it's* to mean "it is" and *its* to mean "belonging to it."

For more help with language, see **L-1** through **L-10**.

Proofreading

This is the final stage of the writing process, the point when you check for misspelled words, mixed-up fonts, missing pages, and so on.

- Use your computer's grammar and spelling checkers, but be aware that they're not very reliable. Computer programs rely on formulas and banks of words—so what they flag (or not) as mistakes may not be accurate. For example, if you were to write "sea you soon," the word *sea* would not be flagged as misspelled.

- Place a ruler or piece of paper under each line as you read. Use your finger or a pencil as a pointer.

- Try beginning with the last sentence and working backward.

- Read your text out loud to yourself—or better, to others. Ask someone else to read your text.

W-3g Collaborating

Even if you do much of your writing alone, you probably spend a lot of time working with others, either face-to-face or online. Here are some guidelines for collaborating successfully.

Working in a group

- For face-to-face meetings, make sure everyone is facing one another and is physically part of the group.
- Be respectful and tactful. This is especially important when collaborating online. Without tone of voice, facial expressions, and other body language, your words carry all the weight. Remember also that what you write may be forwarded to others.
- When collaborating online, decide as a group how best to exchange drafts and comments. Group members may not all have access to the same equipment and software. Name files carefully.
- Each meeting needs an agenda—and careful attention to the clock. Appoint one person as timekeeper and another person as group leader; a third member should keep a record of the discussion and write a summary afterward.

Working on a group writing project

- Define the overall project as clearly as possible, and divide the work into parts.
- Assign each group member specific tasks with deadlines.
- Try to accommodate everyone's style of working, but make sure everyone performs.
- Work for consensus, if not necessarily total agreement.

W-4 Developing Paragraphs

Paragraphs help us organize our writing for our readers. Here one writer recalls when he first understood what a paragraph does.

> I can remember picking up my father's books before I could read. The words themselves were mostly foreign, but I still remember the exact moment when I first understood, with a sudden clarity, the purpose of a paragraph. I didn't have the vocabulary to say "paragraph," but I realized that a paragraph was a fence that held words. The words inside a paragraph worked together for a common purpose. They had some specific reason for being inside the same fence. . . .
>
> —Sherman Alexie, "The Joy of Reading and Writing"

This chapter will help you build "fences" around words that work together on a common topic. It offers tips and examples for composing strong paragraphs.

W-4a Focusing on the Main Point

All the sentences in a paragraph should focus on one main idea, as they do in this paragraph from an article about the Mall of America.

> There is, of course, nothing naturally abhorrent in the human impulse to dwell in marketplaces or the urge to buy, sell, and trade. Rural Americans traditionally looked forward to the excitement and sensuality of market day; Native Americans traveled long distances to barter and trade at sprawling, festive encampments. In Persian bazaars and in the ancient Greek agoras the very soul of the community was preserved and could be seen, felt, heard, and smelled as it might be nowhere else. All over the planet the humblest of people have always gone to market with hope in their hearts and in expectation of something beyond mere goods—seeking a place where humanity is temporarily in ascendance, a palette for the senses, one another.   —David Guterson, "Enclosed. Encyclopedic. Endured. One Week at the Mall of America"

Topic sentences. To help you focus a paragraph on one main point, state that point in a **TOPIC SENTENCE**. Often, but not always, you might start a paragraph with a topic sentence, as in this example from an essay about legalizing the sale of human kidneys.

> Dialysis is harsh, expensive, and, worst of all, only temporary. Acting as an artificial kidney, dialysis mechanically filters the blood of a patient. It works, but not well. With treatment sessions lasting three hours, several times a week, those dependent on dialysis are, in a sense, shackled to a machine for the rest of their lives. Adding excessive stress to the body, dialysis causes patients to feel increasingly faint and tired, usually keeping them from work and other normal activities.
> —Joanna MacKay, "Organ Sales Will Save Lives"

Sometimes, you may choose to put the topic sentence at the end of the paragraph. See how this strategy works in another paragraph in the essay about kidneys.

> In a legal kidney transplant, everybody gains except the donor. The doctors and nurses are paid for the operation, the patient receives a new kidney, but the donor receives nothing. Sure, the donor will have the warm, uplifting feeling associated with helping a fellow human being, but this is not enough reward for most people to part with a piece of themselves. In an ideal world, the average person would be altruistic enough to donate a kidney with nothing expected in return. The real world, however, is run by money. We pay men for donating sperm, and we pay women for donating ova, yet we expect others to give away an entire organ with no compensation. If the sale of organs were allowed, people would have a greater incentive to help save the life of a stranger.

Occasionally, the main point is so obvious that you don't need a topic sentence. Especially in **NARRATIVE** writing, you may choose only to imply—not state—the main idea, as in this paragraph from an essay about one Latina writer's difficulty in learning Spanish.

> I came to the United States in 1963 at age 3 with my family and immediately stopped speaking Spanish. College-educated and

seamlessly bilingual when they settled in west Texas, my parents (a psychology professor and an artist) wholeheartedly embraced the notion of the American melting pot. They declared that their two children would speak nothing but *inglés*. They'd read in English, write in English, and fit into Anglo society beautifully.

—Tanya Maria Barrientos, "Se Habla Español"

Sticking to the main point. Whether or not you announce the main point in a topic sentence, be sure that every sentence in a paragraph relates to that point. Edit out any sentences that stray off topic, such as those crossed out below.

In "Se Habla Español," Tanya Maria Barrientos notes some of the difficulties she encounters as a Latina who is not fluent in Spanish. ~~Previous generations of immigrants were encouraged to speak only English.~~ When someone poses a question to her in Spanish, she often has to respond in English. In other instances, she tries to speak Spanish but falters over the past and future tenses. Situations like these embarrass Barrientos and make her feel left out of a community she wants to be part of. ~~Native Guatemalans who are bilingual do not have such problems.~~

W-4b Strategies for Developing the Main Point

A good paragraph provides enough good details to develop its main point—to fill out and support that point. Following are some common strategies for fleshing out and organizing paragraphs—and sometimes even for organizing an entire essay.

Analyzing cause and effect. Sometimes, you can develop a paragraph on a topic by analyzing what CAUSES it—or what its EFFECTS might be. The following paragraph about air turbulence identifies some of its causes.

A variety of factors can cause turbulence, which is essentially a disturbance in the movement of air. Thunderstorms, the jet stream, and mountains are some of the more common natural culprits, while what is known as wake turbulence is created by another plane. "Clear air turbulence" is the kind that comes up unexpectedly; it is difficult to detect because there is no moisture or particles to reveal the movement of air.

—Susan Stellin, "The Inevitability of Bumps"

Classifying and dividing. When we CLASSIFY something, we group it with things that share similar characteristics. See how two social scientists use classification to explain the ways that various types of social network websites (SNSs) make user profiles visible.

The visibility of a profile varies by site and according to user discretion. By default, profiles on *Friendster* and *Tribe.net* are crawled by search engines, making them visible to anyone, regardless of whether or not the viewer has an account. Alternatively, *LinkedIn* controls what a viewer might see based on whether she or he has a paid account. Sites like *MySpace* allow users to choose whether they want their profile to be public or "friends only." *Facebook* takes a different approach—by default, users who are part of the same "network" can view each other's profiles, unless a profile owner has decided to deny permission to those in their network. Structural variations around visibility and access are one of the primary ways that SNSs differentiate themselves from each other.

—danah boyd and Nicole Ellison,
"Social Network Sites: Definition, History, and Scholarship"

As a writing strategy, DIVISION is a way of separating something into parts. See how the following paragraph divides the concept of pressure into four kinds.

I see four kinds of pressure working on college students today: economic pressure, parental pressure, peer pressure, and self-induced pressure. It is easy to look around for villains—to blame the colleges for charging too much money, the professors for assigning too much work, the parents for pushing their children too far, the students for driving themselves too hard. But there are no villains; only victims.

—William Zinsser, "College Pressures"

Comparing and contrasting. Comparing things looks at their similarities; contrasting them focuses on their differences—though often we use the word *comparison* to refer to both strategies. You can structure a paragraph that COMPARES AND CONTRASTS in two ways. One is to shift back and forth between each item *point by point*, as in this paragraph contrasting the attention given to a football team and to academic teams.

> The football team from Mountain View High School won the Arizona state championship last year. Again. Unbeknownst to the vast majority of the school's student body, so did the Science Bowl Team, the Speech and Debate Team, and the Academic Decathlon team. The football players enjoyed the attentions of an enthralled school, complete with banners, assemblies, and even video announcements in their honor, a virtual barrage of praise and downright deification. As for the three champion academic teams, they received a combined total of around ten minutes of recognition, tacked onto the beginning of a sports assembly. Nearly all of the graduating seniors will remember the name and escapades of their star quarterback; nearly none of them will ever even realize that their class produced Arizona's first national champion in Lincoln-Douglas Debate. After all, why should they? He and his teammates were "just the nerds."   —Grant Penrod, "Anti-Intellectualism: Why We Hate the Smart Kids"

Another way to compare and contrast two items is to use the *block method*, covering all the details about one and then all the details about the other. See how this approach works in the following example, which contrasts photographs of Bill Clinton and Hillary Clinton on the opening day of the 1994 baseball season.

> The next day photos of the Clintons in action appeared in newspapers around the country. Many papers, including the *New York Times* and the *Washington Post*, chose the same two photos to run. The one of Bill Clinton showed him wearing an Indians cap and warm-up jacket. The President, throwing lefty, had turned his shoulders sideways to the plate in preparation for delivery. He was bringing the ball forward from behind his head in a clean-looking throwing action as the photo was snapped. Hillary Clinton was pictured wearing a dark jacket, a scarf, and an oversized Cubs

hat. In preparation for her throw she was standing directly facing the plate. A right-hander, she had the elbow of her throwing arm pointed out in front of her. Her forearm was tilted back, toward her shoulder. The ball rested on her upturned palm. As the picture was taken, she was in the middle of an action that can only be described as throwing like a girl.

—James Fallows, "Throwing Like a Girl"

Another way to make a comparison is with an **ANALOGY**, explaining something unfamiliar by comparing it with something familiar. See how one writer uses analogy to explain the way DNA encodes genetic information.

Although the complexity of cells, tissues, and whole organisms is breathtaking, the way in which the basic DNA instructions are written is astonishingly simple. Like more familiar instruction systems such as language, numbers, or computer binary code, what matters is not so much the symbols themselves but the order in which they appear. Anagrams, for example, "derail" and "redial," contain exactly the same letters but in a different order, and so the words they spell out have completely different meanings. . . . In exactly the same way the order of the four chemical symbols in DNA embodies the message. "ACGGTA" and "GACAGT" are DNA anagrams that mean completely different things to a cell, just as "derail" and "redial" have different meanings for us.

—Bryan Sykes, "So, What Is DNA and What Does It Do?"

Defining. When you **DEFINE** something, you put it in a general category and then add characteristics that distinguish it from others in that group. The following paragraph provides brief definitions of three tropical fruits.

My grandfather died some years ago and, as is natural, my memories of our childhood spitting games receded from memory until this May, when I visited a friend's house in Mérida, in the Yucatán peninsula of Mexico. I walked onto a patio speckled with dark stains, as if the heavens had been spitting down on it. I looked up; there were the two trees responsible. One was a lollipop mango tree. Lollipop mangos are little heart-shaped mangos that you eat not by peeling and slicing the flesh, but by biting off their heads and sucking out the juices. The other was a nispero tree. A nispero (called a loquat in English) is a golf-ball-sized tropical fruit, with a thin rind the color of a deer's coat and sweet golden flesh. Beyond the patio, I saw a mammee tree, which bears large, football-shaped fruit. The fruit's flesh is just as sweet as the nispero's, but it's much more suggestive—with its carmine hues and its ominous single black seed. My friend's black-spotted patio would have made my grandmother pull out all three of her mop buckets.

—Ernesto Mestre-Reed, "A Spitting Image of Cuba"

Describing. A DESCRIPTIVE paragraph provides specific details to show what something looks like—and perhaps how it sounds, feels, smells, and tastes. Here a paragraph weaves together details of background, appearance, and speech to create a vivid impression of Chuck Yeager, the first pilot to break the sound barrier.

Yeager grew up in Hamlin, West Virginia, a town on the Mud River not far from Nitro, Hurricane, Whirlwind, Salt Rock, Mud, Sod, Crum, Leet, Dollie, Ruth, and Alum Creek. His father was a gas driller (drilling for natural gas in the coalfields), his older brother was a gas driller, and he would have been a gas driller had he not enlisted in the Army Air Force in 1941 at the age of eighteen. In 1943, at twenty, he became a flight officer, i.e., a non-com who was allowed to fly, and went to England to fly fighter planes over France and Germany. Even in the tumult of the war Yeager was somewhat puzzling to a lot of other pilots. He was a short, wiry, but muscular little guy with dark curly hair and a tough-looking face that seemed (to strangers) to be saying: "You best not be lookin' me in the eye, you peckerwood, or I'll put four more holes in your nose." But that wasn't what was puzzling. What was puzzling was the way Yeager talked. He seemed to talk with some older forms of English elocution, syntax, and conjugation that had been preserved uphollow in the Appalachians. There were people up there who never said they disapproved of anything, they said: "I don't hold with it." In the present tense they were willing to *help* out, like anyone else; but in the past tense they only *holped*. "H'it weren't nothin' I hold with, but I holped him out with it, anyways."

—Tom Wolfe, *The Right Stuff*

Explaining a process. Sometimes you might write a paragraph that explains a process —telling someone how to do something, such as how to parallel park—or how something is done, such as how bees make honey. Cookbooks explain many processes step-by-step, as in this explanation of how to pit a mango.

> The simplest method for pitting a mango is to hold it horizontally, then cut it in two lengthwise, slightly off-center, so the knife just misses the pit. Repeat the cut on the other side so a thin layer of flesh remains around the flat pit. Holding a half, flesh-side up, in the palm of your hand, slash the flesh into a lattice, cutting down to, but not through, the peel. Carefully push the center of the peel upward with your thumbs to turn it inside out, opening the cuts of the flesh. Then cut the mango cubes from the peel.   —Paulette Mitchell, *Vegetarian Appetizers*

Narrating. When you write a **NARRATIVE** paragraph in an essay, you tell a story to support a point. In the following paragraph, one author tells about being mistaken for a waitress and how that incident of stereotyping served "as a challenge" that provoked her to read her poetry with new confidence.

> One such incident that has stayed with me, though I recognize it as a minor offense, happened on the day of my first public poetry reading. It took place in Miami in a boat-restaurant where we were having lunch before the event. I was nervous and excited as I walked in with my notebook in my hand. An older woman motioned me to her table. Thinking (foolish me) that she wanted me to autograph a copy of my brand-new slender volume of verse, I went over. She ordered a cup of coffee from me, assuming that I was the waitress. Easy enough to mistake my poems for menus, I suppose. I know that it wasn't an intentional act of cruelty, yet of all the good things that happened that day, I remember that scene most clearly, because it reminded me of what I had to overcome before anyone would take me seriously. In retrospect, I understand that my anger gave my reading fire, that I have almost always taken doubts in my abilities as a challenge—and that the result is, most times, a feeling of satisfaction at having won a convert when I see the cold, appraising eyes warm to my words, the body language change, the smile that indicates that I have opened some avenue for communication. That day I read to that

woman and her lowered eyes told me that she was embarrassed at her little faux pas, and when I willed her to look up at me, it was my victory, and she graciously allowed me to punish her with my full attention. We shook hands at the end of the reading, and I never saw her again. She has probably forgotten the whole thing but maybe not.   —Judith Ortiz Cofer, *The Latin Deli*

Using examples. Illustrating a point with one or more examples is a common way to develop a paragraph, like the following one, which uses lyrics as examples to make a point about the similarities between two types of music.

> On a happier note, both rap and [country-and-western] feature strong female voices as well. Women rappers are strong, confident, and raunchy: "I want a man, not a boy/to approach me/Your lame game really insults me. . . . I've got to sit on my feet to come down to your level," taunt lady rappers Entice and Barbie at Too Short in their duet/duel, "Don't Fight the Feeling." Likewise, Loretta Lynn rose to C&W fame with defiant songs like "Don't Come Home a-Drinkin' with Lovin' on Your Mind" and "Your Squaw Is on the Warpath Tonight."
> —Denise Noe, "Parallel Worlds: The Surprising Similarities (and Differences) of Country-and-Western and Rap"

W-4c Making Paragraphs Flow

There are several ways to make your paragraphs **COHERENT** so that readers can follow your train of thought. Repetition, parallelism, and transitions are three strategies for making paragraphs flow.

Repetition. One way to help readers follow your train of thought is to repeat key words and phrases, as well as pronouns referring to those key words.

> Not that long ago, blogs were one of those annoying buzz words that you could safely get away with ignoring. The word *blog*—it works as both noun and verb—is short for *Web log*. It was coined in 1997 to describe a website where you could post daily scribblings, journal-style, about whatever you like—mostly critiquing and linking to other articles online

that may have sparked your thinking. Unlike a big media out-let, bloggers focus their efforts on narrow topics, often rising to become de facto watchdogs and self-proclaimed experts. Blogs can be about anything: politics, sex, baseball, haiku, car repair. There are blogs about blogs.   —Lev Grossman, "Meet Joe Blog"

Instead of repeating one word, you can use synonyms.

Predictably, the love of cinema has waned. People still like going to the movies, and some people still care about and expect something special, necessary from a film. And wonderful films are still being made.... But one hardly finds anymore, at least among the young, the distinctive cinephilic love of movies, which is not simply love of but a certain *taste* in films.
—Susan Sontag, "A Century of Cinema"

Parallel structures. Putting similar items into the same grammatical structure helps readers see the connection among those elements and follow your sentences—and your thoughts.

The disease was bubonic plague, present in two forms: one that infected the bloodstream, causing the buboes and internal bleeding and was spread by contact; and a second, more virulent pneumonic type that infected the lungs and was spread by respiratory infection. The presence of both at once caused the high mortality and speed of contagion. So lethal was the disease that cases were known of persons going to bed well and dying before they woke, of doctors catching the illness at a bedside and dying before the patient. So rapidly did it spread from one to another that to a French physician, Simon de Covino, it seemed as if one sick person "could infect the whole world."
—Barbara Tuchman, "'This Is the End of the World':
The Black Death"

Transitions help readers follow your train of thought—and move from sentence to sentence, paragraph to paragraph. Here are some common ones:

- *To show causes and effects*: accordingly, as a result, because, consequently, hence, so, then, therefore, thus

- *To show comparison*: along the same lines, also, in the same way, like, likewise, similarly

- *To show contrasts or exceptions:* although, but, even though, however, in contrast, instead, nevertheless, nonetheless, on the contrary, on the one hand . . . on the other hand, still, yet

- *To show examples:* for example, for instance, indeed, in fact, of course, such as

- *To show place or position:* above, adjacent to, below, beyond, elsewhere, here, inside, near, outside, there

- *To show sequence:* again, also, and, and then, besides, finally, first, furthermore, last, moreover, next, too

- *To show time:* after, as soon as, at first, at last, at the same time, before, eventually, finally, immediately, later, meanwhile, next, simultaneously, so far, soon, then, thereafter

- *To signal a summary or conclusion:* as a result, as we have seen, finally, in a word, in any event, in brief, in conclusion, in other words, in short, in the end, in the final analysis, on the whole, therefore, thus, to summarize

See how Julia Alvarez uses several transitions to show time and to move her ideas along.

> Yolanda, the third of the four girls, became a schoolteacher but not on purpose. For years after graduate school, she wrote down *poet* under profession in questionnaires and income tax forms, and later amended it to *writer*-slash-*teacher.* Finally, acknowledging that she had not written much of anything in years, she announced to her family that she was not a poet anymore.   — Julia Alvarez, *How the Garcia Girls Lost Their Accents*

Transitions can also help readers move from paragraph to paragraph; they can even signal connections between paragraphs.

> Today the used-book market is exceedingly well organized and efficient. Campus bookstores buy back not only the books that will be used at their university the next semester but also those that will not. Those that are no longer on their lists of required books they resell to national wholesalers, which in turn sell them to college bookstores on campuses where they will be required. This means that even if a text is being adopted for the first time at a particular college, there is almost certain to be an ample supply of used copies.

As a result, publishers have the chance to sell a book to only one of the multiple students who eventually use it. Hence, publishers must cover their costs and make their profit in the first semester their books are sold—before used copies swamp the market. That's why the prices are so high.

—Michael Granof, "Course Requirement: Extortion"

W-4d When to Start a New Paragraph

Paragraphs may be long or short, and there are no strict rules about how many sentences are necessary for a well-developed paragraph. But while a brief, one- or two-sentence paragraph can be used to set off an idea you want to emphasize, too many short paragraphs can make your writing choppy. Here are some reasons for beginning a new paragraph:

- to introduce a new subject or idea
- to signal a new speaker (in dialogue)
- to emphasize an idea
- to give readers a needed pause

W-4e Opening and Closing Paragraphs

A good opening engages readers and provides some indication of what's to come; a good closing leaves them feeling satisfied—that the story is complete, the questions have been answered, the argument has been made.

Opening paragraphs. Sometimes, you may begin with a general statement that provides context or background for your topic, and then proceed to state your THESIS. In the following opening paragraph, the writer begins with a generalization about academic architecture, then ends with a specific thesis stating what the rest of the essay will argue.

Academic architecture invariably projects an identity about campus and community to building users and to the world beyond.

Some institutions desire new buildings to be stand-alone statements, with ultramodern exteriors to symbolize the cutting-edge research to be conducted within. Yet in other cases, the architectural language established in surrounding precedents may be more appropriate, even for high-tech facilities. Simon Hall, a new $46.6 million interdisciplinary science building on the Indiana University campus, designed by Flad Architects of Madison, Wisconsin, inserts state-of-the-art research infrastructure in a building mass and exterior crafted to respond to their surroundings in the established vernacular of the historic Bloomington campus.

—Gregory Hoadley, "Classic Nuance:
Simon Hall at Indiana University"

OTHER WAYS OF OPENING AN ESSAY

- with an ANECDOTE
- with a quotation
- with a question
- with a startling fact or opinion

Concluding paragraphs. One approach is to conclude by summarizing the text's argument. The following paragraph reiterates the writer's main point and then issues a call for action.

The bottom line is that drastically reducing both crime rates and the number of people behind bars is technically feasible. Whether it is politically and organizationally feasible to achieve this remains an open question. It would be tragic if the politics proved prohibitive, but it would be genuinely criminal if we didn't even try.   —Mark A. R. Kleiman, "The Outpatient Prison"

OTHER WAYS OF CONCLUDING AN ESSAY

- by discussing the implications of your argument
- by asking a question
- by referring to something discussed at the beginning
- by proposing action

》 **SEE W-3f** for help editing paragraphs.

W-5 Designing What You Write

Whether you're putting together your résumé, creating a website for your intramural soccer league, or writing a research essay for a class, you need to think about how to design what you write. Sometimes you can rely on established design conventions: in academic writing, there are specific guidelines for headings, margins, and line spacing. (This book includes guidelines for **MLA**, **APA**, **Chicago**, and **CSE** styles. If you're unsure what specific style is required for your discipline, check with your instructor.)

But often you'll have to make design decisions on your own—and not just about words and spacing but also about integrating your written text with visuals (and sometimes video and audio clips and hyperlinks) in the most attractive and effective way. No matter what your text includes, its design will influence how your audience responds to it and therefore how well it achieves your purpose. This chapter offers advice on designing print and online texts to suit your **PURPOSE**, **AUDIENCE**, and the rest of your **WRITING CONTEXT**.

W-5a Some Basic Principles of Design

Be consistent. To keep readers oriented as they browse multipage documents or websites, use design elements consistently. In a print academic essay, choose a single font for your main text and use boldface or italics for headings. In writing for the web, place navigation buttons and other major elements in the same place on every page. In a presentation, use the same background and font for each slide unless there's a good reason for differences.

Keep it simple. Help readers see quickly—even intuitively—what's in your text and where to find specific information. Add headings to help them see the parts, use consistent colors and fonts to help them recognize key elements, set off steps in lists, and use white space to set off blocks of text or highlight certain elements. Resist the temptation to fill pages with unnecessary graphics or animations.

Aim for balance. Create balance through the use of margins, images, headings, and spacing. MLA, APA, *Chicago*, and CSE styles have specific design guidelines for academic research papers that cover these elements. A website or magazine might balance a large image with a narrow column of text or use PULL QUOTES and illustrations to break up columns of dense vertical text.

Use color and contrast carefully. Academic readers usually expect black text on a white background, with perhaps one other color for headings. Presentation slides and webpages are most readable with dark text on a plain, light-colored background. Make sure your audience will be able to distinguish any color variations in your text well enough to grasp your meaning. Remember that an online text with several colors might be printed out and read in black and white and that not everyone can see all colors; red-green contrasts can be particularly challenging for some people.

Use available templates. To save time and simplify design decisions, take advantage of templates. In *Microsoft Word*, for example, you can customize font, spacing, indents, and other features that will automatically be applied to your document. Websites that host personal webpages and presentation software also offer templates that you can use or modify.

W-5b Some Elements of Design

Whatever your text, you have various design decisions to make. The following guidelines will help you make those decisions.

Fonts. The fonts you choose will affect how well readers can read your text. For most academic writing, you'll want to use 10- or 11- or 12-point type. It's usually a good idea to use a serif font (such as Times New Roman or Bookman) for your main text, reserving sans serif (such as Calibri, **Verdana**, or Century Gothic) for headings and parts you want to highlight. Decorative fonts (such as Chiller) should be used sparingly. If you use more than one font, use each one consistently: one for headings, one for captions, one for the main body of your text. You won't often need more than two or three fonts in any one text.

Every common font has regular, **bold,** and *italic* forms. In general, use regular for the main text, bold for major headings, and italic for titles of books and other long works. If, however, you are following a specific discipline's style, be sure you conform to its requirements.

Layout. Layout is the way text is arranged on a page. An academic essay, for example, will usually have a title centered at the top and one-inch margins all around. Items such as lists, tables, headings, and images should be arranged consistently.

Line spacing. Generally, academic writing is double-spaced, whereas letters and résumés are usually single-spaced. In addition, you'll often need to add an extra space to set off parts of a text—lists, for instance, or headings.

Paragraphs. In general, indent paragraphs five spaces when your text is double-spaced; either indent or skip a line between paragraphs that are single-spaced. When preparing a text intended for online use, single-space your document, skip a line between paragraphs, and begin each paragraph flush left (no indent).

Lists. Use a list format for information that you want to set off and make easily accessible. Number the items when the sequence matters (in instructions, for example); use bullets when the order is not important. Set off lists with an extra line of space above and below, and add extra space between the items on a list if necessary for legibility.

White space and margins. To make your text attractive and readable, use white space to separate its various parts. In general, use one-inch margins for the text of an essay or report. Unless you're following a format that has specific guidelines (such as APA), include space above headings, above and below lists, and around photos, graphs, and other visuals.

Headings. Headings make the structure of a text easier to follow and help readers find specific information. Some academic fields require standard headings—announcing a list of WORKS CITED, for example, to follow MLA format. Whenever you include headings, you need to decide how to phrase them, what fonts to use, and where to position them.

Phrase headings consistently. Make your headings succinct and parallel in structure. For example, you might make all the headings nouns (*Mushrooms*), noun phrases (*Kinds of Mushrooms*), gerund phrases (*Recognizing Kinds of Mushrooms*), or questions (*How Do I Identify Mushrooms?*). Whatever form you decide on, use it consistently.

Make headings visible. Consider setting headings in bold or italics, or with an underline—or in a different, or slightly larger, font. When you have several levels of headings, use capitalization, bold, and italics to distinguish among the various levels:

> **First-Level Head**
> *Second-Level Head*
> Third-level head

Some academic fields have specific requirements about formatting headings; see the **MLA**, **APA**, **Chicago**, and **CSE** chapters for details.

Position headings appropriately. If you're following APA or MLA format, center first-level headings. If you are not following a prescribed format, you get to decide where to position the headings: centered, flush with the left margin, or even alongside the text, in a wide left-hand margin. Position each level of head consistently.

W-5c Visuals

Visuals (including video) can help make a point in ways that written words alone cannot. In print documents, you can often use photos, charts, graphs, and diagrams. Online or in spoken presentations, your options expand to include video and printed handouts. But choose carefully—and be sure that any items you incorporate contribute to your point and are appropriate for your purpose and audience

Photographs can support an argument, illustrate events and processes, present other points of view, and help readers place your information in time and space. A discussion of Google Glass might be clearer when accompanied by this photo.

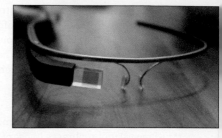

Tables are useful for displaying numerical information concisely, especially when several items are being compared. Presenting information in columns and rows permits readers to find data and identify relationships among the items.

ECONOMY WATCH

A snapshot of key figures for the world's largest economies.

COUNTRY	GDP in billions in 2010	GDP GROWTH Y/year (%)	CURRENT ACC'T/GDP in 2010 (%)	INFLATION Year over year (%)	JOBLESS (%)
U.S.	$14,658	2.0†	-3.2	3.5	8.6
Euro zone	12,474*	1.4	-0.2*	3.0	10.3
China	5,878	9.1	5.2	5.5	4.1§
Japan	5,459	5.6†	3.6	-0.1	4.5
Germany	3,316	2.5	5.3	2.8†	6.9
France	2,583	1.7	-2.1	2.5†	9.7
Britain	2,247	0.5	-2.5	5.0	8.3
Italy	2,055	0.8	-2.1*	3.7†	8.5
Brazil	1,601*	2.1	-1.5*	6.6	5.8
Canada	1,574	3.5†	-3.1	2.3	7.4
India	1,538	6.9	-3.2	9.7	n.a.
Russia	1,222*	4.8	4.1*	6.8	6.4
Mexico	1,039	4.5	-0.7*	3.5	5.0
South Korea	833*	3.5	3.9*	4.2	3.1

*Actual figures at 2009 **harmonised figures †Quarter on quarter annualised §Urban end September*

Pie charts can be used to show how a whole is divided into parts or how parts of a whole relate to one another. Percentages in a pie chart should always add up to 100. Each segment should be labeled clearly, as in these two charts about English football league finances.

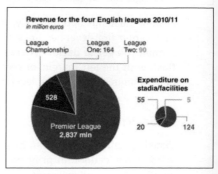

Revenue for the four English leagues 2010/11
in million euros

League Championship   League One: 164   League Two: 90

528

Premier League
2,837 mln

Expenditure on stadia/facilities

55 ⌐ 5

20   124

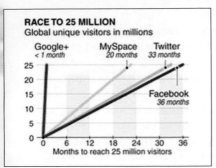

RACE TO 25 MILLION
Global unique visitors in millions

Line graphs are a good way of showing changes in data over time. Each line here represents a different social-networking site. Plotting the lines together enables readers to compare the data at different points in time. Be sure to label the x and y axes and limit the number of lines to four at the most.

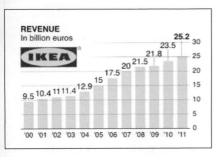

REVENUE
In billion euros

Bar graphs are useful for comparing quantitative data—measurements of how much or how many. Bars can be horizontal or vertical; this one uses vertical bars to show IKEA's earnings over the course of twelve years. Some software offers 3-D and other special effects, but simple graphs are often easier to read.

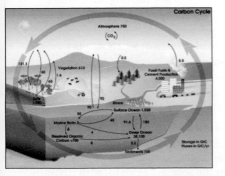

Diagrams and flowcharts are ways of showing relationships and processes. This diagram shows how carbon moves between the Earth and its atmosphere. Flowcharts can be made by using widely available templates; diagrams, on the other hand, can range from simple drawings to works of art.

SOME TIPS FOR USING VISUALS

- *Choose visuals that relate directly to your subject,* support your assertions, and add information that words alone can't provide as clearly or easily. Avoid clip art.
- *In academic writing, number each image,* using separate sequences for FIGURES and tables: *Fig. 1, Table 1.*
- *Refer to the visual before it appears.* Position images as close as possible to the relevant discussion. Explain the information you're presenting—don't expect it to speak for itself: "As Table 1 shows, Italy's economic growth rate has been declining for thirty years."
- *Provide a title or caption for each image* to identify it and explain its significance for your text: "Table 1. Italian Economic Growth Rate, 1980–2010."
- *Label the parts of charts, graphs, and diagrams clearly*—sections of a pie chart, colors in a line graph, items in a diagram—to ensure that your audience will understand what they show.
- DOCUMENT *any visual you found or adapted from another source.* If you use data to create a graph or chart, include source information directly below.
- *Consider linking to a file rather than embedding it.* Large files may be hard to upload without altering quality and can clog email inboxes. Linking also allows readers to see the original context.
- *Integrate a video clip* by pasting its URL into your text or adding an image from the video that you've hyperlinked to the source. To include your own video, upload it to *YouTube*; choose the Private setting to limit access.
- *Obtain permission* if you publish a visual in any form, including on the web. If you're in doubt about whether or not you can use an item, check "fair use" guidelines online.

If you alter a visual in some way—such as darkening a photo or cropping to include only a portion of it—tell readers what you've changed and why. Be sure to represent the original content accurately, and provide relevant information about the source. Be careful with charts and graphs as well—changing the scale on a bar graph, for example, may mislead readers.

W-6 Giving Presentations

Whether in class as part of a research project, on campus in a campaign for student government, or at a wedding in a toast to the newlyweds, you may be called on to give spoken presentations —sometimes, in combination with print and electronic media. Whatever the occasion, you need to make your points clear and memorable. This chapter offers guidelines to help you prepare and deliver effective presentations.

W-6a Key Elements of Spoken Presentations

A clear structure. Spoken texts need a clear organization so that your audience can follow you. The beginning needs to engage their interest, make clear what you will talk about, and perhaps forecast the central points of your talk. The main part should focus on a few key points—only as many as your audience can be expected to absorb. The ending should leave your audience something to remember, think about, or do.

In the Gettysburg Address, Abraham Lincoln follows a chronological structure. He begins with a reference to the past ("Four score and seven years ago"), segues to the present ("Now we are engaged in a great civil war"), looks to the future ("to the great task remaining before us"), and ends with a dramatic resolution: "that government of the people, by the people, for the people, shall not perish from the earth."

Signpost language to keep your audience on track. Provide cues, especially TRANSITIONS from one point to the next, to help your audience follow what you're saying. Sometimes, you'll also want to SUMMARIZE a complex point.

A tone to suit the occasion. Lincoln was speaking at a serious, formal event, the dedication of a national cemetery, and his TONE was **FORMAL** and solemn. In a presentation to a panel of professors, you probably would want to avoid too much slang and speak in complete sentences. Speaking on the same topic to a neighborhood group, however, you would likely want to speak more **INFORMALLY**.

Repetition and parallel structure can lend power to a presentation, making it easy to follow—and likely to be remembered. In the Gettysburg Address, the repetition and **PARALLEL** structure in "We can not dedicate—we can not consecrate—we can not hallow" create a rhythm that engages listeners and at the same time unifies the text—one reason these words stay with us more than 150 years after they were written and delivered.

Slides and other media. Depending on the topic and occasion, you may need to use slides, video or audio clips, handouts, flip charts, whiteboards, and so on to present certain information or highlight key points.

W-6b Tips for Composing a Presentation

Budget your time. A five-minute presentation calls for about two and a half double-spaced pages of writing, and ten minutes means four or five pages. Your introduction and conclusion should each take about one-tenth of the total time available; audience responses (if the format allows), about one-fifth; and the main part of the talk, the rest.

Organize and draft your presentation. Structure and word your presentation so that your audience can easily follow it—and remember what you say.

- *Draft an introduction* that engages your audience's interest and tells them what to expect. Depending on the **WRITING CONTEXT**, you may decide to begin with humor, with an **ANECDOTE**, or with something about the occasion for your talk. Provide any background information the audience needs, summarize your main points, and outline how you'll proceed.

- *In the main part of your talk, present your key points* in more detail, and support them with REASONS and EVIDENCE. If in drafting you find you have too many points for the time available, leave out the less important ones.

- *Let your listeners know when you're concluding* (but try to avoid saying "in conclusion"). Then restate your main points, and explain why they're important. Thank your listeners, and offer to take questions and comments if the format allows.

Consider whether to use visuals. Especially when you're presenting complex information, it helps to let your audience see it as well as hear it. Remember, though, that visuals should be a means of conveying information, not mere decoration.

- *Slides* are useful for listing main points and projecting illustrations, tables, and graphs.

- *Videos, animations, and audio* can add additional information.

- *Flip charts, whiteboards, or chalkboards* enable you to create visuals as you speak or to track audience comments.

- *Posters* can serve as the main part of a presentation, providing a summary of your points. You then offer only a brief introduction and answer questions.

- *Handouts* can provide additional information, lists of works cited, or copies of your slides.

What visual tools (if any) you decide to use is partly determined by how your presentation will be delivered: face to face? through a podcast? a web conference? Make sure that any necessary equipment, programs, and electrical and internet connections are available—and that they work. You may also have to move furniture or the screen to make sure everyone can see your visuals. Finally, have a backup plan. Computers fail; the internet may not work. Have an alternative in case of problems.

Presentation software. *PowerPoint* or other presentation software enables you to include images, video, and sound in addition to writ-

- Appeared overconfident
- Ran a lackluster, "safe" campaign
- Was perceived as stuffy and aloof
- Made several blunders
- Would not address issues

This slide about the 1948 presidential election uses a sans-serif font and includes an image. Using red is fine, as long as the contrast is clear and the text will be legible to those who can't see the color.

ten text. Prezi allows you to arrange slides in various designs, and zoom in and out. Here are some tips for writing and designing slides.

- *Use lists or images, not paragraphs.* Use slides to emphasize your main points, not to reproduce your talk. A list of brief points, presented one by one, reinforces your words; charts and images can provide additional information that the audience can take in quickly.

- *Make your text easy for the audience to read.* FONTS should be at least 18 points. On slides, sans serif fonts like Arial and Helvetica are easier to read than serif fonts like Times New Roman. Avoid using all capital letters, which are hard to read.

- *Choose colors carefully.* Your text and illustrations need to contrast with the background. Dark content on a light background is easier to see and read than the reverse. And remember that not everyone sees all colors; be sure your audience doesn't need to see particular colors in order to get your meaning. Red-green and blue-yellow contrasts are hard for some people to see.

- *Use bells and whistles sparingly, if at all.* Decorative backgrounds, letters that fade in and out or dance across the screen, and sound effects can be more distracting than helpful; use them only if they help to make your point.

- *Mark your text.* Indicate in your notes each place where you need to advance to the next slide.

Handouts. Label handouts with your name and the date and title of the presentation. Unless your audience needs to consult them during the presentation, distribute them after you've finished.

W-6c Delivering a Presentation

Practice. Practice, practice, and then practice some more. The better you know your talk, the more confident you'll be. Your audience will respond positively to that confidence. If you're reading a prepared text rather than using notes, practice by recording it as you read it; listen for spots that sound as if you're reading, and try to sound more relaxed. Time your talk to be sure you don't go beyond your limit. If possible, practice with a small group of friends to get used to having an audience.

Speak clearly. If listeners miss important words or phrases because you don't pronounce them distinctly, your talk will not succeed. Often you'll have to make yourself speak more slowly than usual.

Pause for emphasis. In writing, you have white space and punctuation to show readers where an idea or discussion ends. When speaking, a pause helps to signal the end of a thought, gives the audience a moment to consider what you've just said, or prepares them for a surprising or amusing statement.

Stand up (or sit up) straight, and look at your audience. If you're in the same room as your audience, try to maintain eye contact. If that's uncomfortable, fake it: focus on the wall just above someone in the back of the room. If you stand or sit up straight, you'll project confidence in what you're saying—and your audience will trust that you know what you're talking about.

Use gestures for emphasis. To overcome any nervousness and stiffness, take some deep breaths, try to relax, and move your arms and the rest of your body as you would if you were talking to a friend. Use your hands for emphasis; watch politicians on C-SPAN to see how people who speak on a regular basis use gestures as part of their delivery.

>> **SEE W-1** for help analyzing your writing context. See **W-3** for guidelines on drafting, revising, editing, and proofreading.
To read an example presentation, go to **digital.wwnorton.com /littleseagull3**.

W-7   Arguments

Everything we say or do presents some kind of argument, takes some kind of position. Often we take overt positions: "Everyone in the United States is entitled to affordable health care." "Photoshopped images should carry disclosure notices." In college course work, you are constantly called on to argue positions: in an English class, you may argue for a certain interpretation of a poem; in a business course, you may argue for the merits of a flat tax. All of those positions are arguable—people of goodwill can agree or disagree with them. This chapter provides a description of the key elements of an essay that argues a position and tips for writing one.

W-7a Key Elements of an Argument

A clear and arguable position. At the heart of every argument is a CLAIM with which people may reasonably disagree. Some claims are not arguable because they're matters of taste or opinion ("I love kale"), of fact ("The first *Star Wars* movie came out in 1977"), or belief or faith ("There is life after death"). To be arguable, a position must reflect one of at least two points of view, making reasoned argument necessary: file sharing should (or should not) be considered fair use; selling human organs should be legal (or illegal). In college writing, you will often argue not that a position is correct but that it is plausible—that it is reasonable, supportable, and worthy of being taken seriously.

Necessary background information. Sometimes, we need to provide some background on a topic so that readers can understand what is being argued. To argue that file sharing should be considered fair use, for example, you might begin by describing the rise in file sharing and explaining fair-use laws.

Good reasons. By itself, a position does not make an argument; the argument comes when a writer offers reasons to support the position. There are many kinds of good REASONS. You might argue that file sharing should be fair use by comparing, showing many examples of so-called piracy in other media. You might base an argument in favor of legalizing the sale of human organs on the fact that transplants save lives and that regulation would protect impoverished people who currently sell their organs on the black market.

Convincing evidence. Once you've given reasons for your position, you then need to offer EVIDENCE for your reasons: facts, statistics, testimony, anecdotes, textual examples, and so on. For example, to support your position that fast food should be taxed, you might cite a nutrition expert who links obesity to fast food, offer facts that demonstrate the health-care costs of widespread obesity, and provide statistics that show how taxation affects behavior.

Appeals to readers' values. Effective arguments appeal to readers' values and emotions. For example, arguing that legalizing organ sales will save the lives of those in need of transplants appeals to compassion—a deeply held value. To appeal to readers' emotions, you might describe the plight of those who are dying in want of a transplant. Keep in mind, however, that emotional appeals can make readers feel manipulated—and then less likely to accept an argument.

A trustworthy TONE. Readers need to trust the person who's making the argument. There are many ways of establishing yourself (and your argument) as trustworthy: by providing facts that demonstrate your knowledge of the subject, by indicating that you have some experience with it, by demonstrating that you've considered perspectives other than your own, and by showing that you're fair and honest.

Careful consideration of other positions. No matter how reasonable you are in arguing your position, others may disagree or hold other positions. So you need to acknowledge any likely COUNTER-ARGUMENTS and, if possible, refute them. For example, you might acknowledge that some people object to file sharing because they think "piracy" is inherently wrong, but then you could counter that some types of content piracy have historically been productive for an industry in general, including the pirated firms—and give examples.

W-7b Tips for Writing an Argument

Choosing a topic. A fully developed argument requires significant work and time, so choosing a topic in which you're interested is very important. Widely debated topics such as animal rights or gun control can be difficult to write on if you have no personal connection to them. Better topics include those that interest you right now, are focused, and have some personal connection to your life. Here's one good way to GENERATE IDEAS for a topic that meets those three criteria:

Start with your roles in life. Make four columns with the headings "Personal," "Family," "Public," and "School." Then list the roles you play in life that relate to each heading. Under "School," for example, your list might include *college student, dorm resident, chemistry major,* and *work-study employee.*

Identify issues that interest you. Pick a few of the roles you list, and identify the issues that interest or concern you. Try wording each issue as a question starting with *should: Should college cost less than it does? Should student achievement be measured by standardized tests?*

Try framing your topic as a problem: *Why has college tuition risen so rapidly in recent years? What would be better than standardized tests for measuring student achievement?* This strategy will help you think about the issue and find a clear focus for your essay.

Choose one issue to write about. It is a preliminary choice; if you find later that you have trouble writing about it, you'll be able to go back to your list and choose another.

Generating ideas and text. Most essays that successfully argue a position share certain features that make them interesting and persuasive. Remember that your goal is to stake out a position and convince your readers that it's plausible.

Explore the issue. Write out whatever you know about the issue, perhaps by FREEWRITING or making an OUTLINE. Consider what interests you about the topic and what more you may need to learn in order to write about it. It may help to do some preliminary research; start with one general source of information (a news magazine or *Wikipedia*, for example) to find out the main questions raised about your issue and to get some ideas about how you might argue it. Make sure your issue is arguable—and worth arguing about.

Draft a THESIS. Once you've explored the issue thoroughly, decide your position on it, and write it out as a sentence—for example, "Baseball players who use steroids should not be eligible for the Hall of Fame." In most cases you'll then want to qualify your thesis—to acknowledge that yours is not the only plausible position, and to limit your topic and make it manageable. There are various ways to qualify your thesis: *in certain circumstances, under certain conditions, with these limitations,* and so on. For example, "Though baseball players who use steroids should not be eligible for the Hall of Fame, their records and achievements will still stand."

Come up with good REASONS. You need to convince your readers that your thesis is plausible. Start by stating your position and then answering the question *why?*

> **THESIS:**   Baseball players who use steroids should not be eligible for the Hall of Fame.
>
> **REASON:**   (Because) Using steroids gives athletes unfair advantages.

Keep in mind that you will likely have a further reason, a principle that underlies the reason you give for your CLAIM.

> **UNDERLYING REASON:**   Gaining an unfair advantage is cheating.
>
> **UNDERLYING REASON:**   Cheating is wrong.

This analysis can continue indefinitely as the underlying reasons grow more and more general and abstract. When you've listed several reasons, consider which are the most persuasive ones given your PURPOSE and AUDIENCE.

Find EVIDENCE to support your reasons. Here are some kinds of evidence you can offer as support: facts; statistics; testimony by authorities and experts; ANECDOTES; case studies and observations; textual evidence; and visual evidence like photos, graphs, and videos.

Identify other positions. Think about positions that differ from yours and about the reasons that might be given for those positions. Even if you can't refute such doubts about and objections to your position, you need to acknowledge them to show that you've considered other perspectives. To refute other positions, state them as clearly and as fairly as you can, and then show why you believe they are wrong. Perhaps the reasoning is faulty or the supporting evidence is inadequate. Acknowledge their merits, if any, but emphasize their shortcomings.

Ways of organizing an argument. Sometimes, you'll want to give all the reasons for your argument first, followed by discussion of all the counterarguments. Alternatively, you might discuss each reason and any counterargument to it together. And be sure to consider the order in which you discuss your reasons. Usually, what comes last makes the strongest impression on readers, and what comes in the middle makes the weakest impression.

[Reasons to support your argument, followed by counterarguments]

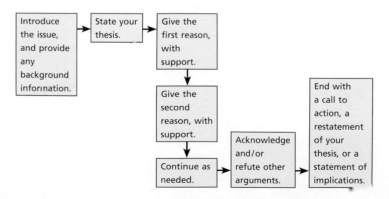

[Reason / counterargument, reason / counterargument]

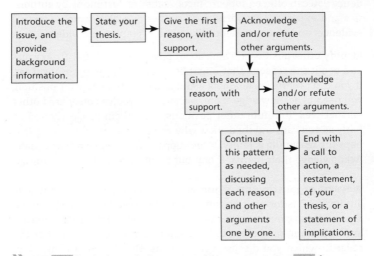

| Introduce the issue, and provide background information. | → | State your thesis. | → | Give the first reason, with support. | → | Acknowledge and/or refute other arguments. |

| Give the second reason, with support. | → | Acknowledge and/or refute other arguments. |

| Continue this pattern as needed, discussing each reason and other arguments one by one. | → | End with a call to action, a restatement, of your thesis, or a statement of implications. |

>> **SEE W-1** for help analyzing your writing context. See **W-3** for guidelines on drafting, revising, editing, and proofreading your argument. See **W-16b** for guidelines on analyzing an argument. To read an example argument essay, go to **digital.wwnorton.com /littleseagull3**.

W-8   Rhetorical Analyses

Both the *Huffington Post* and *National Review* cover the same events, but they each interpret them differently. All toothpaste ads claim to make teeth "the whitest." Those are just a couple of examples that demonstrate why we need to be careful, analytical readers of magazines and newspapers, websites, ads, political documents, even textbooks—to understand not only what texts say but also how they say it. Assignments in many disciplines call for a rhetorical analysis: you may be asked to analyze the use of color and space in Edward Hopper's painting *Nighthawks* for an art history course, or to analyze a set of data to find the standard deviation in a statistics course. This chapter describes the key elements of an essay that analyzes a text and provides tips for writing one.

W-8a Key Elements of a Rhetorical Analysis

A summary of the text. Your readers may not know the text you are analyzing, so you need to include it or tell them about it before you can analyze it. A well-known text such as the Gettysburg Address may require only a brief description, but less well-known texts require a more detailed SUMMARY. For an analysis of several advertisements, for example, you'd likely show several ads and also describe them in some detail.

Attention to the context. All texts are part of ongoing conversations, controversies, or debates, so to understand a text, you need to understand its larger context. To analyze the lyrics of a new hip-hop song, you might need to introduce other artists that the lyrics refer to or explain how the lyrics relate to aspects of hip-hop culture.

A clear interpretation or judgment. Your goal is to lead readers through a careful examination of the text to some kind of interpretation or reasoned judgment, generally announced clearly in a THESIS statement. When you interpret something, you explain what you think it means. If you're analyzing the TV show *Family Guy*, you might argue that a particular episode is a parody of the political controversy over health care. In an analysis of a cologne advertisement, you might explain how the ad encourages consumers to objectify themselves.

Reasonable support for your conclusions. You'll need to support your analysis with EVIDENCE from the text itself and sometimes from other sources. You might support your interpretation by quoting passages from a written text or referring to images in a visual text. To argue that Barack Obama's eulogy for Reverend Pinckney aligns him with Martin Luther King Jr. and Abraham Lincoln, you might trace the ways his wording echoes that of "I Have a Dream" and Lincoln's second inaugural address, for example. Note that the support you offer need only be "reasonable"—there is never only one way to interpret something.

W-8b Tips for Writing a Rhetorical Analysis

Choosing a text to analyze. Most of the time, you will be assigned a text or a type of text to analyze: the work of a political philosopher in a political science class, a speech in a history or communications course, a painting or sculpture in an art class, and so on. If you must choose a text to analyze, look for one that suits the assignment—one that is neither too large or complex to analyze thoroughly nor too brief or limited to generate sufficient material. You might also analyze three or four texts by examining elements common to all.

Generating ideas and text. In analyzing a text, your goal is to understand what it says, how it works, and what it means. To do so, you may find it helpful to follow a certain sequence for your analysis: read, respond, summarize, analyze, and draw conclusions.

Read to see what the text says. Start by reading carefully, noting the main ideas, key words and phrases, and anything that seems noteworthy or questionable.

Once you have a sense of what the text says, consider your initial response. What's your reaction to the argument, the tone, the language, the images? Do you find the text difficult? puzzling? Do you agree with what the writer says? Whatever your reaction, think about how you react—and why.

Then consolidate your understanding of the text by SUMMARIZING or DESCRIBING it in your own words.

Decide what you want to analyze. Think about what you find most interesting about the text and why. Does the language interest you? the imagery? the larger context? Something else? You might begin your analysis by exploring what attracted your notice.

Think about the larger context. All texts are part of larger conversations, and academic texts include documentation partly to weave in voices from the conversation. Being aware of that larger context can help you better understand what you're reading; here are some things to consider:

- *What larger conversation does the text respond to?* What's motivated the writer? Does he or she respond to something others have said?

- *Who else cares about this topic?* Those cited could be assumed to care, but does the author indicate who else cares—and why the topic matters in the first place?

- *Where is the writer coming from?* Is there any terminology that suggests that he or she is allied with a particular intellectual school or academic discipline? Words like *false consciousness* or *hegemony,* for instance, would suggest that the text was written by a Marxist scholar.

Consider what you know about the writer or artist. The credentials, other work, reputation, stance, and beliefs of the person who created the text are all useful windows into understanding it. Write a sentence or two summarizing what you know about the creator and how that information affects your understanding of the text.

Study how the text works. Written texts are made up of various components, including words, sentences, headings, punctuation—and sometimes images as well. Visual texts might be made up of images, lines, angles, color, light and shadow, and sometimes words. Look for patterns in the way these elements are used. Write a sentence or two describing the patterns you discover and how they contribute to what the text says.

Analyze the argument. An important part of understanding any text is to recognize its ARGUMENT —what the writer or artist wants the audience to believe, feel, or do.

- *What is the claim?* What is the main point the writer is trying to make? Is there a clearly stated THESIS, or is it merely implied?

- *What support does the writer offer for the claim?* What REASONS are given to support the claim, and what EVIDENCE backs up those reasons? Are the reasons plausible and sufficient?

- *How evenhandedly does the writer present the issues?* Are the arguments appropriately qualified? Is there any mention of COUNTER-ARGUMENTS —and if so, how does the writer deal with them?

- *What authorities or other sources of information are cited?* How credible and current are they?

- *Do you see any logical FALLACIES?* Arguments that rely on faulty reasoning can seem plausible, and they can be persuasive—but they're misleading.

After considering these questions, write a sentence or two summarizing the argument and your reactions to it.

Come up with a thesis. Once you've studied the text thoroughly, you need to identify your analytical goal. Do you want to show that the text has a certain meaning? uses certain techniques to achieve its purposes? tries to influence its audience in particular ways? relates to some larger context in some significant manner? Something else? Come up with a tentative thesis to guide you—but be aware that your thesis may change as you work.

Ways of organizing a rhetorical analysis. Consider how to organize the information you've gathered to best support your thesis. Your analysis might be structured in at least two ways. You might discuss patterns or themes that run through the text. Alternatively, you might analyze each text or section of text separately.

[Thematically]

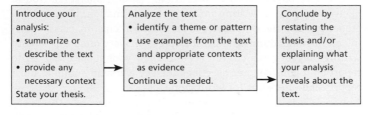

Introduce your analysis:
• summarize or describe the text
• provide any necessary context
State your thesis.

Analyze the text
• identify a theme or pattern
• use examples from the text and appropriate contexts as evidence
Continue as needed.

Conclude by restating the thesis and/or explaining what your analysis reveals about the text.

[Part by part, or text by text]

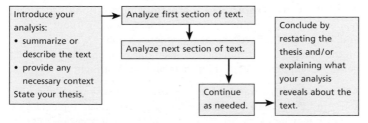

Introduce your analysis:
• summarize or describe the text
• provide any necessary context
State your thesis.

Analyze first section of text.

Analyze next section of text.

Continue as needed.

Conclude by restating the thesis and/or explaining what your analysis reveals about the text.

>> **SEE W-1** for help analyzing your writing context. See **W-3** for guidelines on drafting, revising, editing, and proofreading a textual analysis. To read an example rhetorical analysis, go to **digital.wwnorton.com/littleseagull3**.

W-9　Reports

Many kinds of writing report information. Newspapers report on local and world events; textbooks give information about biology, history, writing; websites provide information about products (jcrew.com), people (lebronjames.com), institutions (smithsonian.org). You've likely done a lot of writing that reports information, from a third-grade report on the water cycle to an essay for a history class reporting on migrants during the Great Depression. Very often this kind of writing calls for research: you need to know your subject in order to report on it. This chapter describes the key elements found in most reports and offers tips for writing one.

W-9a　Key Elements of a Report

A tightly focused topic. The goal of this kind of writing is to inform readers about something without digressing—and without, in general, bringing in the writer's own opinions. If you're writing a report on the causes of air turbulence, for example, you probably shouldn't get into complaints about the delays on your last flight.

Accurate, well-researched information. Reports usually require some research. The kind of research depends on the topic. Library research may be necessary for some topics—for a report on migrant laborers during the Great Depression, for example. Most current topics, however, require internet research. Some topics may require FIELD RESEARCH — interviews, observations, and so on. For a report on local farming, for example, you might interview some local farmers.

Various writing strategies. You'll usually use a number of organizing STRATEGIES — to describe something, explain a process, and so on. For example, a report on the benefits of exercise might require that you classify types of exercise, analyze the effects of each type, and compare the benefits of each.

Clear definitions. Reports need to provide clear **DEFINITIONS** of any key terms that the audience may not know. For a report on the 2008 financial crisis for a general audience, for example, you might need to define terms such as *mortgage-backed security* and *predatory lending*.

Appropriate design. Some information is best presented in paragraphs, but other information may be easier to present (and to read) in lists, tables, diagrams, and other **VISUALS**. Numerical data, for instance, can be easier to understand in a table than in a paragraph. A photograph can help readers see a subject, such as an image of someone texting while driving in a report on car accidents.

W-9b Tips for Writing a Report

Choosing a topic. If you get to choose your topic, consider what interests you and what you wish you knew more about. The possible topics for informational reports are limitless, but the topics that you're most likely to write well on are those that engage you. They may be academic in nature or reflect your personal interests, or both.

If your topic is assigned, be sure to understand what you're required to do. Some assignments are specific: "Explain the physics of roller coasters." If, however, your assignment is broad—"Explain some aspect of the US government"—try focusing on a more limited aspect of that topic, preferably one that interests you: federalism, the electoral college, filibusters. Even if an assignment seems to offer little flexibility, you will need to decide how to research the topic and how to develop your report to appeal to your audience. And sometimes even narrow topics can be shaped to fit your own interests.

Generating ideas and text. Start by exploring whatever you know or want to know about your topic, perhaps by **FREEWRITING**, **LOOPING**, or **CLUSTERING**, all activities that will help you come up with ideas. Then you'll need to narrow your focus.

Narrow your topic. You may know which aspect of the topic you want to focus on, but often you'll need to do some research first—and that research may change your thinking and your focus. Start with sources that can give you a general sense of the subject, such as a *Wikipedia* entry or an interview with an expert. Your goal at this point is to find topics to report on and then to focus on one that you will be able to cover.

Come up with a tentative thesis. Once you narrow your topic, write out a statement saying what you plan to report on or explain. A good THESIS is potentially interesting (to you and your readers) and limits your topic enough to be manageable. For a report on the benefits of exercise, for instance, your thesis might be "While weight lifting can build strength and endurance, regular cardiovascular exercise offers greater overall health benefits."

Do any necessary research. Focus your efforts by OUTLINING what you expect to discuss. Identify any aspects you'll need to research. Think about what kinds of information will be most informative for your audience, and be sure to consult multiple sources and perspectives. Revisit and finalize your thesis in light of your research findings.

Ways of organizing a report

[Reports on topics that are unfamiliar to readers]

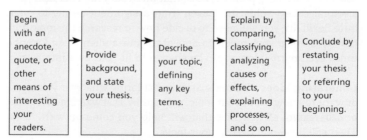

Begin with an anecdote, quote, or other means of interesting your readers. → Provide background, and state your thesis. → Describe your topic, defining any key terms. → Explain by comparing, classifying, analyzing causes or effects, explaining processes, and so on. → Conclude by restating your thesis or referring to your beginning.

[Reports on an event]

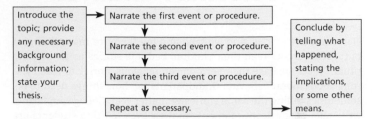

[Reports that compare by the block method]

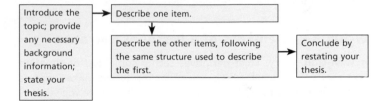

[Reports that compare by the point-by-point method]

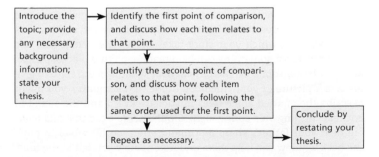

>> **SEE W-1** for help analyzing your writing context. See **W-3** for guidelines on drafting, revising, editing, and proofreading your report. To read an example report, go to **digital.wwnorton.com /littleseagull3**.

W-10   Personal Narratives

Narratives are stories, and we read and tell them for many different purposes. Parents read their children bedtime stories as an evening ritual. Preachers base their sermons on religious stories to teach lessons about moral behavior. Grandparents tell how things used to be, sometimes telling the same stories year after year. College applicants write about significant moments in their lives. Writing students are often called on to compose narratives to explore their personal experiences. This chapter describes the key elements of personal narratives and provides tips for writing one.

W-10a Key Elements of a Personal Narrative

A well-told story. Most narratives set up some sort of situation that needs to be resolved. That need for resolution makes readers want to keep reading. You might write about a challenge you've overcome, for example, such as learning a new language or dealing with some kind of discrimination.

Vivid detail. Details can bring a narrative to life by giving readers vivid mental images of the sights, sounds, smells, tastes, and textures of the world in which your story takes place. The details you use when DESCRIBING something can help readers picture places, people, and events; DIALOGUE can help them hear what is being said. To give readers a picture of your childhood home in the country, you might describe the gnarled apple trees in your backyard and the sound of crickets chirping on a spring night. Similarly, dialogue that lets readers hear your father's sharp reprimand after you hit a ball through the back window can help them understand how you felt at the time. Depending on your topic and your MEDIUM, you may want to provide some of the details in audio or visual form.

Some indication of the narrative's significance. Narratives usually have a point; you need to make clear why the incident matters to you, or how the narrative supports a larger argument. You may reveal its significance in various ways, but try not to state it too directly, as if it were a kind of moral of the story. A story about the lasting impression of a conversation with your grandfather about the novel he started but never finished would likely be less effective if you were to end by saying, "He taught me to value creative writing."

W-10b Tips for Writing a Personal Narrative

Choosing a topic. In general, it's a good idea to focus on a single event that took place during a relatively brief period of time:

- an event that was interesting, humorous, or embarrassing
- something you found (or find) especially difficult or challenging
- the origins of an attitude or belief you hold
- a memory from your childhood that remains vivid

Make a list of possible topics, and then choose one that you think will be interesting to you and to others—and that you're willing to share.

Generating ideas and text. Start by writing out what you remember about the setting and those involved, perhaps BRAINSTORMING, LOOPING, or QUESTIONING to help you generate ideas.

Describe the setting. List the places where your story unfolds. For each place, write informally for a few minutes, DESCRIBING what you remember seeing, hearing, smelling, tasting, and feeling.

Think about the key people. Narratives include people whose actions play an important role in the story. To develop your understanding of the people in your narrative, you might begin by describing them—their movements, their posture, their bearing, their facial expressions. Then try writing several lines of DIALOGUE between two people in your narrative, including distinctive words or phrases they used. If you can't remember an actual conversation, make up one that could have happened.

Write about what happened. At the heart of every good narrative is the answer to the question "What happened?" The action may be as dramatic as winning a championship or as subtle as a conversation between two friends; both contain action, movement, or change that the narrative dramatizes for readers. Try narrating the action using active and specific verbs (*pondered*, *shouted*, *laughed*) to capture what happened.

Consider the significance. You need to make clear why the event you are writing about matters. How did it change or otherwise affect you? What aspects of your life now can you trace to that event? How might your life have been different if this event had not happened?

Ways of organizing a personal narrative. Don't assume that the only way to tell your story is just as it happened. That's one way—starting at the beginning of the action and continuing to the end. You might also start in the middle—or even at the end.

[Chronologically, from beginning to end]

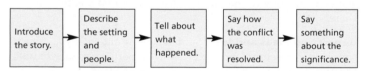

| Introduce the story. | Describe the setting and people. | Tell about what happened. | Say how the conflict was resolved. | Say something about the significance. |

[Beginning in the middle]

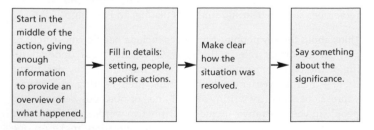

| Start in the middle of the action, giving enough information to provide an overview of what happened. | Fill in details: setting, people, specific actions. | Make clear how the situation was resolved. | Say something about the significance. |

[Beginning at the end]

Start by telling how the story ends up; then introduce the subject.	Go back to the beginning of the story, telling what happens chronologically and describing the setting and people.	Conclude by saying something about the story's significance.

>> **SEE W-1** for help analyzing your writing context. See **W-3** for guidelines on drafting, revising, editing, and proofreading your narrative. To read an example narrative, go to **digital.wwnorton .com/littleseagull3**.

W-11   Literary Analyses

Literary analyses are essays in which we examine literary texts closely to understand their messages, interpret their meanings, and appreciate their writers' techniques. You might look for a pattern in the images of blood in Shakespeare's *Macbeth* or point out the differences between Stephen King's *The Shining* and Stanley Kubrick's screenplay based on that novel. In both cases, you go below the surface to deepen your understanding of how the texts work and what they mean. This chapter describes the key elements expected in most literary analyses and provides tips for writing one.

W-11a Key Elements of a Literary Analysis

An arguable THESIS. In a literary analysis, you are arguing that your ANALYSIS of a work is valid. Your thesis, then, should be arguable. You might argue, for example, that the dialogue between two female characters in a short story reflects current stereotypes about gender roles. But a mere summary—"In this story, two women discuss their struggles to succeed"—would not be arguable and therefore is not a good thesis. (See W-7a for help developing an arguable thesis.)

Careful attention to the language of the text. Specific words, images, METAPHORS —these are the foundation of a text's meaning, and are where analysis begins. You may also bring in contextual information or refer to similar texts, but the words, phrases, and sentences that make up the text you're analyzing are your primary source. That's what literature teachers mean by "close reading": reading with the assumption that every word of a text is meaningful.

Attention to patterns or themes. Literary analyses are usually built on evidence of meaningful patterns or themes within a text or among several texts. For example, you might analyze how the images of snow, ice, and wind and the repetition of the word *nothing* contribute to a sense of loneliness and desolation in a poem about a winter scene.

A clear INTERPRETATION. When you write a literary analysis, you show one way the text may be understood, using evidence from the text and, sometimes, relevant contextual evidence to support what you think the text means.

MLA style. Literary analyses usually follow MLA style.

W-11b Tips for Writing a Literary Analysis

Generating ideas and text. Start by considering whether your assignment specifies a particular kind of analysis or critical approach. Look for words that say what to do: *analyze*, *compare*, *interpret*, and so on. Then you'll want to take a close look at the literary work.

Choose a method for analyzing the text. If your assignment doesn't specify a particular method, three common approaches are to focus on the text itself; on your own experience reading it; and on other cultural, historical, or literary contexts:

- *The text itself.* Trace the development and expression of themes, characters, and language through the work. How do they help to create particular meaning, tone, or effects?

- *Your own response as a reader.* Explore the way the text affects you as you read through it. Read closely, noticing how the elements of the text shape your responses, both intellectual and emotional. How has the author evoked your response?

- *Context.* Analyze the text as part of some larger context—as part of a certain time or place in history or of a certain culture; or as one of many other texts like it, a representative of a genre.

Read the work more than once. When you first experience a piece of literature, you usually focus on the story, the plot, the overall meaning. By experiencing the work repeatedly, you can see how its effects are achieved, what the pieces are and how they fit together, where different patterns emerge, and how the author crafted the work.

Compose a strong thesis. The THESIS of a literary analysis should be specific, limited, and open to potential disagreement. In addition, it should be ANALYTICAL, not EVALUATIVE. Your goal is not to pass judgment but to suggest one way of seeing the text.

Do a close reading. Find specific, brief passages that support your interpretation; then analyze those passages in terms of their language, their context, and your reaction to them as a reader. Do a close reading, questioning as you go:

- What does each word (phrase, passage) mean exactly? Why does the writer choose *this* language, *these* words?

- What images or metaphors are used? What is their effect?

- What patterns of language, imagery, or plot do you see? If something is repeated, what significance does the pattern have?

- What words, phrases, or passages connect to a larger context?

- How do these various elements of language, image, and pattern support your thesis?

Support your argument with evidence. The parts of the text you examine in your close reading become the evidence you use to support your interpretation. Treat your analysis like any other ARGUMENT: discuss how the text creates an effect or expresses a theme, and then show EVIDENCE from the text—significant plot or structural elements; important characters; patterns of language, imagery, or action—to back up your argument.

Paying attention to matters of style. Literary analyses have certain conventions for using pronouns and verbs. In informal papers, it's okay to use the first person: "I believe Frost's narrator provides little basis for claiming that one road is 'less traveled.'" In more formal essays, make assertions directly: "Frost's narrator provides no basis for claiming that one road is 'less traveled.'" Discuss textual features in the present tense even if quotations from the text are in another tense. Describe the historical context of the setting in the past tense.

One way of organizing a literary analysis

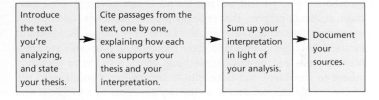

| Introduce the text you're analyzing, and state your thesis. | Cite passages from the text, one by one, explaining how each one supports your thesis and your interpretation. | Sum up your interpretation in light of your analysis. | Document your sources. |

>> **SEE** **W-1** for help analyzing your writing context. See **W-16** for more help reading with a critical eye. For guidelines on drafting, revising, editing, and proofreading, see **W-3**. To read an example literary analysis, go to **digital.wwnorton.com/littleseagull3**.

W-12 Proposals

You need a car, so you propose paying half the cost of a car and insurance if your parents will pay the other half. Lovers propose marriage; students propose that colleges provide healthier food options in campus cafeterias. These are all examples of proposals, ideas put forward that offer solutions to some problem. All proposals are arguments: when you propose something, you are trying to persuade others to consider—and hopefully to accept—your solution to the problem. This chapter describes the key elements of a proposal and provides tips for writing one.

W-12a Key Elements of Proposals

A well-defined problem. Some problems are self-evident and relatively simple, and you would not need much persuasive power to make people act. While some might not see a problem with colleges discarding too much paper, for example, most are likely to agree that recycling is a good thing. Other issues are more controversial: some people see them as problems while others do not. For example, some believe that motorcycle riders who do not wear helmets risk serious injury and also raise the cost of health care for all of us, but others think that wearing a helmet—or not—should be a personal choice; you would have to present arguments to convince your readers that not wearing a helmet is indeed a problem needing a solution. Any written proposal must establish that there is a problem—and that it's serious enough to require a solution.

A solution to the problem. Once you have defined the problem, you need to describe the solution you are suggesting and to explain it in enough detail for readers to understand what you are proposing. Sometimes you might suggest several possible solutions, analyze their merits, and then say which one you think will most likely solve the problem.

A convincing argument for your proposed solution. You need to provide evidence to convince readers that your solution is feasible—and that it will, in fact, solve the problem. If, for example, you're proposing that motorcycle riders be required to wear helmets, you might provide data about the serious injuries suffered by those not wearing helmets—and note that insurance rates are tied to the costs of dealing with such injuries. Sometimes you'll want to explain in detail how your proposed solution would work.

A response to questions readers may have. You need to consider any questions readers may have about your proposal—and to show how its advantages outweigh any disadvantages. A proposal for recycling paper, for example, would need to address questions about the costs of recycling bins and separate trash pickups.

A call to action. The goal of a proposal is to persuade readers to accept your proposed solution—and perhaps to take some kind of action. You may want to conclude your proposal by noting the outcomes likely to result from following your recommendations.

An appropriate tone. Since you're trying to persuade readers to act, your tone is important. Readers will always react better to a reasonable, respectful presentation than to anger or self-righteousness.

W-12b Tips for Writing a Proposal

Choosing a topic. Choose a problem that can be solved. Large, complex problems such as poverty, hunger, or terrorism usually require large, complex solutions. Most of the time, focusing on a smaller problem or a limited aspect of a large problem will yield a more manageable proposal. Rather than tackling the problem of world poverty, for example, think about the problem faced by people in your community who have lost jobs and need help until they find employment.

Generating ideas and text. Most successful proposals share certain features that make them persuasive. Remember that your goal is to identify a problem that matters, come up with a feasible solution, and convince readers that it will solve the problem.

Explore several possible solutions to the problem. Many problems can be solved in more than one way, and you need to show your readers that you've examined several potential solutions. You may develop solutions on your own; more often, though, you'll need to do RESEARCH to see how others have solved—or tried to solve—similar problems. Don't settle on a single solution too quickly; you'll need to compare the advantages and disadvantages of several solutions in order to argue convincingly for one.

Decide on the most desirable solution(s). One solution may be head and shoulders above others, but be open to rejecting all the possible solutions on your list and starting over if you need to, or to combining two or more potential solutions in order to come up with an acceptable fix.

Think about why your solution is the best one. What has to be done to enact it? What will it cost? What makes you think it can be done? Why will it work better than others?

Ways of organizing a proposal. You can organize a proposal in various ways, but you should always begin by establishing that there is a problem. You may then identify several possible solutions before recommending one of them or a combination of several. Sometimes, however, you might discuss only a single solution.

[Several possible solutions]

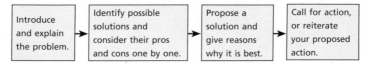

| Introduce and explain the problem. | → | Identify possible solutions and consider their pros and cons one by one. | → | Propose a solution and give reasons why it is best. | → | Call for action, or reiterate your proposed action. |

[A single solution]

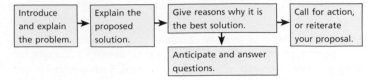

Introduce and explain the problem. → Explain the proposed solution. → Give reasons why it is the best solution. → Call for action, or reiterate your proposal.

Anticipate and answer questions.

>> **SEE W-1** for help analyzing your writing context. See **W-3** for guidelines on drafting, revising, editing, and proofreading your argument. To read an example proposal, go to **digital.wwnorton.com/littleseagull3**.

W-13 Reflections

Sometimes we write essays just to think about something—to specu-late, ponder, probe; to play with an idea; to develop a thought; or simply to share something that's on our mind. Such essays are our attempt to think something through by writing about it and to share our thinking with others. If such essays make an argument, it is about things we're thinking about more than about what we believe to be "true." This chapter describes the key elements of a reflective essay and tips for writing one.

W-13a Key Elements of a Reflection

A topic that intrigues you. A reflective essay has a dual pur-pose: to ponder something you find interesting or puzzling and to share your thoughts with an audience. Your topic may be any-thing that interests you—someone you're curious about, some-thing that happened that's got you thinking, some idea you want to contemplate. Whatever your subject, your goal is to explore it in a way that will interest others. One way to do that is to start by considering your own experience and then moving on to think about more universal experiences that your readers may share. For example, you might write about your dog, and in doing so you could raise questions and offer insights about the ways that people and animals interact.

Some kind of structure. A reflective essay can be organized in many ways, but it needs to have a clear structure. Whether you move from detail to detail or focus your reflection on one central question or insight about your subject, all your ideas need to relate, one way or another. The challenge is to keep your readers interested as you explore your topic and to leave them satisfied that the journey was interesting and thought-provoking.

Specific details. You'll need to provide concrete details to help readers understand and connect with your subject. In an essay about his dog, Jonathan Safran Foer offers a wealth of DESCRIPTIVE details ("She mounts guests, eats my son's toys . . . lunges at skateboarders and Hasids. . . ."). ANECDOTES can bring your subject to life, as Foer shows when he tells us that sometimes his dog will "tear into a full sprint" and that "Other dog owners can't help but watch her. Every now and then someone will cheer her on." You might explore CAUSES (why are Labrador Retrievers so popular?) or make COMPARISONS (how's your dog better than all the others?). Details such as these will help your readers understand and care about your subject.

A questioning, speculative tone. In a reflective essay, you're usually looking for answers, not providing them neatly organized and ready for consumption. So your tone will often be tentative and open, demonstrating a willingness to entertain, try out, accept, and reject various ideas as your essay progresses from beginning to end, maybe even asking questions for which you can provide no direct answers.

W-13b Tips for Writing a Reflection

Choosing a topic. Choose a subject you want to explore. Make a list of things that you think about, wonder about, find puzzling or annoying. They may be big things (work, relationships) or little things (a friend's quirky behavior, an everyday event). Begin by FREEWRITING to see what comes to mind as you write, and then try CLUSTERING to see how your ideas relate to one another.

Generating ideas and text. Start by exploring your topic, perhaps by BRAINSTORMING, LOOPING, QUESTIONING, even doodling—all activities that will help you come up with ideas.

Explore your subject in detail. Reflections often include descriptive details that provide a base for the speculations to come. Foer, for example, DESCRIBES the many ways he encounters dogs in New York:

"Retrievers in elevators, Pomeranians on No. 6 trains, Bull mastiffs crossing the Brooklyn Bridge." You may also use other STRATEGIES to explore your subject: DEFINING, COMPARING, CLASSIFYING, and so on.

Back away. Ask yourself why your subject matters: why is it important or intriguing or otherwise significant? You may try LISTING or OUTLINING possible answers, or you may want to start DRAFTING to see where it takes your thinking. Your goal is to think on screen or paper about your subject, to see where it leads you.

Think about how to keep readers with you. Reflections must be carefully crafted so that readers can follow your train of thought. It's a good idea to sketch out a rough THESIS to help focus your thoughts. Even if you don't include the thesis in the essay itself, every part of the essay should in some way relate to it.

Ways of organizing a reflective essay. Reflections may be organized in many ways because they mimic the way we think, sometimes associating one idea with another in ways that make sense but do not necessarily follow the kinds of logical progression found in academic arguments or reports. Here are two ways you might organize a reflection.

[Exploring a subject using various strategies]

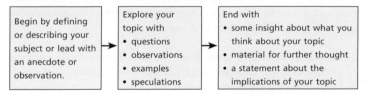

Begin by defining or describing your subject or lead with an anecdote or observation.

→

Explore your topic with
• questions
• observations
• examples
• speculations

→

End with
• some insight about what you think about your topic
• material for further thought
• a statement about the implications of your topic

[Presenting a series of reflections on your subject]

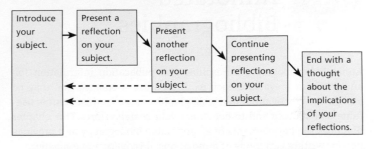

>> **SEE W-1** for help analyzing your writing context. See **W-3** for guidelines on drafting, revising, editing, and proofreading your reflection. To read an example reflective essay, go to **digital .wwnorton.com/littleseagull3**.

W-14 Annotated Bibliographies

Annotated bibliographies describe, give publication information for, and sometimes evaluate each work on a list of sources. You may be assigned to create annotated bibliographies to weigh the potential usefulness of sources and to document your search efforts. This chapter describes the key elements of an annotated bibliography and provides tips for writing two kinds of annotations: *descriptive* and *evaluative*.

Descriptive annotations simply SUMMARIZE the contents of each work, without comment or evaluation. They may be very short, just long enough to capture the flavor of the work, like this excerpt from a bibliography of books and articles on teen films, documented with **MLA** style and published in the *Journal of Popular Film and Television*.

> Doherty, Thomas. *Teenagers and Teenpics: The Juvenilization of American Movies in the 1950s.* Unwin Hyman, 1988.
> A historical discussion of the identification of teenagers as a targeted film market.
>
> Foster, Harold M. "Film in the Classroom: Coping with Teen Pics." *English Journal*, vol. 76, no. 3, Mar. 1987, pp. 86-88.
> An evaluation of the potential of using teen films such as *Sixteen Candles* and *The Karate Kid* to instruct adolescents on the difference between film as communication and film as exploitation.
>   —Michael Benton, Mark Dolan,
>   and Rebecca Zisch, "Teen Film$"

Evaluative annotations offer opinions on each source as well as describe it. They are often helpful in assessing how useful a source will be for your own writing. The following evaluative annotation is from an **APA**-style bibliography written by a student.

> Gore, A. (2006). *An inconvenient truth: The planetary emergency of global warming and what we can do about it.* New York, NY: Rodale.

This publication, which is based on Gore's slide show on global warming, stresses the urgency of the global warming crisis. It centers on how the atmosphere is very thin and how greenhouse gases such as carbon dioxide are making it thicker. The thicker atmosphere traps more infrared radiation, causing warming of the Earth. Gore argues that carbon dioxide, which is created by burning fossil fuels, cutting down forests, and producing cement, accounts for 80% of greenhouse gas emissions. He includes several examples of problems caused by global warming. Penguins and polar bears are at risk because the glaciers they call home are quickly melting. Coral reefs are being bleached and destroyed when their inhabitants overheat and leave. Global warming is now affecting human's lives as well. For example, many highways in Alaska are only frozen enough to be driven on fewer than 80 days of the year. In China and elsewhere, record-setting floods and droughts are taking place. Hurricanes are on the rise. This source's goal is to inform its audience about the global warming crisis and to inspire change. It is useful because it relies on scientific data that can be referred to easily and it provides a solid foundation for me to build on. For example, it explains how carbon dioxide is produced and how it is currently affecting plants and animals. This evidence could potentially help my research on how humans are biologically affected by global warming. It will also help me structure my essay, using its general information to lead into the specifics of my topic. For example, I could introduce the issue by explaining the thinness of the atmosphere and the effect of greenhouse gases, then focus on carbon dioxide and its effects on organisms.

—Jessica Ann Olson, "Global Warming"

W-14a Key Elements of Annotated Bibliographies

A statement of scope. You may need a brief introductory statement to explain what you're covering. This might be one paragraph or several—but it should establish a context for the bibliography and announce your purpose for compiling it.

Complete bibliographic information. Provide all the information about each source using one documentation system (**MLA**, **APA**, **Chicago**, **CSE**, or another one) so that your readers or other researchers will be able to find the source easily.

A concise description of the work. A good annotation describes each item as carefully and objectively as possible, giving accurate, specific information and showing that you understand the source—and how it relates to your topic.

Relevant commentary. If you write an evaluative bibliography, your comments should be relevant to your purpose and audience. To achieve relevance, consider what questions a potential reader might have about the sources. Your evaluation might also focus on the text's suitability as a source for your writing.

Consistent presentation. All annotations should be consistent in content, sentence structure, and format. If you're evaluating, don't evaluate some sources and just describe others. If one annotation is written in complete sentences, they should all be. Also be sure to use one documentation style—and to treat all book titles consistently, all italicized and following a consistent capitalization style.

W-14b Tips for Annotating a Bibliography

Generating ideas and text. You'll need to do some research to locate potential sources for your bibliography. As you consider which to include, keep your **AUDIENCE** and **PURPOSE** in mind.

Decide what sources to include. Though you may be tempted to include every source you find, a better strategy is to include only those sources that you or your readers may find useful in researching your topic. Consider these qualities:

- *Appropriateness.* Is this source relevant to your topic? Is it a **PRIMARY** or **SECONDARY** source? Is it general or specialized?

- *Credibility.* Are the author and the publisher or sponsor reputable? Do their ideas agree with those in other sources you've read?

- *Balance.* Does the source present enough evidence? Does it show any particular bias? Does it present COUNTERARGUMENTS?

- *Timeliness.* Does the source reflect current thinking or research?

Decide whether the bibliography should be descriptive or evaluative. If you're writing a descriptive bibliography, your reading goal will be just to understand and capture each writer's message clearly. If you're writing an evaluative bibliography, you'll also need to assess the source as you read in order to include your own opinions of it.

Read carefully. To write an annotation, you must understand the source's argument, but for some assignments, you may have neither the time nor the need to read the whole text. To quickly determine whether a source is likely to serve your needs, first check the publisher or sponsor; then read the preface, abstract, or introduction; skim the table of contents or the headings; and read the parts that relate specifically to your topic.

Research the writer, if necessary. You may need to find information about the writer's credentials; try looking him or her up online or in *Contemporary Authors.* In any case, information about the writer should take up no more than one sentence in your annotation.

Summarize the work. Sumarize it as objectively as possible: even if you are writing an evaluative annotation, you can evaluate the central point of a work better by stating it clearly first. Your SUMMARY should be concise, but try to be specific and detailed enough to give readers a clear understanding not only of the scope and content of the source, but also of the author's perspective on the topic. *If you're writing a descriptive annotation, you're done after completing this step.*

If you're writing an evaluative bibliography, EVALUATE your sources in terms of their usefulness for your project, their STANCE, and their overall credibility. If you can generalize about the worth of the entire work, fine. You may find, however, that some parts are useful while others are not, and your evaluation should reflect that mix.

Ways of organizing an annotated bibliography. Depending on their purpose, annotated bibliographies may or may not include an introduction. Consult the documentation system you're using for details about alphabetizing works appropriately.

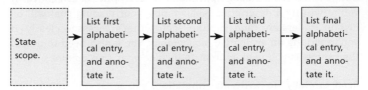

Sometimes an annotated bibliography needs to be organized into several subject areas (or genres, periods, or some other category); if so, the entries are listed alphabetically within each category.

[Multicategory bibliography]

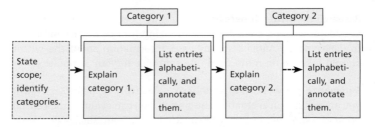

>> **SEE** W-1 for help analyzing your writing context. See W-3 for guidelines on drafting, revising, editing, and proofreading your bibliography. For help finding and evaluating sources, see R-1 and R-2. To read an example annotated bibliography, go to **digital.wwnorton.com/littleseagull3**.

W-15 Abstracts

Abstracts are brief summaries written to give readers the gist of a report or presentation. You may be required to include an abstract in a REPORT or as a preview of a presentation you plan to give at an academic or professional conference. This chapter provides tips for writing three common kinds: *informative*, *descriptive*, and *proposal*.

Informative abstracts state in one paragraph the essence of a whole paper about a study or a research project. That one paragraph must mention all the main points or parts of the paper: a description of the study or project, its methods, the results, and the conclusions. Here is an example of the abstract accompanying a seven-page essay that appeared in 2002 in the *Journal of Clinical Psychology*:

The relationship between boredom proneness and health-symptom reporting was examined. Undergraduate students (N = 200) completed the Boredom Proneness Scale and the Hopkins Symptom Checklist. A multiple analysis of covariance indicated that individuals with high boredom-proneness total scores reported significantly higher ratings on all five subscales of the Hopkins Symptom Checklist (Obsessive-Compulsive, Somatization, Anxiety, Interpersonal Sensitivity, and Depression). The results suggest that boredom proneness may be an important element to consider when assessing symptom reporting. Implications for determining the effects of boredom proneness on psychological- and physical-health symptoms, as well as the application in clinical settings, are discussed.   —Jennifer Sommers and Stephen J. Vodanovich,
"Boredom Proneness"

Descriptive abstracts are usually much briefer than informative abstracts; they provide a quick overview that invites the reader to read the whole paper. They usually do not summarize the entire paper, give or discuss results, or set out the conclusion or its implications. A descriptive abstract of the boredom-proneness essay might simply include the first sentence from the informative abstract plus a final sentence of its own:

> The relationship between boredom proneness and health-symptom reporting was examined. The findings and their application in clinical settings are discussed.

Proposal abstracts contain the same basic information as informative abstracts. You prepare them to persuade someone to let you write on a topic, pursue a project, conduct an experiment, or present a paper at a scholarly conference; often the abstract is written before the paper itself. Titles and other aspects of the proposal deliberately reflect the theme of the proposed work, and you may use the future tense to describe work not yet completed. Here is a possible proposal for doing research on boredom and health problems:

> Undergraduate students will complete the Boredom Proneness Scale and the Hopkins Symptom Checklist. A multiple analysis of covariance will be performed to determine the relationship between boredom-proneness total scores and ratings on the five subscales of the Hopkins Symptom Checklist (Obsessive-Compulsive, Somatization, Anxiety, Interpersonal Sensitivity, and Depression).

W-15a Key Elements of an Abstract

A summary of basic information. An informative abstract includes enough information to substitute for the report itself; a descriptive abstract offers only enough information to let the audience decide whether to read further; and a proposal abstract gives an overview of the planned work.

Objective description. Abstracts present information on the contents of a report or a proposed study; they do not present arguments about or personal perspectives on those contents.

Brevity. Although the length of abstracts may vary, journals and organizations often restrict them to 120–200 words—meaning you must carefully select and edit your words.

W-15b Tips for Writing an Abstract

Generating ideas and text. Unless you are writing a proposal abstract, you should write the paper first. You can then use the finished work as the guide for the abstract, which should follow the same basic structure.

Copy and paste key statements. If you've already written the work, highlight your THESIS, objective, or purpose; basic information on your methods; your results; and your conclusion. Copy and paste those sentences into a new document to create a rough draft.

Pare down the rough draft. SUMMARIZE the key ideas, editing out any nonessential words and details. Introduce the overall scope of your study, and include any other information that seems crucial to understanding your work. In general, you probably won't want to use "I"; an abstract should cover ideas, not say what you personally think or will do.

Conform to any length requirements. In general, an informative abstract should be at most 10 percent as long as the original and no longer than the maximum length allowed. Descriptive abstracts should be shorter still, and proposal abstracts should conform to the requirements of the organization calling for the proposal.

Ways of organizing an abstract

[An informative abstract]

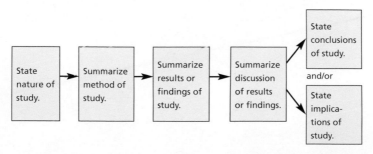

[A descriptive abstract]

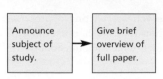

Announce subject of study. → Give brief overview of full paper.

[A proposal abstract]

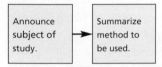

Announce subject of study. → Summarize method to be used.

》 **SEE W-1** for help analyzing your writing context. See **W-3** for guidelines on drafting, revising, editing, and proofreading your abstract. To read an example abstract, go to **digital.wwnorton .com/littleseagull3**.

W-16   Reading Strategies

We read newspapers and websites to learn about the events of the day. We read cookbooks to find out how to make brownies; we read textbooks to learn about history, biology, and other academic topics. We read short stories for pleasure—and, in literature classes, to analyze plot, theme, and the like. And as writers, we read our own drafts to make sure they say what we mean. In other words, we read for many different purposes. This chapter offers strategies for reading texts—and the arguments they make—with a critical eye.

W-16a Reading with a Critical Eye

Different texts require different strategies. Some can be read quickly, if you're reading to get a general overview. But most of the time you'll need to read carefully, skimming to get the basic ideas, then reading again to absorb the details. Following are some strategies for reading with a critical eye.

What do you know about the topic—and what do you want to learn? It always helps to approach new information in the context of what we already know. Before you begin reading, BRAINSTORM what you already know about the topic. List any terms or phrases that come to mind, and group them into categories. Then, or after reading a few paragraphs, list any questions that you expect, want, or hope to be answered as you read, and number them according to their importance to you. Finally, after you read the whole text, list what you learned from it. Compare your second and third lists to see what you still want or need to know—and what you learned that you didn't expect.

Preview the text. Start by skimming to get the basic ideas; read the title and subtitle, any headings, the first and last paragraphs, the first sentences of all the other paragraphs. Study any visuals.

Consider the writing context. What is the PURPOSE of the text—to inform? persuade? entertain? Who is the intended AUDIENCE? If you're not a member of that group, are there terms or concepts you'll need to look up? What is the GENRE—a report? an analysis? something else? What do you know about the writer, and what is his or her STANCE—critical? objective? something else? Is the text print or electronic—and how does the MEDIUM affect what it says?

Think about your initial response. Read the text to get a sense of it; then jot down brief notes about your initial reaction, and think about why you reacted as you did. What aspects of the text account for this reaction?

Annotate. Highlight key words and phrases, connect ideas with lines or symbols, and write comments or questions in the margins. What you annotate depends on your purpose. If you're analyzing an argument, you might underline any thesis statement and the reasons and evidence that support it. If you're looking for patterns, try highlighting each one in a different color.

One simple way of annotating is to use a coding system, such as a check mark to indicate passages that confirm what you already thought, an X for ones that contradict your previous thinking, a question mark for ones that are puzzling or confusing, an exclamation point or asterisk for ones that strike you as important, and so on. You might also circle new words that you need to look up.

Play the believing and doubting game. Regardless of how you actually feel about what the writer says, LIST or FREEWRITE as many reasons as you can think of for believing it, given the writer's perspective, and then as many as you can for doubting it. This exercise helps you consider new ideas and question your current ideas—as well as clarify where you stand in relation to the ideas in the text.

Analyze how the text works. Outline the text paragraph by paragraph. If you're interested in analyzing its ideas, identify what each paragraph *says*. Are there any patterns in the topics the writer addresses? How has the writer arranged ideas, and how does that arrangement develop the topic? If, however, you're concerned with the way the ideas are presented, pay attention to what each paragraph *does*: does it introduce a topic? provide background? describe something? entice you to read further?

Summarize. Restate a text's main ideas in your own words, leaving out most examples and other details. This approach can help you both to see the relationships among those ideas and to understand what they're saying.

Identify patterns. Look for notable patterns in the text: recurring words and their synonyms, repeated phrases and metaphors, and types of sentences. Does the author rely on any particular writing strategies? Is the evidence offered more opinion than fact? nothing but statistics? Is there a predominant pattern to how sources are presented? As quotations? paraphrases? summaries? In visual texts, are there any patterns of color, shape, and line? What isn't there that you would expect to find? Is there anything that doesn't really fit in?

Consider the larger context. All texts are part of a conversation with other texts, and that larger context can help you better understand what you're reading. What's motivating the writer? What other arguments is he or she responding to? Who is cited?

Be persistent with difficult texts. For texts that are especially challenging or uninteresting, first try skimming the headings, the abstract or introduction, and the conclusion to look for something that relates to knowledge you already have. Then read through the text once just to understand what it's saying and again to look for parts that relate to other parts, to other texts or course information, or to other knowledge you have. Treat such a text as a challenge: "I'm going to keep working on this until I make sense of it."

W-16b Analyzing an Argument

All texts make some kind of argument, claiming something and then offering reasons and evidence as support for the claim. As a critical reader, you need to look closely at the argument a text makes.

- *What is the claim?* What is the main point the writer is trying to make? Is there a clearly stated THESIS, or is it merely implied?

- *What support does the writer offer for the claim?* What REASONS are given to support the claim, and what EVIDENCE backs up those reasons? Are the reasons plausible and sufficient?

- *How evenhandedly does the writer present the issues?* Are the arguments appropriately qualified? Is there any mention of COUNTER-ARGUMENTS —and if so, how does the writer deal with them?

- *What authorities or other sources of information are cited?* How credible and current are they?

- *How does the writer address you as the reader?* Does the writer assume that you know something about what's being discussed? Does his or her language include you, or not? (Hint: if you see the word *we*, do you feel included?)

Be sure to check for FALLACIES, arguments that rely on faulty reasoning. Such arguments can seem plausible, and they can be persuasive —but they're misleading.

W-16c Reading Visual Texts

Photos, drawings, graphs, diagrams, and charts are frequently used to help convey important information and often make powerful arguments themselves. So learning to read and interpret visual texts is just as necessary as it is for written texts.

Take visuals seriously. Remember that VISUALS are texts themselves, not just decoration. When they appear as part of a written text, they may introduce information not discussed elsewhere in the text.

Or they might illustrate concepts hard to grasp from words alone. In either case, it's important to pay close attention to any visuals in a written text.

Looking at any title, caption, or other written text that's part of a visual will help you understand its main idea. It might also help to think about its purpose: Why did the writer include it? What information does it add or emphasize? What argument is it making?

How to read charts and graphs. To read the information in charts and graphs, you need to look for different things depending on what type of chart or graph you're considering. A line graph, for example, usually contains certain elements: title, legend, x-axis, y-axis, and source information. Figure 1 shows one such graph taken from a sociology textbook.

Other types of charts and graphs include some of these same elements. But the specific elements vary according to the different

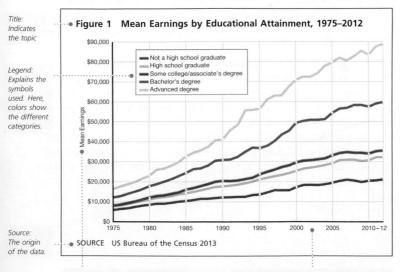

Title: Indicates the topic

Figure 1   Mean Earnings by Educational Attainment, 1975–2012

Legend: Explains the symbols used. Here, colors show the different categories.

Legend:
- Not a high school graduate
- High school graduate
- Some college/associate's degree
- Bachelor's degree
- Advanced degree

Mean Earnings (y-axis): $0, $10,000, $20,000, $30,000, $40,000, $50,000, $60,000, $70,000, $80,000, $90,000

x-axis: 1975, 1980, 1985, 1990, 1995, 2000, 2005, 2010–12

Source: The origin of the data.

SOURCE   US Bureau of the Census 2013

Y-axis: Defines the independent variable (something that doesn't change depending on other factors).

X-axis: Defines the dependent variable (something that changes depending on other factors).

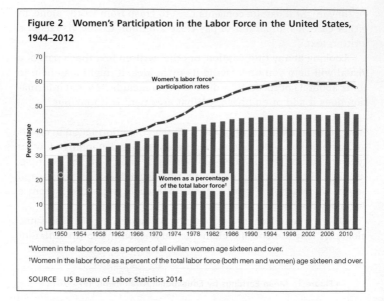

Figure 2   Women's Participation in the Labor Force in the United States, 1944–2012

*Women in the labor force as a percent of all civilian women age sixteen and over.

†Women in the labor force as a percent of the total labor force (both men and women) age sixteen and over.

SOURCE   US Bureau of Labor Statistics 2014

kinds of information being presented, and some charts and graphs can be challenging to read. For example, the chart in Figure 2, from the same textbook, includes elements of both bar and line graphs to depict two trends at once: the red line shows the percentage of women who were in the US labor force from 1948 to 2012, and the blue bars show the percentage of US workers who were women during that same period. Both trends are shown in two-year increments. To make sense of this chart, you need to read the title, the y-axis labels, and the labels and their definitions carefully.

Research

Research is formalized curiosity.
It is poking and prying with a purpose.

— ZORA NEALE HURSTON

R-1 Doing Research

We do research all the time, for many different reasons. We search the web for information about a new computer, ask friends about the best place to get coffee, try on several pairs of jeans before deciding which ones to buy. When you write something that uses statistics, theories, or other information from sources, you're doing research. This chapter will help you to get started with the kind of research you'll need to do for academic work.

R-1a Considering the Context for Your Research

When you begin a research project, you need to consider your purpose and the overall context for your project.

- What is your PURPOSE for the project? If it's part of an assignment, does it specify a GENRE of writing—to argue for a position? report on a topic? analyze something? do something else?

- Who is your AUDIENCE, and what do they know about your topic? Will you need to provide background information? What kinds of evidence will your audience find persuasive? What attitudes do they hold, and how can you best appeal to them?

- What kinds of sources will you need to find to learn about your topic? Think about your own STANCE on the topic—are you objective? skeptical? confused? indifferent?

- Do you get to choose your MEDIUM? If so, which media will best reach your audience, and how will they affect the kind of information you search for?

- How much time do you have to complete the project? Is there a due date? How much time will your project take, and how can you best schedule your time in order to complete it?

R-1b Choosing a Topic, Narrowing Its Focus

If you need to choose a topic for your research project, consider your interests. What do you want to learn more about? If your topic is assigned, read the assignment carefully to make sure you understand what it asks you to do. If the assignment offers only broad guidelines, identify the requirements and range of possibilities, and define your topic within those constraints.

As you consider topics, look to narrow your focus to be specific enough to cover in a research paper. For example, "fracking and the environment" is probably too broad; a better topic might be "the potential environmental risks from fracking." Narrowing your topic will make it easier to find and manage specific information that you can address in your project.

Doing some preliminary research can help you explore your topic and start to articulate a research question that will drive your research—and starting in the library can save you time in the long run. Reference librarians can direct you to the most appropriate reference works, and library catalogs and databases provide sources that have been selected by experts. General encyclopedias and other reference works can provide an overview of your topic, while more specialized encyclopedias cover subjects in greater depth and provide other scholarly references for further research.

Be sure to keep a WORKING BIBLIOGRAPHY that lists any sources you consult. Include all the information you'll need later to follow the documentation style you'll use when you write. Some databases include documentation entries in several styles that you can simply copy and paste. You'll find more on documentation in the chapters on MLA, APA, *Chicago*, and CSE styles.

R-1c Posing a Research Question, Drafting a Tentative Thesis

Posing a research question. Once you have narrowed your topic, you need to come up with a research question—a specific question that you will then work to answer through your research. Generate a list of questions beginning with *What? When? Where? Who? How? Why? Would? Could?* and *Should?* For example, here are some questions about the tentative topic "the potential environmental risks from fracking":

What are the environmental effects of fracking?
Who should determine when and where fracking can be done?
Should fracking be expanded?

Select one question, and use it to help guide your research.

Drafting a tentative thesis. When your research has led you to a possible answer to your question, try to formulate your answer as a tentative THESIS. Here are three tentative thesis statements, each one based on a previous research question about fracking:

> By injecting sand, water, and chemicals into rock, fracking may pollute drinking water and air.
>
> The federal government should strictly regulate the production of natural gas by fracking.
>
> Fracking can greatly increase our supplies of natural gas, but other methods of producing energy should still be pursued.

A tentative thesis will help guide your research, but you should be ready to revise it as you continue to learn about your subject and consider many points of view. If you hold too tightly to a tentative thesis, you risk focusing only on evidence that supports your own views—but research should be a process of inquiry in which you approach a topic with an open mind, ready to learn.

R-1d Finding Appropriate Sources

You'll need to choose from many sources for your research—from reference works, books, periodicals, and the web to surveys, interviews, and other kinds of field research that you yourself conduct. Which sources you turn to will depend on your topic. If you're researching a literary topic, you might consult biographical reference works and scholarly works of criticism. If you're researching a current issue, you would likely consult newspapers and other periodicals, books, and perhaps blogs on your topic. For a report on career opportunities in psychology, you might interview someone working in the field.

Primary and secondary sources. Check your assignment to see if you are required to use primary or secondary sources—or both. Primary sources are original works, such as historical documents, literary works, eyewitness accounts, diaries, letters, and lab studies, as well as your own original field research. Secondary sources include scholarly books and articles, reviews, biographies, and other works that interpret or discuss primary sources.

Whether a source is considered primary or secondary sometimes depends on your topic and purpose. If you're analyzing a poem, a critic's article analyzing the poem is a secondary source—but if you're investigating the critic's work, the article would be a primary source.

Scholarly and popular sources. In many of your college courses, you'll be expected to rely primarily on scholarly sources, ones written by experts for knowledgeable readers and that treat their subjects in depth. Popular sources, on the other hand, are written for a general audience, and while they may discuss scholarly research, they are more likely to summarize that research than to report on it in detail. That said, the distinction can be blurry: many scholars write books for a general readership that are informed by those authors' own scholarship. Even if it's not a requirement, citing scholarly sources will contribute to your own authority as a writer, demonstrating that you are familiar with important research and scholarship and that your own writing is informed by it.

HOW TO DETERMINE IF A SOURCE IS SCHOLARLY

- *What's the title?* Catchy, provocative titles usually signal that a source is popular, not scholarly. Compare Nicholas Carr's "Is Google Making Us Stupid?" (published in the *Atlantic*) with Cynthia Selfe's "Technology and Literacy: A Story about the Perils of Not Paying Attention" (published in *College Composition and Communication,* a scholarly journal).

- *Who's the author?* Scholarly sources are written by authors with academic credentials; popular sources are most often written by journalists or staff writers.

Scholarly Source

Published in an academic journal.

Journal List · NIH Public Access · Author Manuscript · PMC3719 ISSN

NIH Public Access
Author Manuscript
Accepted for publication in a peer reviewed journal

About Author manuscripts   Submit a manuscript

Formats:
Article | PubReader | ePub (beta) | PDF (338K)

J Res Pers. Author manuscript; available in PMC 2015 August 1.   PMCID: PMC3940996
Published in final edited form as: NIHMSID: NIHMS826286
J Res Pers. 2010 August 1; 44(4): 478–484.
doi: 10.1016/j.jrp.2010.05.001

Sounds like a Narcissist: Behavioral Manifestations of Narcissism in Everyday Life

Nicholas S. Holtzman, Simine Vazire, and Matthias R. Mehl

Author information ▸   Copyright and License information ▸

See other articles in PMC that cite the published article.

Related citations in PubMed

Irresistibility and the self-defeating behavior of narcissists.
[Pers Soc Psychol Rev. 2006]

Why are narcissists so charming at first sight? Decoding the narcissism-popularity link at zero acquaintance [J Pers Soc Psychol. 2010]

The performance of narcissists rises and falls with perceived opportunity for glory.
[J Pers Soc Psychol. 2002]

An empirical typology of narcissism and mental health in late adolescence.
[J Adolesc. 2005]

Animal models of obsessive compulsive disorder: rationale to understanding psychology and [Psychiatr Clin North Am. 2006]

See reviews...
See all...

Includes an abstract.

Abstract

Go to: ▸

Little is known about narcissists' everyday behavior. The goal of this study was to describe how narcissism is manifested in everyday life. Using the Electronically Activated Recorder (EAR), we obtained naturalistic behavior from participants' everyday lives. The results suggest that the defining characteristics of narcissism that have been established from questionnaire and laboratory-based studies are borne out in narcissists' day-to-day behaviors. Narcissists do indeed behave in more extraverted and less agreeable ways than non-narcissists, skip class more (among narcissists high in exploitativeness/entitlement only), and use more sexual language. Furthermore, we found that the link between narcissism and disagreeable behavior is strengthened when controlling for self-esteem, thus extending prior questionnaire-based findings (Paulhus, Robins, Trzesniewski, & Tracy, 2004) to observed, real-world behavior.

Keywords: narcissism, behavior, personality traits, sexual behavior, language use

Cited by other articles in PMC

Evidence for the criterion validity and clinical utility of the Pathological Narcissism Inventory [Assessment. 2012]

See all...

Cites academic research with consistent documentation style.

Narcissists love attention. Lucky for them, they have recently received a considerable amount of it from academic psychologists, especially in laboratory settings (e.g., Beck, Schmukle, & Egloff, 2010; Kuhmann & Baumeister, 1998; Campbell, Foster, & Finkel, 2002; Miller et al., 2009). This laboratory research has led to several wide-reaching theories about why narcissists do what they do (Holtzman & Strube, 2010; Morf & Rhodewalt, 2001; Vazire & Campbell, 2009; Vazire & Funder, 2006). Despite all this attention from researchers, however, we still know little about what narcissists actually do in their everyday lives. The aim of this paper is to help create an empirical basis for a more complete understanding of narcissism by exploring behavioral manifestations of narcissism in everyday life. Thus, we intend to answer a simple, yet largely unanswered question: What do narcissists do on a day-to-day basis?

Links
MedGen
PubMed

Recent activity
Turn Off   Clear

Sounds like a Narcissist: Behavioral Manifestations of Narcissism in Everyday Li...   PMC

See more...

Does self-love lead to love for others? A story of narcissistic game playing [J Pers Soc Psychol. 2002]

Interpersonal and intrapsychic adaptiveness of trait self-enhancement: a mixed blessing? [J Pers Soc Psychol. 1998]

Describes research methods, includes numerical data.

Method

Go to: ▸

Participants

Participants were 80 undergraduate students at the University of Texas at Austin (79 provided valid EAR data), recruited mainly from introductory psychology courses and by flyers in the psychology department. The sample was 54% female, and the ethnic composition of the sample was 65% White, 22% Asian, 12% Latino, and 3% of another ethnicity. Participants ranged from 18 to 24 years old (M = 18.7, SD = 1.4). Participants were compensated $50. Data from this sample were also reported in Vazire and Mehl (2008), where further information can be found about the study.

Knowing me, knowing you: the accuracy and unique predictive validity of self-ratings and other-ratings [J Pers Soc Psychol. 2008]

Narcissistic Personality Inventory (NPI)

The NPI is a 40-item test of narcissism that is reliable and well-validated (Raskin & Terry, 1988). The items on this forced-choice test contain pairs of statements such as "Sometimes I tell good stories" (non-narcissistic) versus "Everybody likes to hear my stories" (narcissistic). In our study, the NPI exhibited good reliability (α = .83). As seen in Table 1, we also calculated means and reliabilities for four facets (Emmons, 1987).

A principal-components analysis of the Narcissistic Personality inventory and further evidence of its r [J Pers Soc Psychol. 1988]

Narcissistic theory and measurement
[J Pers Soc Psychol. 1987]

Table 1
Means, Standard Deviations, Gender-Differences, and Reliabilities for the NPI and NPI Facets

Multiple authors who are academics.

Contributor Information

Go to: ▸

Nicholas S. Holtzman, Washington University in St. Louis.

Simine Vazire, Washington University in St. Louis.

Matthias R. Mehl, University of Arizona.

Includes complete references list.

References

Go to: ▸

1. Beck MD, Schmukle SC, Egloff B. Why are narcissists so charming at first sight? Decoding the narcissism-popularity link at zero acquaintance. Journal of Personality and Social Psychology. 2010;98:132–145. [PubMed]

2. Baumeister RF, Vohs KD, Funder DC. Psychology as the science of self-reports and finger movements: Whatever happened to actual behavior? Perspectives on Psychological Science. 2007;2:396–403.

Popular Source

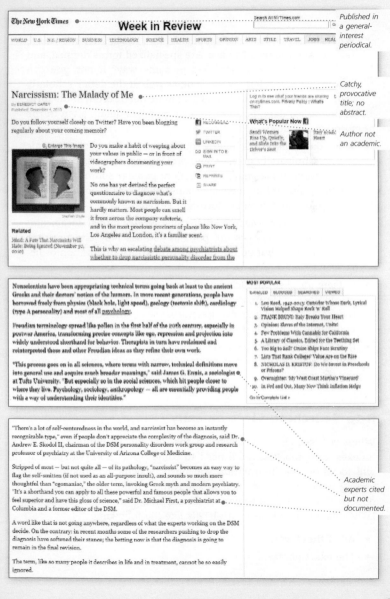

The New York Times

Week in Review

WORLD U.S. N.Y. / REGION BUSINESS TECHNOLOGY SCIENCE HEALTH SPORTS OPINION ARTS STYLE TRAVEL JOBS REAL

Narcissism: The Malady of Me

By BENEDICT CAREY
Published: December 4, 2010

Do you follow yourself closely on Twitter? Have you been blogging regularly about your coming memoir?

Do you make a habit of weeping about your values in public — or in front of videographers documenting your work?

No one has yet devised the perfect questionnaire to diagnose what's commonly known as narcissism. But it hardly matters. Most people can smell it from across the company cafeteria, and in the most precious precincts of places like New York, Los Angeles and London, it's a familiar scent.

This is why an escalating debate among psychiatrists about whether to drop narcissistic personality disorder from the

Related

Mind: A Fate That Narcissists Will Hate: Being Ignored (November 30, 2010)

Nonscientists have been appropriating technical terms going back at least to the ancient Greeks and their doctors' notion of the humors. In more recent generations, people have borrowed freely from physics (black hole, light speed), geology (tectonic shift), cardiology (type A personality) and most of all psychology.

Freudian terminology spread like pollen in the first half of the 20th century, especially in postwar America, transforming precise concepts like ego, repression and projection into widely understood shorthand for behavior. Therapists in turn have reclaimed and reinterpreted these and other Freudian ideas as they refine their own work.

"This process goes on in all sciences, where terms with narrow, technical definitions move into general use and acquire much broader meanings," said James G. Ennis, a sociologist at Tufts University. "But especially so in the social sciences, which hit people closer to where they live. Psychology, sociology, anthropology — all are essentially providing people with a way of understanding their identities."

"There's a lot of self-centeredness in the world, and narcissist has become an instantly recognizable type," even if people don't appreciate the complexity of the diagnosis, said Dr. Andrew E. Skodol II, chairman of the DSM personality disorders work group and research professor of psychiatry at the University of Arizona College of Medicine.

Stripped of most — but not quite all — of its pathology, "narcissist" becomes an easy way to flag the self-smitten (if not used as an all-purpose insult), and sounds so much more thoughtful than "egomaniac," the older term, invoking Greek myth and modern psychiatry. "It's a shorthand you can apply to all these powerful and famous people that allows you to feel superior and have this gloss of science," said Dr. Michael First, a psychiatrist at Columbia and a former editor of the DSM.

A word like that is not going anywhere, regardless of what the experts working on the DSM decide. On the contrary: in recent months some of the researchers pushing to drop the diagnosis have softened their stance; the betting now is that the diagnosis is going to remain in the final revision.

The term, like so many people it describes in life and in treatment, cannot be so easily ignored.

MOST POPULAR

E-MAILED BLOGGED SEARCHED VIEWED

1. Lou Reed, 1942-2013: Outsider Whose Dark, Lyrical Vision Helped Shape Rock 'n' Roll
2. FRANK BRUNI: Italy Breaks Your Heart
3. Opinion: Slaves of the Internet, Unite!
4. Few Problems With Cannabis for California
5. A Library of Classics, Edited for the Teething Set
6. Too Big to Sail? Cruise Ships Face Scrutiny
7. Lists That Rank Colleges' Value Are on the Rise
8. NICHOLAS D. KRISTOF: Do We Invest in Preschools or Prisons?
9. Overnighter: 'My West Coast Martha's Vineyard'
10. In Fed and Out, Many Now Think Inflation Helps

Go to Complete List »

95

- *Who's the intended audience?* Consider how much prior knowledge readers are assumed to have. Are specialized terms defined, and are the people cited identified in some way? If not, you can assume it's a scholarly work. Look as well at the detail: scholarly sources describe methods and give more detail, often in the form of numerical data; popular sources give less detail, often in the form of anecdotes.

- *Who's the publisher?* Scholarly sources are published by academic journals, university presses, and professional organizations such as the Modern Language Association; popular sources are published by general interest magazines such as *Time* or *Fortune* or trade publishers such as Norton or Penguin.

- *Does it cite other academic studies and include formal documentation?* Scholarly sources do; popular sources may cite previous academic work but do not include in-text documentation or list references.

- *Is there an abstract?* Scholarly journal articles often begin with an abstract or summary of the article; popular magazine articles may include a tag line giving some sense of what the article covers, but less than a formal summary.

- *If it's online, what's the URL?* Scholarly sources have URLs that end in *.edu, .org,* or *.gov;* popular sources usually have URLs ending in *.com.*

R-1e Searching Electronically

When you search for subjects on the web or in library catalogs, indexes, or databases, you'll need to come up with KEYWORDS that will focus on the information you need. Specific commands vary among search sites and databases, but most offer advanced-search options that allow you to narrow (or expand) your search by typing keywords into text boxes with labels like the following:

- All of these words
- The exact phrase

- Any of these words
- None of these words

In addition, you may filter the results to include only full-text articles (articles that are available in full online); only certain domains (such as *.edu*, for educational sites; *.gov*, for government sites; or *.org*, for nonprofit sites); and, in library databases, only scholarly, peer-reviewed sites.

Some databases may require that you use various symbols or Boolean operators (AND, OR, NOT) to combine search functions. See the databases' advanced-search instructions for help with such symbols, which may be called "field tags."

If a search turns up too many sources, be more specific (*homeopathy* instead of *medicine*). If your original keywords don't generate good results, try synonyms (*home remedy* instead of *folk medicine*). Keep in mind that searching requires flexibility, both in the words you use and in the methods you try.

R-1f Reference Works

Every library has a reference section, where you'll find encyclopedias, dictionaries, atlases, almanacs, bibliographies, and other reference works that can provide an overview as you begin your search. For some topics, you might find specialized reference works such as the *Film Encyclopedia* or *Dictionary of Philosophy*, which provide in-depth information on a single field or topic and can often lead you to more specific sources. Many reference works are also online, but some may be available only in the library. *Wikipedia* can often serve as a starting point for preliminary research and includes links to other sources, but since its information can be written and rewritten by anyone, make sure to consult other reference works as well.

You should also look for bibliographies, which list published works on particular topics along with the information you'll need to find each work. You can find bibliographies in many scholarly articles and books. Check with a reference librarian for help finding bibliographies on your research topic.

R-1g Searching the Library Catalog for Books

The library catalog is your main source for finding books, and most catalogs can be accessed through the library's website. You can search the catalog by author, title, subject, or keyword. A **KEYWORD** search will yield books the library has on the topic and may also provide related subject headings that could lead to other useful materials. Library catalogs supply a call number, which identifies a print book's location on the shelves. Many books in the catalog are also available online, and some may be downloaded to a computer or mobile device.

R-1h Searching Indexes and Databases for Periodicals

To find journal, magazine, and newspaper articles, you need to search periodical indexes and databases. Indexes list articles by topics; databases usually provide full texts or abstracts. While some databases and indexes are freely available online, most must be accessed through a library. For articles published before 1980, you may need to check print indexes such as *The Reader's Guide to Periodical Literature*.

A reference librarian can help you determine which databases will be most helpful to you, but here are some useful ones:

GENERAL INDEXES AND DATABASES

Academic Search Complete indexes and contains articles from journals.

EBSCOhost provides databases of abstracts and complete articles from periodicals and government documents.

InfoTrac offers full-text articles from scholarly and popular sources, including the *New York Times*.

JSTOR archives many scholarly journals but not current issues.

LexisNexis contains articles from many kinds of sources—newspapers; business, legal, and medical sources; and references such as the *World Almanac*.

ProQuest Central provides full-text articles from periodicals and newspapers from 1971 to the present.

SINGLE-SUBJECT INDEXES AND DATABASES

BIOSIS Previews provides abstracts and indexes for over 5,500 sources on biological sciences, the environment, and agriculture.

ERIC is the database of the US Department of Education.

Humanities International Index contains bibliographies for over 2,200 humanities journals.

MLA International Bibliography indexes scholarly articles on modern languages, literature, folklore, and linguistics.

PsycINFO indexes scholarly literature in psychology.

To search a database, start with a **KEYWORD** search. If a keyword does not lead to enough sources, try a synonym; if it leads to too many sources, try narrowing your search using the strategies discussed in **R-1e**. When you access a source through a database, the URL may not be stable, so it's good to record the URL of the database homepage. Even better, look for a **PERMALINK** on **DOI** number to copy and paste into your list of sources.

R-1i Searching the Web

The web contains countless sites sponsored by governments, educational institutions, organizations, businesses, and individuals. Because it is so vast and dynamic, however, finding information can be a challenge. There are several ways to search the web:

- *Keyword searches.* *Google, Bing, Yahoo!,* and many other search sites scan the web looking for the keywords you specify.

- *Metasearches.* *Yippy, Dogpile,* and *SurfWax* let you use several search sites simultaneously. They are best for searching broadly; use a single site to obtain the most precise results.

- *Academic searches.* For peer-reviewed academic writing in many disciplines, try *Google Scholar*; or use *Scirus* for scientific, technical, and medical documents.

- *Searches on social media.* Use **HASHTAGS** (#) to search the contents of posts and tweets.

Although many websites provide authoritative information, web content varies greatly in its stability and reliability: what you see on a site today may be different (or gone) tomorrow, so save copies of pages you use, and evaluate carefully what you find there (see R-2). Following are a few of the many resources available on the web.

Directories. You can find information put together by specialists at *The Voice of the Shuttle* (a guide to online resources in the humanities); the *WWW Virtual Library* (a catalog of websites on numerous subjects, compiled by subject specialists); or in subject directories such as those provided by *Google* and *Yahoo!*

News sites. Many newspapers, magazines, and radio and TV stations have websites that provide both up-to-the-minute information and also archives of older news articles. Through *Google News* and *NewsLink,* for example, you can access current news worldwide, and *Google News Archive Search* has files extending back to the 1700s.

Government sites. Many government agencies and departments maintain websites where you can find government reports, statistics, legislative information, and other resources. *USA.gov* offers resources from the US government.

Audio, video, and image collections. Your library likely subscribes to various databases where you can find and download audio, video, and image files. *AP Images* provides access to photographs taken for the Associated Press; *Artstor* is a digital library of images; *Naxos Music Library* contains more than 60,000 recordings.

Digital archives. You can find primary sources from the past, including drawings, maps, recordings, speeches, and historic documents at sites maintained by the National Archives, the Library of Congress, the New York Public Library, and others.

R-1j Field Research

Sometimes you'll need to go beyond the information you find in published sources and gather your own data by doing field research. Three kinds of field research that you might consider are interviews, observations, and surveys.

Interviews. Some kinds of writing—a PROFILE of a living person, for instance—almost require that you conduct an interview, whether it's face-to-face or by telephone, email, or videoconference.

1. *Before the interview,* email or phone to contact the person, stating your purpose for the request. If you wish to record the interview, ask for permission. Write out questions in advance—and bear in mind that open-ended questions are likely to elicit a more extended response than those that can be answered with a simple *yes* or *no.*

2. *At the interview,* note the full name of the person and the date, time, and place. Take notes, even if you are recording the interview, and don't take more time than you agreed to beforehand.

3. *After the interview,* flesh out your notes with details right away, and send a thank-you note or email.

Observations. Some writing projects are based on information you get by observing something.

1. *Before observing,* think about your research purpose. How does this observation relate to your research goals, and what do you expect to find? If necessary, set up an appointment, and ask your subjects' permission to observe them. You may also need to get your school's permission.

2. *While observing,* divide your notebook pages or document into two columns, and make notes only in the left column. Describe

who is there, what they are doing, what they look like, what they say, and any other relevant details. Also note details about the setting.

3. *After observing,* use the right column of your notes to fill in additional details. Then analyze your notes, looking for patterns. What did you learn? Did anything surprise or puzzle you?

Surveys. One way of gathering information from a large number of people is to use a questionnaire.

1. *Start by thinking* about your research question and what you can learn with a survey.

2. *Decide whom you'll send it to* and how you'll reach them: face-to-face? on the phone? on a website such as *SurveyMonkey?* via email?

3. *Write questions* that require specific answers and can be answered easily. Multiple-choice questions will be easier to tally than open-ended questions.

4. *Write an introduction* that explains the survey's purpose. Be sure to give a due date and to say thank you.

5. *Test your questions* on several people, making sure that the questions and any instructions are clear.

R-2   Evaluating Sources

Searching the *Health Source* database for information on the incidence of meningitis among college students, you find seventeen articles. A *Google* search on the same topic produces over ten thousand hits. How do you decide which ones to read? This chapter presents advice on evaluating potential sources and reading those you choose critically.

R-2a Considering Whether a Source Might Be Useful

As you consider potential sources, keep your PURPOSE in mind. If you're trying to persuade readers to believe something, be sure to find sources representing various stances; if you're reporting on a topic, you may need sources that are more factual or informative. Reconsider your AUDIENCE. What kinds of sources will they find persuasive? If you're writing for readers in a particular field, what counts as EVIDENCE in that field? The following questions can help you select reliable and useful sources:

- **Is it relevant?** How well does it relate to your purpose? What would it add to your work? To see what it covers, look at the title and at any introductory material (such as a preface or an abstract).

- **What are the author's credentials?** Has the author written other works on this subject? Is he or she known for a particular position on it? If the credentials are not stated, you might do a search to see what else you can learn about him or her.

- **What is the STANCE?** Does the source cover various points of view or advocate only one perspective? Does its title suggest a certain slant? If it's online, check to see whether it includes links to other sites and, if so, what their perspectives are. You'll want to consult sources with various viewpoints.

- **Who is the publisher?** If the source is a book, what kind of company published it; if an article, what kind of periodical did it appear in? Books published by university presses and articles in scholarly journals are reviewed by experts before they are published. But books and articles written for the general public do not undergo rigorous review or fact-checking.

- **If it's a website, who is the sponsor?** Is the site maintained by an organization, an interest group, a government agency, or an individual? Look for clues in the URL: *.edu* is used mostly by colleges and universities, *.gov* by government agencies, *.org* by nonprofit organizations, *.mil* by the military, and *.com* by commercial organizations. What is the site's purpose: to argue a position? to present information even-handedly? to sell something?

- *At what level is it written?* Can you understand it? Texts written for a general audience might be easier to understand but not authoritative enough for academic work. Scholarly texts will be more authoritative but may be hard to comprehend.

- *How current is it?* Check to see when books and articles were published and when websites were last updated. (If a site lists no date, see if links to other sites still work; if not, the site is probably too dated to use.) A recent publication date or update, however, does not necessarily mean that a potential source is good—some topics require current information; others call for older sources.

- *Is it cited in other works?* If so, you can probably assume that some other writers regard it as trustworthy.

- *Is it available?* If it's a book and your school's library doesn't have it, can you get it through interlibrary loan?

- *Does it include other useful information?* Is there a bibliography that might lead you to other sources? How current or authoritative are the sources it cites?

R-2b Reading Sources with a Critical Eye

Approach your sources with an open mind, but consider their arguments with a critical eye. Pay attention to what they say, to the reasons and evidence they offer to support what they say, and to whether they address viewpoints other than their own. Assume that each author is responding to some other argument.

- *What ARGUMENTS does the author make?* Does he or she present several different positions or argue for a particular position? What arguments is he or she responding to?

- *How persuasive do you find the argument to be?* What REASONS and EVIDENCE does the author provide? Are there references or links—and if so, are they CREDIBLE? Are any of the author's assumptions questionable? How thoroughly does he or she consider alternative arguments?

- *What is the author's* STANCE*?* Does it seem objective, or does the content or language reveal a particular bias? Are opposing views considered and treated fairly?

- *Do you recognize ideas you've run across in other sources?* Does the source leave out any information or perspective that other sources include—or does it include any that they leave out?

- *Does this source support or challenge your own position—or does it do both?* Does it support a different argument altogether? Does it represent a position you need to address? Don't reject a source just because it challenges your views.

- *What can you tell about the intended* AUDIENCE *and* PURPOSE*?* Are you a member of the audience addressed—and if not, does that affect the way you interpret what you read? Is the main purpose to inform readers about a topic or to argue a certain point?

R-3   Synthesizing Ideas

Whatever topic you are researching, you need to constantly synthesize the information you find—that is, to sift through your sources in order to identify patterns, themes, and main points—and then use these data to help generate your own ideas. This chapter focuses on going beyond what your sources say to inspire and support what you want to say.

R-3a Reading for Patterns and Connections

Your task as a writer is to find as much information as you can on your topic and then to study the data you find to determine what you think and to support what you yourself then write. Read with an open mind, taking careful notes to help you see patterns, themes, and connections among your sources. Pay attention to your first reactions: you'll likely have many ideas to work with, but your first thoughts can often lead somewhere interesting. Here are some questions that can help you discover patterns and connections:

- Which sources make the strongest arguments? What makes them so strong?
- Which arguments do you agree with? disagree with?
- Are there any arguments, distinctive terms, themes, or data that you see in more than one source?
- Are there any disagreements among sources? Are there any that you need to address in what you write?
- How have your sources affected your thinking on your topic? Have you discovered new questions you need to investigate?
- Have you found the information you need that will achieve your PURPOSE, appeal to your AUDIENCE, and suit your MEDIUM?

The ideas and insights that emerge from this questioning can become the basis for your own ideas—and for what *you* have to say about the topic.

R-3b Moving from What Your Sources Say to What You Say

As you work to make sense of what your sources say, you'll be figuring out what you yourself think—where you stand on your topic and what you want to say. You'll have some understanding of what others believe, which will affect what you think. But when you formulate your own argument, you'll need to be careful to draw from your sources to support *what you think*, to weave their ideas in with your ideas.

Entering the conversation. As you read and think about your topic, you'll come to understand the concepts, interpretations, and controversies relating to it—and you'll become aware that there's a larger conversation going on. When you formulate your own ideas on the topic, you'll begin to find your way into that conversation. This is the exciting part of a research project, for when you write out your own ideas on the topic, you will find yourself entering that conversation. Remember that your STANCE as an author needs to be clear: simply stringing together the words and ideas of others isn't enough. You need to show readers how your source materials relate to one another and to your THESIS.

R-4 Integrating Sources, Avoiding Plagiarism

When you include the ideas and words of others in your writing, you need to clearly distinguish those ideas and words from your own and give credit to their authors. This chapter will help you with the specifics of integrating source materials into your writing and acknowledging your sources appropriately.

R-4a Incorporating the Words and Ideas of Others into Your Text

When you incorporate source materials into your own writing, you'll need to decide how to do so—whether to quote, paraphrase, or summarize. You might follow this rule of thumb: QUOTE texts when the wording is worth repeating, when you want to cite the exact words of a known authority on your topic, when his or her opinions challenge or disagree with those of others, or when the source is one you want to emphasize. PARAPHRASE texts that are not worth quoting but that contain details you need to include. SUMMARIZE passages whose main points are important but whose details are not.

In addition, you'll need to introduce any words or ideas that are not your own with a SIGNAL PHRASE in order to clearly distinguish what your sources say from what you have to say.

R-4b Quoting

Quoting is a way of weaving someone's exact words into your text. When you quote, you reproduce the source exactly, though you can omit unnecessary details (adding ELLIPSES to show that you've done so) or modify the quotation to make it fit smoothly into your text (enclosing any changes in BRACKETS).

Incorporate short quotations into your text, enclosed in quotation marks. What counts as a short quotation varies, however; consult the chapters on MLA, APA, *Chicago*, or CSE for guidelines in each of those styles. The following examples are shown in MLA style.

> Gerald Graff argues that colleges leave many students with "the misconception that the life of the mind is a secret society for which only an elite few qualify" (1).

To quote three lines or less of poetry in MLA style, run them in with your text, enclosed in quotation marks. Separate lines with slashes, leaving one space on each side of the slash. Include the line numbers in parentheses at the end of the quotation.

> Emma Lazarus almost speaks for the Statue of Liberty with the words inscribed on its pedestal: "Give me your tired, your poor, / Your huddled masses yearning to breathe free, / The wretched refuse of your teeming shore" (10-12).

Set off long quotations block style. Longer quotations should not be run in with quotation marks but instead are set off from your text and indented from the left margin. Block quotations are usually introduced by a full sentence. Again, what counts as long varies across disciplines; consult the chapters on MLA, APA, *Chicago*, or CSE for specific guidelines on when to format a quotation as a block and how much to indent. Whatever style you're following, do not add quotation marks; the indent signals that you are quoting someone's exact words. Remember to document the source, using the format required by the style you're following. Here is an example shown in MLA style, indented one-half inch from the left margin:

> Organizations such as Oxfam rely on visual representations of the poor. What better way to get our attention? asks Diana George:
>> In a culture saturated by the image, how else do we convince Americans that—despite the prosperity they see all around them—there is real need out there? The solution for most nonprofits has been to show the despair. To do that they must represent poverty as something that can be seen and easily recognized: fallen down shacks and trashed out public housing, broken windows, dilapidated porches, barefoot kids with stringy hair, emaciated old women and men staring out at the camera with empty eyes. (210)

If you quote four lines or more of poetry in MLA style, they also need to be set off in a block:

> Emily Dickinson, like many poets, asserts that we cannot know truth directly but must apprehend it through indirect means:
>> Tell all the Truth but tell it slant—
>> Success in Circuit lies
>> Too bright for our infirm Delight
>> The Truth's superb surprise (1-4)

Indicate any omissions with ellipses, inserting three ellipsis dots with space around each one to indicate deleted words. Be careful not to distort your source's meaning.

> In her essay, Antonia Peacocke argues that *Family Guy* provides an astute satire of American society, though she concedes that it does sometimes "seem to cross . . . the line of indecency" (266).

If you omit a sentence or more in the middle of a quotation, put a period before the three ellipsis dots.

> According to Kathleen Welch, "Television is more acoustic than visual. . . . One can turn one's gaze away from the television, but one cannot turn one's ears from it without leaving the area where the monitor leaks its aural signals into every corner" (102).

Indicate any additions or changes with brackets. Sometimes, you'll need to change or add words to make a quotation fit grammatically within your sentence, or you'll want to add a comment. Here the writer changes the word *our* to *their* so that the quotation fits grammatically into her own text:

> Writing about the dwindling attention of some composition scholars to the actual teaching of writing, Susan Miller notes that "few discussions of writing pedagogy take it for granted that one of [their] goals is to teach how to write" (480).

In this example, brackets are used to add an explanatory word:

> As Barbosa notes, Chico Buarque's lyrics include "many a metaphor of *saudades* [yearning] so characteristic of fado music" (207).

Keep in mind that too many ellipses and brackets can make a text choppy and hard to read, so it's best to keep such editing to a minimum.

>> **SEE P-4** for guidance in using other punctuation inside or outside quotation marks.

R-4c Paraphrasing

When you paraphrase, you restate material from a source in your own words, using your own sentence structure. Paraphrase when the source material is important but the original wording is not. Because it includes all the main points and details of the source material, a paraphrase is usually about the same length as the original.

Here is an excerpt from a source, followed by a paraphrase:

ORIGINAL SOURCE

In 1938, in a series of now-classic experiments, exposure to synthetic dyes derived from coal and belonging to a class of chemicals called aromatic amines was shown to cause bladder cancer in dogs. These results helped explain why bladder cancers had become so prevalent among dyestuffs workers. With the invention of mauve in 1854, synthetic dyes began replacing natural plant-based dyes in the coloring of cloth and leather. By the beginning of the twentieth century, bladder cancer rates among this group of workers had skyrocketed, and the dog experiments helped unravel this mystery.
—Sandra Steingraber, "Pesticides, Animals, and Humans," p. 976

PARAPHRASE

Biologist Sandra Steingraber explains that pathbreaking experiments in 1938 demonstrated that dogs exposed to aromatic amines (chemicals used in coal-derived synthetic dyes) developed cancers of the bladder that were similar to cancers common among dyers in the textile industry. After mauve, the first synthetic dye, was invented in 1854, leather and cloth manufacturers replaced most natural dyes made from plants with synthetic dyes, and by the early 1900s textile workers had very high rates of bladder cancer. The experiments with dogs revealed the connection (976).

Now see two examples that demonstrate some of the challenges of paraphrasing. The paraphrase below borrows too much of the original language or changes it only slightly, as the words and phrases highlighted in yellow show.

Now-classic experiments in 1938 showed that when dogs were exposed to aromatic amines, chemicals used in synthetic dyes derived from coal, they developed bladder cancer. Similar cancers were prevalent among dyestuffs workers, and these experiments helped to explain why. Mauve, a synthetic dye, was invented in 1854, after which cloth and leather manufacturers replaced most of the natural plant-based dyes with synthetic dyes. By the early twentieth century, this group of workers had skyrocketing rates of bladder cancer, a mystery the dog experiments helped to unravel (Steingraber 976).

This next paraphrase uses different language but follows the sentence structure of Steingraber's text too closely.

In 1938, several pathbreaking experiments showed that being exposed to synthetic dyes that are made from coal and belong to a type of chemicals called aromatic amines caused dogs to get bladder cancer. These results helped researchers identify why cancers of the bladder had become so common among textile workers who worked with dyes. With the development of mauve in 1854, synthetic dyes began to be used instead of dyes based on plants in the dyeing of leather and cloth. By the end of the nineteenth century, rates of bladder cancer among these workers had increased dramatically, and the experiments using dogs helped clear up this oddity (Steingraber 976).

It can be a challenge to write a paraphrase without inadvertently copying some of the original text's wording or sentence structures, especially when you're paraphrasing complex or unfamiliar ideas. One common mistake many writers make is to start by copying a passage directly from a source and then changing it: adding some words or deleting some words, replacing others with synonyms, altering sentence structures. The result is PATCHWRITING, patching together passages from another source; even if the source is documented, patchwriting is considered plagiarism.

To avoid problems of this kind, read over the original passages you're paraphrasing carefully, but do not look at them while you're writing. Use your own words and sentence structure. If you use any words from the original, put them in quotation marks. And be sure to indicate the source: the wording may be yours, but the ideas and information come from another source; name the author and include DOCUMENTATION.

R-4d Summarizing

A summary states the main ideas in a source concisely and in your own words. Unlike a paraphrase, a summary does *not* present the details, and it is generally as brief as possible. Summaries may boil down an entire book or essay into a single sentence, or they may take a paragraph or more to present the main ideas. Here, for example, is a summary of the original excerpt from Steingraber (see p. 111):

Steingraber explains that experiments with dogs demonstrated that aromatic amines, chemicals used in synthetic dyes, can cause bladder cancer (976).

As with a paraphrase, if you include any language from the original, put it in quotation marks—and indicate the source, naming the author and including DOCUMENTATION.

R-4e Using Signal Phrases to Introduce Source Materials

You need to introduce quotations, paraphrases, and summaries with a signal phrase, usually letting readers know who the author is and, if need be, something about his or her credentials. Consider this sentence:

Professor and textbook author Elaine Tyler May argues that many high school history books are far too bland to interest young readers (531).

The signal phrase ("Professor and textbook author Elaine Tyler May") tells readers who is making the assertion and why she has the authority to speak on the topic.

Signal verbs. The language you use in a signal phrase can be neutral, like *X says* or *according to Y*. Or it can suggest something about the STANCE—the source's or your own. The example above referring to the textbook author uses the verb *argues*, suggesting that what she says is disputable (or that the writer believes it is).

SOME COMMON SIGNAL VERBS

acknowledge	claim	disagree	observe
admit	comment	dispute	point out
advise	conclude	emphasize	reason
agree	concur	grant	reject
argue	confirm	illustrate	report
assert	contend	imply	respond
believe	declare	insist	suggest
charge	deny	note	think

Though X *says* or *according to* Y will sometimes be the most appropriate phrasing, you can usually make your writing more precise and lively by choosing verbs that better signal the stance of the source you're citing—and by varying the placement of your signal phrases. In addition, you can include information about authors' institutional affiliations and academic or professional specialties as well as other context that lets your readers judge the **CREDIBILITY** of your sources. For example:

> Suzanne Clark, professor of English at the University of Oregon, argues that . . .
>
> Science writer Isaac McDougal questions whether . . .
>
> Writing in *Psychology Today*, Amanda Chao-Fitz speculates that . . .

If your primary language isn't English, some uses of these verbs may seem odd to you. For example:

> In other words, the data suggest that . . .
>
> Our theory challenges common assumptions about . . .
>
> Their hypothesis supposes . . .

In many languages, it's unheard of for data to "suggest" anything or for a theory to "challenge" assumptions or anything else; only people can do those things. But in English, abstract nouns—a paper, new data, these conclusions—can perform "human" actions as well, and are often paired with the signal verbs above.

Verb tenses. Each documentation style has its own conventions regarding the verbs that are used in signal phrases.

MLA requires present tense verbs (*notes, contends*) in signal phrases that introduce source material. If, however, you mention the date when the source was written, the verb should be in the past tense.

> As Benjamin Franklin <u>notes</u> in *Poor Richard's Almanack*, "He that cannot obey, cannot command" (739).
>
> In a 2012 interview, Susan Miller <u>said</u> that "if you want to know how power works, you must understand how language works—and that's what the study of rhetoric is all about" (36).

APA uses the past tense or **PRESENT PERFECT** to introduce quotations or to present research results.

> Dowdall, Crawford, and Wechsler (1998) <u>observed</u> that women at women's colleges are less likely to engage in binge drinking than are women at coeducational colleges (p. 713).

> Dowdall, Crawford, and Wechsler (1998) <u>have observed</u> that . . . .

But to discuss the implications of an experiment or conclusions that are generally agreed on, APA requires the use of the present tense: *the findings of the study <u>suggest</u>, most researchers <u>concur</u>.*

Chicago uses the present tense (*As Eric Foner <u>notes</u>*) or **PRESENT PERFECT** (*As Eric Foner <u>has noted</u>*) to introduce most quotations. Use the past tense, however, when you are focusing on the fact that the action took place in the past: *Just before signing the Declaration of Independence, John Adams <u>wrote</u> to his wife.*

CSE uses the past tense or **PRESENT PERFECT** to refer to research from the past (*Gillen's 2005 paper <u>argued</u>, his early studies <u>have demonstrated</u>*) or to discuss methods (*our subjects <u>received</u>*) or findings: *his earlier studies (1999, 2003) <u>showed</u>.* Use the present tense, however, when citing research reports: *Gillen (2010) <u>provides</u> the most detailed evidence.*

Statistics and facts. You may introduce a statistic or a specific fact with a signal phrase—but you don't need to. Most of the time, it will be clear that you are documenting only the statistic or fact. The following examples introduce statistics with and without a signal phrase in **MLA** style.

> Puzzanchera notes that almost half of the people arrested for arson in 2008—47 percent—were juveniles (2).

> Almost half of the people arrested for arson in 2008—47 percent—were juveniles (Puzzanchera 2).

R-4f Acknowledging Sources

When you insert into your text any information that you've obtained from others, your reader needs to know where your source's words or ideas begin and end. Usually, you should introduce a source by naming the author in a SIGNAL PHRASE and follow it with brief DOCUMENTATION; then provide full publication information in your WORKS CITED, REFERENCES, or BIBLIOGRAPHY. Conventions for acknowledging sources vary across disciplines, however; see the chapters on MLA, APA, Chicago, and CSE for specific advice.

Material that needs acknowledgment

- Direct quotations (unless they're well known), paraphrases, and summaries
- Controversial statements
- Information that may not be common knowledge
- The opinions and ideas of others
- Any information that you didn't generate or create yourself— charts, graphs, interviews, statistics, visuals
- Help from others

Material that doesn't need acknowledgment. Widely available information and common knowledge do not require acknowledgment—but what constitutes common knowledge isn't always clear. When in doubt, provide documentation or ask your instructor for advice. You generally do not need to document the following material:

- Facts that most readers are likely to know or that are found in reference sources (such as the date when Michael Jackson died)
- Information that you see mentioned in several sources
- Well-known quotations
- Material that you created or gathered yourself, such as photos you took or data from your own field research (make sure, however, that readers know the work is yours)

A good rule of thumb: *when in doubt, acknowledge your source*. You won't be criticized for documenting too much—but you may invite charges of plagiarism by documenting too little.

R-4g Avoiding Plagiarism

When you use the words or ideas of others, you need to acknowledge them; if you don't credit your sources, you are guilty of plagiarism. Plagiarism is often unintentional, as when a writer paraphrases someone else's ideas in language that is close to the original. It is essential, therefore, to know what constitutes plagiarism: (1) using another writer's words or ideas without acknowledging and documenting the source, (2) using another writer's exact words without quotation marks, and (3) paraphrasing or summarizing another writer's text by using language or sentence structures that are too close to the originals. The following practices will help you avoid plagiarizing.

- *Take careful notes*, clearly labeling quotations and using your own phrasing and sentence structure in paraphrases and summaries.

- *Know what sources you must document*, and give credit to them both in the text and in a works-cited list (MLA), a references list (APA or CSE), or a bibliography (*Chicago*).

- *Be especially careful with online material*—copying source material directly into a document you are writing, and then forgetting to put quotation marks around it or document it, is all too easy. Like other sources, information from the web must be acknowledged.

- *Check all paraphrases and summaries* to be sure they are in your words and sentence structures—and that you put quotation marks around any of the source's original phrasing.

- *Check to see that all quotations are documented* and enclosed in quotation marks (or indented as a block); it's not enough to do just one or the other.

Whether it's deliberate or accidental, plagiarism has consequences. Students who plagiarize fail courses or might even be expelled from school. If you're having trouble completing an assignment, seek assistance from your instructor or your school's writing center.

R-4h Understanding Documentation Styles

When we write up the results of a research project, we cite the sources we use and acknowledge those sources through DOCUMENTATION. Documenting our sources not only helps establish our credibility as researchers and writers, but it also enables our readers to find our sources themselves (if they wish to).

The Little Seagull Handbook provides guidelines on four documentation styles, each of which is commonly used in specific disciplines.

- MLA (Modern Language Association): mainly used in English, foreign languages, and other humanities
- APA (American Psychological Association): mainly used in psychology and other social sciences
- Chicago (University of Chicago Press): mainly used in history, philosophy, and other humanities
- CSE (Council of Science Editors): mainly used in physical and biological sciences and mathematics

Each system has two parts: (1) an acknowledgment of each quotation, paraphrase, or summary in the text and (2) a detailed list of sources at the end of the text. Although the specific guidelines for the styles differ, they all require that you provide basic information about the authors, titles, and publication of your sources. To help you see the crucial parts of each source documentation in this book, the examples throughout the following chapters are color-coded: brown for author and editor, yellow for title, and gray for publication information: place of publication, name of publisher, date of publication, page number(s), medium of publication, and so on.

MLA Style

MLA style calls for (1) brief in-text documentation and (2) complete bibliographic information in a list of works cited at the end of your text. The models and examples in this chapter draw on the eighth edition of the *MLA Handbook*, published by the Modern Language Association in 2016. For additional information, visit **style.mla.org**.

A DIRECTORY TO MLA STYLE

In-Text Documentation 122

1. Author named in a signal phrase   123
2. Author named in parentheses   123
3. Two or more works by the same author   123
4. Authors with the same last name   124
5. Two or more authors   124
6. Organization or government as author   124
7. Author unknown   125
8. Literary works   125
9. Work in an anthology   126
10. Encyclopedia or dictionary   126
11. Legal and historical documents   126
12. Sacred text   127
13. Multivolume work   127
14. Two or more works cited together   127
15. Source quoted in another source   128
16. Work without page numbers   128
17. An entire work or a one-page article   128

Notes   129

List of Works Cited   129

CORE ELEMENTS   129

AUTHORS AND OTHER CONTRIBUTORS   134

1. One author   134

2. Two authors   134

3. Three or more authors   134

4. Two or more works by the same author   135

5. Author and editor or translator   135

6. No author or editor   135

7. Organization or government as author   136

ARTICLES AND OTHER SHORT WORKS   136

Documentation Map: Article in a Print Journal   137
Documentation Map: Article in an Online Magazine   138
Documentation Map: Journal Article Accessed through a Database   140

8. Article in a journal   136

9. Article in a magazine   139

10. Article in a newspaper   139

11. Article accessed through a database   141

12. Entry in a reference work   141

13. Editorial   142

14. Letter to the editor   142

15. Review   143

16. Comment on an online article   143

BOOKS AND PARTS OF BOOKS   144

Documentation Map: Print Book   145

17. Basic entries for a book   144

18. Anthology   144

19. Work in an anthology   144

20. Multivolume work   146

21. Book in a series   146

22. Graphic narrative   147

23. Sacred text   147

24. Edition other than the first   147

25. Republished work   147

26. Foreword, introduction, preface, or afterword   148

27. Published letter   148

28. Paper at a conference   148

29. Dissertation   149

WEBSITES   149

Documentation Map: Work on a Website   150

30. Entire website   149

31. Work on a website   151

32. Blog entry   151

33. Wiki   151

PERSONAL COMMUNICATION AND SOCIAL MEDIA   151

34. Personal letter   151

35. Email   151

36. Text message   152

37. Post to an online forum   152

38. Post to *Twitter*, *Facebook*, or other social media   152

AUDIO, VISUAL, AND OTHER SOURCES   153

39. Advertisement   153

40. Art   153

41. Cartoon   154

42. Court case   154

43. Film   154

44. Interview   155

45. Map   155

46. Musical score   156

47. Online video   156

48. Oral presentation   156

49. Podcast   156

50. Radio program   157

51. Sound recording   157

52. TV show   157

53. Video game   158

Formatting a Research Paper   158
Sample Research Paper   160

Throughout this chapter, you'll find color-coded templates and examples to help you see how writers include source information in their texts and in their lists of works cited: tan for author, editor, translator, and other contributors; yellow for titles; gray for publication information—date of publication, page number(s) or other location information, and so on.

MLA-a In-Text Documentation

Brief documentation in your text tells your readers what you took from a source and where in the source you found the information.

You have three options for citing a source in your text: quoting, paraphrasing, and summarizing. As you cite each source, you will need to decide whether or not to name the author in a signal phrase— "as Toni Morrison writes"—or in parentheses—(Morrison 24).

author   title   publication

The first examples below show basic in-text documentation of a work by one author. Variations on those examples follow. The examples illustrate the MLA style of using quotation marks around titles of short works and italicizing titles of long works.

1. AUTHOR NAMED IN A SIGNAL PHRASE

If you mention the author in a signal phrase, put only the page number(s) in parentheses. Do not write *page* or *p*.

> McCullough describes John Adams's hands as those of someone used to manual labor (18).

2. AUTHOR NAMED IN PARENTHESES

If you do not mention the author in a signal phrase, put his or her last name in parentheses along with the page number(s). Do not use punctuation between the name and the page number(s).

> Adams is said to have had "the hands of a man accustomed to pruning his own trees, cutting his own hay, and splitting his own firewood" (McCullough 18).

Whether you use a signal phrase and parentheses or parentheses only, try to put the parenthetical documentation at the end of the sentence or as close as possible to the material you've cited—without awkwardly interrupting the sentence. Notice that in the example above, the parenthetical reference comes after the closing quotation marks but before the period at the end of the sentence.

3. TWO OR MORE WORKS BY THE SAME AUTHOR

If you cite multiple works by one author, include the title of the work you are citing either in the signal phrase or in parentheses. Give the full title if it's brief; otherwise, give a short version.

> Kaplan insists that understanding power in the Near East requires "Western leaders who know when to intervene, and do so without illusions" (*Eastward* 330).

Put a comma between author and title if both are in the parentheses.

> Understanding power in the Near East requires "Western leaders
> who know when to intervene, and do so without illusions"
> (Kaplan, *Eastward* 330).

4. AUTHORS WITH THE SAME LAST NAME

Give the author's first and last names in any signal phrase, or add
the author's first initial in the parenthetical reference.

> *Imaginative* applies not only to modern literature but also to
> writing of all periods, whereas *magical* is often used in writing
> about Arthurian romances (A. Wilson 25).

5. TWO OR MORE AUTHORS

For a work with two authors, name both, either in a signal phrase
or in parentheses.

> Carlson and Ventura's stated goal is to introduce Julio Cortázar,
> Marjorie Agosín, and other Latin American writers to an
> audience of English-speaking adolescents (v).

For a work by three or more authors, name the first author followed
by *et al.*

> One popular survey of American literature breaks the contents
> into sixteen thematic groupings (Anderson et al. A19-24).

6. ORGANIZATION OR GOVERNMENT AS AUTHOR

Acknowledge the organization either in a signal phrase or in parentheses. It's acceptable to shorten long names.

> The US government can be direct when it wants to be. For
> example, it sternly warns, "If you are overpaid, we will recover
> any payments not due you" (Social Security Administration 12).

7. AUTHOR UNKNOWN

If you don't know the author, use the work's title or a shortened version of the title in the parenthetical reference.

> A powerful editorial in last week's paper asserts that healthy liver donor Mike Hurewitz died because of "frightening" faulty postoperative care ("Every Patient's Nightmare").

8. LITERARY WORKS

When referring to literary works that are available in many different editions, give the page numbers from the edition you are using, followed by information that will let readers of any edition locate the text you are citing.

NOVELS. Give the page and chapter number, separated by a semicolon.

> In *Pride and Prejudice,* Mrs. Bennet shows no warmth toward Jane when she returns from Netherfield (105; ch. 12).

VERSE PLAYS. Give act, scene, and line numbers, separated with periods.

> Macbeth continues the vision theme when he says, "Thou hast no speculation in those eyes / Which thou dost glare with" (3.3.96-97).

POEMS. Give the part and the line numbers (separated by periods). If a poem has only line numbers, use the word *line*(s) only in the first reference.

> Whitman sets up not only opposing adjectives but also opposing nouns in "Song of Myself" when he says, "I am of old and young, of the foolish as much as the wise, / . . . a child as well as a man" (16.330-32).

One description of the mere in *Beowulf* is "not a pleasant place" (line 1372). Later, it is labeled "the awful place" (1378).

9. WORK IN AN ANTHOLOGY

Name the author(s) of the work, not the editor of the anthology—either in a signal phrase or in parentheses.

"It is the teapots that truly shock," according to Cynthia Ozick in her essay on teapots as metaphor (70).

In *In Short: A Collection of Creative Nonfiction*, readers will find both an essay on Scottish tea (Hiestand) and a piece on teapots as metaphors (Ozick).

10. ENCYCLOPEDIA OR DICTIONARY

Acknowledge an entry in an encyclopedia or dictionary by giving the author's name, if available. For an entry without an author, give the entry's title in parentheses. If entries are arranged alphabetically, no page number is needed.

According to *Funk & Wagnall's New World Encyclopedia*, early in his career Kubrick's main source of income came from "hustling chess games in Washington Square Park" ("Kubrick, Stanley").

11. LEGAL AND HISTORICAL DOCUMENTS

For legal cases and acts of law, name the case or act in a signal phrase or in parentheses. Italicize the name of a legal case.

In 2005, the Supreme Court confirmed in *MGM Studios, Inc. v. Grokster, Ltd.* that peer-to-peer file sharing is copyright infringement.

Do not italicize the titles of laws, acts, or well-known historical documents such as the Declaration of Independence. Give the title and any relevant articles and sections in parentheses. It's fine to use common abbreviations such as *art.* or *sec.* and to abbreviate well-known titles.

The president is also granted the right to make recess appointments (US Const., art. 2, sec. 2).

12. SACRED TEXT

When citing a sacred text such as the Bible or the Qur'an for the first time, give the title of the edition, and in parentheses give the book, chapter, and verse (or their equivalent), separated by periods. MLA recommends abbreviating the names of the books of the Bible in parenthetical references. Later citations from the same edition do not have to repeat its title.

> The wording from *The New English Bible* follows: "In the beginning of creation, when God made heaven and earth, the earth was without form and void, with darkness over the face of the abyss, and a mighty wind that swept over the surface of the waters" (Gen. 1.1-2).

13. MULTIVOLUME WORK

If you cite more than one volume of a multivolume work, each time you cite one of the volumes, give the volume *and* the page number(s) in parentheses, separated by a colon and a space.

> Sandburg concludes with the following sentence about those paying last respects to Lincoln: "All day long and through the night the unbroken line moved, the home town having its farewell" (4: 413).

If your works cited list includes only a single volume of a multivolume work, give just the page number in parentheses.

14. TWO OR MORE WORKS CITED TOGETHER

If you're citing two or more works closely together, you will sometimes need to provide a parenthetical reference for each one.

> Tanner (7) and Smith (viii) have looked at works from a cultural perspective.

If you include both in the same parentheses, separate the references with a semicolon.

> Critics have looked at both *Pride and Prejudice* and *Frankenstein* from a cultural perspective (Tanner 7; Smith viii).

15. SOURCE QUOTED IN ANOTHER SOURCE

When you are quoting text that you found quoted in another source, use the abbreviation *qtd. in* in the parenthetical reference.

> Charlotte Brontë wrote to G. H. Lewes: "Why do you like Miss Austen so very much? I am puzzled on that point" (qtd. in Tanner 7).

16. WORK WITHOUT PAGE NUMBERS

For works without page numbers, including many online sources, identify the source using the author or other information either in a signal phrase or in parentheses.

> Studies show that music training helps children to be better at multitasking later in life ("Hearing the Music").

If the source has chapter, paragraph, or section numbers, use them with the abbreviations *ch* , *par.*, or *sec.*: ("Hearing the Music," par. 2). Alternatively, you can refer to a heading on a screen to help readers locate text.

> Under the heading "The Impact of the Railroad," Rawls notes that the transcontinental railroad was called an iron horse and a greedy octopus.

For an audio or a video recording, give the hours, minutes, and seconds (separated by colons) as shown on the player: (00:05-08:30).

17. AN ENTIRE WORK OR A ONE-PAGE ARTICLE

If you cite an entire work rather than a part of it, or if you cite a single-page article, there's no need to include page numbers.

> Throughout life, John Adams strove to succeed (McCullough).

MLA-b Notes

Sometimes you may need to give information that doesn't fit into the text itself—to thank people who helped you, to provide additional details, to refer readers to other sources, or to add comments about sources. Such information can be given in a *footnote* (at the bottom of the page) or an *endnote* (on a separate page with the heading *Notes* just before your works cited list). Put a superscript number at the appropriate point in your text, signaling to readers to look for the note with the corresponding number. If you have multiple notes, number them consecutively throughout your paper.

TEXT

This essay will argue that small liberal arts colleges should not recruit athletes and, more specifically, that giving student athletes preferential treatment undermines the larger educational goals.[1]

NOTE

   1. I want to thank all those who have contributed to my thinking on this topic, especially my classmates and my teacher Marian Johnson.

MLA-c List of Works Cited

A works cited list provides full bibliographic information for every source cited in your text. See page 160 for guidelines on formatting this list and page 168 for a sample works cited list.

Core Elements

MLA style provides a list of "core" elements for documenting sources in a works cited list. Not all sources will include each of these elements; include as much information as is available for any title you cite. For guidance about specific sources you need to document, see the templates and examples on pages 134–58, but here are some general guidelines for how to treat each of the core elements.

CORE ELEMENTS FOR ENTRIES IN A WORKS CITED LIST

- Author
- Title of the source
- Title of any "container," MLA's term for a larger work in which the source is found—an anthology, a website, a journal or magazine, a database, even a streaming service like *Netflix*
- Editor, translator, director, or other contributors
- Version
- Volume and issue numbers
- Publisher (or sponsor)
- Date of publication
- Location of the source: page numbers, URL, **PERMALINK,** DOI, etc.

The above order is the general order MLA recommends, but there will be exceptions. To document a translated essay that you found in an anthology, for instance, you'd identify the translator after the title of the essay rather than after that of the anthology. Remember that your goal is to tell readers what sources you've consulted and where they can find them. Providing this information is one way you can engage with readers—and enable them to join in the conversation with you and your sources.

AUTHORS AND OTHER CONTRIBUTORS

- If there is one author, put the last name first, followed by a comma and the first name: Morrison, Toni.
- If there are two authors, list the first author last name first and the second one first name first: Lunsford, Andrea, and Lisa Ede. Put their names in the order given in the work. For three or more authors, give the first author's name followed by *et al.*: Greenblatt, Stephen, et al.
- Include any middle names or initials: Toklas, Alice B.

- If there's no known author, start the entry with the title.

- If you're citing an editor, translator, or other contributors, specify their role. If there are multiple contributors, put the one whose work you wish to highlight before the title, and list any others you want to mention after the title. For contributors named before the title, specify their role after the name: Fincher, David, director. For those named after the title, specify their role first: directed by David Fincher.

TITLES

- Include any subtitles and capitalize all the words except for articles (*a, an, the*), prepositions (*to, at, from,* and so on), and coordinating conjunctions (*and, but, for, or, nor, yet*)—unless they are the first or last word of a title or subtitle.

- Italicize the titles of books, periodicals, and other long works: *Pride and Prejudice, Wired.*

- Put quotation marks around the titles of articles and other short works: "Letter from Birmingham Jail."

- To document a source that has no title, describe it without italics or quotation marks: Letter to the author, Review of rap concert.

VERSIONS

- If you cite a source that's available in more than one version, specify the one you consulted in your works cited entry. Write ordinal numbers with numerals, and abbreviate *edition*: 2nd ed. Write out names of specific versions, and capitalize if the name is a **PROPER NOUN**: King James Version, unabridged version, director's cut.

NUMBERS

- If you cite a book that's published in multiple volumes, indicate the volume number. Abbreviate *volume*, and write the number as a numeral: vol. 2.

- Indicate any volume and issue numbers of journals, abbreviating both *volume* and *number*: vol. 123, no. 4.

PUBLISHERS

- Write publishers' names in full, but omit business words like *Inc.* or *Company*.

- For university presses, use U for "University" and P for "Press": Princeton UP, U of California P.

DATES

- Whether to give just the year or to include the month and day depends on the source. Give the full date that you find there. If the date is unknown, simply omit it

- Abbreviate the months except for May, June, and July: Jan., Feb., Mar., Apr., Aug., Sept., Oct., Nov., Dec.—9 Sept. 2016.

- For books, give the year of publication: 1948. If a book lists more than one date, use the most recent one.

- Periodicals may be published annually, monthly, seasonally, weekly, or daily. Give the full date that you find in the periodical: 2011, Apr. 2011, Spring 2011, 16 Apr. 2011.

- For online sources, use the copyright date or the most recent update, giving the full date that you find in the source. If the source does not give a date, use the date of access: Accessed 6 June 2016. And if the source includes the time when it was posted or updated, give the time along with the date: 18 Oct. 2016, 9:20 a.m.

- Because online sources may change or even disappear, the date of access can be important for indicating the exact version you've cited. Some instructors may require this information, so we've included access dates in this chapter's guidelines for specific kinds of sources, but check with your instructor to see if you're required to include this information.

LOCATION

- For most print articles and other short works, give a page number or range of pages: p. 24, pp. 24-35. For articles that are not on consecutive pages, give the first page number with a plus sign: pp. 24+.

author   title   publication

- Indicate the location of most online sources by giving their URL, omitting *http://* or *https://*. If a source has a permalink (a stable version of its URL), give that instead. Some of the scholarly journal articles you'll find in a database provide a DOI number instead; if so, give that.

- For physical objects that you find in a museum, archive, or some other place, give the name of the place and its city: Menil Collection, Houston. Omit the city if it's part of the place's name: Boston Public Library.

- For performances or other live presentations, name the venue and its city: Mark Taper Forum, Los Angeles. Omit the city if it's part of the place's name: Berkeley Repertory Theatre.

PUNCTUATION

- Use a period after the author name(s) that start an entry (Morrison, Toni.) and the title of the source you're documenting (*Beloved*.)

- Use a comma between the author's last and first names: Ede, Lisa.

- Some URLs will not fit on one line. MLA does not specify where to break a URL, but we recommend breaking it before a punctuation mark. Do not add a hyphen.

- Sometimes you'll need to provide information about more than one work for a single source—for instance, when you cite an article from a periodical that you access through a database. MLA refers to the periodical and database (or any other entity that holds a source) as "containers" and specifies certain punctuation. Use commas between elements within each container, and put a period at the end of each container. For example:

Semuels, Alana. "The Future Will Be Quiet." *The Atlantic*, Apr. 2016, pp. 19-20. *ProQuest*, search.proquest.com/docview /1777443553?accountid+42654. Accessed 5 Apr. 2016.

The guidelines that follow will help you document kinds of sources you're likely to use. The first section shows how to acknowledge authors and other contributors and applies to all kinds of sources—print, online, or others. Later sections show how to treat titles, publication information, location, and access information for many specific kinds of sources. In general, provide as much information as possible for each source—enough to tell readers how to find a source if they wish to access it themselves.

Authors and Other Contributors

When you name authors and other contributors in your citations, you are crediting them for their work and letting readers know who's in on the conversation. The following guidelines for citing authors and other contributors apply to all sources you cite: in print, online, or in some other media.

1. ONE AUTHOR

Author's Last Name, First Name. *Title*. Publisher, Date.

Anderson, Curtis. *The Long Tail: Why the Future of Business Is Selling Less of More*. Hyperion, 2006.

2. TWO AUTHORS

1st Author's Last Name, First Name, and 2nd Author's First and Last Names. *Title*. Publisher, Date.

Lunsford, Andrea, and Lisa Ede. *Singular Texts/Plural Authors: Perspectives on Collaborative Writing*. Southern Illinois UP, 1990.

3. THREE OR MORE AUTHORS

1st Author's Last Name, First Name, et al. *Title*. Publisher, Date.

Sebranek, Patrick, et al. *Writers INC: A Guide to Writing, Thinking, and Learning*. Write Source, 1990.

4. TWO OR MORE WORKS BY THE SAME AUTHOR

Give the author's name in the first entry, and then use three hyphens in the author slot for each of the subsequent works, listing them alphabetically by the first important word of each title.

> Author's Last Name, First Name. *Title That Comes First*
> > *Alphabetically.* Publisher, Date.
> - - -. *Title That Comes Next Alphabetically.* Publisher, Date.
> Kaplan, Robert D. *The Coming Anarchy: Shattering the Dreams of*
> > *the Post Cold War.* Random House, 2000.
> - - -. *Eastward to Tartary: Travels in the Balkans, the Middle East,*
> > *and the Caucasus.* Random House, 2000.

5. AUTHOR AND EDITOR OR TRANSLATOR

> Author's Last Name, First Name. *Title.* Role by First and Last Names,
> > Publisher, Date.
> Austen, Jane. *Emma.* Edited by Stephen M. Parrish, W. W. Norton,
> > 2000.
> Dostoevsky, Fyodor. *Crime and Punishment.* Translated by Richard
> > Pevear and Larissa Volokhonsky, Vintage Books, 1993.

Start with the editor or translator if you are focusing on that contribution rather than the author's.

> Pevear, Richard, and Larissa Volokhonsky, translators. *Crime and*
> > *Punishment.* By Fyodor Dostoevsky, Vintage Books, 1993.

6. NO AUTHOR OR EDITOR

When there's no known author or editor, start with the title.

> *The Turner Collection in the Clore Gallery.* Tate Publications, 1987.
> "Being Invisible Closer to Reality." *The Atlanta Journal-Constitution,*
> > 11 Aug. 2008, p. A3.

7. ORGANIZATION OR GOVERNMENT AS AUTHOR

Organization Name. *Title.* Publisher, Date.

Diagram Group. *The Macmillan Visual Desk Reference.* Macmillan, 1993.

For a government publication, give the name of the government first, followed by the names of any department and agency.

United States, Department of Health and Human Services, National Institute of Mental Health. *Autism Spectrum Disorders.* Government Printing Office, 2004.

When the organization is both author and publisher, start with the title and list the organization only as the publisher.

Stylebook on Religion 2000: A Reference Guide and Usage Manual. Catholic News Service, 2002.

Articles and Other Short Works

Articles, essays, reviews, and other shorts works are found in journals, magazines, newspapers, other periodicals, and books—all of which you may find in print, online, or in a database. For most short works, you'll need to provide information about the author, the titles of both the short work and the longer work, any page numbers, and various kinds of publication information, all explained below.

8. ARTICLE IN A JOURNAL

PRINT

Author's Last Name, First Name. "Title of Article." *Name of Journal*, Volume, Issue, Date, Pages.

Cooney, Brian C. "Considering *Robinson Crusoe's* 'Liberty of Conscience' in an Age of Terror." *College English,* vol. 69, no. 3, Jan. 2007, pp. 197-215.

Documentation Map (MLA)

ARTICLE IN A PRINT JOURNAL

Marge Simpson, Blue-Haired Housewife: ← Title of article
Defining Domesticity on *The Simpsons*

JESSAMYN NEUHAUS ← Author

MORE THAN TWENTY SEASONS AFTER ITS DEBUT AS A SHORT ON *THE
Tracy Ullman Show* in 1989, pundits, politicians, scholars,
journalists, and critics continue to discuss and debate the
meaning and relevance of *The Simpsons* to American society. For
academics and educators, the show offers an especially dense pop culture text, inspiring articles and anthologies examining *The Simpsons* in
light of American religious life, the representation of homosexuality in
cartoons, and the use of pop culture in the classroom, among many
other topics (Dennis; Frank; Henry "The Whole World's Gone Gay";
Hobbs; Kristiansen). Philosophers and literary theorists in particular
are intrigued by the quintessentially postmodern self-aware form and
content of *The Simpsons* and the questions about identity, spectatorship,
and consumer culture it raises (Alberti; Bybee and Overbeck; Glynn;
Henry "The Triumph of Popular Culture"; Herron; Hull; Irwin et al.;
Ott; Parisi).

Simpsons observers frequently note that this TV show begs one of the
fundamental questions in cultural studies: can pop culture ever provide
a site of individual or collective resistance or must it always ultimately
function in the interests of the capitalist dominant ideology? Is *The
Simpsons* a brilliant satire of virtually every cherished American myth
about public and private life, offering dissatisfied Americans the opportunity to critically reflect on contemporary issues (Turner 435)? Or
is it simply another TV show making money for the Fox Network? Is
The Simpsons an empty, cynical, even nihilistic view of the world, lull-
ing its viewers into laughing hopelessly at the pointless futility of

Volume

Name of Journal → *The Journal of Popular Culture*, Vol. 43, No. 4, 2010 ← Year
© 2010, Wiley Periodicals, Inc.

Issue

Neuhaus, Jessamyn. "Marge Simpson, Blue-Haired Housewife:
Defining Domesticity on *The Simpsons.*" *The Journal of
Popular Culture,* vol. 43, no. 4, 2010, pp. 761-81.

Documentation Map (MLA)
ARTICLE IN AN ONLINE MAGAZINE

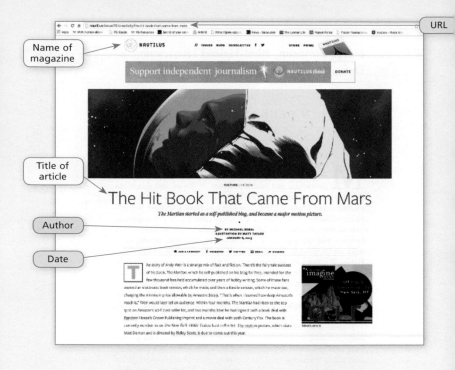

Name of magazine

URL

Title of article

Author

Date

Segal, Michael. "The Hit Book That Came from Mars." *Nautilus*,
    8 Jan. 2015, nautil.us/issue/20/creativity/the-hit-book-that
    -came-from-mars. Accessed 10 Oct. 2016.

ONLINE

Author's Last Name, First Name. "Title of Article." *Name of Journal*,
    Volume, Issue, Date, Pages (if any), URL. Accessed Day Month
    Year.

Gleckman, Jason. "Shakespeare as Poet or Playwright? The Player's
    Speech in *Hamlet*." *Early Modern Literary Studies,* vol. 11, no.
    3, Jan. 2006, purl.oclc.org/emls/11-3/glechaml.htm. Accessed 31
    Mar. 2015.

9. ARTICLE IN A MAGAZINE

PRINT

Author's Last Name, First Name. "Title of Article." *Name of*
    Magazine, Date, Pages.

Neyfakh, Leon. "The Future of Getting Arrested." *The Atlantic,*
    Jan.-Feb. 2015, pp. 26+.

ONLINE

Author's Last Name, First Name. "Title of Article." *Name of*
    Magazine, Date on web, Pages (if any), URL. Accessed Day
    Month Year.

Khazan, Olga. "Forgetting and Remembering Your First Language."
    The Atlantic, 24 July 2014, www.theatlantic.com/international
    /archive/2014/07/learning-forgetting-and-remembering-your
    -first-language/374906/. Accessed 2 Apr. 2015.

10. ARTICLE IN A NEWSPAPER

PRINT

Author's Last Name, First Name. "Title of Article." *Name of*
    Newspaper, Date, Pages.

Saulny, Susan, and Jacques Steinberg. "On College Forms, a Question
    of Race Can Perplex." *The New York Times*, 14 June 2011, p. A1.

Documentation Map (MLA)

JOURNAL ARTICLE ACCESSED THROUGH A DATABASE

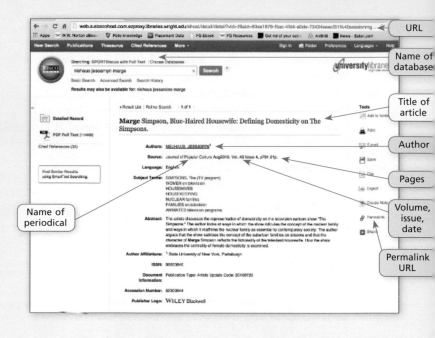

URL

Name of database

Title of article

Author

Pages

Name of periodical

Volume, issue, date

Permalink URL

Neuhaus, Jessamyn. "Marge Simpson, Blue-Haired Housewife:
    Defining Domesticity on The Simpsons." *Journal of Popular
    Culture*, vol. 43, no. 4, Aug. 2010, pp. 761-81. *SPORT
    Discus with Full Text*, http://eds.a.ebscohost.com.ezproxy
    .libraries.wright.edu/eds/detail/detail?vid=3&sid=1115d897
    -ef7a-478f-83ad80b949f71078%40sessionmgr4009&hid=4110
    &bdata=JnNpdGU9ZWRzLWxpdmU%3d#. Accessed 24 Mar.
    2016.

To document a particular edition of a newspaper, list the edition (*late ed.*, *natl. ed.*, and so on) after the date. If a section of the newspaper is numbered, put that detail after the edition information.

> Burns, John F., and Miguel Helft. "Under Pressure, YouTube Withdraws Muslim Cleric's Videos." *The New York Times,* 4 Nov. 2010, late ed., sec. 1, p. 13.

ONLINE

> Author's Last Name, First Name. "Title of Article." *Name of Newspaper,* Date on web, URL. Accessed Day Month Year.
>
> Banerjee, Neela. "Proposed Religion-Based Program for Federal Inmates Is Canceled." *The New York Times,* 28 Oct. 2006, www.nytimes.com/2006/10/28/us/28prison.html?_r=0. Accessed 4 Apr. 2015.

11. ARTICLE ACCESSED THROUGH A DATABASE

> Author's Last Name, First Name. "Title of Article." *Name of Periodical,* Volume, Issue, Date, Pages. Name of Database, DOI or URL. Accessed Day Month Year.
>
> Stalter, Sunny. "Subway Ride and Subway System in Hart Crane's 'The Tunnel.'" *Journal of Modern Literature,* vol. 33, no. 2, Jan. 2010, pp. 70-91. *JSTOR,* doi: 10.2979/jml.2010.33.2.70. Accessed 30 Mar. 2015.

12. ENTRY IN A REFERENCE WORK

PRINT

> Author's Last Name, First Name (if any). "Title of Entry." *Title of Reference Book,* edited by Editor's First and Last Names (if any), Edition number, Publisher, Date, Pages.
>
> "California." *The New Columbia Encyclopedia,* edited by William H. Harris and Judith S. Levey, 4th ed., Columbia UP, 1975, pp. 423-24.

"Feminism." *Longman Dictionary of American English*, Longman,
1983, p. 252.

If there's no author given, start with the title of the entry.

ONLINE

Document online reference works the same as print ones, adding the
URL and access date after the date of publication.

"Baseball." *The Columbia Electronic Encyclopedia,* edited by
Paul Lagassé, 6th ed., Columbia UP, 2012. www.infoplease
.com/encyclopedia. Accessed 25 May 2016.

13. EDITORIAL

PRINT

"Title of Editorial." Editorial. *Name of Periodical*, Date, Page.

"Gas, Cigarettes Are Safe to Tax." Editorial. *The Lakeville Journal,* 17
Feb. 2005, p. A10.

ONLINE

"Title of Editorial." Editorial. *Name of Periodical*, Date on web, URL.
Accessed Day Month Year.

"Keep the Drinking Age at 21." Editorial. *Chicago Tribune*,
28 Aug. 2008, articles.chicagotribune.com/2008-08-26
/news/0808250487_1_binge-drinking-drinking-age-alcohol
-related-crashes. Accessed 26 Apr. 2015.

14. LETTER TO THE EDITOR

Author's Last Name, First Name. "Title of Letter (if any)." Letter.
Name of Periodical, Date on web, URL. Accessed Day Month
Year.

Pinker, Steven. "Language Arts." Letter. *The New Yorker,* 4 June
2012, www.newyorker.com/magazine/2012/06/04/language
-arts-2. Accessed 6 Apr. 2015.

author   title   publication

15. REVIEW

PRINT

Reviewer's Last Name, First Name. "Title of Review." *Review of
    Title*, by Author's First and Last Names. *Name of
    Periodical*, Date, Pages.

Frank, Jeffrey. "Body Count." Review of *The Exception,* by Christian
    Jungersen. *The New Yorker,* 30 July 2007, pp. 86-87.

If a review has no author or title, start with what's being reviewed:

Review of *Ways to Disappear,* by Idra Novey. *The New Yorker,* 28
    Mar. 2016, p. 79.

ONLINE

Reviewer's Last Name, First Name. "Title of Review." *Review of
    Title*, by Author's First and Last Names. *Name of Periodical*,
    Date, URL. Accessed Day Month Year.

Donadio, Rachel. "Italy's Great, Mysterious Storyteller." Review
    of *My Brilliant Friend*, by Elena Ferrante. *The New York
    Review of Books*, 18 Dec. 2014, www.nybooks.com
    /articles/2014/12/18/italys-great-mysterious-storyteller.
    Accessed 28 Sept. 2015.

16. COMMENT ON AN ONLINE ARTICLE

Commenter. Comment on "Title of Article." *Name of Periodical*,
    Date posted, Time posted, URL. Accessed Day Month Year.

Nick. Comment on "The Case for Reparations." *The Atlantic*, 22 May
    2014, 3:04 p.m., www.theatlantic.com/business/archive/2014/05
    /how-to-comment-on-reparations/371422/#article-comments.
    Accessed 8 May 2015.

Books and Parts of Books

For most books, you'll need to provide information about the author, the title, the publisher, and the year of publication. If you found the book inside a larger volume, a database, or some other work, be sure to specify that as well.

17. BASIC ENTRIES FOR A BOOK

PRINT

Author's Last Name, First Name. *Title*. Publisher, Year of
publication.

Watson, Brad. *Miss Jane*. W. W. Norton, 2016.

EBOOK

Document an ebook as you would a print book, but add information about the ebook—or the type of ebook if you know it.

Watson, Brad. *Miss Jane.* Ebook, W. W. Norton, 2016.

Watson, Brad. *Miss Jane.* Kindle ed., W. W. Norton, 2016.

IN A DATABASE

Author's Last Name, First Name. *Title*. Publisher, Year of
publication. *Name of Database*, DOI or URL. Accessed Day
Month Year.

Anderson, Sherwood. *Winesburg, Ohio*. B. W. Huebsch, 1919.
Bartleby.com, www.bartleby.com/156/. Accessed 8 Apr. 2015.

18. ANTHOLOGY

Last Name, First Name, editor. *Title*. Publisher, Year of publication.

Hall, Donald, editor. *The Oxford Book of Children's Verse in America*.
Oxford UP, 1985.

19. WORK IN AN ANTHOLOGY

Author's Last Name, First Name. "Title of Work." *Title of
Anthology*, edited by First and Last Names, Publisher, Year of
publication, Pages.

Documentation Map (MLA)

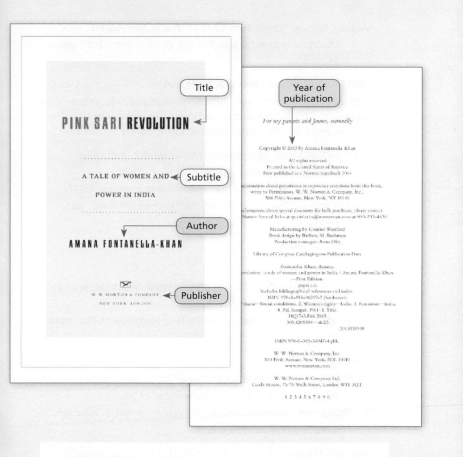

Fontanella-Khan, Amana. *Pink Sari Revolution: A Tale of Women and Power in India.* W. W. Norton, 2013.

Achebe, Chinua. "Uncle Ben's Choice." *The Seagull Reader:*
Literature, edited by Joseph Kelly, W. W. Norton, 2005, pp.
23-27.

TWO OR MORE WORKS FROM ONE ANTHOLOGY

Prepare an entry for each selection by author and title, followed by
the anthology editors' last names and the pages of the selection. Then
include an entry for the anthology itself (see no. 18).

Author's Last Name, First Name. "Title of Work." Anthology
Editors' Last Names, Pages.

Hiestand, Emily. "Afternoon Tea." Kitchen and Jones, pp. 65-67.

Ozick, Cynthia. "The Shock of Teapots." Kitchen and Jones, pp.
68-71.

20. MULTIVOLUME WORK

ALL VOLUMES

Author's Last Name, First Name. *Title of Work.* Publisher, Year(s) of
publication. Number of vols.

Churchill, Winston. *The Second World War.* Houghton Mifflin, 1948-
53. 6 vols.

SINGLE VOLUME

Author's Last Name, First Name. *Title of Work.* Vol. number,
Publisher, Year of publication. Number of vols.

Sandburg, Carl. *Abraham Lincoln: The War Years.* Vol. 2, Harcourt,
Brace & World, 1939. 4 vols.

21. BOOK IN A SERIES

Author's Last Name, First Name. *Title of Book.* Edited by First and
Last Names, Publisher, Year of publication. Series Title.

Walker, Alice. *Everyday Use.* Edited by Barbara T. Christian, Rutgers
UP, 1994. Women Writers: Texts and Contexts.

author   title   publication

22. GRAPHIC NARRATIVE

> Author's Last Name, First Name. *Title*. Publisher, Year of publication.
> Bechdel, Alison. *Fun Home: A Family Tragicomedy*. Houghton Mifflin, 2006.

If the work has both an author and an illustrator, start with the one whose work is more relevant to your research, and label the role of anyone who's not an author.

> Pekar, Harvey. *Bob & Harv's Comics*. Illustrated by R. Crumb, Running Press, 1996.
> Crumb, R., illustrator. *Bob & Harv's Comics*. By Harvey Pekar, Running Press, 1996.

23. SACRED TEXT

If you cite a specific edition of a religious text, you need to include it in your works cited list.

> *The New English Bible with the Apocrypha*. Oxford UP, 1971.
> *The Torah: A Modern Commentary*. Edited by W. Gunther Plaut, Union of American Hebrew Congregations, 1981.

24. EDITION OTHER THAN THE FIRST

> Author's Last Name, First Name. *Title*. Name *or* number of edition, Publisher, Year of publication.
> Fowler, H. W. *A Dictionary of Modern English*. 2nd ed., Oxford UP, 1965.

25. REPUBLISHED WORK

> Author's Last Name, First Name. *Title*. Year of original publication. Current publisher, Year of republication.
> Bierce, Ambrose. *Civil War Stories*. 1909. Dover, 1994.

26. FOREWORD, INTRODUCTION, PREFACE, OR AFTERWORD

Part Author's Last Name, First Name. Name of Part. *Title of Book*,
  by Author's First and Last Names, Publisher, Year of
  publication, Pages.

Tanner, Tony. Introduction. *Pride and Prejudice*, by Jane Austen,
  Penguin, 1972, pp. 7-46.

27. PUBLISHED LETTER

Letter Writer's Last Name, First Name. Letter to First and Last
  Names. Day Month Year. *Title of Book*, edited by First and
  Last Names, Publisher, Year of publication, Pages.

White, E. B. Letter to Carol Angell. 28 May 1970. *Letters of E. B.
  White,* edited by Dorothy Lobarno Guth, Harper & Row, 1976,
  p. 600.

28. PAPER AT A CONFERENCE

PAPER PUBLISHED IN CONFERENCE PROCEEDINGS

Author's Last Name, First Name. "Title of Paper." *Title of Published
  Conference Proceedings*, edited by First and Last
  Names, Publisher, Year of publication, Pages.

Flower, Linda. "Literate Action." *Composition in the Twenty-first
  Century: Crisis and Change,* edited by Lynn Z. Bloom et al.,
  Southern Illinois UP, 1996, pp. 249-60.

PAPER HEARD AT A CONFERENCE

Author's Last Name, First Name. "Title of Paper." Title of
  Conference, Day Month Year, Location, City.

Hern, Katie. "Inside an Accelerated Reading and Writing Classroom."
  Conference on Acceleration in Developmental Education, 15
  June 2016, Sheraton Inner Harbor Hotel, Baltimore.

29. DISSERTATION

> Author's Last Name, First Name. *Title.* Year. Institution, PhD
> > dissertation. *Name of Database*, URL. Accessed Day Month Year.
>
> Simington, Maire Orav. *Chasing the American Dream Post World*
> > *War II: Perspectives from Literature and Advertising*. 2003.
> > Arizona State University, PhD dissertation. *ProQuest*, search
> > .proquest.com/docview/305340098?accountid=42654. Accessed
> > 5 Oct. 2016.

For an unpublished dissertation, end with the institution and a description of the work.

> Kim, Loel. *Students Respond to Teacher Comments: A Comparison*
> > *of Online Written and Voice Modalities*. 1998. Carnegie
> > Mellon U, PhD dissertation.

Websites

Many sources are available in multiple media—for example, a print periodical that is also on the web and contained in digital databases—but some are published only on websites. This section covers the latter.

30. ENTIRE WEBSITE

> Last Name, First Name, role. *Title of Site.* Publisher, Date, URL.
> > Accessed Day Month Year.
>
> Zalta, Edward N., principal editor. *Stanford Encyclopedia of*
> > *Philosophy.* Metaphysics Research Lab, Center for the Study of
> > Language, Stanford U, 1995-2015, plato.stanford.edu/index
> > .html. Accessed 21 Apr. 2015.

PERSONAL WEBSITE

> Author's Last Name, First Name. *Title of Site.* Date, URL. Accessed
> > Day Month Year.
>
> Heath, Shirley Brice. *Shirley Brice Heath.* 2015, shirleybriceheath.net.
> > Accessed 6 June 2015.

Documentation Map (MLA)

WORK ON A WEBSITE

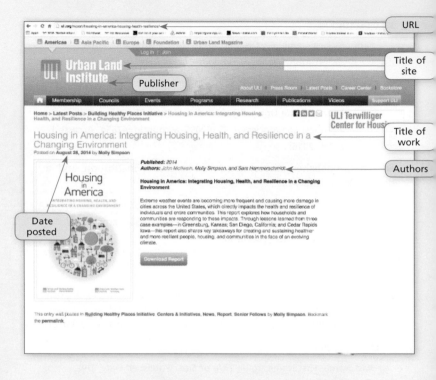

URL

Title of site

Publisher

Title of work

Authors

Date posted

McIlwain, John, et al. "Housing in America: Integrating Housing,
     Health, and Resilience in a Changing Environment." *Urban
     Land Institute*, Urban Land Institute, 28 Aug. 2014, uli.org
     /report/housing-in-america-housing-health-resilience.
     Accessed 17 Sept. 2015.

31. WORK ON A WEBSITE

> Author's Last Name, First Name (if any). "Title of Work." *Title of
>   Site*, Publisher, Date, URL. Accessed Day Month Year.

> "Global Minnesota: Immigrants Past and Present." *Immigration
>   History Research Center*, U of Minnesota, 2015, cla.umn.edu
>   .ihrc. Accessed 25 May 2016.

32. BLOG ENTRY

> Author's Last Name, First Name. "Title of Blog Entry." *Title of
>   Blog*, Date, URL. Accessed Day Month Year.

> Hollmichel, Stefanie. "Bringing Up the Bodies." *So Many Books,*
>   10 Feb. 2014, somanybooksblog.com/2014/02/10/bring-up
>   -the-bodies/. Accessed 12 Feb. 2014.

Document a whole blog as you would an entire website (no. 30) and
a comment on a blog as you would a comment on an online article
(no. 16).

33. WIKI

> "Title of Entry." *Title of Wiki*, Publisher, Date, URL. Accessed Day
>   Month Year.

> "Pi." *Wikipedia*, Wikimedia Foundation, 28 Aug. 2013, en.wikipedia
>   .org/wiki/Pi. Accessed 25 Oct. 2013.

Personal Communication and Social Media

34. PERSONAL LETTER

> Sender's Last Name, First Name. Letter to the author. Day Month Year.

> Quindlen, Anna. Letter to the author. 11 Apr. 2013.

35. EMAIL

> Sender's Last Name, First Name. "Subject Line." Received by First
>   and Last Names, Day Month Year.

Smith, William. "Teaching Grammar—Some Thoughts." Received by
Richard Bullock, 19 Nov. 2013.

36. TEXT MESSAGE

Sender's Last Name, First Name. Text message. Received by First and
Last Names, Day Month Year.

Douglass, Joanne. Text message. Received by Kim Yi, 4 June 2015.

37. POST TO AN ONLINE FORUM

Author. "Subject line" *or* "Full text of short untitled post." *Name of
Forum*, Day Month Year, URL.

@somekiryu. "What's the hardest part about writing for you?"
Reddit, 22 Apr. 2016, redd.it/4fyni0.

38. POST TO *TWITTER*, *FACEBOOK*, OR OTHER SOCIAL MEDIA

Author. "Full text of short untitled post" *or* "Title" or Descriptive
label. *Name of Site*, Day Month Year, Time, URL.

@POTUS (Barack Obama). "I'm proud of the @NBA for taking a
stand against gun violence. Sympathy for victims isn't
enough—change requires all of us speaking up." *Twitter,*
23 Dec. 2015, 1:21 p.m., twitter.com/POTUS/status
/679773729749078016.

Black Lives Matter. "Rise and Grind! Did you sign this petition yet?
We now have a sign on for ORGANIZATIONS to lend their
support." *Facebook,* 23 Oct. 2015, 11:30 a.m., www.facebook
.com/BlackLivesMatter/photos/a.294807204023865.1073741829
.180212755483311/504711973033386/?type=3&theater.

@quarterlifepoetry. Illustrated poem about girl at Target. *Instagram,*
22 Jan. 2015, www.instagram.com/p/yLO6fSurRH/.

Audio, Visual, and Other Sources

39. ADVERTISEMENT

PRINT

Name of Product or Company. Advertisement *or* Description of ad.
      Title of Periodical, Date, Page.

Cal Alumni Association. Sports Merchandise ad. *California*, Spring
      2016, p. 3.

AUDIO OR VIDEO

Name of Product or Company. Advertisement *or* Description of ad.
      Date. *Name of Host Site*, URL. Accessed Day Month Year.

Chrysler. Super Bowl commercial. 6 Feb. 2011. *YouTube*, www
      .youtube.com/watch?v=SKLZ254Y_jtc. Accessed 1 May 2015.

40. ART

ORIGINAL

Artist's Last Name, First Name. *Title of Art*. Year created, Site, City.

Van Gogh, Vincent. *The Potato Eaters*. 1885, Van Gogh Museum,
      Amsterdam.

REPRODUCTION

Artist's Last Name, First Name. *Title of Art*. Year created. *Title of Book*,
      by First and Last Names, Publisher, Year of publication, Page.

Van Gogh, Vincent. *The Potato Eaters*. 1885. *History of Art: A Survey
      of the Major Visual Arts from the Dawn of History to the
      Present Day,* by H. W. Janson, Prentice-Hall/Harry N. Abrams,
      1969, p. 508.

ONLINE

Artist's Last Name, First Name. *Title of Art*. Year created. *Name of
      Site*, URL. Accessed Day Month Year.

Warhol, Andy. *Self-portrait.* 1979. *J. Paul Getty Museum,* www.getty
    .edu/art/collection/objects/106971/andy-warhol-self-portrait
    -american-1979/. Accessed 20 Jan. 2015.

41. CARTOON

PRINT

Author's Last Name, First Name. "Title of Cartoon." *Title of*
    Periodical, Date, Page. Cartoon.

Chast, Roz. "The Three Wise Men of Thanksgiving." *The New Yorker,*
    1 Dec. 2003, p. 174. Cartoon.

ONLINE

Author's Last Name, First Name. "Title of Cartoon." *Title of Site,*
    Date, URL. Accessed Day Month Year. Cartoon.

Munroe, Randall. "Up Goer Five." *xkcd,* 12 Nov. 2012, xkcd
    .com/1133/. Accessed 22 Apr. 2015. Cartoon.

42. COURT CASE

First Plaintiff v. First Defendant. *United States Reports* citation.
    Name of Court, Year of decision. Name of Source Site.
    Publisher, URL. Accessed Day Month Year.

District of Columbia v. Heller. 554 US 570. Supreme Court of the US,
    2008. Legal Information Institute, Cornell U Law School,
    www.law.cornell.edu/supct/html/07-290.ZS.html. Accessed 3
    June 2016.

43. FILM

Name individuals based on the focus of your project—the director,
the screenwriter, the cinematographer, or someone else. If your essay
focuses on one or more contributors, you may put their names before
the title.

Title of Film. Role by First and Last Names, Production Studio, Date.
Breakfast at Tiffany's. Directed by Blake Edwards, Paramount, 1961.

STREAMING

Title of Film. Role by First and Last Names, Production Studio,
Date. *Streaming Service*, URL. Accessed Day Month Year.

Interstellar. Directed by Christopher Nolan, Paramount, 2014.
Amazon Prime Video, www.amazon.com/Interstellar-Matthew
-McConaughey/dp/B00TU9UFTS. Accessed 2 May 2015.

44. INTERVIEW

If the interviewer's name is known and relevant to your argument,
include it after the word "Interview" or the title: Interview by Stephen
Colbert.

BROADCAST

Subject's Last Name, First Name. Interview *or* "Title of Interview."
Title of Program, Network, Day Month Year.

Gates, Henry Louis, Jr. Interview. *Fresh Air,* NPR, 9 Apr. 2002.

PUBLISHED

Subject's Last Name, First Name. Interview *or* "Title of Interview."
Title of Publication, Date, Pages.

Stone, Oliver. Interview. *Esquire,* Nov. 2004, pp. 170-71.

PERSONAL

Subject's Last Name, First Name. Personal interview. Day Month Year.

Roddick, Andy. Personal interview. 17 Aug. 2013.

45. MAP

If the title doesn't make clear it's a map, add a label at the end.

"Title of Map." Publisher, URL. Accessed Day Month Year.

"National Highway System." US Department of Transportation
Federal Highway Administration, www.fhwa.dot.gov/planning
/images/nhs.pdf. Accessed 10 May 2015. Map.

46. MUSICAL SCORE

> Composer's Last Name, First Name. *Title of Composition.* Year of
>   composition. Publisher, Year of publication.
>
> Stravinsky, Igor. *Petrushka.* 1911. W. W. Norton, 1967.

47. ONLINE VIDEO

> Author's Last Name, First Name. *Title. Name of Host Site,* Date,
>   URL. Accessed Day Month Year.
>
> Westbrook, Adam. *Cause/Effect: The Unexpected Origins of Terrible
>   Things. Vimeo,* 9 Sept. 2014, vimeo.com/105681474. Accessed
>   20 Dec. 2015.

48. ORAL PRESENTATION

> Presenter's Last Name, First Name. "Title of Presentation."
>   Sponsoring Institution, Date, Location.
>
> Cassin, Michael. "Nature in the Raw—The Art of Landscape
>   Painting." Berkshire Institute for Lifelong Learning, 24 Mar.
>   2005, Clark Art Institute, Williamstown.

49. PODCAST

If you accessed a podcast online, give the URL and date of access; if
you accessed it through a service such as *iTunes* or *Spotify*, indicate
that instead.

> Last Name, First Name, role. "Title of Episode." *Title of Program,*
>   season, episode, Sponsor, Date, URL. Accessed Day Month Year.
>
> Koenig, Sarah, host. "DUSTWUN." *Serial,* season 2, episode 1, WBEZ,
>   10 Dec. 2015, serialpodcast.org/season-two/1/dustwun.
>   Accessed 23 Apr. 2016.
>
> Foss, Gilad, author and performer. "Aquaman's Brother-in-Law."
>   *Superhero Temp Agency,* season 1, episode 1, 16 Apr. 2015.
>   *iTunes.*

50. RADIO PROGRAM

Last Name, First Name, role. "Title of Episode." *Title of Program*,
Station, Day Month Year of broadcast, URL. Accessed Day
Month Year.

Glass, Ira, host. "In Defense of Ignorance." *This American Life*,
WBEZ, 22 Apr. 2016, thisamericanlife.org/radio-archives
/episode/585/in-defense-of-ignorance. Accessed 2 May 2016.

51. SOUND RECORDING

ONLINE

Last Name, First Name. "Title of Work." *Title of Album*, Distributor,
Date. *Name of Audio Service.*

Simone, Nina. "To Be Young, Gifted and Black." *Black Gold*, RCA
Records, 1969. *Spotify.*

CD

Last Name, First Name. "Title of Work." *Title of Album*, Distributor,
Date.

Brown, Greg. "Canned Goods." *The Live One,* Red House, 1995.

52. TV SHOW

Name contributors based on the focus of your project—director, writers, actors, or others. And if there's a key contributor, you might
include his or her name and role before the title of the episode.

"Title of Episode." *Title of Program*, role by First and Last Names,
season, episode, Network, Day Month Year.

"The Silencer." *Criminal Minds,* written by Erica Messer, season 8,
episode 1, NBC, 26 Sept. 2012.

DVD

"Title of Episode." Broadcast Year. *Title of DVD*, role by First and
Last Names, season, episode, Production Studio, Release Year,
disc number.

"The Pants Tent." 2003. *Curb Your Enthusiasm: Season One,*
       performance by Larry David, season 1, episode 1, HBO Video,
       2006, disc 1.

ONLINE

"Title of Episode." *Title of Program*, role by First and Last Names (if
       any), season, episode, Production Studio, Day Month Year.
       Name of Host Site, URL. Accessed Day Month Year.
"Shadows in the Glass." *Marvel's Daredevil*, season 1, episode 8,
       Netflix, 10 Apr. 2015. *Netflix*, www.netflix.com/watch
       /80018198. Accessed 3 Nov. 2015.

53. VIDEO GAME

Last Name, First Name, role. Title of Game. Distributor, Date of
       release. Gaming System or Platform.
Metzen, Chris, and James Waugh, writers. *StarCraft II: Legacy of the
       Void.* Blizzard Entertainment, 2015. OS X.

MLA-d Formatting a Research Paper

Name, course, title. MLA does not require a separate title page.
In the upper left-hand corner of your first page, include your name,
your professor's name, the name of the course, and the date. Center
the title of your paper on the line after the date; capitalize it as you
would a book title.

Page numbers. In the upper right-hand corner of each page, one-
half inch below the top of the page, include your last name and the
page number. Number pages consecutively throughout your paper.

Font, spacing, margins, and indents. Choose a font that is easy to
read (such as Times New Roman) and that provides a clear contrast
between regular and italic text. Double-space the entire paper, includ-

ing your works cited list. Set one-inch margins at the top, bottom, and sides of your text; do not justify your text. The first line of each paragraph should be indented one-half inch from the left margin.

Long quotations. When quoting more than three lines of poetry, more than four lines of prose, or dialogue between characters in a drama, set off the quotation from the rest of your text, indenting it one-half inch (or five spaces) from the left margin. Do not use quotation marks, and put any parenthetical documentation *after* the final punctuation.

> In *Eastward to Tartary*, Kaplan captures ancient and
> contemporary Antioch for us:
>> At the height of its glory in the Roman-Byzantine age,
>> when it had an amphitheater, public baths, aqueducts,
>> and sewage pipes, half a million people lived in Antioch.
>> Today the population is only 125,000. With sour relations
>> between Turkey and Syria, and unstable politics
>> throughout the Middle East, Antioch is now a backwater—
>> seedy and tumbledown, with relatively few tourists. I
>> found it altogether charming. (123)
> In the first stanza of Arnold's "Dover Beach," the exclamations
> make clear that the speaker is addressing someone who is also
> present in the scene:
>> Come to the window, sweet is the night air!
>> Only, from the long line of spray
>> Where the sea meets the moon-blanched land,
>> Listen! You hear the grating roar
>> Of pebbles which the waves draw back, and fling. (6-10)

Be careful to maintain the poet's line breaks. If a line does not fit on one line of your paper, put the extra words on the next line. Indent that line an additional quarter inch (or two spaces).

Illustrations. Insert illustrations close to the text that discusses them. For tables, provide a number (*Table* 1) and a title on separate lines above the table. Below the table, provide a caption and information about the source. For graphs, photos, and other figures, provide a figure number (*Fig.* 1), caption, and source information below the figure. If you give only brief source information (such as a parenthetical note), or if the source is cited elsewhere in your text, include it in your list of works cited. Be sure to make clear how any illustrations relate to your point.

List of Works Cited. Start your list on a new page, following any notes. Center the title and double-space the entire list. Begin each entry at the left margin, and indent subsequent lines one-half inch (or five spaces). Alphabetize the list by authors' last names (or by editors' or translators' names, if appropriate). Alphabetize works with no author or editor by title, disregarding *A*, *An*, and *The*. To cite more than one work by a single author, list them as in no. 4 on page 135.

MLA-e Sample Research Paper

The following report was written by Dylan Borchers for a first-year writing course. It's formatted according to the guidelines of the MLA (**style.mla.org**).

Sample Research Paper, MLA Style

Last name and page number.

1"

Dylan Borchers

Professor Bullock

English 102, Section 4

4 May 2012

Against the Odds:

Harry S. Truman and the Election of 1948

Title centered.

Just over a week before Election Day in 1948, a *New York Times* article noted "[t]he popular view that Gov. Thomas E. Dewey's election as President is a foregone conclusion" (Egan). This assessment of the race between incumbent Democrat Harry S. Truman and Dewey, his Republican challenger, was echoed a week later when *Life* magazine published a photograph whose caption labeled Dewey "The Next President" (Photo of Truman 37). In a *Newsweek* survey of fifty prominent political writers, each one predicted Truman's defeat, and *Time* correspondents declared that Dewey would carry 39 of the 48 states (Donaldson 210). Nearly every major media outlet across the United States endorsed Dewey and lambasted Truman. As historian Robert H. Ferrell observes, even Truman's wife, Bess, thought he would be beaten (270).

Double-spaced throughout.

1"

1"

Author named in signal phrase, page numbers in parentheses.

The results of an election are not so easily predicted, as the famous photograph in fig. 1 shows. Not only did Truman win the election, but he won by a significant margin, with 303 electoral votes and 24,179,259 popular votes, compared to Dewey's 189 electoral votes and 21,991,291 popular votes (Donaldson 204-07). In fact, many historians and political analysts argue that Truman would have won by an even greater margin had third-party Progressive candidate Henry A. Wallace not split the Democratic

1"

Borchers   2

Fig. 1. President Harry S. Truman holds up an edition of the *Chicago Daily Tribune* that mistakenly announced "Dewey Defeats Truman." (Rollins).

vote in New York State and Dixiecrat Strom Thurmond not won four states in the South (McCullough 711). Although Truman's defeat was heavily predicted, those predictions themselves, Dewey's passiveness as a campaigner, and Truman's zeal turned the tide for a Truman victory.

In the months preceding the election, public opinion polls predicted that Dewey would win by a large margin. Pollster Elmo Roper stopped polling in September, believing there was no reason to continue, given a seemingly inevitable Dewey landslide. Although the margin narrowed as the election drew near, the other pollsters predicted a Dewey win by at least 5 percent (Donaldson 209). Many

1"   Borchers   3

historians believe that these predictions aided the president in the long run. First, surveys showing Dewey in the lead may have prompted some of Dewey's supporters to feel overconfident about their candidate's chances and therefore to stay home from the polls on Election Day. Second, these same surveys may have energized Democrats to mount late get-out-the-vote efforts ("1948 Truman-Dewey Election"). Other analysts believe that the overwhelming predictions of a Truman loss also kept at home some Democrats who approved of Truman's policies but saw a Truman loss as inevitable. According to political analyst Samuel Lubell, those Democrats may have saved Dewey from an even greater defeat (Hamby, *Man* 465). Whatever the impact on the voters, the polling numbers had a decided effect on Dewey.

    Historians and political analysts alike cite Dewey's overly cautious campaign as one of the main reasons Truman was able to achieve victory. Dewey firmly believed in public opinion polls. With all indications pointing to an easy victory, Dewey and his staff believed that all he had to do was bide his time and make no foolish mistakes. Dewey himself said, "When you're leading, don't talk" (Smith 30). Each of Dewey's speeches was well crafted and well rehearsed. As the leader in the race, he kept his remarks faultlessly positive, with the result that he failed to deliver a solid message or even mention Truman or any of Truman's policies. Eventually, Dewey began to be perceived as aloof and stuffy. One observer compared him to the plastic groom on top of a wedding cake (Hamby, "Harry S. Truman"), and others noted his stiff, cold demeanor (McCullough 671-74).

Paragraphs indent ½ inch or 5 spaces.

Two works cited within the same sentence.

As his campaign continued, observers noted that Dewey seemed uncomfortable in crowds, unable to connect with ordinary people. And he made a number of blunders. One took place at a train stop when the candidate, commenting on the number of children in the crowd, said he was glad they had been let out of school for his arrival. Unfortunately for Dewey, it was a Saturday ("1948: The Great Truman Surprise"). Such gaffes gave voters the feeling that Dewey was out of touch with the public.

Title used when there's no known author.

Again and again through the autumn of 1948, Dewey's campaign speeches failed to address the issues, with the candidate declaring that he did not want to "get down in the gutter" (Smith 515). When told by fellow Republicans that he was losing ground, Dewey insisted that his campaign not alter its course. Even *Time* magazine, though it endorsed and praised him, conceded that his speeches were dull (McCullough 696). According to historian Zachary Karabell, they were "notable only for taking place, not for any specific message" (244). Dewey's numbers in the polls slipped in the weeks before the election, but he still held a comfortable lead over Truman. It would take Truman's famous whistle-stop campaign to make the difference.

Few candidates in US history have campaigned for the presidency with more passion and faith than Harry Truman. In the autumn of 1948, he wrote to his sister, "It will be the greatest campaign any President ever made. Win, lose, or draw, people will know where I stand" (91). For thirty-three days, Truman traveled the nation, giving hundreds of speeches from the back of the *Ferdinand Magellan* railroad car. In the same letter, he described the

Borchers   5

pace: "We made about 140 stops and I spoke over 147 times, shook hands with at least 30,000 and am in good condition to start out again tomorrow for Wilmington, Philadelphia, Jersey City, Newark, Albany and Buffalo" (91). McCullough writes of Truman's campaign:

> No President in history had ever gone so far in quest of support from the people, or with less cause for the effort, to judge by informed opinion. . . . As a test of his skills and judgment as a professional politician, not to say his stamina and disposition at age sixty-four, it would be like no other experience in his long, often difficult career, as he himself understood perfectly. More than any other event in his public life, or in his presidency thus far, it would reveal the kind of man he was. (655)

He spoke in large cities and small towns, defending his policies and attacking Republicans. As a former farmer and relatively late bloomer, Truman was able to connect with the public. He developed an energetic style, usually speaking from notes rather than from a prepared speech, and often mingled with the crowds that met his train. These crowds grew larger as the campaign progressed. In Chicago, over half a million people lined the streets as he passed, and in St. Paul the crowd numbered over 25,000. When Dewey entered St. Paul two days later, he was greeted by only 7,000 supporters ("1948 Truman-Dewey Election"). Reporters brushed off the large crowds as mere curiosity seekers wanting to see a president (McCullough 682). Yet Truman persisted, even if he often seemed to be the only one who thought he could win. By

Quotations of more than 4 lines indented $\frac{1}{2}$ inch (5 spaces) and double-spaced.

Parenthetical reference after final punctuation.

going directly to the American people and connecting with them, Truman built the momentum needed to surpass Dewey and win the election.

The legacy and lessons of Truman's whistle-stop campaign continue to be studied by political analysts, and politicians today often mimic his campaign methods by scheduling multiple visits to key states, as Truman did. He visited California, Illinois, and Ohio 48 times, compared with 6 visits to those states by Dewey. Political scientist Thomas M. Holbrook concludes that his strategic campaigning in those states and others gave Truman the electoral votes he needed to win (61, 65).

The 1948 election also had an effect on pollsters, who, as Elmo Roper admitted, "couldn't have been more wrong." *Life* magazine's editors concluded that pollsters as well as reporters and commentators were too convinced of a Dewey victory to analyze the polls seriously, especially the opinions of undecided voters (Karabell 256). Pollsters assumed that undecided voters would vote in the same proportion as decided voters—and that turned out to be a false assumption (Karabell 257). In fact, the lopsidedness of the polls might have led voters who supported Truman to call themselves undecided out of an unwillingness to associate themselves with the losing side, further skewing the polls' results (McDonald et al. 152). Such errors led pollsters to change their methods significantly after the 1948 election.

Work by 3 or more authors is shortened using et al.

After the election, many political analysts, journalists, and historians concluded that the Truman upset was in fact a victory for the American people, who, the *New Republic* noted, "couldn't be ticketed by the polls, knew its own mind and had picked the rather unlikely but courageous figure of Truman to carry its banner" (T.R.B. 3). How "unlikely" is unclear, however; Truman biographer Alonzo Hamby notes that "polls of scholars consistently rank Truman among the top eight presidents in American history" (*Man* 641). But despite Truman's high standing, and despite the fact that the whistle-stop campaign is now part of our political landscape, politicians have increasingly imitated the style of the Dewey campaign, with its "packaged candidate who ran so as not to lose, who steered clear of controversy, and who made a good show of appearing presidential" (Karabell 266). The election of 1948 shows that voters are not necessarily swayed by polls, but it may have presaged the packaging of candidates by public relations experts, to the detriment of public debate on the issues in future presidential elections.

1"   Borchers   8

Works Cited

Donaldson, Gary A. *Truman Defeats Dewey*. UP of Kentucky, 1999.

Egan, Leo. "Talk Is Now Turning to the Dewey Cabinet." *The New York Times*, 20 Oct. 1948, p. 8E, www.nytimes.com /timesmachine/1948/10/26/issue.html. Accessed 18 Apr. 2012.

Ferrell, Robert H. *Harry S. Truman: A Life*. U of Missouri P, 1994.

Hamby, Alonzo L., editor. "Harry S. Truman: Campaigns and Elections." *American President*, Miller Center, U of Virginia, 11 Jan. 2012, millercenter.org/president/biography/truman -campaigns-and-elections. Accessed 17 Mar. 2012.

- - -. *Man of the People: A Life of Harry S. Truman*. Oxford UP, 1995.

Holbrook, Thomas M. "Did the Whistle-Stop Campaign Matter?" *PS: Political Science and Politics,* vol. 35, no. 1, Mar. 2002, pp. 59-66.

Karabell, Zachary. *The Last Campaign: How Harry Truman Won the 1948 Election*. Alfred A. Knopf, 2000.

McCullough, David. *Truman*. Simon and Schuster, 1992.

McDonald, Daniel G., et al. "The Spiral of Silence in the 1948 Presidential Election." *Communication Research,* vol. 28, no. 2, Apr. 2001, pp. 139-55.

"1948: The Great Truman Surprise." *The Press and the Presidency*, Dept. of Political Science and International Affairs, Kennesaw State U, 29 Oct. 2003, kennesaw.edu/pols.3380/pres/1984.html. Accessed 10 Apr. 2012.

"1948 Truman-Dewey Election." *American Political History*, Eagleton Institute of Politics, Rutgers, State U of New Jersey, 1995-2012, www.eagleton.rutgers.edu/research/americanhistory /ap_trumandewey.php. Accessed 18 Apr. 2012.

Photo of Truman in San Francisco. "The Next President Travels by
       Ferry Boat over the Broad Waters of San Francisco Bay." *Life*,
       1 Nov. 1948, p. 37. Google Books, books.google.com/books?id
       =ekoEAAAAMBAJ&printsec=frontcover#v=onepage&q&f=false.
       Accessed 20 Apr. 2012.

Rollins, Byron. "President Truman with *Chicago Daily Tribune*
       Headline of 'Dewey Defeats Truman.'" Associated Press,
       4 Nov. 1948. Harry S. Truman Library & Museum, www
       .trumanlibrary.org/photographs/view.php?id=25248. Accessed
       20 Apr. 2012.

Roper, Elmo. "Roper Eats Crow; Seeks Reason for Vote Upset."
       Evening Independent, 6 Nov. 1948, p. 10. Google News, news
       .google.com/newspapers?nid=PZE8UkGerEcC&dat=19481106
       &printsec=frontpage&hl=en. Accessed 13 Apr. 2012.

Smith, Richard Norton. *Thomas E. Dewey and His Times*. Simon and
       Schuster, 1982.

T.R.B. "Washington Wire." *The New Republic*, 15 Nov. 1948, pp. 3-4.
       EBSCOhost, search.ebscohost.com/login.aspx?direct=true&db
       =tsh&AN=14779640&site=ehost-live. Accessed 20 Apr. 2012.

Truman, Harry S. "Campaigning, Letter, October 5, 1948." *Harry S.
       Truman*, edited by Robert H. Ferrell, CQ P, 2003, p. 91.

*Every source
used is in the
list of works
cited.*

APA Style

American Psychological Association (APA) style calls for (1) brief documentation in parentheses near each in-text citation and (2) complete documentation in a list of references at the end of your text. The models in this chapter draw on the *Publication Manual of the American Psychological Association*, 6th edition (2010). Additional information is available at **www.apastyle.org** and at **blog.apastyle.org**.

A DIRECTORY TO APA STYLE

In-Text Documentation   173

1. Author named in a signal phrase   173
2. Author named in parentheses   174
3. Authors with the same last name   174
4. Two authors   175
5. Three or more authors   175
6. Organization or government as author   175
7. Author unknown   176
8. Two or more works cited together   176
9. Two or more works by one author in the same year   176
10. Source quoted in another source   176
11. Work without page numbers   177
12. An entire work   177
13. Personal communication   178
14. Social media   178

Notes   178

Reference List   179

PRINT BOOKS   179

Documentation Map: Print Book   180

1. One author   181

2. Two or more works by the same author   181

3. Two or more authors   181

4. Organization or government as author   182

5. Author and editor   182

6. Edited collection   182

7. Work in an edited collection   183

8. Unknown author   183

9. Edition other than the first   183

10. Translation   183

11. Multivolume work   184

12. Article in a reference book   184

PRINT PERIODICALS   184

13. Article in a journal paginated by volume   185

14. Article in a journal paginated by issue   185

15. Article in a magazine   186

16. Article in a newspaper   186

17. Interview in a periodical   186

18. Article by an unknown author   186

19. Book review   187

20. Letter to the editor   187

ONLINE SOURCES   187

Documentation Map: Work from a Nonperiodical Website   189
Documentation Map: Article with DOI from a Journal   190
Documentation Map: Article with DOI Available through a Database   194

21. Work from a nonperiodical website   188

22. Article in an online periodical   191

23. Comment on an online article   191

24. Article available through a database   192

25. Article or chapter in a web document or an online reference work   192

26. Electronic book   192

27. Wiki entry   193

28. Blog entry   193

29. Online video   193

30. Podcast   195

31. Episode from a TV show or other series found online   195

PERSONAL COMMUNICATION AND SOCIAL MEDIA   195

32. Personal letter, email, text message, or conversation   195

33. Post to an online forum   195

34. Post to *Twitter*, *Facebook*, and other social media   196

AUDIO, VISUAL, MULTIMEDIA, AND OTHER SOURCES   196

35. Film, video, or DVD   196

36. Music recording   196

37. Proceedings of a conference   196

38. Television program   197

39. Computer software   197

40. Government document   197

41. Dissertation   198

42. Technical or research report   198

43. Video game   198

44. Data set or graph   199

45. Map   199

46. Advertisement   199

author   title   publication

SOURCES NOT COVERED BY APA   200

Formatting a Paper   200
Sample Pages   203

Throughout this chapter, you'll find models and examples that are color-coded to help you see how writers include source information in their texts and reference lists: brown for author or editor, yellow for title, gray for publication information: place of publication, publisher, date of publication, page number(s), and so on.

APA-a In-Text Documentation

Brief documentation in your text makes clear to your reader precisely what you took from a source and, in the case of a quotation, precisely where (usually, on which page) in the source you found the text you are quoting. (See p. 177, no. 11, for works without page numbers.)

PARAPHRASES and SUMMARIES are more common than QUOTATIONS in APA-style projects. See R-4 for more on all three kinds of citation. As you cite each source, you will need to decide whether to name the author in a signal phrase—"as McCullough (2001) wrote"—or in parentheses—"(McCullough, 2001)." Note that APA requires you to use the past tense or present perfect tense for verbs in SIGNAL PHRASES: "Moss (2003) argued," "Moss (2003) has argued."

1. AUTHOR NAMED IN A SIGNAL PHRASE

If you are quoting, you must give the page number(s). You are not required to give the page number(s) with a paraphrase or a summary, but APA encourages you to do so, especially if you are citing a long or complex work; most of the models in this chapter do include page numbers.

AUTHOR QUOTED

Put the date in parentheses right after the author's name; put the page in parentheses as close to the quotation as possible.

> McCullough (2001) described John Adams as having "the hands of
> a man accustomed to pruning his own trees, cutting his own hay,
> and splitting his own firewood" (p. 18).

Notice that in this example the parenthetical reference with the page
number comes *after* the closing quotation marks but *before* the period
at the end of the sentence.

AUTHOR PARAPHRASED OR SUMMARIZED

Put the date in parentheses right after the author's name; follow the
date with the page.

> John Adams' hands were those of a laborer, according to
> McCullough (2001, p. 18).

2. AUTHOR NAMED IN PARENTHESES

If you do not mention an author in a signal phrase, put his or her
name, a comma, and the year of publication in parentheses as close
as possible to the quotation, paraphrase, or summary.

AUTHOR QUOTED

Give the author, date, and page in one pair of parentheses, or split
the information between two pairs of parentheses.

> One biographer (McCullough, 2001) has said John Adams had
> "the hands of a man accustomed to pruning his own trees,
> cutting his own hay, and splitting his own firewood" (p. 18).

AUTHOR PARAPHRASED OR SUMMARIZED

Give the author, date, and page in one pair of parentheses toward the
beginning or the end of the paraphrase or summary.

> John Adams' hands were those of a laborer (McCullough, 2001, p. 18).

3. AUTHORS WITH THE SAME LAST NAME

If your reference list includes more than one person with the same last
name, include initials in all documentation to distinguish the authors
from one another.

Eclecticism is common in contemporary criticism (J. M. Smith, 1992, p. vii).

4. TWO AUTHORS

Always mention both authors. Use *and* in a signal phrase, but use an ampersand (&) in parentheses.

Carlson and Ventura (1990) wanted to introduce Julio Cortázar, Marjorie Agosín, and other Latin American writers to an audience of English-speaking adolescents (p. v).

According to the Peter Principle, "In a hierarchy, every employee tends to rise to his level of incompetence" (Peter & Hull, 1969, p. 26).

5. THREE OR MORE AUTHORS

In the first reference to a work by three to five persons, name all contributors. In subsequent references, name the first author followed by *et al.*, Latin for "and others." Whenever you refer to a work by six or more contributors, name only the first author, followed by *et al.* Use *and* in a signal phrase, but use an ampersand (&) in parentheses.

Faigley, George, Palchik, and Selfe (2004) have argued that where there used to be a concept called *literacy,* today's multitude of new kinds of texts has given us *literacies* (p. xii).

Faigley et al. (2004) have also argued that images are an integral part of communication today (p. xiii).

Peilen et al. (1990) supported their claims about corporate corruption with startling anecdotal evidence (p. 75).

6. ORGANIZATION OR GOVERNMENT AS AUTHOR

If an organization name is recognizable by its abbreviation, give the full name and the abbreviation the first time you cite the source. In subsequent references, use only the abbreviation. If the organization does not have a familiar abbreviation, always use its full name.

FIRST REFERENCE

(American Psychological Association [APA], 2008)

SUBSEQUENT REFERENCES

(APA, 2008)

7. AUTHOR UNKNOWN

Use the complete title if it is short; if it is long, use the first few words of the title under which the work appears in the reference list.

> *Webster's New Biographical Dictionary* (1988) identifies William James as "American psychologist and philosopher" (p. 520).

> A powerful editorial asserted that healthy liver donor Mike Hurewitz died because of "frightening" faulty postoperative care ("Every Patient's Nightmare," 2007).

8. TWO OR MORE WORKS CITED TOGETHER

If you cite multiple works in the same pair of parentheses, order them alphabetically, separated by semicolons.

> Many researchers have argued that what counts as "literacy" is not necessarily learned at school (Heath, 1983; Moss, 2003).

9. TWO OR MORE WORKS BY ONE AUTHOR IN THE SAME YEAR

If your list of references includes more than one work by the same author published in the same year, order them alphabetically by title, adding lowercase letters ("a," "b," and so on) to the year, as on p. 167, no. 2. Then use the year plus letter in your text.

> Kaplan (2000b, p. 127) described orderly shantytowns in Turkey that did not resemble the other slums he visited.

10. SOURCE QUOTED IN ANOTHER SOURCE

When you cite a source that was quoted in another source, let the reader know that you used a secondary source by adding the words *as cited in.*

author   title   publication

During the meeting with the psychologist, the patient stated repeatedly that he "didn't want to be too paranoid" (as cited in Oberfield & Yasik, 2004, p. 294).

11. WORK WITHOUT PAGE NUMBERS

Instead of page numbers, some electronic works have paragraph numbers, which you should include (preceded by the abbreviation *para.*) if you are referring to a specific part of such a source.

Russell's dismissals from Trinity College at Cambridge and from City College in New York City have been seen as examples of the controversy that marked his life (Irvine, 2006, para. 2).

In sources with neither page nor paragraph numbers, refer readers to a particular part of the source if possible, perhaps indicating a heading and the paragraph under the heading.

One analyst (Greenstein, 2006) concluded, "The early republic presented chief executives with the political equivalent of a Rorschach test" ("Washington, Adams, and Jefferson Compared," para. 1).

12. AN ENTIRE WORK

You do not need to give a page number if you are directing readers' attention to an entire work.

Throughout his life, John Adams strove to succeed (McCullough, 2001).

When you are citing an entire website, give the URL in the text. You do not need to include the website in your reference list. To cite part of a website, see no. 21 on page 188.

Beyond providing diagnostic information, the website for the Alzheimer's Association includes a variety of resources for family and community support of patients suffering from Alzheimer's disease (http://www.alz.org).

13. PERSONAL COMMUNICATION

Document email, telephone conversations, interviews, personal letters, and other personal texts as *personal communication,* along with the person's initial(s), last name, and the date. You do not need to include such personal communications in your reference list.

> L. Strauss (personal communication, December 6, 2013) told about visiting Yogi Berra when they both lived in Montclair, New Jersey.

14. SOCIAL MEDIA

For an archived social-media source, document the source with author and date, both in the text and in your reference list (see pp. 195–96, nos. 33 and 34).

POST TO AN ONLINE FORUM

> A Stanford sleep specialist posting to *Reddit* identified three potential causes of poor sleep: "poor timing, poor quality, [and] poor quantity" (Velma, 2015).

TWITTER

> POTUS tweeted his approval of the National Basketball Association's anti–gun violence stance (Obama, 2015).

FACEBOOK

> Its social-media campaign called not only for individuals but also for organizations to support the movement (Black Lives Matter, 2015).

APA-b Notes

You may need to use content notes to give an explanation or information that doesn't fit into your text. To signal a content note, place a superscript numeral at the appropriate point in your text. Include this information as a footnote, or put the notes on a separate page with the heading *Notes*, after your reference list. If you have multiple notes, number them consecutively throughout your text. Here is an example from *In Search of Solutions: A New Direction in Psychotherapy* (2003).

TEXT WITH SUPERSCRIPT

An important part of working with teams and one-way mirrors is taking the consultation break, as at Milan, BFTC, and MRI.[1]

CONTENT NOTE

[1]It is crucial to note here that while working within a team is fun, stimulating, and revitalizing, it is not necessary for successful outcomes. Solution-oriented therapy works equally well when working solo.

APA-c Reference List

A reference list provides full bibliographic information for every source cited in your text with the exception of entire websites and personal communications. See page 202 for guidelines on organizing and formatting such a list; for a sample reference list, see page 207.

Print Books

For most books, you'll need to provide the author, the publication date, the title and any subtitle, and the place of publication and publisher.

KEY DETAILS FOR DOCUMENTING PRINT BOOKS

- **AUTHORS:** Use the author's last name, but replace the first and middle names with initials (D. R. Kinder for Donald R. Kinder).
- **DATES:** If more than one year is given, use the most recent one.
- **TITLES:** Capitalize only the first word and proper nouns and proper adjectives in titles and subtitles. Italicize titles of books.

Documentation Map (APA)
PRINT BOOK

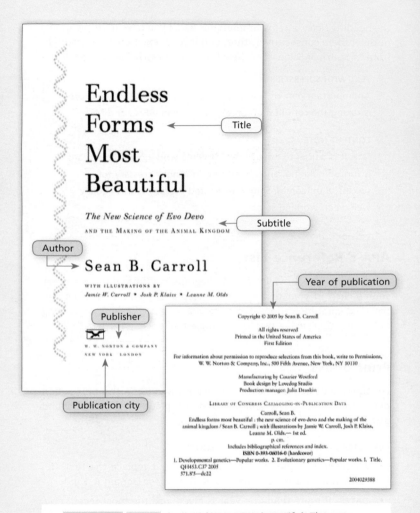

Carroll, S. B. (2005). *Endless forms most beautiful: The new science of evo devo and the making of the animal kingdom.* New York, NY: Norton.

- **PUBLICATION PLACE:** Give city followed by state (abbreviated) or country if outside the United States; include the province for Canadian cities (for example, Boston, MA; London, England; Toronto, Ontario, Canada). If more than one city is given, use the first. Do not include the state or country if the publisher is a university whose name includes that information.

- **PUBLISHER:** Use a shortened form of the publisher's name (Norton for W. W. Norton), but retain *Association*, *Books*, and *Press* (American Psychological Association, Princeton University Press).

1. ONE AUTHOR

Author's Last Name, Initials. (Year of publication). *Title.* Publication
     City, State *or* Country: Publisher.

Lewis, M. (2003). *Moneyball: The art of winning an unfair game.*
     New York, NY: Norton.

2. TWO OR MORE WORKS BY THE SAME AUTHOR

If the works were published in different years, list them chronologically.

Lewis, B. (1995). *The Middle East: A brief history of the last 2,000*
     years. New York, NY: Scribner.

Lewis, B. (2003). *The crisis of Islam: Holy war and unholy terror.* New
     York, NY: Modern Library.

If the works were published in the same year, list them alphabetically by title, adding "a," "b," and so on to the year.

Kaplan, R. D. (2000a). *The coming anarchy: Shattering the dreams of*
     the post cold war. New York, NY: Random House.

Kaplan, R. D. (2000b). *Eastward to Tartary: Travels in the Balkans, the*
     Middle East, and the Caucasus. New York, NY: Random House.

3. TWO OR MORE AUTHORS

For two to seven authors, include all names.

> First Author's Last Name, Initials, Next Author's Last Name, Initials, &
> Final Author's Last Name, Initials. (Year of publication). *Title.*
> Publication City, State *or* Country: Publisher.

Levitt, S. D., & Dubner, S. J. (2005). *Freakonomics: A rogue economist
explores the hidden side of everything.* New York, NY: Morrow.

For a work by eight or more authors, name just the first six authors,
followed by three ellipses, and end with the final author (see no. 22
for an example from an online magazine article).

4. ORGANIZATION OR GOVERNMENT AS AUTHOR

Sometimes an organization or a government agency is both author
and publisher. If so, use the word *Author* as the publisher.

> Organization Name *or* Government Agency. (Year of publication).
> *Title.* Publication City, State *or* Country: Publisher.

Catholic News Service. (2002). *Stylebook on religion 2000: A
reference guide and usage manual.* Washington, DC: Author.

5. AUTHOR AND EDITOR

> Author's Last Name, Initials. (Year of edited edition). *Title.* (Editor's
> Initials Last Name, Ed.). Publication City, State *or* Country:
> Publisher. (Original work[s] published year[s])

Dick, P. F. (2008). *Five novels of the 1960s and 70s.* (J. Lethem, Ed.).
New York, NY: Library of America. (Original works published
1964-1977)

6. EDITED COLLECTION

> First Editor's Last Name, Initials, Next Editor's Last Name, Initials, &
> Final Editor's Last Name, Initials. (Eds.). (Year of edited
> edition). *Title.* Publication City, State *or* Country: Publisher.

Raviv, A., Oppenheimer, L., & Bar-Tal, D. (Eds.). (1999). *How children
understand war and peace: A call for international peace
education.* San Francisco, CA: Jossey-Bass.

7. WORK IN AN EDITED COLLECTION

Author's Last Name, Initials. (Year of publication). Title of work. In Initials Last Name (Ed.), *Title of collection* (pp. page numbers). Publication City, State *or* Country: Publisher.

Harris, I. M. (1999). Types of peace education. In A. Raviv, L. Oppenheimer, & D. Bar-Tal (Eds.), *How children understand war and peace: A call for international peace education* (pp. 46-70). San Francisco, CA: Jossey-Bass.

8. UNKNOWN AUTHOR

Title. (Year of publication). Publication City, State *or* Country: Publisher.

Webster's new biographical dictionary. (1988). Springfield, MA: Merriam-Webster.

If the title page of a work lists the author as *Anonymous*, treat the reference-list entry as if the author's name were Anonymous, and alphabetize it accordingly.

9. EDITION OTHER THAN THE FIRST

Author's Last Name, Initials. (Year). *Title* (name *or* number ed.). Publication City, State *or* Country: Publisher.

Burch, D. (2008). *Emergency navigation: Find your position and shape your course at sea even if your instruments fail* (2nd ed.). Camden, ME: International Marine/McGraw-Hill.

10. TRANSLATION

Author's Last Name, Initials. (Year of publication). *Title* (Translator's Initials Last Name, Trans.). Publication City, State *or* Country: Publisher. (Original work published Year)

Hugo, V. (2008). *Les misérables* (J. Rose, Trans.). New York, NY: Modern Library. (Original work published 1862)

11. MULTIVOLUME WORK

Author's Last Name, Initials. (Year). *Title* (Vols. numbers). Publication
   City, State *or* Country: Publisher.

Nastali, D. P., & Boardman, P. C. (2004). *The Arthurian annals: The
   tradition in English from 1250 to 2000* (Vols. 1-2). New York,
   NY: Oxford University Press USA.

ONE VOLUME OF A MULTIVOLUME WORK

Author's Last Name, Initials. (Year). *Title of whole work* (Vol.
   number). Publication City, State *or* Country: Publisher.

Spiegelman, A. (1986). *Maus* (Vol. 1). New York, NY: Random House.

12. ARTICLE IN A REFERENCE BOOK

UNSIGNED

Title of entry. (Year). In *Title of reference book* (Name *or* number
   ed., Vol. number, pp. page numbers). Publication City, State *or*
   Country: Publisher.

Macrophage. (2003). In *Merriam-Webster's collegiate dictionary* (11th
   ed., p. 745). Springfield, MA: Merriam-Webster.

SIGNED

Author's Last Name, Initials. (Year). Title of entry. In *Title of
   reference book* (Vol. number, pp. page numbers). Publication
   City, State *or* Country: Publisher.

Wasserman, D. E. (2006). Human exposure to vibration. In
   International encyclopedia of ergonomics and human factors
   (Vol. 2, pp. 1800-1801). Boca Raton, FL: CRC.

Print Periodicals

For most articles, you'll need to provide information about the author,
the date, the article title and any subtitle, the periodical title, and any
volume or issue number and inclusive page numbers.

author   title   publication

KEY DETAILS FOR DOCUMENTING PRINT PERIODICALS

- **AUTHORS:** List authors as you would for a book (see p. 179).

- **DATES:** For journals, give year only. For magazines and newspapers, give year followed by a comma and then month or month and day.

- **TITLES:** Capitalize article titles as you would for a book (see p. 179). Italicize the names of periodicals, and capitalize the first and last words and all principal words. Do not capitalize *a, an, the,* or any prepositions or coordinating conjunctions unless they begin the title of the periodical.

- **VOLUME AND ISSUE:** For journals and magazines, give volume or volume and issue, depending on the journal's pagination method. For newspapers, do not give volume or issue.

- **PAGES:** Use *p.* or *pp.* for a newspaper article but not for a journal or magazine article. If an article does not fall on consecutive pages, give all the page numbers (for example, 45, 75-77 for a journal or magazine; pp. C1, C3, C5-C7 for a newspaper).

13. ARTICLE IN A JOURNAL PAGINATED BY VOLUME

Author's Last Name, Initials. (Year). Title of article. *Title of Journal, volume,* page number(s).

Gremer, J. R., Sala, A., & Crone, E. E. (2010). Disappearing plants: Why they hide and how they return. *Ecology, 91,* 3407-3413.

14. ARTICLE IN A JOURNAL PAGINATED BY ISSUE

Author's Last Name, Initials. (Year). Title of article. *Title of Journal, volume*(issue), page number(s).

Weaver, C., McNally, C., & Moerman, S. (2001). To grammar or not to grammar: That is *not* the question! *Voices from the Middle, 8*(3), 17-33.

15. ARTICLE IN A MAGAZINE

If a magazine is published weekly, include the month and day. If there are a volume number and an issue number, include them after the magazine title.

> Author's Last Name, Initials. (Year, Month Day). Title of article. *Title of Magazine, volume*(issue), page number(s).
>
> Gregory, S. (2008, June 30). Crash course: Why golf carts are more hazardous than they look. *Time, 171*(26), 53.

If a magazine is published monthly, include the month(s) only.

16. ARTICLE IN A NEWSPAPER

If page numbers are consecutive, separate them with a hyphen. If not, separate them with a comma.

> Author's Last Name, Initials. (Year, Month Day). Title of article. *Title of Newspaper,* p(p). page number(s).
>
> Schneider, G. (2005, March 13). Fashion sense on wheels. *The Washington Post,* pp. F1, F6.

17. INTERVIEW IN A PERIODICAL

For an interview in a newspaper, omit volume and issue numbers.

> Interviewee's Last Name, Initials. (Year, Month Day). Title of interview. [Interview by Initials Last Name]. *Title of Periodical,* volume(issue), page numbers *or* p(p). page number(s).
>
> Wolfson, E. (2015, July 24). I believed we could win. [Interview by J. Rutenberg] *New York Times Magazine,* p. 22.

18. ARTICLE BY AN UNKNOWN AUTHOR

> Title of article. (Year, Month Day). *Title of Periodical, volume*(issue), page number(s).

Hot property: From carriage house to family compound. (2004,
    December). *Berkshire Living, 1*(1), 99.

19. BOOK REVIEW

Reviewer's Last Name, Initials. (Date of publication). Title of review
    [Review of the book *Title,* by Author's Initials Last Name].
    Title of Periodical, volume(issue), page number(s).
Brandt, A. (2003, October). Animal planet [Review of the book
    Intelligence of apes and other rational beings, by D. R. Rumb
    & D. A. Washburn]. *National Geographic Adventure, 5*(10), 47.

If the review does not have a title, place the bracketed information
immediately after the date.

20. LETTER TO THE EDITOR

Author's Last Name, Initials. (Date of publication). Title of letter
    [Letter to the editor]. *Title of Periodical, volume*(issue), page
    number(s) *or* p(p). page number(s).
Hitchcock, G. (2008, August 3). Save our species [Letter to the
    editor]. *San Francisco Chronicle,* p. P-3.

No need for volume or issue numbers if your source is a newspaper.

Online Sources

Not every online source gives you all the data that APA would like to
see in a reference entry. Ideally, you will be able to list an author's or
editor's name; date of first electronic publication or most recent revision; title of document; information about print publication if any; and
retrieval information: DOI (Digital Object Identifier, a string of letters
and numbers that identifies an online document) or URL. In some cases,
additional information about electronic publication may be required
(title of site, retrieval date, name of sponsoring institution).

KEY DETAILS FOR DOCUMENTING ONLINE SOURCES

- **AUTHORS:** List authors as you would for a print book or periodical (see p. 179).

- **TITLES:** For websites and electronic documents, articles, or books, capitalize titles and subtitles as you would for a book (see p. 179); capitalize periodical titles as you would for a print periodical (see p. 185).

- **DATES:** After the author, give the year of publication on the web or of its most recent revision. If those dates aren't available, use *n.d.* to mean "no date." For undated content or content that may change (for example, a wiki entry), include the month, day, and year that you retrieved the document. No need to include the retrieval date for content that's unlikely to change.

- **DOI OR URL:** Include the DOI instead of the URL in the reference whenever one is available. If no DOI is available, provide the URL of the home page or menu page. When a URL or DOI won't fit on the line, break it after a double slash or before any punctuation. Do not break *http://*, and do not add a period at the end.

?1. WORK FROM A NONPERIODICAL WEBSITE

Author's Last Name, Initials. (Date of publication). Title of work.
Title of site. DOI *or* Retrieved Month Day, Year [if necessary],
from URL

Cruikshank, D. (2009, June 15). Unlocking the secrets and powers of
the brain. *National Science Foundation*. Retrieved from http://
www.nsf.gov/discoveries/disc_summ.jsp?cntn_id=114979&org
=NSF

When citing an entire website, include the URL in parentheses within the text, as shown on page 177, no. 12. Do not include the website in your list of references.

Documentation Map (APA)

WORK FROM A NONPERIODICAL WEBSITE

Rudebusch, G. D. (2001, October 19). Has a recession already
   started? *Federal Reserve Bank of San Francisco.* Retrieved
   April 3, 2008, from http://www.frbsf.org/publications
   /economics/letter/2001/el2001-29.html

Documentation Map (APA)

ARTICLE WITH DOI FROM A JOURNAL

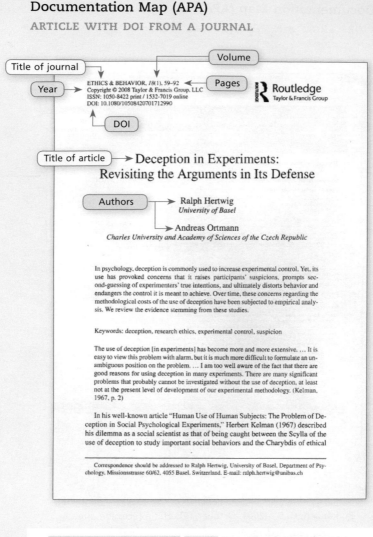

Title of journal

Volume

Year

Pages

ETHICS & BEHAVIOR, 18(1), 59–92
Copyright © 2008 Taylor & Francis Group, LLC
ISSN: 1050-8422 print / 1532-7019 online
DOI: 10.1080/10508420701712990

R Routledge
Taylor & Francis Group

DOI

Title of article → **Deception in Experiments:
Revisiting the Arguments in Its Defense**

Authors → Ralph Hertwig
University of Basel

→ Andreas Ortmann
Charles University and Academy of Sciences of the Czech Republic

In psychology, deception is commonly used to increase experimental control. Yet, its use has provoked concerns that it raises participants' suspicions, prompts second-guessing of experimenters' true intentions, and ultimately distorts behavior and endangers the control it is meant to achieve. Over time, these concerns regarding the methodological costs of the use of deception have been subjected to empirical analysis. We review the evidence stemming from these studies.

Keywords: deception, research ethics, experimental control, suspicion

The use of deception [in experiments] has become more and more extensive. … It is easy to view this problem with alarm, but it is much more difficult to formulate an unambiguous position on the problem. … I am too well aware of the fact that there are good reasons for using deception in many experiments. There are many significant problems that probably cannot be investigated without the use of deception, at least not at the present level of development of our experimental methodology. (Kelman, 1967, p. 2)

In his well-known article "Human Use of Human Subjects: The Problem of Deception in Social Psychological Experiments," Herbert Kelman (1967) described his dilemma as a social scientist as that of being caught between the Scylla of the use of deception to study important social behaviors and the Charybdis of ethical

Correspondence should be addressed to Ralph Hertwig, University of Basel, Department of Psychology, Missionsstrasse 60/62, 4055 Basel, Switzerland. E-mail: ralph.hertwig@unibas.ch

Hertwig, R., & Ortmann, A. (2008). Deception in experiments: Revisiting the arguments in its defense. *Ethics & Behavior, 18,* 59-92. doi:10.1080/10508420701712990

22. ARTICLE IN AN ONLINE PERIODICAL

When available, include the volume number and issue number as you would for a print source. If no DOI has been assigned, provide the URL of the home page or menu page of the journal or magazine, even for articles that you access through a database.

ARTICLE IN AN ONLINE JOURNAL

Author's Last Name, Initials. (Year). Title of article. *Title of Journal,*
　　volume(issue), pages. DOI *or* Retrieved from URL

Corbett, C. (2007). Vehicle-related crime and the gender gap.
　　Psychology, Crime & Law, 13, 245-263. doi:10.1080
　　/10683160600822022

ARTICLE IN AN ONLINE MAGAZINE

Author's Last Name, Initials. (Year, Month Day). Title of article. *Title*
　　of Magazine, volume(issue). DOI *or* Retrieved from URL

Barreda, V. D., Palazzesi, L., Tellería, M. C., Katinas, L., Crisci, J. N.,
　　Bromer, K., . . . Bechis, F. (2010, September 24). Eocene
　　Patagonia fossils of the daisy family. *Science, 329*(5999).
　　doi:10.1126/science.1193108

ARTICLE IN AN ONLINE NEWSPAPER

If the article can be found by searching the site, give the URL of the home page or menu page.

Author's Last Name, Initials. (Year, Month Day). Title of article. *Title*
　　of Newspaper. Retrieved from URL

Collins, G. (2012, September 12). Game time. *The New York Times.*
　　Retrieved from http://www.nytimes.com

23. COMMENT ON AN ONLINE ARTICLE

If the writer of the comment does not provide a real name, use the screen name without brackets.

Writer's Real Last Name, Initials. [Writer's screen name]. (Year,
　　Month Day). Re: Title of article [Comment]. *Name of*
　　periodical. Retrieved from URL

Whirled Peas. (2016, May 27). Re: How kids learn resilience
[Comment]. *The Atlantic*. Retrieved from http://www
.theatlantic.com/magazine/archive/2016/06/how-kids-really
-succeed/480744/#article-comments

24. ARTICLE AVAILABLE THROUGH A DATABASE

When no DOI is provided, give either the name of the database or
its homepage URL.

Author's Last Name, Initials. (Year). Title of article. *Title of Journal*,
volume(issue), pages. DOI *or* Retrieved from Name of
database *or* URL

Simpson, M. (1972). Authoritarianism and education: A comparative
approach. *Sociometry, 35*(2), 223-234. Retrieved from http://
www.jstor.org

25. ARTICLE OR CHAPTER IN A WEB DOCUMENT OR AN ONLINE REFERENCE WORK

For a chapter in a web document or an article in an online reference
work, give the URL of the chapter or entry if no DOI is provided.

Author's Last Name, Initials. (Year). Title of entry. In Initials Last Name
(Ed.), *Title of reference work*. DOI *or* Retrieved from URL

Korfmacher, C. (2006). Personal identity. In J. Fieser & B. Dowden
(Eds.), *Internet encyclopedia of philosophy*. Retrieved from
http://www.iep.utm.edu/person-i/

26. ELECTRONIC BOOK

Author's Last Name, Initials. (Year). *Title of book*. DOI *or* Retrieved
from URL

O'Connor, M. R. (2015). Ressurection science: Conservation,
de-extinction and the precarious future of wild things.
Retrieved from http://books.google.com

For an ebook based on a print version, include a description of the digital format in brackets after the book title.

> Blain, M. (2009). *The sociology of terror: Studies in power, subjection, and victimage ritual* [Adobe Digital Editions version]. Retrieved from http://www.powells.com/sub /AdobeDigitalEditionsPolitics.html?sec_big_link=1

27. WIKI ENTRY

Give the entry title and the date of posting, or *n.d.* if there is no date. Then include the retrieval date, the name of the wiki, and the URL for the entry.

> Title of entry. (Year, Month Day). Retrieved Month Day, Year, from Title of wiki: URL
>
> Discourse. (n.d.). Retrieved November 8, 2013, from Psychology Wiki: http://psychology.wikia.com/wiki/Discourse

28. BLOG ENTRY

> Author's Last Name, Initials. (Year, Month Day). Title of post [Blog post]. Retrieved from URL
>
> Collins, C. (2009, August 19). Butterfly benefits from warmer springs? [Blog post]. Retrieved from http://www.intute.ac.uk /blog/2009/08/19/butterfly-benefits-from-warmer-springs/

29. ONLINE VIDEO

> Last Name, Initials (Writer), & Last Name, Initials (Producer). (Year, Month Day posted). *Title* [Descriptive label]. Retrieved from URL
>
> Coulter, J. (Songwriter & Performer), & Booth, M. S. (Producer). (2006, September 23). *Code monkey* [Video file]. Retrieved from http://www.youtube.com/watch?v=v4Wy7gRGgeA

Documentation Map (APA)

ARTICLE WITH DOI AVAILABLE THROUGH A DATABASE

Goelitz, A. (2007). Exploring dream work at end of life.
Dreaming, 17(3), 159-171. doi:10.1037/1053-079717.3.159

30. PODCAST

> Writer's Last Name, Initials. (Writer), & Producer's Last Name, Initials.
>> (Producer). (Year, Month Day). Title of podcast. *Title of site*
>> *or program* [Audio podcast]. Retrieved from URL
>
> Britt, M. A. (Writer & Producer). (2009, June 7). Episode 97: Stanley
>> Milgram study finally replicated. *The Psych Files Podcast* [Audio
>> podcast]. Retrieved from http://www.thepsychfiles.com/

31. EPISODE FROM A TV SHOW OR OTHER SERIES FOUND ONLINE

> Last Name, Initials. (Writer), & Last Name, Initials. (Director). (Year).
>> Title of episode [Kind of episode]. In Initials. Last Name
>> (Producer), *Title of series.* Retrieved from URL
>
> Arnold, M. (Writer), & Wong, F. (Director). (2012). Carpe diem [TV
>> series episode]. In B. Laatsch (Producer), *Video game high*
>> *school.* Retrieved from www.rocketjump.com/?video=vghs
>> -episode-6

Personal Communication and Social Media

32. PERSONAL LETTER, EMAIL, TEXT MESSAGE, OR CONVERSATION

Personal communication generally does not need to be included on a
reference list—only in your text (see p. 178, no. 13).

33. POST TO AN ONLINE FORUM

> Last Name, Initials. (Year, Month Day). Title of post [Post to Name
>> of forum]. Retrieved from URL
>
> Verma, N. (2015, March 4). IamA Stanford trained sleep doctor, treated
>> conditions like apnea, insomnia, exploding head syndrome,
>> restless legs syndrome, narcolepsy. AMA! [Post to Reddit].
>> Retrieved from www.reddit.com /r/IAmA/comments
>> /2xws1w/iama_stanford_trained_sleep_doctor_treated_sleep/

34. POST TO *TWITTER, FACEBOOK*, AND OTHER SOCIAL MEDIA

Last Name, Initials. [*Twitter* handle *or* full first name on *Facebook*].
    (Year, Month Day). Title of post *or* Content of post up to 40
    words [Kind of post]. Retrieved from URL

Obama, B. [Barack]. (2016, June 21). This is the only planet we've
    got, and we have to do everything we can to protect it—
    including action to fight climate change [Facebook post].
    Retrieved from www.facebook.com/barackobama

If the writer gives only a screen name, give that as the name.

Audio, Visual, Multimedia, and Other Sources

35. FILM, VIDEO, OR DVD

Last Name, Initials (Producer), & Last Name, Initials (Director). (Year).
    Title [Motion picture]. Country: Studio.

Wallis, H. B. (Producer), & Curtiz, M. (Director). (1942). *Casablanca*
    [Motion picture]. United States: Warner.

36. MUSIC RECORDING

Composer's Last Name, Initials. (Year of copyright). Title of song. On
    Title of album [Medium]. City, State *or* Country: Label.

Veloso, C. (1997). Na baixado sapateiro. On *Livros* [CD]. Los Angeles,
    CA: Nonesuch.

37. PROCEEDINGS OF A CONFERENCE

Author's Last Name, Initials. (Year of publication). Title of paper. In
    Proceedings Title (pp. page numbers). Publication City, State
    or Country: Publisher.

Heath, S. B. (1997). Talking work: Language among teens. In
    Symposium about Language and Society—Austin (pp. 27-45).
    Austin: Department of Linguistics at the University of Texas.

author   title   publication

38. TELEVISION PROGRAM

> Last Name, Initials (Writer), & Last Name, Initials (Director). (Year).
> Title of episode [Descriptive label]. In Initials Last Name
> (Producer), *Series title*. City, State *or* Country: Network.

Dunkle, R. (Writer), & Lange, M. (Director). (2012). Hit [Television
series episode]. In E. A. Bernero (Executive Producer), *Criminal
minds*. New York, NY: NBC.

39. COMPUTER SOFTWARE

> Title and version number [Computer software]. (Year). Publication
> City, State *or* Country: Publisher.

OS X Yosemite [Computer software]. (2014). Cupertino, CA: Apple
Inc.

40. GOVERNMENT DOCUMENT

> Government Agency. (Year of publication). *Title.* Publication City,
> State *or* Country: Publisher.

US Department of Health and Human Services, Centers for Disease
Control and Prevention. (2009). *Fourth national report on
human exposure to environmental chemicals.* Washington, DC:
Government Printing Office.

ONLINE GOVERNMENT DOCUMENT

> Government Agency. (Year of publication). *Title* (Publication No. [if
> any]). Retrieved from URL

US Department of Health and Human Services, National Institutes of
Health, National Institute of Mental Health. (2006). *Bipolar
disorder* (NIH Publication No. 06-3679). Retrieved from http://
www.nimh.nih.gov/health/publications/bipolar-disorder
/nimh-bipolar-adults.pdf

41. DISSERTATION

Include the database name and accession number for dissertations that you retrieve from a database.

> Author's Last Name, Initials. (Year). *Title of dissertation* (Doctoral
> dissertation). Retrieved from Name of database. (accession
> number)
>
> Knapik, M. (2008). *Adolescent online trouble-talk: Help-seeking in*
> *cyberspace* (Doctoral dissertation). Retrieved from ProQuest
> Dissertation and Theses database. (AAT NR38024)

For a dissertation that you access on the web, include the name of the institution after *Doctoral dissertation*. For example: (Doctoral dissertation, University of North Carolina). End your documentation with *Retrieved from* and the URL.

42. TECHNICAL OR RESEARCH REPORT

> Author's Last Name, Initials. (Year). *Title of report* (Report number).
> Publication City, State *or* Country: Publisher.
>
> Elsayed, T., Namata, G., Getoor, L., & Oard., D. W. (2008). *Personal*
> *name resolution in email: A heuristic approach* (Report No.
> LAMP-TR-150). College Park: University of Maryland.

43. VIDEO GAME

When there is no author, start with the title and put the date after the brackets.

> Last Name, Initials. (Year). Title of Video Game [Video game].
> Publication City, State *or* Country: Publisher.
>
> Barone, E. (2016). Stardew Valley [Video game]. London, England:
> Chucklefish.
>
> Call of Duty: Black Ops 3 [Video game]. (2015). Santa Monica, CA:
> Activision.

If you accessed the game online, give the URL instead of the city and publisher.

> Call of Duty: Black Ops 3 [Video game]. (2015). Retrieved from
>   https://www.callofduty.com/blackops3

44. DATA SET OR GRAPH

> Last Name, Initials *or* Organization name. (Year, Month Day). Title
>   of data set *or* graph [Data set *or* Graph]. Retrieved from URL
> Caumont, A. (2014, February 11). Median annual earnings among
>   full-time workers ages 25 to 32, in 2012 dollars [Graph].
>   Retrieved from www.pewresearch.org/fact-tank/2014/02/11/6
>   -key-findings-about-going-to-college/
> Pew Research Center. (2014, December 22). *Higher Education,*
>   *Gender & Work* [Data set]. Retrieved from www
>   .pewsocialtrends.org/category/datasets/?download=20041

45. MAP

> Last Name, Initials *or* Organization Name (Cartographer). (Year).
>   Title of map.
> Touring Club Italiano (Cartographer). (1987). Toscana.

If the map is available online, follow the example below. APA recommends giving the retrieval date because maps may change over time.

> Google (Cartographer). (n.d.). Portland, Oregon. Retrieved July 25,
>   2015, from www.google.com/maps/place/Portland,OR

46. ADVERTISEMENT

PRINT

> Name of Product *or* Company. (Year, Month Day). Advertisement *or*
>   Description of ad. *Title of Periodica*l, *volume*(issue), page
>   number(s).

Harvard University Press. (2015, September/October). Advertisement.
Foreign Affairs, *94*(5), 35.

ONLINE

Name of Product or Company. (Year, Month Day). Advertisement *or*
Description of ad. Retrieved from URL

Chrysler. (2011, February 5). Super Bowl commercial. Retrieved from
https://www.youtube.com/watch?v=SKL254Y_jtc

Sources Not Covered by APA

To document a source for which APA does not provide guidelines, look
at models similar to the source you have cited. Give any information
readers will need in order to find it themselves—author; date of publication; title; publisher; information about electronic retrieval (DOI or
URL); and any other pertinent information. You might want to test your
reference note yourself, to be sure it will lead others to your source.

APA-d Formatting a Paper

Title page. APA generally requires a title page. At the upper left-hand
corner of the page, include "Running head:" and a shortened version
of your title in capital letters. The page number (1) should go in the
upper right-hand corner. Center the full title of the paper, your name,
and the name of your school on separate lines about halfway down the
page. You may add an "Author Note" at the bottom of the page to provide course information, acknowledgments, or contact information.

Page numbers. Use a shortened title in capital letters in the upper
left-hand corner of each page; place the page number in the upper
right-hand corner. Number pages consecutively throughout your paper.

Font, spacing, margins, and indents. Use a serif font (such as
Times New Roman or Bookman) for the text, and a sans serif font
(such as Calibri or Verdana) for figure labels. Double-space the entire
paper, including any notes and your list of references. Leave one-inch

margins at the top, bottom, and sides of your text; do not justify the text. The first line of each paragraph should be indented one-half inch (or five to seven spaces) from the left margin.

Headings. Though they are not required in APA style, headings can help readers follow your text. The first level of heading should be bold, centered, and capitalized as you would any other title; the second level of heading should be bold and flush with the left margin; the third level should be bold and indented, with only the first letter and proper nouns capitalized and with a period at the end of the heading, with the text following on the same line.

First Level Heading

Second Level Heading

    Third level heading.

Abstract. An abstract is a concise summary of your paper that introduces readers to your topic and main points. Most scholarly journals require an abstract; check with your instructor about his or her preference. Put your abstract on the second page, with the word *Abstract* centered at the top. Unless your instructor specifies a length, limit your abstract to 250 words or fewer.

Long quotations. Indent quotations of more than forty words one-half inch from the left margin. Do not use quotation marks, and place the page number(s) in parentheses *after* the end punctuation.

> Kaplan (2000b) captured ancient and contemporary Antioch for us:
>
> > At the height of its glory in the Roman-Byzantine age, when it had an amphitheater, public baths, aqueducts, and sewage pipes, half a million people lived in Antioch. Today the population is only 125,000. With sour relations between Turkey and Syria, and unstable politics throughout the Middle East, Antioch is now a backwater—seedy and tumbledown, with relatively few tourists. (p. 123)

Antioch's decline serves as a reminder that the fortunes of cities can change drastically over time.

List of references. Start your list on a new page after the text but before the notes. Center the title, and double-space the entire list. Each entry should begin at the left margin, and subsequent lines should be indented one-half inch (or five to seven spaces). Alphabetize the list by authors' last names (or by editors' names, if appropriate). Alphabetize works that have no author or editor by title, disregarding *A, An,* and *The.* Be sure every source listed is cited in the text; do not include sources that you consulted but did not cite.

Illustrations. For each table, provide a number (*Table 1*) and a descriptive title on separate lines above the table; below the table, include a note with information about the source. For figures—charts, diagrams, graphs, photos, and so on—include a figure number (*Figure 1*)

Table 1

Hours of Instruction Delivered per Week

	American classrooms	Japanese classrooms	Chinese classrooms
First grade			
Language arts	10.5	8.7	10.4
Mathematics	2.7	5.8	4.0
Fifth grade			
Language arts	7.9	8.0	11.1
Mathematics	3.4	7.8	11.7

Note. From "Peeking Out from Under the Blinders: Some Factors We Shouldn't Forget in Studying Writing," by J. R. Hayes, 1991, National Center for the Study of Writing and Literacy (Occasional Paper No. 25). Retrieved from National Writing Project website: http://www.nwp.org

and information about the source in a note below the figure. Number tables and figures separately, and be sure to discuss any illustrations so that readers know how they relate to the rest of your text.

APA-e Sample Pages

The following sample pages are from "Early Word Production: A Study of One Child's Word Productions," a paper written by Katryn Sheppard for a psychology course at Portland State University. They are formatted according to the guidelines of the *Publication Manual of the American Psychological Association*, 6th edition (2010). To read the complete paper, go to **digital.wwnorton.com/littleseagull3**.

Sample Title Page, APA Style

"Running head:" and shortened title.

Page number. 1

Title, name, and school name.

Early Word Production:

A Study of One Child's Word Productions

Katryn Sheppard

Portland State University

Sample Abstract, APA Style

EARLY WORD PRODUCTION 2

Heading centered.

Abstract

Early word production, one of the initial stages of language development in children, plays an important role in the development of later language skills. This study identifies the word classes and number of words spoken in a recorded interaction (Bloom, 1973) by one normally developing child of sixteen months and analyzes aspects of the child's speech, with the goal of noting if the characteristics observed were supported by the existing research on early word production or if they deviated from those findings. The words that I analyzed fell into six categories: nouns, spatial terms, adjectives, negatives, social phrases, and verbs. Although the frequency with which the child used words from some of these categories reflected the expectations established by previous research, her use of words in other categories was less predictable. Noting word usage in the six categories led to an analysis of the functions that those categories served in the child's semantic communication at this early stage of language development.

No paragraph indent

Two spaces after end punctuation.

250 words or fewer.

Sample Page of Research Paper, APA Style

EARLY WORD PRODUCTION   3

Title centered. • Early Word Production: A Study of One Child's Word Productions

First-level headings are centered, bold, and capitalized. • **Introduction**

Each step in the course of language development and
acquisition in children provides a foundation for later skills and
eventual mastery of the language. Early word production, a stage
of language development in which children have only a few words

Double-spaced throughout in their vocabularies, provides the foundation for later vocabulary
building and language production and has been shown to be
closely linked to later language performance skills (Walker,

Source with fewer than six authors. • Greenwood, Hart, & Carta, 1994). The early word production stage
is therefore worthy of examination, as it "signals that children
have a new tool that will enable them to learn about and

Page number of exact quote. • participate more fully in their society" (Uccelli & Pan, 2013, p. 95).

Because so few words are produced by children in this early
stage, the analysis of their word production focuses on the
particular word classes and how frequently each class of words
appears in speech. When examining typically developing English-
speaking children who have few words in their productive

Source with more than six authors. • vocabulary, Bates et al. (1994) found that the words produced were
most often nouns, while other categories more seldom appeared.
These less frequent categories included verbs and closed-class
words. Closed-class words are function words, which include the
categories of articles, conjunctions, numbers, pronouns, and
prepositions; they are called closed-class words because new
members cannot be added to these categories.

Paragraph indent ½" (5-7 spaces). • Reporting on the most common kinds of the nouns uttered in
early vocabularies, Nelson (1973) found that children "began by

Sample Page of Reference List, APA Style

References •···

Heading centered.

Anglin, J. M. (1995). Classifying the world through language: •··
    Functional relevance, cultural significance, and category
    name learning. *International Journal of Intercultural Relations,*
    19(2), 161-181. Retrieved from http://www.sciencedirect •···
    .com/science/journal/01471767

Alphabetized by authors' last name.

All lines after the first are indented ½" (5-7 spaces).

Bates, E., Marchman, V., Thal, D., Fenson, L., Dale, P., Reznick, J. S.,
    & Hartung, J. (1994). Developmental and stylistic variation
    in the composition of early vocabulary. *Journal of Child*
    Language, 21(1), 85-123. Retrieved from http://search.proquest •···
    .com/docview/58280873?accountid=13265

Article accessed through a database.

Bloom, L. (1973). *One word at a time: The use of single-word utterances*
    before syntax. The Hague, Netherlands: Mouton.

Bowerman, M. (2007). Containment, support, and beyond:
    Constructing topological spatial categories in first language
    acquisition. In M. Aurnague, M. Hickmann, & L. Vieu (Eds.), •···
    The categorization of spatial entities in language and cognition (pp.
    177-203). Amsterdam, Netherlands: John Benjamins.

Work from an edited collection.

Brown, R. (1973). *A first language: The early stages.* Cambridge, MA:
    Harvard University Press.

MacWhinney, B. (2000). *The CHILDES Project: Tools for analyzing talk.*
    (3rd ed.). Mahwah, NJ: Lawrence Erlbaum.

Nelson, K. (1973). Structure and strategy in learning to talk.
    Monographs of the Society for Research in Child Development,
    38(1), 1-135. Retrieved from http://onlinelibrary.wiley
    .com/journal/10.1111/%28ISSN%291540-5834

All sources listed are cited in the text.

Chicago Style

The University of Chicago Press presents two systems of documentation. This chapter shows the notes-and-bibliography system, which calls for (1) a superscript number for each in-text citation, (2) a correspondingly numbered footnote or endnote, and (3) an end-of-paper bibliography. The models in this chapter draw on *The Chicago Manual of Style*, 16th edition (2010) and Kate L. Turabian's *A Manual for Writers of Research Papers, Theses, and Dissertations*, 8th edition (2013). Additional information about CMS style is available at **www.chicagomanualofstyle.org** and within that site at "Chicago Style Q&A."

A DIRECTORY TO *CHICAGO* STYLE

PRINT BOOKS   211

Documentation Map: Print Book   213

  1. One author   212

  2. Multiple authors   214

  3. Organization or corporation as author   214

  4. Author and editor   215

  5. Editor only   215

  6. Part of a book   216

  7. Unknown author   217

  8. Translation   217

  9. Edition other than the first   218

10. Volume of a multivolume work   218

11. Dictionary or encyclopedia entry   219

12. Letter in a published collection   219

13. Book in a series   220

14. Sacred text   220

15. Source quoted in another source   220

PRINT PERIODICALS 221

Documentation Map: Article in a Print Journal 224
Documentation Map: Article in a Print Magazine 225

16. Article in a journal 221

17. Article in a magazine 222

18. Article in a newspaper 222

19. Unsigned article 222

20. Book review 223

ONLINE SOURCES 226

Documentation Map: Article Accessed through a Database 230
Documentation Map: Work from a Website 233

21. Article in an online journal 227

22. Article in an online magazine 227

23. Article in an online newspaper 228

24. Article accessed through a database 228

25. Ebook 229

26. Website 231

27. Blog entry 232

28. Video 234

29. Podcast 234

30. Email or posting to an online forum 235

OTHER KINDS OF SOURCES 235

31. Broadcast interview 235

32. Sound recording 236

33. Video or DVD 237

34. Government publication 237

SOURCES NOT COVERED BY *CHICAGO* 238

Formatting a Paper 238
Sample Pages 240

Throughout this chapter, you'll find models that are color-coded to help you see how writers include source information in their notes and bibliographies: brown for author or editor, yellow for title, gray for publication information—place of publication, publisher, date of publication, page number(s), and so on.

CMS-a Documenting with Notes and Bibliography

Put a superscript number in your text to indicate to your reader that you are citing material from a source. The superscript should follow the **QUOTATION**, **PARAPHRASE**, or **SUMMARY** of the source you are citing, as in the example below. Note that CMS requires you to use the present tense for verbs in **SIGNAL PHRASES**.

> **IN-TEXT CITATION**
>
> Kaplan insists that understanding power in the Near East requires "Western leaders who know when to intervene, and do so without illusions."[1]

The superscript number directs your reader to a footnote or an endnote that gives more information about the source; these in-text references are numbered sequentially throughout your text. Here is the note that documents the quote from Kaplan's book.

> **NOTE WHEN YOU FIRST CITE A SOURCE**
>
> 1. Robert D. Kaplan, *Eastward to Tartary: Travels in the Balkans, the Middle East, and the Caucasus* (New York: Random House, 2000), 330.

If you cite the same source later in your paper, give a shorter form of the note that lists just the author's last name, an abbreviated title, and the page(s) cited.

> **SUBSEQUENT NOTES**
>
> 4. Kaplan, *Eastward*, 332.

If you cite the same source in two consecutive notes, simply change the page number in the second note and use *Ibid.*, a Latin abbreviation meaning "in the same place." When your next citation is to the same page of that source, use just *Ibid*.

> 5. Ibid., 334.
> 6. Ibid.

BIBLIOGRAPHY

The bibliography at the end of your paper is an alphabetical list of the sources you've cited or consulted. Here is how Kaplan's book would appear in a bibliography.

> Kaplan, Robert D. *Eastward to Tartary: Travels in the Balkans, the Middle East, and the Caucasus.* New York: Random House, 2000.

If your bibliography includes all the works referenced in the notes, *Chicago* suggests that your notes be brief. It's a good idea to check your instructor's preference, however.

CMS-b Note and Bibliography Models

Because *Chicago* style requires notes and a bibliography for documentation, this chapter provides examples of both. See page 240 for guidelines on preparing notes and a bibliography; for samples, see pages 243–44.

Print Books

For most books, you'll need to provide information about the author; the title and any subtitle; and the place of publication, publisher, and year of publication. Treat pamphlets and brochures like books, giving whatever information is available.

KEY DETAILS FOR DOCUMENTING PRINT BOOKS

- **AUTHORS:** Include the author's middle name or initial, if any.
- **TITLES:** Capitalize the first and last words and all principal words of titles and subtitles. Italicize book titles. Use quotation marks around titles of chapters or other short works within books.

- **PUBLICATION PLACE:** If there's more than one city, use only the first. If a city may be unfamiliar or could be confused with another of the same name, give the state, province, or country. For the US capital, use "Washington, DC." Do not list the state or country if that information is part of the publisher's name.

- **PUBLISHER:** Omit *The* at the start of a publisher's name, along with abbreviations such as *Inc.* If you shorten a publisher's name (e.g., *Wiley* for *John Wiley*), be consistent.

1. ONE AUTHOR

NOTE

1. Author's First Name Last Name, *Title* (Publication City: Publisher, Year of publication), Page(s).

1. Erik Larson, *The Devil in the White City: Murder, Mayhem, and Madness at the Fair That Changed America* (New York: Crown, 2003), 113.

BIBLIOGRAPHY

Author's Last Name, First Name. *Title.* Publication City: Publisher, Year of publication.

Larson, Erik. *The Devil in the White City: Murder, Mayhem, and Madness at the Fair That Changed America.* New York: Crown, 2003.

TWO OR MORE WORKS BY THE SAME AUTHOR

If you include more than one work by the same author, give the author's name in the first entry, and then use a long dash (three-em dash or six hyphens) in the author slot for each of the subsequent works, listing them alphabetically by the first important word of each title.

Caro, Robert A. *Master of the Senate*. New York: Knopf, 2002.

———. *The Passage of Power.* New York: Knopf, 2012.

Documentation Map (*Chicago*)

PRINT BOOK

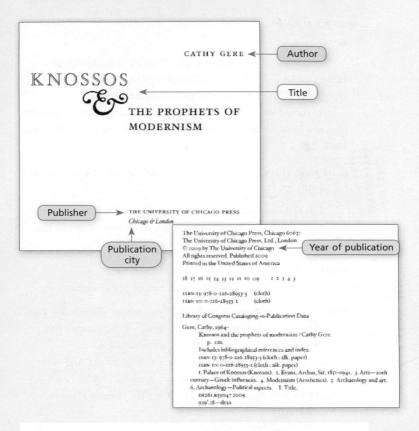

NOTE

    1. Cathy Gere, *Knossos & the Prophets of Modernism*
(Chicago: University of Chicago Press, 2009), 18.

BIBLIOGRAPHY

Gere, Cathy. *Knossos & the Prophets of Modernism.* Chicago:
    University of Chicago Press, 2009.

2. MULTIPLE AUTHORS

NOTE

2. First Author's First Name Last Name, Next Author's First Name Last Name, and Third Author's First Name Last Name, *Title* (Publication City: Publisher, Year of publication), Page(s).

2. Ronald W. Walker, Richard E. Turley Jr., and Glen M. Leonard, *Massacre at Mountain Meadows* (New York: Oxford University Press, 2008), 225.

For more than three authors, give the first author's name followed by *et al.*, Latin for "and others."

2. David Goldfield et al., *Twentieth-Century America: A Social and Political History* (Upper Saddle River, NJ: Pearson Prentice Hall, 2005), 376.

BIBLIOGRAPHY

Give all authors' names for works with ten or fewer authors.

First Author's Last Name, First Name, Next Author's First Name Last Name, . . . and Final Author's First Name Last Name. *Title*. Publication City: Publisher, Year of publication.

Goldfield, David, Carl F. Abbott, Jo Ann E. Argersinger, and Peter H. Argersinger. *Twentieth-Century America: A Social and Political History.* Upper Saddle River, NJ: Pearson Prentice Hall, 2005.

For more than ten authors, give the first seven names, followed by *et al.*

3. ORGANIZATION OR CORPORATION AS AUTHOR

NOTE

3. Organization Name, *Title* (Publication City: Publisher, Year of publication), Page(s).

3. Johnson County Historical and Genealogical Society, *Historic*

Sites of Paintsville and Johnson County, Kentucky (Paintsville: East
Kentucky Press, 2012), 27.

BIBLIOGRAPHY

Organization Name. *Title.* Publication City: Publisher, Year of
    publication.

Johnson County Historical and Genealogical Society. *Historic Sites of
    Paintsville and Johnson County, Kentucky.* Paintsville: East
    Kentucky Press, 2012.

4. AUTHOR AND EDITOR

NOTE

    4. Author's First Name Last Name, *Title*, ed. Editor's First
Name Last Name (Publication City: Publisher, Year of publication),
Page(s).

    4. Raphael Lemkin, *Totally Unofficial: The Autobiography of
Raphael Lemkin*, ed. Donna-Lee Frieze (New Haven, CT: Yale
University Press, 2013), 288.

BIBLIOGRAPHY

Author's Last Name, First Name. *Title.* Edited by Editor's First
    Name Last Name. Publication City: Publisher, Year of
    publication.

Lemkin, Raphael. *Totally Unofficial: The Autobiography of Raphael
    Lemkin*. Edited by Donna-Lee Frieze. New Haven, CT: Yale
    University Press, 2013.

5. EDITOR ONLY

NOTE

    5. Editor's First Name Last Name, ed., *Title* (Publication City:
Publisher, Year of publication), Page(s).

    5. Eric Foner and John A. Garraty, eds., *The Reader's Companion
to American History* (Boston: Houghton Mifflin, 1991), xix.

BIBLIOGRAPHY

Editor's Last Name, First Name, ed. *Title.* Publication City: Publisher,
    Year of publication.

Foner, Eric, and John A. Garraty, eds. *The Reader's Companion to
    American History.* Boston: Houghton Mifflin, 1991.

6. PART OF A BOOK

WORK IN AN EDITED COLLECTION OR ANTHOLOGY

NOTE

    6. Author's First Name Last Name, "Title of Work," in *Title
of Book*, ed. Editor's First Name Last Name (Publication City:
Publisher, Year of publication), Page(s).

    6. Lee Sandlin, "Losing the War," in *The New Kings of
Nonfiction,* ed. Ira Glass (New York: Riverhead Books, 2007), 355.

BIBLIOGRAPHY

Author's Last Name, First Name. "Title of Work." In *Title of Book*,
    edited by Editor's First Name Last Name, Page range.
    Publication City: Publisher, Year of publication.

Sandlin, Lee. "Losing the War." In *The New Kings of Nonfiction,*
    edited by Ira Glass, 315-61. New York: Riverhead Books, 2007.

CHAPTER IN A BOOK

NOTE

    6. Author's First Name Last Name, "Title of Chapter," in *Title
of Book* (Publication City: Publisher, Year of publication), Page(s).

    6. Nate Silver, "Less and Less and Less Wrong," in *The Signal
and the Noise* (New York: Penguin Press, 2012), 236-37.

BIBLIOGRAPHY

Author's Last Name, First Name. "Title of Chapter." In *Title of Book*,
    Page range. Publication City: Publisher, Year of publication.

Silver, Nate. "Less and Less and Less Wrong." In *The Signal and the
    Noise*, 232-61. New York: Penguin Press, 2012.

FOREWORD, INTRODUCTION, PREFACE, OR AFTERWORD

NOTE

      6. Part Author's First Name Last Name, part to *Title of Book*, by *or* ed. First Name Last Name (Publication City: Publisher, Year of publication), Page(s).

      6. Tony Tanner, introduction to *Pride and Prejudice*, by Jane Austen (New York: Penguin, 1972), 8.

BIBLIOGRAPHY

Part Author's Last Name, First Name. Part to *Title of Book*, by *or* ed. First Name Last Name, Page range. Publication City: Publisher, Year of publication.

Tanner, Tony. Introduction to *Pride and Prejudice*, by Jane Austen, 7-46. New York: Penguin, 1972.

7. UNKNOWN AUTHOR

NOTE

      7. *Title* (Publication City: Publisher, Year of publication), Page(s).

      7. *All States Tax Handbook* (New York: Thomson Reuters, 2009), 5.

BIBLIOGRAPHY

Title. Publication City: Publisher, Year of publication.

All States Tax Handbook. New York: Thomson Reuters, 2009.

8. TRANSLATION

NOTE

      8. Author's First Name Last Name, *Title*, trans. Translator's First Name Last Name (Publication City: Publisher, Year of publication), Page(s).

      8. Norberto Fuentes, *The Autobiography of Fidel Castro*, trans. Anna Kushner (New York: Norton, 2009), 49.

BIBLIOGRAPHY

Author's Last Name, First Name. *Title.* Translated by Translator's
    First and Last Names. Publication City: Publisher, Year of
    publication.

Fuentes, Norberto. *The Autobiography of Fidel Castro.* Translated by
    Anna Kushner. New York: Norton, 2009.

9. EDITION OTHER THAN THE FIRST

NOTE

9. Author's First Name Last Name, *Title,* name or number of
ed. (Publication City: Publisher, Year of publication), Page(s).

9. Michael D. Coe and Rex Koontz, *Mexico: From the Olmecs to
the Aztecs,* 6th ed. (London: Thames & Hudson, 2008), 186-87.

BIBLIOGRAPHY

Author's Last Name, First Name. *Title.* Name or number of ed.
    Publication City: Publisher, Year of publication.

Coe, Michael D., and Rex Koontz. *Mexico: From the Olmecs to the
    Aztecs.* 6th ed. London: Thames & Hudson, 2008.

10. VOLUME OF A MULTIVOLUME WORK

NOTE

10. Author's First Name Last Name, *Title of Multivolume Work,*
vol. number of individual volume, *Title of Individual Volume*
(Publication City: Publisher, Year of publication), Page(s).

10. Bruce Catton, *The Army of the Potomac,* vol. 2, *Glory Road*
(Garden City, NY: Doubleday, 1952), 169-70.

BIBLIOGRAPHY

Author's Last Name, First Name. *Title of Multivolume Work.* Vol.
    number, *Title of Individual Volume.* Publication City: Publisher,
    Year of publication.

Catton, Bruce. *The Army of the Potomac.* Vol. 2, *Glory Road.* Garden
    City, NY: Doubleday, 1952.

11. DICTIONARY OR ENCYCLOPEDIA ENTRY

Well-known reference works can be documented in a note without any publication information and do not need to be included in your bibliography. Use the abbreviation s.v., meaning "under the word," before the name of the entry.

> 11. *Title,* name or number of ed., s.v. "name of entry."

> 11. *The Random House Dictionary of the English Language*, 2nd ed., s.v. "ethos."

> 11. *The New Encyclopaedia Britannica*, 15th ed., s.v. "Klee, Paul."

12. LETTER IN A PUBLISHED COLLECTION

NOTE

> 12. Sender's First Name Last Name to Recipient's First Name Last Name, Day Month Year, in *Title of Collection,* ed. Editor's First Name Last Name (Publication City: Publisher, Year of publication), Page(s).

> 12. Abigail Adams to John Adams, 14 August 1776, in *My Dearest Friend: Letters of Abigail and John Adams,* ed. Margaret A. Hogan and C. James Taylor (Cambridge, MA: Harvard University Press, 2007), 139-41.

BIBLIOGRAPHY

Sender's Last Name, First Name. Sender's First Name Last Name to Recipient's First Name Last Name, Day Month Year. In *Title of Collection of Letters,* edited by Editor's First Name Last Name, Pages. Publication City: Publisher, Year.

Adams, Abigail. Abigail Adams to John Adams, 14 August 1776. In *My Dearest Friend: Letters of Abigail and John Adams,* edited by Margaret A. Hogan and C. James Taylor, 139-41. Cambridge, MA: Harvard University Press, 2007.

13. BOOK IN A SERIES

NOTE

     13. Author's First Name Last Name, *Title of Book*, Title of Series (Publication City: Publisher, Year of publication), Page(s).

     13. Karen Armstrong, *Buddha*, Penguin Lives (New York: Viking, 2004), 135.

BIBLIOGRAPHY

Author's Last Name, First Name. *Title of Book*. Title of Series. Publication City: Publisher, Year of publication.

Armstrong, Karen. *Buddha*. Penguin Lives. New York: Viking, 2004.

14. SACRED TEXT

Document a sacred work in a note but not in your bibliography. Provide section information, such as book, chapter, and verse—but never a page number. If you are documenting the Bible, identify the version. Translated texts should give the name of the version or translator.

     14. Exod. 6:26-27 (New Revised Standard Version).

     14. Qur'an 19:17-21.

15. SOURCE QUOTED IN ANOTHER SOURCE

Give the author, title, publication, and page information for the source quoted, followed by information on the source where you found it.

NOTE

     15. John Gunther, *Inside USA* (New York: Harper and Brothers, 1947), 259, quoted in Thomas Frank, *What's the Matter with Kansas?* (New York: Henry Holt, 2004), 29.

BIBLIOGRAPHY

Gunther, John. *Inside USA*. New York: Harper and Brothers, 1947. Quoted in Thomas Frank, *What's the Matter with Kansas?* New York: Henry Holt, 2004.

Print Periodicals

For most articles, you'll need to list the author, the article title and any subtitle, the periodical title, volume and issue numbers (for journals), and date information. Include page references only for journals and magazines.

KEY DETAILS FOR DOCUMENTING PRINT PERIODICALS

- **AUTHORS:** If there is more than one author, follow the models for a book with multiple authors (see no. 2).

- **TITLES:** Capitalize article titles and subtitles as you would a work in an edited collection (see no. 6). Use quotation marks around article titles. Italicize periodical titles.

- **VOLUME, ISSUE, AND DATE:** Give Arabic numbers for the volume even if a journal uses roman numerals. If an issue number is given, there's no need to include the month or season in your documentation. Magazines and newspapers are documented by date only.

- **PAGES:** Notes for journal and magazine articles need a specific page number; notes for newspapers do not. For the bibliography, give the full page range for journal and magazine articles that are paged consecutively; omit this information for newspapers and for magazines articles that include pages that continue at the back of an issue.

16. ARTICLE IN A JOURNAL

NOTE

16. Author's First Name Last Name, "Title of Article," *Title of Journal* volume, no. issue (Year): Page(s).

16. Jeremy Adelman, "An Age of Imperial Revolutions," *American Historical Review* 113, no. 2 (2008): 336.

BIBLIOGRAPHY

Author's Last Name, First Name. "Title of Article." *Title of Journal* volume, no. issue (Year): Page range.

Adelman, Jeremy. "An Age of Imperial Revolutions." *American Historical Review* 113, no. 2 (2008): 319-40.

17. ARTICLE IN A MAGAZINE

Include the day for a weekly magazine. For a monthly magazine, give only the month and year with no comma in between.

NOTE

17. Author's First Name Last Name, "Title of Article," *Title of Magazine*, Month Day, Year, Page(s).

17. Tony Horwitz, "One Man's Epic Quest to Visit Every Former Slave Dwelling in the United States," *Smithsonian*, October 2013, 42.

BIBLIOGRAPHY

Author's Last Name, First Name. "Title of Article." *Title of Magazine*, Month Day, Year.

Horwitz, Tony. "One Man's Epic Quest to Visit Every Former Slave Dwelling in the United States." *Smithsonian*, October 2013.

18. ARTICLE IN A NEWSPAPER

NOTE

18. Author's First Name Last Name, "Title of Article," *Title of Newspaper*, Month Day, Year, edition (if any), sec. (if any).

18. Nicholas J. C. Pistor, "Arch Is Endangered Monument, Group Says," *St. Louis Post-Dispatch,* October 10, 2013, early edition, sec. A.

BIBLIOGRAPHY

Author's Last Name, First Name. "Title of Article." *Title of Newspaper*, Month Day, Year, edition (if any), sec. (if any).

Pistor, Nicholas J. C. "Arch Is Endangered Monument, Group Says." *St. Louis Post-Dispatch,* October 10, 2013, early edition, sec. A.

19. UNSIGNED ARTICLE

When the author is unknown, put the article title first in notes. In the bibliography entry, put the name of the periodical first.

author   title   publication

NOTE

19. "Title of Article," *Title of Newspaper*, Month Day, Year, edition (if any), sec. (if any).

19. "The Next Campaign," *New York Times,* November 8, 2010, New York edition, sec. A.

BIBLIOGRAPHY

Title of Newspaper. "Title of Article." Month Day, Year, edition (if any), sec. (if any).

New York Times. "The Next Campaign." November 8, 2010, New York edition, sec. A.

20. BOOK REVIEW

NOTE

20. Reviewer's First Name Last Name, review of *Title of Book*, by Author's First Name Last Name, *Title of Periodical* volume, no. issue (Year): Page(s).

20. Gary K. Waite, review of *The Path of the Devil: Early Modern Witch Hunts*, by Gary Jensen, *American Historical Review* 113, no. 2 (2008): 453.

BIBLIOGRAPHY

Reviewer's Last Name, First Name. Review of *Title of Book*, by Author's First Name Last Name. *Title of Periodical* volume, no. issue (Year): Page range.

Waite, Gary K. Review of *The Path of the Devil: Early Modern Witch Hunts,* by Gary Jensen. *American Historical Review* 113, no. 2 (2008): 453-54.

For a review in a magazine or newspaper, replace the volume and issue numbers with the publication date, as in nos. 17 and 18.

Documentation Map (*Chicago*)

ARTICLE IN A PRINT JOURNAL

Author

Title of article → Syria: The Change That Never Came

Title of journal

LINDSAY A. GIFFORD

CURRENT HISTORY

December 2009   Vol. 108, No. 722

Volume and issue

CONTENTS

395   Year ast's New Power Dynamics . . . . *Anoushiravan Ehteshami*
US military intervention and the rise of Iran have dramatically reshuffled national rivalries and the balance of power in the region.

402   "Moderates" Redefined: How To Deal with Political Islam . . . . *Emile Nakhleh*
To engage the Muslim world, Washington needs to work not just with governments, but with mainstream Islamic political parties.

410   Fixing the Mideast's Economies . . . . *Hossein Askari*
Oil riches have brought more conflict and corruption than sustainable development. What the region needs is effective institutions. *Fourth in a series on changing relations between governments and markets.*

417   Syria: The Change That Never Came . . . . *Lindsay A. Gifford*
Bashar al-Assad, when he inherited the Syrian presidency from his father in 2001, proposed gradual economic and political reforms. They have yet to materialize.

Year

Page

NOTE

16. Lindsay A. Gifford, "Syria: The Change That Never Came," *Current History* 108, no. 722 (2009): 417.

BIBLIOGRAPHY

Gifford, Lindsay A. "Syria: The Change That Never Came." *Current History* 108, no. 722 (2009): 417-23.

Documentation Map (*Chicago*)

ARTICLE IN A PRINT MAGAZINE

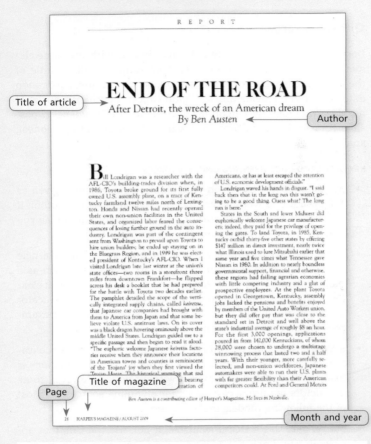

Title of article →

END OF THE ROAD

After Detroit, the wreck of an American dream
By Ben Austen ← Author

Bill Londrigan was a researcher with the AFL-CIO's building-trades division when, in 1986, Toyota broke ground for its first fully owned U.S. assembly plant, on a tract of Kentucky farmland twelve miles north of Lexington. Honda and Nissan had recently opened their own non-union facilities in the United States, and organized labor feared the consequences of losing further ground in the auto industry. Londrigan was part of the contingent sent from Washington to prevail upon Toyota to hire union builders; he ended up staying on in the Bluegrass Region, and in 1999 he was elected president of Kentucky's AFL-CIO. When I visited Londrigan late last winter at the union's state offices—two rooms in a storefront three miles from downtown Frankfort—he flipped across his desk a booklet that he had prepared for the battle with Toyota two decades earlier. The pamphlet detailed the scope of the vertically integrated supply chains, called *keiretsu*, that Japanese car companies had brought with them to America from Japan and that some believe violate U.S. antitrust laws. On its cover was a black dragon hovering ominously above the middle United States. Londrigan guided me to a specific passage and then began to read it aloud. "The euphoric welcome Japanese keiretsu factories receive when they announce their locations in American towns and counties is reminiscent of the Trojans' joy when they first viewed the Trojan Horse. The historical meaning that sad

Americans, or has at least escaped the attention of U.S. economic development officials."

Londrigan waved his hands in disgust. "I said back then that in the long run this wasn't going to be a good thing. Guess what? The long run is here."

States in the South and lower Midwest did euphorically welcome Japanese car manufacturers; indeed, they paid for the privilege of opening the gates. To land Toyota, in 1985, Kentucky outbid thirty-five other states by offering $147 million in direct investment, nearly twice what Illinois used to lure Mitsubishi earlier that same year and five times what Tennessee gave Nissan in 1980. In addition to nearly boundless governmental support, financial and otherwise, these regions had failing agrarian economies with little competing industry and a glut of prospective employees. At the plant Toyota opened in Georgetown, Kentucky, assembly jobs lacked the pensions and benefits enjoyed by members of the United Auto Workers union, but they did offer pay that was close to the standard set in Detroit and well above the state's industrial average of roughly $8 an hour. For the first 3,000 openings, applications poured in from 142,000 Kentuckians, of whom 28,000 were chosen to undergo a multistage winnowing process that lasted two and a half years. With their younger, more carefully selected, and non-union workforces, Japanese automakers were able to run their U.S. plants with far greater flexibility than their American competitors could. At Ford and General Motors

Ben Austen is a contributing editor of Harper's Magazine. He lives in Nashville.

Title of magazine

Page ↓

26 HARPER'S MAGAZINE / AUGUST 2009 ← Month and year

NOTE

17. Ben Austen, "End of the Road: After Detroit, the Wreck of an American Dream," *Harper's*, August 2009, 26.

BIBLIOGRAPHY

Austen, Ben. "End of the Road: After Detroit, the Wreck of an American Dream." *Harper's*, August 2009, 26-36.

Online Sources

Documentation for many online sources begins with the same elements you'd provide for a print source: author or editor; title of the work; publisher, place of publication, periodical title, publication date, and so on. Provide a DOI (Digital Object Identifier, a string of numbers that identifies an online document) or URL whenever possible. For websites you'll also need to include the site's title, sponsor, and a URL.

KEY DETAILS FOR DOCUMENTING ONLINE SOURCES

- **AUTHORS:** When no person or separate organization is given as the author of a website, list the site's sponsor as the author. If there is more than one author, list subsequent authors as you would for a book with multiple authors (see no. 2).

- **PAGES OR OTHER LOCATORS:** When an online book or journal article has no page numbers, you may give another locator such as a paragraph number or subsection heading. Be sure to make it clear (with an abbreviation such as *par.,* for example) that the locator you cite is not a page number. See no. 25 (pp. 229, 231) for examples that use part and chapter headings as locators.

- **ACCESS DATES:** *Chicago* requires access dates only when a publication or revision date cannot be determined, or when a source is likely to be updated or removed without notice. However, some instructors require access dates for all online sources, so most of the following models include them.

- **DOI OR URL:** Use a DOI if available; if not, use the URL that appears in your browser's address bar. It is also acceptable to use a **PERMALINK** if one is provided. Break a DOI or URL that won't fit on one line after a colon or a double slash, before a slash or other punctuation mark, or to either side of an equals sign or an ampersand. Do not add a hyphen or break the URL at one. Put a period at the end.

21. ARTICLE IN AN ONLINE JOURNAL

NOTE

   21. Author's First Name Last Name, "Title of Article," *Title of Journal* volume, no. issue (Year): Page(s) *or* other locator, accessed Month Day, Year, DOI *or* URL.

   21. Gary Gerstle, "A State Both Strong and Weak," *American Historical Review* 115, no. 3 (2010): 780, accessed October 7, 2013, doi:10.1086/ahr.115.3.779.

BIBLIOGRAPHY

Author's Last Name, First Name. "Title of Article." *Title of Journal* volume, no. issue (Year): Page(s) *or* other locator. Accessed Month Day, Year. DOI *or* URL.

Gerstle, Gary. "A State Both Strong and Weak." *American Historical Review* 115, no. 3 (2010): 778-85. Accessed October 7, 2013. doi:10.1086/ahr.115.3.779.

22. ARTICLE IN AN ONLINE MAGAZINE

NOTE

   22. Author's First Name Last Name, "Title of Article," *Title of Magazine*, Month Day, Year, accessed Month Day, Year, DOI *or* URL.

   22. Tom D. Crouch, "Amelia Found?," *AmericanHeritage.com*, Summer 2012, accessed May 8, 2013, http://www.americanheritage.com/content/amelia-found.

BIBLIOGRAPHY

Author's Last Name, First Name. "Title of Article." *Title of Magazine*, Month Day, Year. Accessed Month Day, Year. DOI *or* URL.

Crouch, Tom D. "Amelia Found?" *AmericanHeritage.com*, Summer 2012. Accessed May 8, 2013. http://www.americanheritage.com/content/amelia-found.

23. ARTICLE IN AN ONLINE NEWSPAPER

Very lengthy newspaper URLs can be shortened to end after the first single forward slash.

NOTE

23. Author's First Name Last Name, "Title of Article," *Title of Newspaper*, Month Day, Year, accessed Month Day, Year, DOI *or* URL.

23. Quan Truong, "Fundraising Begins for Wheaton Grand Renovation," *Chicago Tribune*, February 27, 2013, accessed March 4, 2013, http://www.chicagotribune.com/.

BIBLIOGRAPHY

Author's Last Name, First Name. "Title of Article." *Title of Newspaper*, Month Day, Year. Accessed Month Day, Year. DOI *or* URL.

Truong, Quan. "Fundraising Begins for Wheaton Grand Renovation." *Chicago Tribune*, February 27, 2013. Accessed March 4, 2013. http://www.chicagotribune.com/.

24. ARTICLE ACCESSED THROUGH A DATABASE

Give the URL of the article if the database supplies a stable one; if there's no stable URL, include the database name and article identification number.

NOTE

24. Author's First Name Last Name, "Title of Article," *Title of Journal* volume, no. issue (Year): Page(s) *or* other locator, accessed Month Day, Year, stable URL *or* Database Name (identification number).

24. David W. Galenson, "Analyzing Artistic Innovation," *Historical Methods* 41, no. 3 (2008): 114, accessed August 23, 2013, Academic Search Premier (34217664).

BIBLIOGRAPHY

Author's Last Name, First Name. "Title of Article." *Title of Journal*
       volume, no. issue (Year): Page range. Accessed Month Day,
       Year. Stable URL *or* Database Name (identification number).
Galenson, David W. "Analyzing Artistic Innovation." *Historical*
       Methods 41, no. 3 (2008): 111-20. Accessed August 23, 2013.
       Academic Search Premier (34217664).

For magazines and newspapers, add the appropriate information
about the month, day, and year as shown in nos. 22 and 23. See page
230 for a journal article accessed through a database.

25. EBOOK

To document a downloaded ebook of a print work, follow the setup
for a print book but indicate the format of the ebook (*PDF ebook, Kindle*
edition). Be aware that the publisher and year may be different from
the print edition's. Because pagination can vary depending on factors
such as text size, notes should include the chapter or section instead
of a page reference.

NOTE

       25. Author's First Name Last Name, *Title* (Publication City:
Publisher, Year of publication), Format, locator.
       25. Erik Larson, *In the Garden of Beasts: Love, Terror, and an*
American Family in Hitler's Berlin (New York: Crown, 2011), Kindle
edition, pt. 1, under "Dread."

BIBLIOGRAPHY

Author's Last Name, First Name. *Title.* Publication City: Publisher,
       Year of publication. Format.
Larson, Erik. *In the Garden of Beasts: Love, Terror, and an*
       American Family in Hitler's Berlin. New York: Crown, 2011.
       Kindle edition.

Documentation Map (*Chicago*)

ARTICLE ACCESSED THROUGH A DATABASE

Database title — ProQuest

Title of article — Crime, Clairvoyance and the Weimar Police

Page

Author — Wolffram, Heather

Title of journal — Journal of Contemporary History

Volume and issue — 44 4

Year — (Oct 2009): 581.

Publication subject	Political Science, History
ISSN	00220094
CODEN	JCHID7
Source type	Scholarly Journals
Language of publication	English
Document type	Feature
Document feature	References
ProQuest document ID	233047167

Database ID number

NOTE

24. Heather Wolffram, "Crime, Clairvoyance and the Weimar Police," *Journal of Contemporary History* 44, no. 4 (2009): 581, accessed November 8, 2016, ProQuest (233047167).

BIBLIOGRAPHY

Wolffram, Heather. "Crime, Clairvoyance and the Weimar Police." *Journal of Contemporary History* 44, no. 4 (2009): 581–601. Accessed November 8, 2016. ProQuest (233047167).

For a book consulted online, include a DOI or URL at the end of the reference.

NOTE

25. Mark Rowlands, *Can Animals Be Moral?* (Oxford: Oxford Scholarship Online, 2013), under "The Problem," doi:10.1093/acprof:oso/9780199842001.003.0002.

BIBILIOGRAPHY

Rowlands, Mark. *Can Animals Be Moral?* Oxford: Oxford Scholarship Online, 2013. doi:10.1093/acprof:oso/9780199842001.003.0002.

26. WEBSITE

According to the *Chicago Manual of Style*, titles of sites don't call for italics unless they are "analogous to books." For many sites, the author, the title, and the sponsor of the site are one and the same. If that is the case, simply give the name once at the start of your entry. If no author is given, list the sponsor as the author, and do not repeat its name after the title of the website.

WHOLE WEBSITE

NOTE

26. Author's First Name Last Name *or* Organization Name, Title of Site, Sponsor, Year of publication *or* last modification, accessed Month Day, Year, URL.

26. National Oceanic and Atmospheric Administration, National Weather Service, US Department of Commerce, 2016, accessed June 25, 2016, www.weather.gov.

BIBLIOGRAPHY

Author's Last Name, First Name *or* Organization Name. Title of Site. Sponsor. Year of publication *or* last modification. Accessed Month Day, Year. URL.

National Oceanic and Atmospheric Administration. National Weather Service. US Department of Commerce. 2016. Accessed June 25, 2016. www.weather.gov.

WORK FROM A WEBSITE

NOTE

26. Author's First Name Last Name *or* Organization Name, "Title of Work," Title of Site, Sponsor, Month Day, Year of publication *or* modification, accessed Month Day, Year, URL.

26. David P. Silverman and Zahi Hawass, "The Story of King Tut," The Field Museum, 2010, accessed August 5, 2013, http://www .fieldmuseum.org/tut/story.asp.

BIBLIOGRAPHY

Author's Last Name, First Name *or* Organization Name. "Title of Work." Title of Site. Sponsor. Month Day, Year of publication *or* modification. Accessed Month Day, Year. URL.

Silverman, David P., and Zahi Hawass. "The Story of King Tut." The Field Museum. 2010. Accessed August 5, 2013. http://www .fieldmuseum.org/tut/story.asp.

27. BLOG ENTRY

If a blog is sponsored by a larger publication, include the publication's title in italics. Omit (*blog*) if that word is included in the title.

NOTE

27. Author's First Name Last Name, "Title of Entry," *Title of Blog* (blog), Month Day, Year, accessed Month Day, Year, URL.

27. Daniel Adkins, "The Premier Hotspot of St. Louis," *History Happens Here* (blog), August 29, 2011, accessed April 27, 2013, http://www.historyhappenshere.org/archives/3992.

BIBLIOGRAPHY

Author's Last Name, First Name. "Title of Entry." *Title of Blog* (blog). Month Day, Year. Accessed Month Day, Year. URL.

Adkins, Daniel. "The Premier Hotspot of St. Louis." *History Happens Here* (blog). August 29, 2011. Accessed April 27, 2013. http://www.historyhappenshere.org/archives/3992.

Documentation Map (*Chicago*)

WORK FROM A WEBSITE

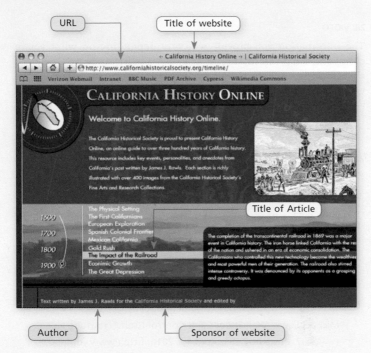

URL — Title of website

Title of Article

Author — Sponsor of website

NOTE

    26. James J. Rawls, "The Impact of the Railroad," California History Online, California Historical Society, accessed February 22, 2010, http://www.californiahistoricalsociety.org/timeline/.

BIBLIOGRAPHY

Rawls, James J. "The Impact of the Railroad." California History Online. California Historical Society. Accessed February 22, 2010. http://www.californiahistoricalsociety.org/timeline/.

28. VIDEO

The information you provide will vary depending on what you're citing and what information is available. For instance, you may not always find complete author information for online videos. If the video has an author, give his or her name first. If it was posted under a pseudonym or by someone else, indicate that as well.

NOTE

> 28. Author's First Name Last Name (if any), "Title of Video," Medium, duration, posted by "Online Pseudonym" *or* Other Publisher, Date of online publication, URL.

> 28. "Michael Lewis: Wall Street Can't Control Itself," YouTube video, 9:57, posted by CBS, April 19, 2010, http://www.youtube.com /watch?v=M93YUdbAVDA&feature=fvst.

BIBLIOGRAPHY

Author's Last Name, First Name (if any). "Title of Video."
> Medium, Duration. Posted by "Online Pseudonym" *or* Other Publisher. Date of online publication. URL.

"Michael Lewis: Wall Street Can't Control Itself." YouTube video,
> 9:57. Posted by CBS. April 19, 2010. http://www.youtube .com/watch?v=M93YUdbAVDA&feature=fvst.

29. PODCAST

NOTE

> 29. Author's *or* Speaker's First Name Last Name, "Title of Podcast," *Title of Site*, Sponsor, medium, Month Day, Year of posting, accessed Month Day, Year, URL.

> 29. Marideth Sisco, "Safety in the Middle of the Road," *These Ozark Hills,* Ozarks Public Radio (KSMU), podcast audio, July 30, 2009, accessed March 3, 2010, http://www.ksmu.org/index .php?option=com_content&task=view&id=4927&Itemid=74.

BIBLIOGRAPHY

Author's *or* Speaker's Last Name, First Name. "Title of Podcast." *Title of Site*. Sponsor. Medium. Month Day, Year of posting. Accessed Month Day, Year. URL.

Sisco, Marideth. "Safety in the Middle of the Road." *These Ozark Hills*. Ozarks Public Radio (KSMU). Podcast audio. July 30, 2009. Accessed March 3, 2010. http://www.ksmu.org/index .php?option=com_content&task=view&id=4927&Itemid=74.

30. EMAIL OR POSTING TO AN ONLINE FORUM

Include these sources in notes but not in a bibliography.

EMAIL

30. Writer's First Name Last Name, email message to author, Month Day, Year.

30. Ana Cooke, email message to author, February 22, 2013.

POSTING TO AN ELECTRONIC FORUM

30. Writer's First Name Last Name to Name of Forum, Month Day, Year, accessed Month Day, Year, URL.

30. David Elbert to New American Folk Music Listserv, July 3, 1998, accessed March 3, 2013, http://www.folkmusic.org/archives /fm/0492.html.

Other Kinds of Sources

31. BROADCAST INTERVIEW

NOTE

31. Subject's First Name Last Name, interview by First Name Last Name, *Title of Program*, Network, Month Day, Year.

31. Clive Davis, interview by Don Gonyea, *Weekend Edition Saturday*, NPR, February 22, 2013.

BIBLIOGRAPHY

Subject's Last Name, First Name. Interview by Interviewer's First Name
Last Name. *Title of Program.* Network, Month Day, Year.

Davis, Clive. Interview by Don Gonyea. *Weekend Edition Saturday.*
NPR, February 22, 2013.

32. SOUND RECORDING

NOTE

32. Composer's *or* Author's First Name Last Name, *Title of
Work,* other appropriate information about the performer,
conductor, recording, etc., Recording Company identifying number
of recording, year of release, medium.

32. Giuseppe Verdi, *Rigoletto*, London Symphony Orchestra,
conducted by Richard Bonynge, with Joan Sutherland, Luciano
Pavarotti, Sherrill Milnes, et al., recorded at Kingsway Hall, June
1971, London 414269, 1990, MP3 file.

BIBLIOGRAPHY

Composer's *or* Author's Last Name, First Name. *Title of Work.* Other
appropriate information about the performer, conductor,
recording, etc. Recording Company identifying number of
recording, year of release, medium.

Verdi, Giuseppe. *Rigoletto*. London Symphony Orchestra. Richard
Bonynge. With Joan Sutherland, Luciano Pavarotti, Sherrill
Milnes, et al. Recorded at Kingsway Hall, June 1971. London
414269, 1990, MP3 file.

To document a particular person's work, start with that name.

32. Bruce Springsteen, vocal performance of "Shenandoah," by
Pete Seeger, on *We Shall Overcome: The Seeger Sessions*, Columbia
82867, 2006, compact disc.

To document a speech or lecture, begin with the speaker's name.

      32. Lt. Ernest H. Shackleton, "My South Polar Expedition" (speech), March 30, 1910, Edison Amberol cylinder, 4M-473, July 1910, Thomas Edison National Historical Park, "Documentary Recordings and Political Speeches," MP3 file, http://www.nps.gov/edis /photosmultimedia/documentary-recordings-and-political-speeches.htm.

33. VIDEO OR DVD

To document a particular person's work, start with that name.

NOTE

      33. Writer's First Name Last Name, *Title,* directed by First Name Last Name (Original release year; City: Studio, Year of recording release), Medium.

      33. Chris Terrio, *Argo,* directed by Ben Affleck (2012; Burbank, CA: Warner Home Video, 2013), DVD.

BIBLIOGRAPHY

Writer's Last Name, First Name. *Title.* Directed by First Name Last Name. Original release year. City: Studio, Year of recording release. Medium.

Terrio, Chris. *Argo.* Directed by Ben Affleck. 2012. Burbank, CA: Warner Home Video, 2013. DVD.

34. GOVERNMENT PUBLICATION

Most government publications can be documented like a work by an organization or corporation (no. 3) or a work by an unknown author (no. 7).

NOTE

      34. *The 9/11 Commission Report: Final Report of the National Commission on Terrorist Attacks upon the United States*, official government ed. (Washington, DC: US Government Printing Office, 2004), 33.

BIBLIOGRAPHY

*The 9/11 Commission Report: Final Report of the National
    Commission on Terrorist Attacks upon the United States,*
    official government ed. Washington, DC: US Government
    Printing Office, 2004.

Sources Not Covered by *Chicago*

To document a source for which *Chicago* does not provide guidelines, look for models similar to the source you have cited. Give any
information readers will need in order to find your source themselves—author, title, publisher, date of publication, information
about electronic retrieval (such as the URL and date of access), and
any other pertinent information. You might want to try out your reference note yourself, to be sure it will lead others to your source.

CMS-c Formatting a Paper

Name, course, title. Type the title of your paper about one-third of
the way down the page; capitalize it as you would the title of a book.
Place your name several lines below the title, along with information
such as the title of your course, your instructor's name, and the date.
Center each element on the title page on a separate line.

Page numbers. Number all pages consecutively, but do not put
a page number on the title page. If your instructor asks you to
include your name, the date, or draft number alongside the page
number, place the page number and this information in either the
upper-right-hand or bottom-right-hand corner of the page; if all you
need is a page number, you may also follow this setup or simply
center it at the top or bottom of the page.

Spacing and margins. Double-space the main text of the paper as
well as block quotations, table titles, captions, footnotes, endnotes,
and the bibliography. Set one-inch margins on all sides.

author   title   publication

Long quotations. When quoting five or more lines or two or more paragraphs, set off the quotation as a block, indenting it one-half inch (or five spaces) from the left margin. Double-space the quotation and do not add extra line space above or below it. Block quotations should not be enclosed in quotation marks.

> Bruce Catton describes the end of the US Civil War:
>> The end of the war was like the beginning, with the army marching down the open road under the spring sky, seeing a far light on the horizon. Many lights had died in the windy dark but far down the road there was always a gleam, and it was as if a legend had been created to express some obscure truth that could not otherwise be stated. Everything had changed, the war and the men and the land they fought for, but the road ahead had not changed. It went on through the trees and past the little towns and over the hills, and there was no getting to the end of it.[1]

Poetry should be set off when you're quoting two or more lines.

> By referring to him as both "Captain" and "father," Walt Whitman makes clear the strong sense of identification he has felt with the now-fallen Lincoln:
>> My Captain does not answer, his lips are pale and still,
>> My father does not feel my arm, he has no pulse nor will.[2]

Illustrations. You may wish to include figures and tables. Figures include charts, diagrams, graphs, maps, photographs, and other illustrations. Figures and tables should be numbered and given a title (Figure 1. A Map of Columbus, Ohio, 2010; Table 1. Telephone Ownership, 1900–20). Any illustration that comes from another source should include documentation—*Source:* David Siegel, *Creating Killer Web Sites* (Indianapolis, IN: Hayden Books, 1996), 72. If you've created the illustration yourself with data from another source, add "Data from" before the author's name. Put the title above the illustration and any source note below. Position illustrations as soon as possible after they are discussed in your text—and be sure to explain how they relate to your point.

Notes. You may choose to give notes as footnotes at the bottom of the page on which you cite the source or as endnotes that are grouped at the end of your text under the heading *Notes*. For both footnotes and endnotes, indent the first line one-half inch (five spaces); do not indent subsequent lines. Footnotes and endnotes should be double-spaced.

Bibliography. Start your list on a new page at the end of your paper, following any notes. Center the heading. Double-space each entry. Each entry should begin at the left margin, and subsequent lines should be indented one-half inch (or five spaces). Alphabetize the list by authors' or editors' last names; for works with no author or editor, or for multiple works by the same author, use the first important words of titles. If you include multiple works by the same author, use a three-em dash (or six hyphens) in place of the author's name in every entry after the first.

CMS-d Sample Pages

The following sample pages are from "History at Home: Leighton House, Sambourne House, and the Heritage Debate," written by Erika Graham for a museum studies course and internship during a study-abroad program in London. They are formatted according to the guidelines of the *Chicago Manual of Style*, 16th edition, and *A Manual for Writers of Research Papers, Theses, and Dissertations*, 8th edition. To read Graham's complete research paper, go to **digital.wwnorton.com /littleseagull3**.

author   title   publication

Sample Title Page, *Chicago* Style

History at Home:

Leighton House, Sambourne House, and the Heritage Debate •········· *Title.*

Erika Graham

Grinnell-in-London Internship   •·················· *Name, course information, and date.*

December 3, 2013

Sample Page of Research Paper, *Chicago* Style

Page number.

Double-spaced throughout.

1″

In the Royal Borough of Kensington and Chelsea, many Victorian houses remain standing, for this part of London was favored by many artists of the day. Two of these buildings have since become museums: Leighton House, home to Frederic Lord Leighton, P.R.A., and Linley Sambourne House, residence of the premier cartoonist for *Punch* magazine and his family. Though managed by the same team of curators and staff, the houses have distinct characters, which stem from the finery of their interiors: Sambourne House sports almost entirely original furnishings and decor, while Leighton House has been painstakingly restored to its intended grandeur as a "palace of art."

1″

But although it might not be apparent to an average visitor overwhelmed by these displays, both museums are unavoidably involved in the fierce debate that surrounds all sites that present "the past." This debate is multifaceted, but all strands return eventually to the issue of whether or not such presentations can educate the visitor—the key role of the museum. As museum-

Author in signal phrase; superscript number to cite source.

studies scholar Eilean Hooper-Greenhill observes, "Knowledge is now well understood as the commodity that museums offer."[1] The details of this knowledge vary by museum; we will here be focusing on the transmission of historical knowledge. The history museum, however, has an interesting place in the discourse on museum education, for not everyone accepts that these institutions fulfill their didactic role. The accusation runs that some history museums have abandoned their educational duties by moving beyond the glass case format to display history in context through reconstruction, preservation, and, most feared of all, living history

1″

Sample Endnotes, *Chicago* Style

21

Notes •·································

Heading centered.

1. Eilean Hooper-Greenhill, *Museums and the Shaping of* •·············· Knowledge, Heritage: Care-Preservation-Management (London: Routledge, 1992), 2.

First line indented; subsequent lines flush left.

2. Emma Barker, "Heritage and the Country House," in *Contemporary Cultures of Display,* ed. Emma Barker (New Haven, CT: Yale University Press, 1999), 206.

Double-spaced.

3. G. Ellis Burcaw, *Introduction to Museum Work,* 3rd ed. •············ (London: AltaMira Press, 1997), 177; Beth Goodacre and Gavin Baldwin, *Living the Past: Reconstruction, Recreation, Re-Enactment and Education at Museums and Historical Sites* (London: Middlesex University Press, 2002), 44.

Multiple sources in a note separated by semicolons.

4. Kevin Walsh, *The Representation of the Past: Museums and Heritage in the Post-Modern World,* Heritage: Care-Preservation-Management (London: Routledge, 1992), 102; Paul Greenhalgh, "Education, Entertainment and Politics: Lessons from the Great International Exhibitions," in *The New Museology,* ed. Peter Vergo (London: Reaktion Books, 1989).

Page number omitted in a reference to the source as a whole.

5. Though a criticism here, not everyone believes this modification is a bad thing. For example, see Kevin Moore, *Museums and Popular Culture,* Contemporary Issues in Museum Culture (London: Cassell, 1997).

Shortened note for second citation.

6. Goodacre and Baldwin, *Living,* 9 (italics added).

7. Walsh, *Representation,* 94; Peter J. Fowler, *The Past in Contemporary Society: Then, Now,* Heritage: Care-Preservation-Management (London: Routledge, 1992), 5.

8. Walsh, *Representation,* 102.

Sample Bibliography, *Chicago* Style

24

Bibliography •⋯⋯⋯⋯⋯⋯⋯⋯⋯⋯⋯ *Heading centered.*

Alphabetized by author's last name.

Barker, Emma. "Heritage and the Country House." In *Contemporary Cultures of Display,* edited by Emma Barker, 200-228. New Haven, CT: Yale University Press, 1999.

First line flush left; subsequent lines indented.

Burcaw, G. Ellis. *Introduction to Museum Work.* 3rd ed. London: AltaMira Press, 1997.

Fowler, Peter J. *The Past in Contemporary Society: Then, Now.* Heritage: Care-Preservation-Management. London: Routledge, 1992.

Double-spaced.

Goodacre, Beth, and Gavin Baldwin. *Living the Past: Reconstruction, Recreation, Re-Enactment and Education at Museums and Historical Sites.* London: Middlesex University Press, 2002.

Greenhalgh, Paul. "Education, Entertainment and Politics: Lessons from the Great International Exhibitions." In *The New Museology,* edited by Peter Vergo, 74-98. London: Reaktion Books, 1989.

Handler, Richard. "Authenticity." *Anthropology Today* 2, no. 1 (1986):

DOI.

2-4. Accessed September 30, 2013. doi:10.2307/3032899.

3-em dash or 6 hyphens replace author's name for subsequent works by the same author.

———. "Heritage and Hegemony: Recent Works on Historic Preservation and Interpretation." *Anthropological Quarterly* 60, no. 3 (1987): 137-41. Accessed October 22, 2013. http://www .jstor.org/stable/i274779.

Hooper-Greenhill, Eilean. *Museums and the Shaping of Knowledge.* Heritage: Care-Preservation-Management. London: Routledge, 1992.

James, Simon. "Imag(in)ing the Past: The Politics and Practicalities of Reconstructions in the Museum Gallery." In *Making Early Histories in Museums,* edited by Nick Merriman, 117-35. London: Leicester University Press, 1999.

CSE Style

Many courses in the sciences will require you to follow the documentation style recommended by the Council of Science Editors (CSE) in *Scientific Style and Format: The CSE Manual for Authors, Editors, and Publishers*. This chapter provides models for documenting sources using the style recommended in the eighth edition of the *CSE Manual*, published in 2014. For more guidance on following CSE style, go to **www.scientificstyleandformat.org/tools.html**.

A DIRECTORY TO CSE STYLE

PRINT BOOKS   248

Documentation Map: Print Book   250

1. One author   249
2. Multiple authors   249
3. Organization or corporation as author   249
4. Editor   251
5. Work in an edited collection   251
6. Chapter of a book   251
7. Paper or abstract from conference proceedings   251
8. Edition other than the first   252

PRINT PERIODICALS   252

Documentation Map: Article in a Print Journal   253

9. Article in a journal   252
10. Article in a magazine   254
11. Article in a newspaper   254

ONLINE SOURCES   254

Documentation Map: Article Accessed through a Database   257

12. Online book   255

13. Article accessed through a database   255

14. Article in an online journal   256

15. Article in an online newspaper   256

16. Website   256

17. Part of a website   258

18. Image or infographic   258

19. Podcast or webcast   259

20. Video   259

21. Blog entry   259

22. Social media post   260

SOURCES NOT COVERED BY CSE   260

Formatting a Paper   260

Sample Pages   262

Throughout this chapter, models are color-coded to help you see how writers present source information in their texts and in reference lists: brown for author or editor; yellow for title; gray for publication information, which may include place of publication, publisher, date of publication, volume and issue numbers, section and page numbers, and so on.

CSE-a In-Text Documentation

The *CSE Manual* offers three ways of indicating in your text that you are citing material from a source. You can use any of these styles, but CSE recommends citation–sequence style.

Citation–Sequence Style calls for you to put a number (either a superscript or a number in parentheses) after any reference to a source. Number sources in the order you mention them—the first source you mention is numbered 1, the second one is numbered 2, and so on. Once you number a source, use that same number each time you mention that source: if your first reference to a source is numbered 3, every citation of that source thereafter should be numbered 3 regardless of where it appears in your paper.

Citation–Name Style calls for you first to alphabetize your list of references and then number the sources consecutively in the order they appear on the list: the first source on the list—say, Ackerman— is number 1, the second—perhaps, Bond—is number 2, and so on. Then put the appropriate number (either a superscript or a number in parentheses) after each mention of that source. So if Zuefle is the tenth source on your alphabetical list of references, every citation of the same work by this author will get Zuefle[10], even if Zuefle is the first source you cite in your paper.

Name–Year Style calls for you to give the author's last name and the year of publication in parentheses after any mention of a source. If you mention the author's name in a SIGNAL PHRASE, you need to put only the year in parentheses. For instance:

> Atherosclerosis seems to predate our modern lifestyles (Singer 2009).
>
> Singer (2009) questions whether atherosclerosis is inevitable.

If a work has two authors, give both names (Davidson and Lyon 1987). For three or more authors, give only the first author, followed by *et al.*, a Latin abbreviation meaning "and others" (Rathus et al. 2010). If you include more than one work in parentheses, separate them with a semicolon (Gilder 2008; Singer 2009).

CSE-b List of References

The in-text documentation corresponds to the sources you give at the end of your paper in a list of references. How you arrange sources in your References, whether you number them, and where you put publication dates depend on which style you use.

- *In citation–sequence style,* arrange and number the sources in the order in which you first cite them in your text. Put the date for a book at the end of the publication information; put the date for a periodical article after the periodical's title.

- *In citation–name style,* arrange and number the sources in alphabetical order. Put the date for a book at the end of the publication information and the date for a periodical article after its title.

- *In name–year style,* arrange the sources alphabetically, and do not number them. Put the date after the name(s) of the author(s).

The models and examples that follow demonstrate citation–sequence style. See page 262 for guidelines on organizing and formatting a list of references and pages 264–65 for samples from a paper using citation–sequence style.

Print Books

For most books, you'll need to provide information about the author; the title and any subtitle; and the place of publication, publisher, and year of publication.

KEY DETAILS FOR DOCUMENTING PRINT BOOKS

- **AUTHORS:** Put each author's last name first, and give initials for first and middle names. Do not add space between initials, and omit punctuation except a period after the final initial.

- **TITLES:** For book and chapter titles, capitalize only the first word, any acronyms, or proper nouns or adjectives. Do not italicize, underline, or put quotation marks around any title.

- **PUBLICATION PLACE:** Place the two-letter abbreviation for state, province, or country within parentheses after the city.
- **PUBLISHER:** Shorten a publisher's name by omitting *the* and abbreviations such as *Inc.*

1. ONE AUTHOR

1. Author's Last Name Initials. Title. Publication City (State): Publisher; Year of publication.

1. Singh S. Big bang: the origin of the universe. New York (NY): Fourth Estate; 2004.

2. MULTIPLE AUTHORS

List up to ten authors, separating them with commas and putting a period after the last author's initials.

2. First Author's Last Name Initials, Next Author's Last Name Initials, Final Author's Last Name Initials. Title. Publication City (State): Publisher; Year of publication.

2. Gaines SM, Eglinton G, Rullkotter J. Echoes of life: what fossil molecules reveal about Earth history. New York (NY): Oxford University Press; 2009.

For a work by eleven or more authors, list the first ten, followed by a comma and *et al.*

3. ORGANIZATION OR CORPORATION AS AUTHOR

3. Organization Name. Title. Publication City (State): Publisher; Year of publication.

3. National Research Council. Black and smokeless powders: technologies for finding bombs and the bomb makers. Washington (DC): National Academy Press; 1998.

Documentation Map (CSE)

PRINT BOOK

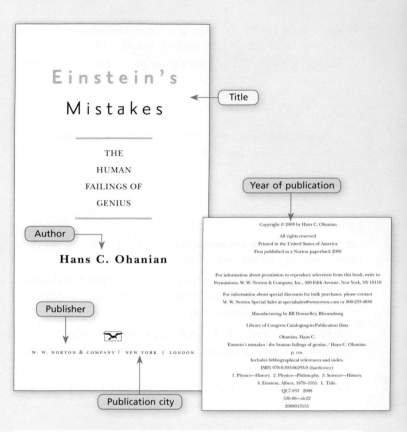

1. Ohanian HC. Einstein's mistakes: the human failings of genius. New York (NY): W. W. Norton; 2008.

4. EDITOR

4. Editor's Last Name Initials, editor. Title. Publication City (State): Publisher; Year of publication.

4. Dawkins R, editor. The Oxford book of modern science writing. New York (NY): Oxford University Press; 2009.

5. WORK IN AN EDITED COLLECTION

5. Author's Last Name Initials. Title of work. Year of publication if earlier than year of collection. In: Editor's Last Name Initials, editor. Title of book. Publication city (State): Publisher; Year of publication of collection. p. Pages.

5. Carson R. The sea around us. 1951. In: Dawkins R, editor. The Oxford book of modern science writing. New York (NY): Oxford University Press; 2009. p. 130–137.

6. CHAPTER OF A BOOK

6. Author's Last Name Initials. Title of book. Publication City (State): Publisher; Year of publication. Chapter number, Title of chapter; p. Pages.

6. Gilder L. The age of entanglement: when quantum physics was reborn. New York (NY): Knopf; 2008. Chapter 13, Solvay 1927; p. 110–127.

7. PAPER OR ABSTRACT FROM CONFERENCE PROCEEDINGS

If you cite an abstract of a paper rather than the paper itself, place *[abstract]* after the paper's title but before the period.

7. Author's Last Name Initials. Title of paper. In: Editor's Last Name Initials, editor. Title of book. Number and Name of Conference; Year Month Day of Conference; Place of Conference. Publication City (State): Publisher; Year of publication. p. Pages.

7. Polivy J. Physical activity, fitness, and compulsive behaviors. In: Bouchard C, Shephard RJ, Stephens T, editors. Physical activity, fitness, and health: international proceedings and consensus statement. 2nd International Consensus Symposium on Physical Activity, Fitness, and Health; 1992 May 5–9; Toronto, Canada. Champaign (IL): Human Kinetics Publishers; 1994. p. 883–897.

8. EDITION OTHER THAN THE FIRST

8. Author's Last Name Initials. Title of book. Name *or* number of ed. Publication City (State): Publisher; Year of publication.

8. Marshak S. Geology. 4th ed. New York (NY): Norton; 2012.

Print Periodicals

For most journal articles, you'll need to list the author, title, and any subtitle of the article; the title of the periodical; the volume and issue numbers; the year; and the inclusive page numbers of the article. Newspaper and some magazine articles have different requirements.

KEY DETAILS FOR DOCUMENTING PRINT PERIODICALS

- **AUTHORS** List authors as you would for a book (nos. 1 and 2).
- **TITLES:** Capitalize only the first word, any acronyms, and proper nouns or adjectives in article titles. Abbreviate titles of journals and capitalize all major words, even if abbreviated. Do not italicize, underline, or put quotation marks around any titles.
- **DATE:** For periodicals with no volume or issue numbers, provide the year, month, and day. Abbreviate months to the first three letters: *Jan, Feb, Mar,* and so on.

9. ARTICLE IN A JOURNAL

9. Author's Last Name Initials. Title of article. Title of Journal. Year;Volume(issue):Pages.

9. Reutemann A, Lucero L, Guarise N, Vigetti AC. Structure of the Cyperaceae inflorescence. Bot Rev. 2012;78(2):184–204.

Documentation Map (CSE)

ARTICLE IN A PRINT JOURNAL

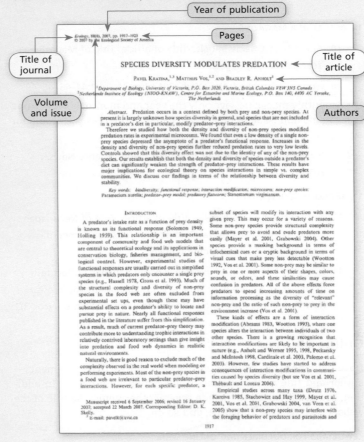

Year of publication

Pages

Title of journal

Title of article

Volume and issue

Authors

9. Kratina P, Vos M, Anholt BR. Species diversity modulates predation. Ecology. 2007;88(8):1917–1923.

10. ARTICLE IN A MAGAZINE

> 10. Author's Last Name Initials. Title of article. Title of Magazine. Year Month Day:Pages.

> 10. Wood, G. Scrubbed. New York. 2013 Jun 24–Jul 1:44–46, 48–49.

For a monthly magazine, give only the year and month. If a magazine has volume and issue numbers, you can give them as you would for a journal.

> 10. Millius S. Virus makes liars of squash plants. Science News. 2010;177(2):8.

11. ARTICLE IN A NEWSPAPER

> 11. Author's Last Name Initials. Title of article. Title of Newspaper (Edition). Year Month Day;Sect. section letter *or* number:first page of article (col. column number).

> 11. Singer N. Artery disease in some very old patients: doctors test mummies at a Cairo museum and find signs of atherosclerosis. New York Times (New England Ed.). 2009 Nov 24;Sect. D:6 (col. 3).

Online Sources

Documentation for online sources begins with basic elements—author and title of the work and publication information. In addition, you usually need to include several other items: the title of the website, access date, URL, DOI, and so on.

KEY DETAILS FOR DOCUMENTING ONLINE SOURCES

- **AUTHORS:** List authors as you would for a book (nos. 1 and 2).
- **TITLES:** Format the titles of books, journals, and articles on the web as you would print sources (see pp. 248 and 252). For titles of other web materials, including homepages, reproduce the wording, capitalization, and punctuation as they appear on the site.

- PUBLICATION CITY: If you cannot identify the city of publication of an online book, write *[place unknown]*.

- PUBLISHER: List as the publisher the person or organization that sponsors the website. If you cannot identify the publisher of an online book, write *[publisher unknown]*.

- DATES: Whenever possible, give three dates: the date a work was first published online or the copyright date; the date of its latest update; and the date you accessed it.

- PAGES, LENGTH: If there are no page numbers, indicate the length in brackets: *[2 screens], [8 paragraphs]*.

- URL, DOI, DOCUMENT NUMBER: Give whatever URL, DOI, and database document number are available, in that order. Break URLs that don't fit on one line after a slash or other punctuation, but do not add a hyphen. Put a period at the end.

12. ONLINE BOOK

12. Author's Last Name Initials. Title. Publication City (State): Publisher; Year of publication [updated Year Month Day; accessed Year Month Day]. URL.

12. Dean L. Blood groups and red cell antigens. Bethesda (MD): National Library of Medicine; 2005 [accessed 2015 Nov 25]. http://www.ncbi.nlm.nih.gov/bookshelf/br.fcgi?book=rbcantigen.

To document a part of an online book, include the title of the part after the publication information (as in no. 6).

13. ARTICLE ACCESSED THROUGH A DATABASE

Include the DOI and document number if the database assigns them.

13. Author's Last Name Initials. Title of article. Title of Periodical. Date of publication [updated Year Month Day; accessed Year Month Day];Volume(issue):Pages *or* [length]. Name of Database. URL. doi: DOI. Database Doc No number.

13. Kemker BE, Stierwalt JAG, LaPointe LL, Heald GR. Effects of a cell phone conversation on cognitive processing performances. J Am Acad Audiol. 2009 [accessed 2015 Nov 29];20(9):582–588. Academic Search Premier. https://web.ebscohost.com/academic/academic-search-premier. Database Doc No 45108388.

14. ARTICLE IN AN ONLINE JOURNAL

14. Author's Last Name Initials. Title of article. Title of Journal. Year of publication [updated Year Month Day; accessed Year Month Day];Volume(issue):Pages *or* [length]. URL.

14. Voelker R. Medical simulation gets real. JAMA. 2009 [accessed 2015 Nov 25];302(20):2190–2192. http://jama.ama-assn.org/cgi/content/full/302/20/2190.

15. ARTICLE IN AN ONLINE NEWSPAPER

15. Author's Last Name Initials. Title of article. Title of Newspaper. Year Month Day of publication [updated Year Month Day; accessed Year Month Day];Pages *or* [length]. URL.

15. Levey NN. Doctors list overused medical treatments. Los Angeles Times. 2013 Feb 20 [accessed 2015 Feb 27];[about 4 screens]. http://www.latimes.com/health/la-na-medical-procedures-20130221,0,6234009.story.

16. WEBSITE

If there is a known author, begin with his or her name before the title of the site. If the author is an organization, begin with the title of the site, and give the organization's name as the publisher.

16. Author's Last Name Initials (if any). Title of Site. Publication City (State): Publisher; Year of publication [updated Year Month Day; accessed Year Month Day]. URL.

author   title   publication

Documentation Map (CSE)

ARTICLE ACCESSED THROUGH A DATABASE

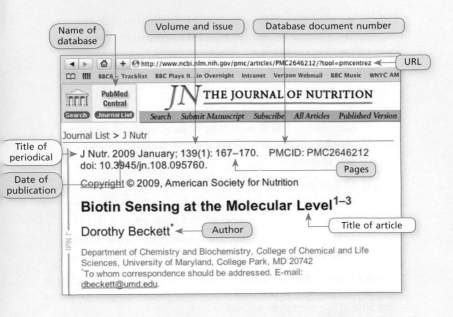

13. Beckett D. Biotin sensing at the molecular level. J Nutr. 2009
    [accessed 2015 Mar 2];139(1):167-170. PubMed Central. http://
    www.ncbi.nlm.nih.gov/pmc. Database Doc No PMC2646212.

16. American Wind Energy Association. Washington (DC): American Wind Energy Association; 1996–2013 [accessed 2015 Mar 17]. http://www.awea.org.

17. PART OF A WEBSITE

17. Title of Site. Publication City (State): Publisher; Year of site publication. Title of part; Date of part publication [updated Year Month Day; accessed Year Month Day]; [length of part]. URL of part.

17. US Environmental Protection Agency. Research Triangle Park (NC): US Environmental Protection Agency, Air Quality Analysis Group; 2011. Nitrogen dioxide; 2011 [updated 2012 Nov 28; accessed 2015 Feb 27];[about 3 screens]. http://www.epa.gov/airtrends/nitrogen.html.

If the author of the part you are citing is different from the author of the site, begin with the author and title of the part and do not give the title of the complete website.

17. Author's Last Name Initials. Title of part. Publication City (State): Publisher; Date of part publication [updated Year Month Day; accessed Year Month Day];[length of part]. URL of part.

17. Macklin SA. PICES Metadata Federation. Sidney (BC): PICES North Pacific Marine Science Organization; 2008 Nov [accessed 2015 May 2];[15 paragraphs]. http://www.pices.int/projects/npem/default.aspx.

18. IMAGE OR INFOGRAPHIC

18. Author's Last Name Initials. Title [image or infographic]. Publication City (State): Publisher or Producer; Date of publication. [updated Year Month Day; accessed Year Month Day]. URL.

author   title   publication

18. Watson JD, Crick FHC. Molecular structure of nucleic acids [image]. London (UK): Nature Publishing Group; 2003 [accessed 2016 Jul 20]. http://www.nature.com/nature/dna50/watsoncrick.pdf.

19. PODCAST OR WEBCAST

19. Host's Last Name Initials. Title of episode [podcast *or* webcast, episode number if any]. Name of series. Producer. Year Month Day of broadcast *or* posting, length. [accessed Year Month Day]. URL.

19. Benson M. Astrogeology—meteorites and spacecraft missions [webcast]. Smithsonian Science How. Smithsonian National Museum of Natural History. 2015 Jun 25, 36:38 minutes. [accessed 2016 Jul 10]. https://qrius.si.edu/explore-science/webcast/astrogeology-meteorites-and-spacecraft-missions.

19. Britt M. Why replications sometimes don't agree with the original study [podcast, episode 246]. The Psych Files. Boot & Eddy Productions. 2015 Sep 4, 12:36 minutes. [accessed 2016 Jul 9]. http://www.thepsychfiles.com/2015/09/ep-246-why-replications-sometimes-dont-agree-with-the-original-study.

20. VIDEO

20. Title of video [video, episode number if any]. Name of series. Producer. Year Month Day of broadcast *or* posting, length. [accessed Year Month Day]. URL.

20. Making North America: origins [video]. NOVA ScienceNOW. WGBH. 2016 Jun 29, 53:04 minutes. [accessed 2016 Jul 10]. http://www.pbs.org/video/2365598165.

21. BLOG ENTRY

21. Author's Last Name Initials. Title of post [blog entry]. Title of blog. Year Month Day of posting, [accessed Year Month Day]. URL.

21. Blair ME. Calls of the forest [blog entry]. Scientist at Work: Notes from the Field. 2013 May 29. [accessed 2016 Jul 10]. http://scientistatwork.blogs.nytimes.com/2013/05/29/calls-of-the-forest.

22. SOCIAL MEDIA POST

22. Author's First Name Last Name *or* Organization's page name. Name of social media site [page type, post type]. Year Month Day, Time posted. [accessed Year Month Date]. URL.

22. Barack Obama. Facebook [profile page, shared link]. 2016 Apr 26, 12:09 p.m. [accessed 2016 Jul 10]. https://www.facebook.com/barackobama.

Sources Not Covered by CSE

To document a source for which CSE does not provide guidelines, look for models similar to the source you have cited. Give any information readers will need in order to find your source themselves—author, title, publisher, date of publication, information about electronic retrieval (such as the database, URL, and date of access), and any other pertinent information. You might want to try your reference note yourself, to be sure it will lead others to your source.

CSE-c Formatting a Paper

Title page. CSE does not provide guidelines for college papers. Check to see whether your instructor prefers a separate title page; if so, include the title of your paper, your name, the name of the course, your instructor's name, and the date. Otherwise, place that information at the top of the first page of your text.

Page numbers and running head. Put the page number and a short version of your title in the top right-hand corner of each page except for the title page.

Margins and line spacing. Leave one-inch margins all around the page. Double-space your text but single-space your list of references, leaving one line space between entries. Some instructors prefer the list of references instead to be double-spaced with no extra spaces between entries; check which style your instructor prefers.

Headings. Especially when your paper is long, or when it has clear parts, headings can help readers to follow your argument. Center headings but without adding any extra space above or below.

Abstract. If you include an **ABSTRACT**, put it on its own page after the title page, with the word *Abstract* centered at the top of the page.

Long quotations. When you are quoting forty or more words, reduce the text size slightly, and set them off from your text, indented a little from the left margin. Do not enclose such quotations in quotation marks. Indicate the source in a sentence that introduces the quotation. Include a superscript or a number in parentheses pointing to the full documentation.

> The simulations identify observable criteria for sympatric speciation and resolve the question of whether Darwin correctly identified the trends he observed in nature.[1]
>
>> How many of those birds and insects in North America and Europe, which differ very slightly from each other, have been ranked by one eminent naturalist as undoubted species, and by another as varieties, or, as they are often called, as geographical races!

FROM LIST OF REFERENCES

1. Darwin C. The origin of species: Darwin's four great books. In: Wilson EO, editor. From so simple a beginning. New York (NY): W. W. Norton; 2006. p. 441–760.

Illustrations. Insert each illustration close to where you mention it in your text. Number and label each one (Table 1, Figure 3), and provide a descriptive title (Figure 5 Bonding in ethylene). Titles use sentence–style capitalization. Figures include charts, graphs, maps, photographs, and other types of illustrations. Number tables and figures consecutively, using separate numbering for tables and for figures.

References. Start your list of sources on a new page at the end of your paper; center the heading *References* at the top of the page. CSE single-spaces entries and separates them with a line space. For citation–sequence style, number entries according to the order in which you first cite them in your text. Align subsequent lines of each entry below the first word of the first line.

CSE-d Sample Pages

The following sample pages are from "Guppies and Goldilocks: Models and Evidence of Two Types of Speciation," a paper written by Pieter Spealman for an undergraduate biology course. They are formatted in the citation–sequence format according to the guidelines of *Scientific Style and Format: The CSE Manual for Authors, Editors, and Publishers,* 8th edition (2014). To read the complete paper, go to **digital.wwnorton.com/littleseagull3**.

Sample Title Page, CSE Style

Title and name centered.

Guppies and Goldilocks: Models and Evidence
of Two Types of Speciation

Pieter Spealman

Course title, instructor's name, date.

Biology 38
Professor Lipke
February 17, 2016

Sample Page of Research Paper, CSE Style

1″
Two Types of Speciation   1

Brief title and page number.

Determining how a given species has arisen is a central question for any field biologist. There are two competing models of speciation: allopatric and sympatric. In 1859, Charles Darwin[1]

Superscript number to mark citation.

asserted that speciation could be sympatric, saying, "I believe that many perfectly defined species have been formed on strictly

Double-spaced text.

continuous areas." One hundred years later, Ernst Mayr[2] contested Darwin's assertion, saying, "All the evidence that has accumulated since Darwin indicates that this assumption [that species have been formed on strictly continuous areas] is unwarranted as far as higher

Words added to a quotation are enclosed in brackets.

animals are concerned." Was Mayr right to condemn Darwin for failing to assess correctly the lessons of nature that he observed in the Galapagos archipelago? The difficulty of determining the provenance of a species—whether it arose through sympatric or allopatric speciation—lies in knowing what to look for. And while recent research employing computer simulations[3] suggests a solution to the problem by providing a set of criteria necessary for sympatric speciation, the results predicted by those simulations did not actually arise in the field study that provides the most comprehensive data available to test the model. Rather than

1″ invalidating the model, however, this research points to the

1″ margin

challenges that complex natural environments pose to the isolation of observable criteria for distinguishing the two types of speciation.

Allopatric and Sympatric: Conditions and Examples

Headings help organize the paper.

The two types of speciation differ in their view of what conditions are crucial in determining whether speciation can occur. Allopatric speciation, which Mayr[2] championed, explains the divergence of species by physical isolation, as when a population

In citation-sequence style, source previously cited uses same number as first citation.

1″

Sample Page of Reference List, CSE Style

Two Types of Speciation   9

Heading centered. ···• References

Entries are single-spaced with a line space between each. Subsequent lines of an entry align below the first word of the first line.

1. Darwin C. The origin of species: Darwin's four great books. In: Wilson EO, editor. From so simple a beginning. New York (NY): W. W. Norton; 2006. p. 441–760.

2. Mayr E. Isolation as an evolutionary factor. Proc Am Philos Soc. 1959;103(2):221–230.

3. van Doorn GS, Edelaar P, Weissing FJ. On the origin of species by natural and sexual selection. Science. 2009;326(5960):1704–1707.

4. Schilthuizen M. Frogs, flies, and dandelions: speciation—the evolution of new species. New York (NY): Oxford University Press; 2001.

5. Grant BR, Grant PR. Darwin's finches: population variation and sympatric speciation. Proc Nat Acad Sci USA. 1979;76(4):2359–2363.

6. Endler JA. Natural selection on color patterns in *Poecilia reticulata*. Evolution. 1980 [accessed 2016 Feb 7];34(1):76–91. JSTOR. http://jstor.org/stable/2408316.

7. Weiner J. The beak of the finch. New York (NY): Vintage; 1994.

8. Smith JM. Sympatric speciation. Am Nat. 1966 [accessed 2016 Feb 7];100(916):637–650. JSTOR. http://jstor.org/stable/2459301.

9. Stewart P. Galapagos: islands that changed the world. New Haven (CT): Yale University Press; 2006.

Citation-sequence style: Sources numbered in the sequence they appear in the text.

Edit

We edit to let the fire show through the smoke.

—ARTHUR PLOTNIK

Editing the Errors That Matter

In writing, as in life, no one's perfect. We make mistakes. Some of our errors are no big deal, barely noticeable, not worth mentioning. Others, however, are more serious—deal breakers, maybe—and we try hard to avoid them. One of the great things about writing is that we have time to edit our work and fix our errors. Our team asked seventy-five writing instructors which errors really matter to them—which ones are most bothersome and do the most damage to a writer's credibility and ideas. Their responses covered a wide gamut, from sentence structure to punctuation. This section focuses on those errors that matter, showing how to spot them in a draft, explaining why they're so troublesome, and suggesting strategies for editing them out.

Editing Sentences 269

E-1a Fragments 270

E-1b Comma splices 272

E-1c Fused sentences 275

E-1d Mixed constructions 278

Editing Pronouns 281

E-2a Pronoun reference 282

E-2b Pronoun-antecedent agreement 285

E-2c Pronoun case 289

Editing Verbs 291

E-3a Subject-verb agreement 292

E-3b Shifts in tense 295

Editing Quotations 298

E-4a Incorporating quotations 299

E-4b Punctuating quotations 301

Editing Commas   304

E-5a   Introductory information   305

E-5b   Essential and nonessential information   307

Editing Words That Are Often Confused   309

E-1   Editing Sentences

Fragments, comma splices, fused sentences, and mixed constructions are all types of sentence-structure errors. Such sentences are usually comprehensible in context, so as long as readers understand the message, what makes them errors? Here's what. Solid sentence structure matters for two reasons:

- The perception of your competence hangs on it: readers don't trust writers who write sloppy sentences.

- Even if a poorly structured sentence can be understood, your readers have to work a little harder to do so, and they may not want to put forth the effort. Your job is to make it easy for readers, to keep them reading smoothly all the way to the end.

Every sentence is composed of one or more CLAUSES, and every clause needs to have a SUBJECT, a VERB, and appropriate punctuation. Don't underestimate those little dots and squiggles; they often make all the difference in how a sentence is read and understood. Consider these two examples:

▶ Let's eat Grandma.

▶ Let's eat, Grandma.

Are you inviting your grandmother to eat a meal right now, or are you inviting someone else to eat *her*? That one little comma in the right place can save grandma's life (or at least make it clear to your readers that you aren't proposing to make a meal of her). This chapter will help you examine your writing with an eye to four common sentence-structure errors: fragments, comma splices, fused sentences, and mixed constructions.

E-1a Fragments

At first glance, a fragment looks like a complete sentence—it begins with a capital letter and concludes with end punctuation—but on closer examination, a key element, usually a **SUBJECT** or a **VERB**, is missing. For example: *Forgot to vote.* Who forgot to vote? We don't know; the subject is missing. *Two bottles of rancid milk.* Wow. That sounds interesting, but what about them? There's no verb, so we don't know. A fragment also occurs when a sentence begins with a **SUBORDINATING WORD** such as *if* or *because*, but the **SUBORDINATE CLAUSE** is not followed by an **INDEPENDENT CLAUSE**. *If the ball game is rained out.* Well, what happens if the ball game is rained out? Again, we don't know.

Checking for fragments

Sometimes writers use fragments for stylistic reasons, but it's best to avoid them in academic writing. To check your text for fragments, examine each sentence one by one, making sure there's both a subject and a verb. (It might take you a while to do this at first, but it will go much faster with practice, and it's worth the time.) Check also for subordinating words (see **S-2a** for a list of common ones), and if there's a subordinate clause, make sure there's also an independent clause.

Editing fragments

Let's look at some fragments and see what we can do about them.

NEEDS A SUBJECT

▶ The Centipedes were terrible last night. *Started late, played three songs, and left.*

Context makes it clear that it was the Centipedes who started late. Still, the italicized part is a fragment because there is no explicit subject. We have two good options here. One is to add a subject to the fragment in order to make the sentence complete; the other is to attach the fragment to a nearby sentence. Both strategies will work, and you can choose whichever sounds better to you.

▶ The Centipedes were terrible last night. ~~Started~~ *They started* late, played three songs, and left.

▶ The Centipedes were terrible last night/ ~~Started~~ *because they started* late, played three songs, and left.

In the first example, we've added a subject, *they*, which refers to the *Centipedes*. In the second, we've attached the fragment to the preceding sentence using a subordinating word, *because*, followed by an explicit subject, *they*.

NEEDS A VERB

▶ Malik heard a knock on the door. *Then a loud thud.*

The example makes sense: we know that Malik heard a loud thud after the knock. But the italicized part is a fragment because between the capital *T* at the beginning and the period at the end, there is no verb. Again, there are two strategies for editing: to add a verb to the fragment in order to make the sentence complete, or to incorporate the fragment into the previous sentence so that its verb can do double duty.

▶ Malik heard a knock on the door. Then *came* a loud thud.

▶ Malik heard a knock on the door/, ~~Then~~ *followed by* a loud thud.

NEEDS MORE INFORMATION

▶ Olga nearly missed her plane. *Because the line at security was so long.* She got flustered and dropped her change purse.

The italicized part of the example above does have a subject and a verb, but it can't stand alone as a sentence because it starts with *because*, a subordinating word that leads readers to expect more information. Did the long security line cause Olga to nearly miss her plane? Or did the long line fluster her? We can't be sure. How you edit this fragment depends on what you're trying to say—and how the ideas relate to one another. For example:

▶ Olga nearly missed her plane, ~~Because~~ *because* the line at security was so long.

▶ Because the line at security was so long, ~~She~~ *she* got flustered and dropped her change purse.

The first option explains why Olga nearly missed her plane, and the second explains why she got flustered and dropped her change purse.

> Edit

The word *if* leads readers to expect a clause explaining what will happen. Consider the following example:

> If you activate the alarm.

This example is a fragment. We need the sentence to show the "what-if": what happens if you activate the alarm? Otherwise, we have an incomplete thought—and readers will be confused.

> The whole lab will be destroyed. If you activate the alarm.
> Spider-Man, you can avert the tragedy.

Will the lab be destroyed if Spider-Man activates the alarm? Or will activating the alarm avert the tragedy? There is no way for readers to know. This example needs to be edited! You try. Edit the example above for both possible interpretations.

》 **SEE S-2** for more on how to edit fragments. Go to **digital.wwnorton .com/littleseagull3** for additional practice.

E-1b Comma Splices

A comma splice looks like a complete sentence in that it starts with a capital letter, concludes with end punctuation, and contains two INDEPENDENT CLAUSES. The problem is that there is only a comma between the two clauses. Here's an example:

▶ It was the coldest day in fifty years, the marching band performed brilliantly.

Both clauses are perfectly clear, and we expect that they are connected in some way—but we don't know how. Did the band play well because of the cold or in spite of it? Or is there no connection at all? In short, comma splices can leave your readers confused.

Checking for comma splices

Writers sometimes use comma splices to create a certain stylistic effect, but it's best to avoid them in academic writing. To check your work for comma splices, look at each sentence one by one and identify the VERBS. Next, look for their SUBJECTS. If you find two or more sets of subjects and verbs that form INDEPENDENT CLAUSES, make sure they are connected appropriately.

Editing comma splices

What are the appropriate ways to connect two independent clauses? Let's look at some of the possibilities.

CHANGE THE COMMA TO A PERIOD

One of your options is to create two separate sentences by inserting a period (.) after the first clause and capitalizing the first letter of the following word.

▶ It was the coldest day in fifty years. ~~the~~ The marching band performed brilliantly.

This might be your preferred choice if you want to write tersely, with short sentences, perhaps to open an essay in a dramatic way. Maybe there is a connection between the two sentences; maybe there's not. Readers will want to keep going in order to find out.

CHANGE THE COMMA TO A SEMICOLON

Another simple way to edit a comma splice is to insert a semicolon (;) between the two clauses.

▶ It was the coldest day in fifty years; the marching band performed brilliantly.

The semicolon lets readers know that there is a definite connection between the weather and the band's brilliant performance, but they can't be certain what it is. The sentence is now correct, if not terribly interesting. You can make the connection clearer and even make the sentence more interesting by adding a TRANSITION (*nevertheless, still, in any event*; see **W-4c** for a complete list).

▶ It was the coldest day in fifty years/; ~nevertheless,~ the marching band performed brilliantly.

ADD A COORDINATING CONJUNCTION

You can also insert a COORDINATING CONJUNCTION (*and, but, or, nor, so, for,* or *yet*) after the comma between the two clauses.

▶ It was the coldest day in fifty years, ~but~ the marching band performed brilliantly.

With this option, the two clauses are separated clearly, and the word *but* indicates that the band played brilliantly in spite of the cold weather.

ADD A SUBORDINATING WORD

Another way to show a relationship between the two clauses is with a SUBORDINATING WORD (*while, however, thus*; see **S-2a** for a full list).

▶ ~Although it~ ~~It~~ was the coldest day in fifty years, the marching band performed brilliantly.

Here, the logical relationship between the two clauses is clear and explicit, and the band's performance becomes the important part of the sentence. But what if you wanted to suggest that the cold weather was responsible for the band playing so well? You could use the same clauses, but with a different subordinating word, as in the example below.

▶ ~Possibly because it~ ~~It~~ was the coldest day in fifty years, the marching band performed brilliantly.

You may also want to experiment with changing the order of the clauses; in many cases, that will cause the emphasis to change. Sometimes, too, changing the order will help you transition to the next sentence.

▶ ~~It~~ was the coldest day in fifty years/. ~~the marching band performed brilliantly~~. Fans huddled together under blankets in the stands.

The marching band performed brilliantly, even though it

> Edit

Consider the following example:

> Transit officials estimate that the new light-rail line will be 20 percent faster than the express bus, the train will cost $1.85 per ride regardless of distance traveled.

Try editing this comma splice in two ways: one that emphasizes the speed of the train and another that emphasizes the cost.

≫ **SEE S-3** for more advice and examples on how to edit comma splices. Go to **digital.wwnorton.com/littleseagull3** for additional practice.

E-1c Fused Sentences

A fused sentence looks like a complete sentence at first glance because it begins with a capital letter, concludes with end punctuation, and contains two **INDEPENDENT CLAUSES**. The reason it is problematic is that there is no explicit connection between the two clauses. A fused sentence will make sense to readers most of the time, but most of the time isn't quite often enough, and you don't want your readers to struggle to understand what you're saying. A sentence can contain more than one independent clause, no problem, but if it does, there needs to be some signal indicating how the clauses relate to one another. That signal could be a punctuation mark, a word that shows how the clauses are related, or both.

Checking for fused sentences

To check your text for fused sentences, look at each sentence one by one and identify any that have more than one INDEPENDENT CLAUSE. Then see how the clauses are connected: is there a word or punctuation mark that indicates how they relate? If not, you've got a fused sentence.

Editing fused sentences

Let's look at a typical fused sentence and some ways it can be edited.

▶ The fire alarm went off the senator spilled her latte all over her desk.

Perfectly clear, right? Or did you have to read it twice to make sure? This example is a fused sentence because it contains two independent clauses but offers no way of knowing where one stops and the next begins, and no indication of how the clauses relate to one another. Here are some options for editing this fused sentence.

ADD A PERIOD

One option is to make the fused sentence into two separate sentences by inserting a period after the first independent clause and capitalizing the first letter of the following clause.

▶ The fire alarm went off. ~~the~~ The senator spilled her latte all over her desk.

Now you have two complete sentences, but they are a little dry and lifeless. Readers may think the two events have nothing to do with one another, or they may think some explanation is missing. In some cases, you may want to choose this solution—if you are merely reporting what happened, for example—but it might not be the best one for this example.

ADD A SEMICOLON

Another option is to insert a semicolon (;) between the two clauses.

▶ The fire alarm went off; the senator spilled her latte all over her desk.

This is another simple way to deal with a fused sentence, although it still doesn't help readers know *how* the two clauses relate. The relationship between the clauses is fairly clear here, but that won't always be the case, so make sure the logical connection between the two clauses is very obvious before you use a semicolon. You can also add a TRANSITION (*nevertheless, still, in any event*; see **W-4c** for a complete list) after the semicolon to make the relationship between the two clauses more explicit.

▶ The fire alarm went off; the senator spilled her latte all over her desk.
  as a result,

ADD A COMMA AND A COORDINATING CONJUNCTION

In order to clarify the relationship between the clauses a little more, you could insert a comma and a COORDINATING CONJUNCTION (*and, but, or, nor, so, for,* or *yet*) between the two clauses.

▶ The fire alarm went off, the senator spilled her latte all over her desk.
  and

Here the division between the two clauses is clearly marked, and readers will generally understand that the latte spilled right after (and the spill was possibly caused by) the fire alarm. With this solution, both clauses have equal importance.

ADD A SUBORDINATING WORD

One of the clearest ways to show the relationship between two clauses is by using a SUBORDINATING WORD (see **S-2a** for a full list).

▶ ~~The~~ fire alarm went off, the senator spilled her latte all over her desk.
  When the

Adding the subordinating word *when* to the first clause makes it clear that the fire alarm caused the senator to spill her latte and also puts emphasis on the spilled coffee. Note that you need to add a comma after the introductory clause. You can also change the order of the two clauses; see how the emphasis changes slightly. Note, too, that in this case, you should not add a comma.

▶ The senator spilled her latte all over her desk the fire alarm went off.
  when

> Edit

Using the editing options explained above, edit the following fused sentence in two different ways. Make one of your solutions short and snappy. In the other solution, show that the banging and the shouting were happening at the same time.

> The moderator banged his gavel the candidates continued to shout at each other.

>> **SEE S-3** for more on how to edit fused sentences. Go to **digital** **.wwnorton.com/littleseagull3** for additional practice.

E-1d Mixed Constructions

A MIXED CONSTRUCTION is a sentence that starts out with one structure and ends up with another one. Such a sentence may be understandable, but more often it leaves readers scratching their heads in confusion. There are many different ways to end up with a mixed construction, and this fact alone makes it difficult to identify one. Here is an example of one common type of mixed construction:

► Décollage is when you take away pieces of an image to create a new image.

The sentence is clear enough, but look again at the word *when*. That word locates an event in time—*I'll call* when *I get there. The baby woke up* when *the phone rang. When the armistice was signed, people everywhere cheered.* In the example above, there is no time associated with décollage; the sentence is simply describing the process. To edit the sentence, replace *when* with a more appropriate word, and adjust the rest of the sentence as needed.

► Décollage is ~~when you take~~ away pieces of an image to create a new image.
       the technique of taking
       ^

Checking for mixed constructions

Let's consider another example:

► Nutritionists disagree about the riskiness of eating raw eggs and also more healthful compared with cooked ones.

What? It's hard to even know where to start. Let's begin by identifying the **VERB(S)**. Take a good look—there's only one verb here, *disagree*. Next, let's identify the **SUBJECT**. Who disagrees? *Nutritionists*. OK, now we have a subject and a verb. What do nutritionists disagree about? It's clear enough that they disagree about *the riskiness of eating raw eggs*, but after that, it gets confusing. Consider the next words: *and also*. Also what? Do nutritionists also disagree that raw eggs are more nutritious than cooked eggs? Or is the writer claiming that raw eggs *are* more healthful? It's impossible to tell, which suggests that we have a mixed construction.

Editing mixed constructions

Let's look at a couple of ways we might edit the sentence about raw eggs. Here's one way:

▶ Nutritionists disagree about the riskiness of eating raw eggs and also
   about their healthfulness
   ~~more healthful~~ compared with cooked ones.
   ^

Notice that we added another *about*, which makes it clear that what follows is also something nutritionists disagree about. Notice, too, that we added the suffix *–ness* to *healthful* so that the word would be **PARALLEL** to *riskiness*. Now the verb *disagree* applies to both *riskiness* and *healthfulness*: nutritionists disagree about the riskiness of eating raw eggs, and they also disagree about the healthfulness of raw eggs compared with cooked ones.

What if the writer's original intention was to claim that raw eggs are more healthful than cooked ones? Since the two parts of the sentence express two different ideas, an editor might choose to simply make the mixed construction into two separate sentences.

▶ Nutritionists disagree about the riskiness of eating raw eggs. ~~and also~~
                                                            Raw eggs are
                                                            ^
   more healthful ~~compared with~~ cooked ones.
                  than
                  ^

Just considering sentence structure, now we have two good sentences, but even though they both focus on raw eggs, the two sentences are not clearly connected. And besides, who is saying that eating raw eggs is more healthful? The author or the nutritionists?

Adding just a couple of words links the sentences together and helps readers follow the ideas.

▶ Nutritionists disagree about the riskiness of eating raw eggs. ~~Raw~~ eggs are more healthful than cooked ones.

Some claim raw ^

Here we've added a new subject, *some* (which refers to nutritionists), and we've also given the second sentence a verb, *claim*. Now the two sentences have a logical sequence and are easier to read. Next, let's look at one other mixed construction:

▶ Because air accumulates under the eggshell is why an egg stands up underwater.

This sentence is more or less clear, but its parts don't fit together properly. What can we do about that? Same procedure as before—first, look for the verbs. This time, it's more complicated because there are three: *accumulates, is,* and *stands up*. Next, we look for the subject of each of the verbs. The first one is easy—*air* accumulates; the subject is *air*. The third one is also simple—*an egg* stands up; the subject is *an egg*. But what is the subject of *is*? That's not such an easy question with this sentence because its structure changes in the middle. So let's try a different approach.

What exactly is this sentence trying to say? It's clear that the point of this sentence is to explain why a submerged egg stands up, and we have two clauses: one that tells us that *an egg stands up underwater* and another that tells us that the egg stands up *because air accumulates under the eggshell*. Now we just have to put them together in an appropriate way.

▶ Because air accumulates under the eggshell, ~~is why~~ an egg stands up underwater.
^

Did you notice that this version is almost exactly the same as the original sentence? The main difference is the words *is why*—which turn out not to be necessary. We now have one **INDEPENDENT CLAUSE** (*an egg stands up underwater*) and one **SUBORDINATE CLAUSE** (*because air accumulates under the eggshell*), with a comma in between. If it sounds better to you, you can reverse the order of the clauses, and the meaning stays the same. Note that you should not use a comma with this option.

▶ An egg stands up underwater because air accumulates under the eggshell.

We can use the same approach for a sentence that starts with a prepositional phrase but changes its structure in the middle: figure out what the sentence is trying to say, identify the phrases and clauses, and edit as needed so that you can put them together in an appropriate way.

▶ ~~For parents~~ of children with a peanut allergy depend on rules that
   ^Parents
   prohibit nuts in school.

> Edit

Try editing the following mixed construction in two ways. First, make one sentence that includes all of the information in the example. Next, present the same information in two separate sentences. Which way do you like better? Why?

> One or two months before mating, male and female eagles together build their nests can be four or five feet in diameter.

≫ Go to **digital.wwnorton.com/littleseagull3** for additional practice.

E-2   Editing Pronouns

Pronouns are some of the smallest words in the language, so you might think they should be among the easiest. Well, no, they're often not. But the good news is that editing your work to make sure all your pronouns are used appropriately is not too complicated. This chapter will give you tools for editing three common pronoun issues: pronoun reference, pronoun-antecedent agreement, and pronoun case.

First, let's clarify the terms. **PRONOUNS**, as you probably know, are words that refer to other words or phrases (and occasionally even whole clauses). They're very useful precisely because they're small and they do a lot of work representing larger units. The words that they represent are their **ANTECEDENTS**. Most frequently, the antecedent is something or somebody that has already been mentioned, and English has very specific conventions for signaling to readers exactly what that antecedent is so that they won't be confused. We call that **PRONOUN REFERENCE**. Let's suppose this next example is the first sentence in a news report.

▶ The Procurement Committee meets today to review the submitted bids, and she will announce the winner tomorrow.

Wait. *She? She* who? It's not clear what *she* refers to, and readers are now lost.

Pronoun **AGREEMENT** is another important convention. Pronouns have to agree with their antecedents in number (*I, we*) and in some cases gender (*he, she, it*). *Mr. Klein misplaced her phone again.* If Mr. Klein is in the habit of losing a specific woman's phone, then perhaps the sentence makes sense. If it's his own phone that he misplaced again, then *her* doesn't agree with its antecedent, Mr. Klein, and readers will get confused.

PRONOUN CASE is a concept that you may never have encountered, but it's one that you use every day, and what's more, you likely do so appropriately and without giving it any thought. For example, you probably say *I bought ice cream* automatically—and would not likely say *Me bought ice cream* or *Coach wants I to play shortstop.* Those two pronouns—*I* and *me*—refer to the same person, but they're not interchangeable. Still, most of the time we automatically choose the appropriate one for the specific context. The difference between those two words is a simple matter of case; read on for more about that.

E-2a Pronoun Reference

Unclear pronoun reference occurs when readers can't be certain what a **PRONOUN** refers to. Usually this confusion arises when there are several possibilities in the same sentence (or sometimes in the previous sentence). Here's an example: *Andrew and Glen competed fiercely for the office of treasurer, but in the end, he won handily.* If Andrew and Glen are both men, the pronoun *he* could refer to either one of them, so who was it that won? We don't know.

Checking for unclear pronoun reference

To check for unclear pronoun reference, you need to first identify each pronoun and then make sure that it points very clearly to its **ANTE-CEDENT**. Often, the meanings of the words provide clues about what the pronoun refers to—but not always. Let's look at three sentences that have very similar structures.

▶ My grandparents ordered pancakes because *they* weren't very hungry.

First, we identify the pronouns: *my* and *they*. *My* clearly refers to the writer, but what about *they*? Although both *pancakes* and *grandparents* are possible antecedents for *they*, we know that the pronoun here has to refer to grandparents because pancakes don't get hungry. Now let's look at another sentence:

▶ My grandparents ordered pancakes because *they* weren't very expensive.

This sentence is almost identical to the first one and has the same pronoun, *they*, but this time, the antecedent has to be *pancakes* because there is no price on grandparents. Sorry to say, though, that antecedents aren't always so obvious. For example:

▶ My grandparents like playing cards with their neighbors because *they* aren't very competitive.

Wait. Who's not very competitive here? The grandparents or the neighbors? Or maybe all of them? We really can't be sure.

Editing unclear pronoun reference

Let's look again at the last example:

▶ My grandparents like playing cards with their neighbors because they aren't very competitive.

To edit this sentence, our best option may be to change the structure, and there are several possibilities:

▶ My grandparents like playing cards with their neighbors, ~~because they~~ ^{who} aren't very competitive.

This option makes clear that the neighbors are the ones who aren't very competitive.

▶ My grandparents, *who aren't very competitive,* like playing cards with their neighbors, *who are also not too* ~~because they aren't very~~ competitive.

Now we know that everybody mentioned here is noncompetitive. You may not think the sentence sounds as good as the original, but at least the meaning is clear. And of course there are usually other options.

The most important objective is to make clear what word or words each pronoun refers to. You don't want to leave your readers guessing. Here is one more example:

▶ After months of posturing and debate, those planning the expensive new football stadium suspended the project, which students loudly celebrated.

What is the antecedent for *which* in this example? You probably interpret this sentence to say that the students celebrated the suspension of the plans to build the stadium, but in fact, that's not really clearly established in the sentence. Another plausible interpretation is that the students celebrated the building of the stadium. Let's reword the sentence and remove *which* in order to make the meaning perfectly clear.

▶ After months of posturing and debate, those planning the expensive new football stadium suspended the project, *and* ~~which~~ students loudly celebrated *the news.*

> Edit

The following sentence uses the words it and *which* to refer to . . . well, it's not exactly clear what they refer to.

> A temperature inversion happens when a layer of warmer air is positioned above a layer of cooler air, which is not how it usually occurs.

You have several options here that would make this sentence better, but try this one: rewrite the sentence to eliminate the need for any pronoun at all.

> >> **SEE S-6b** for more on how to edit unclear pronoun references. Go to **digital.wwnorton.com/littleseagull3** for additional practice.

E-2b Pronoun-Antecedent Agreement

Pronoun-antecedent agreement means that every PRONOUN has to agree with its ANTECEDENT in gender (*he*, *she*, *it*) and number (singular or plural). Some sentences with pronouns that don't agree with their antecedents are relatively easy to understand, and usually readers can figure them out if they think about it, but they shouldn't have to do that extra work. For your academic writing, you need to make sure that all of your pronouns agree with their antecedents.

Checking for pronoun-antecedent agreement

To check for pronoun-antecedent agreement, you need to first identify the pronouns and their antecedents. Then you need to make sure each pronoun agrees with its antecedent in gender and number. Let's look at a couple of examples:

> ▶ Trombones might be very loud, but it was drowned out last night by the cheering of the crowd.

This sentence has only one pronoun: *it*. *Trombones* is the only noun that precedes *it*, so *trombones* has to be the antecedent. Do they agree? We don't have to think about gender in this example, but we do have to think about number. And that's a problem, because the numbers don't match: *trombones* is plural, but *it* is singular.

▶ The table is wobbly because one of her legs is shorter than the others.

In some languages, tables, chairs, and other inanimate objects have grammatical gender, but in English, they don't. The legs of a table are never referred to with masculine or feminine gender.

Editing for pronoun-antecedent agreement

In order to fix the trombone sentence, you can change either the antecedent or the pronoun to make them agree in number. In this case, it is clear that the first CLAUSE refers to trombones in general, and the second clause refers to a specific trombone at a specific event. Assuming that the more important part is the specific event, and that there was only one trombone, let's change the word *trombones* from plural to singular. We can do that easily in this case without really changing the meaning, although sometimes it might be more difficult to do so.

▶ ~~Trombones~~ The trombone might be very loud, but it was drowned out last night by the cheering of the crowd.

Both the pronoun and its antecedent are now singular; that is, they agree in number. Now let's consider several examples where gender is a factor. In the example about the table legs, we simply have to replace the feminine pronoun with the inanimate one.

▶ The table is wobbly because one of ~~her~~ its legs is shorter than the others.

Remember that the gender of English pronouns matters only with *he, him, his; she, her, hers; it, its*. No other English pronouns specify gender. Some languages have more gender-specific pronouns, and some languages have fewer, but let's just stick to English right now.

▶ My mom and dad have an arrangement about sausage pizza— *he* picks off the sausage, and *she* eats *it*.

This sentence has three pronouns—*he, she,* and *it*—and it's quite evident that *he* refers to *dad, she* refers to *mom,* and *it* refers to *sau-*

sage. All the antecedents are clear. But what if we changed the cast of characters in the sentence to two men? It would be confusing to refer to each of them as *he*, so we need a different strategy. One possibility is to use *he* to represent one of the men and to refer to the other man by name. Will that work?

▶ Paul and *his* brother have an arrangement about sausage pizza—Paul picks off the sausage, and *he* eats it.

Who eats the sausage? Paul or his brother? It's still not clear. In this case, our best option is to eliminate the pronoun and refer to both men explicitly both times.

▶ Paul and *his* brother have an arrangement about sausage pizza—
Paul picks off the sausage, and ~~he~~ *his brother* eats it.

If you'd rather not repeat both phrases, and the arrangement itself is more important than which person eats all the sausage, you can try this option:

▶ Paul and *his* brother have an arrangement about sausage pizza—
one of them   *the other one*
~~Paul~~ picks off the sausage, and ~~he~~ eats it.

Now we've got it; everything is clear. As this last edit shows, making pronouns and antecedents agree sometimes requires reworking the structure of a sentence and occasionally even modifying what it says. Pronouns may be small words, but getting them right is hugely important; don't be afraid to make changes in your writing.

Now let's look at some other contexts where making pronouns agree in gender with their antecedents can be complicated. We'll start with one that's pretty straightforward.

▶ Trey noticed a sunflower growing along the path; *he* grabbed *his* phone and took a picture of *it*.

We know that Trey is a man or a boy—*he, his*—and the flower, of course, is inanimate—*it*. In academic writing, inanimate objects are always referred to as *it*, even though in casual speech, we may use gendered pronouns to refer to things such as cars, boats (almost always *she*), and others. What about animals? If you know the sex of an animal, then by all means, refer to it as *he* or *she*. If you don't know the sex, or if the sex isn't pertinent, just use *it*. And what if you're writing about a person whose sex or gender you don't know? That happens, and that's when writing gets complicated. For example:

▶ Anyone who gets three speeding tickets in a year will lose *his* license.

What's wrong with this example? Plenty, unless only men have such a license. If what you are writing applies to both women and men, your pronouns should reflect that reality. One of the easiest solutions is to use plural nouns and pronouns because they do not specify gender:

▶ ~~Anyone~~ who ~~gets~~ three speeding tickets in a year will lose ~~his license~~.
 ^Drivers^   ^get^   ^their licenses^

You may need to tinker a bit with the structure, but the message can remain the same. Another option is to revise the sentence altogether. Here's one possibility:

▶ Getting three speeding tickets in a year will result in the driver's license being revoked.

Another possible solution is to write *his* or *her*:

▶ Anyone who gets three speeding tickets in a year will lose ~~his~~ license.
                                                              ^his or her^

This last solution is fine, although if you have many such instances close together, the writing can start to feel awkward. Another possibility is to employ **SINGULAR THEY**, using *they*, *them*, *their*, or *theirs* with a singular antecedent.

▶ Anyone who gets three speeding tickets in a year will lose ~~his~~ license.
                                                              ^their^

Many of us use singular *they* this way in casual speech, and its use is becoming more and more accepted in some newspapers and magazines and other more formal contexts. Singular *they* is a very tidy solution, but even though it's becoming ever more common, it's still not widely accepted in academic writing. Before you use it in your class work, you might check with your instructor to be sure it will be acceptable in that class.

> Edit

Edit the following sentence in two ways. First, make both the pronoun and its antecedent singular; second, make the pronoun and antecedent plural. Both ways are acceptable, but which way sounds better to you?

> Applicants must file the forms before the deadline and make sure that it's filled out correctly.

>> **SEE S-6a** for more on how to edit for pronoun-antecedent agreement, including advice about how to treat indefinite pronouns such as *everyone* and *anyone* and collective nouns such as *team* and *choir*. Go to **digital.wwnorton.com/littleseagull3** for additional practice.

E-2c Pronoun Case

Pronoun **CASE** refers to the different forms a **PRONOUN** takes in order to indicate how it functions in a sentence. English pronouns have three cases: subject, object, and possessive. Most of the time, we choose the appropriate pronouns automatically, as in the following sentence:

▶ *I* saw *her,* and *she* saw *me,* but *we* didn't see *our* cousin.

This sentence involves two people and six distinct pronouns. I and *me* refer to one person (the writer), *she* and *her* refer to the other person, and *we* and *our* refer to both people. Each of the three pronoun pairs has a distinct role in the sentence. *I*, *she*, and *we* are all subjects; *me* and *her* are objects; and *our* is possessive.

Checking for correct pronoun case

You would probably not ever say *Me saw her* because it wouldn't sound right. In casual speech, though, you might hear (or say) *Me and Bob saw her.* While you might hear or say that in informal conversation, it would not be acceptable in academic writing. Here is a simple and reliable technique for checking your work for case: check for compound subjects like *me and Bob* and cover up everything in the phrase but the pronoun. Read it out loud.

▶ Me ~~and Bob~~ saw her.

Does it sound good to you? Hope not. So how do you change it? Read on.

Editing for pronoun case

To edit for pronoun case, the first step is to identify the pronouns in each sentence. The following example has only one, *us*:

▶ Us first-year students are petitioning for a schedule change.

Remember that the way a pronoun functions in a sentence is the key and that there are three possibilities for case. Is *us* functioning as subject, object, or possessive? In order to answer that question, first we need to identify the verb: *are petitioning*. The subject tells us who (or what) is petitioning—in this sentence, *us first-year students*. If you're not sure if *us* is correct, try it by itself, without *first-year students*.

▶ Us are petitioning for a schedule change.

▶ ~~Us~~ are petitioning for a schedule change.
      We
      ^

We changed *us* to *we* here because it's the subject of the sentence and thus needs to be in the subject case. For more advice on choosing the correct case, see the table in **S-6c**. Now let's look at two more examples: *Pat dated Cody longer than me. Pat dated Cody longer than I.* The only difference between the two sentences is the case of a pronoun, but that little word gives the sentences totally different meanings. How can that tiny detail of case make such a difference? It does so because case lets readers know whether the person—*I* or *me*—is the subject or the object of a verb, and that fact can make all the difference in the world.

▶ Pat dated Cody longer than me.

Look carefully. There's only one verb, *dated*, and its subject is *Pat*. Now notice the pronoun: *me*. That's object case, right? So, according to the example, Pat dated Cody and *me*. Try the next one.

▶ Pat dated Cody longer than I.

Here the pronoun is in subject case: I. Even though it's not followed by a verb, the pronoun tells us that Pat dated Cody and so did I. See **S-6c** for more information about pronoun case.

> ## Edit

Use the technique explained in this section to edit the following sentence for pronoun case.

> Iris was unhappy, but the judges called a tie and gave the award to she and Lu.

≫ **SEE S-6c** for more on how to edit pronoun case. Go to **digital. wwnorton.com/littleseagull3** for additional practice.

E-3   Editing Verbs

Verbs. Are any words more important—or hardworking? Besides specifying actions (*hop, skip, jump*) or states of being (*be, seem*), verbs provide most of the information about *when* (happening now? already happened? might happen? usually happens?), and they also have to link very explicitly to their subjects. That's a lot of work!

Because verbs are so important, verb problems are often easily noticed by readers, and once readers notice a verb problem in your work, they may question your competence as a writer. But if your readers can catch these problems, so can you. This chapter will help you edit your work for two of the most troublesome verb problems: subject-verb agreement and shifts in tense.

E-3a Subject-Verb Agreement

In English, every **VERB** has to agree with its **SUBJECT** in number and person. That may sound complicated, but it's really only third-person singular subjects—*runner, shoe, he, she, it*—that you have to look out for, and even then, only when the verb is in the simple present tense. Still, the third-person present tense is the most common construction in academic writing, so it matters. Take a look at this example:

▶ First the coach enters, then you enter, and then all of the other players enter.

The verb *enter* occurs three times in that sentence, but notice that when its subject is third-person singular—*coach*—an -s follows the **BASE FORM** of the verb, *enter*. In the other two cases, the verb has no such ending. What's so complicated about that? Well, there are two kinds of subjects that cause problems: indefinite pronouns, such as *everyone* and *many*, which may require a singular or plural verb even if their meaning suggests otherwise; and subjects with more than one word, in which the word that has to agree with the verb may be hidden among other words.

Checking for subject-verb agreement

To check for subject-verb agreement, first identify the subjects and their verbs, paying careful attention to **INDEFINITE PRONOUNS** and subjects with more than one word. Then, check to make sure that every subject matches its verb in number and person.

Editing for subject-verb agreement

Let's look at a few common mistakes and see what we can do about them.

INDEFINITE PRONOUNS

Indefinite pronouns are words like *anyone, each, everything,* and *nobody.* When they're used as a subject, they have to agree with the verb. Sometimes that's tricky. For example:

▶ First the coach enters, then you enter, and then each of the other players enter.

We know that the subject of the first clause is *coach* and the subject of the second clause is *you*, but what about the third clause? Is the subject *each*? Or is it *players*? You might be tempted to choose *players* because that's the word closest to the verb *enter*, but that's not correct; the subject is *each*, an indefinite pronoun.

▶ First the coach enters, then you enter, and then each of the other
   players ~~enter~~. *enters*

That -*s* at the end of *enters* is necessary because the **SIMPLE SUBJECT** of the final clause is *each*, which is singular. The phrase *of the other players* is additional information. Now see what happens if we change *each* to *all*:

▶ First the coach enters, then you enter, and then ~~each~~ *all* of the other
   players ~~enters~~. *enter*

Even though the two phrases—*each of the other players* and *all of the other players*—have essentially the same meaning, the word *each* is always singular and requires the verb to have the -*s* ending, while *all* is plural here because it refers to a plural noun, *players*.

 Because *each* refers to the members of a group individually, it is always singular and requires the verb to have the -*s* ending. *All* is plural when it refers to a plural noun, but it's singular when it refers to a singular noun.

▶ *All* of the strawberries *were picked* today.

▶ *All* of the rhubarb *was picked* yesterday.

In the first sentence, *all* refers to the *strawberries* all together, in plural form, while in the second sentence, *all* refers to *rhubarb*, a **NONCOUNT NOUN**, which requires the singular form of the verb. When a subject is an **INDEFINITE PRONOUN**, check **S-5f** to see whether that particular pronoun should take a singular or plural verb.

SUBJECTS WITH MORE THAN ONE WORD

Sometimes a sentence has a subject with more than one word, so you need to determine which of the words is the one that the verb has to agree with and which words simply provide extra information.

To do that, pull the subject apart to find which word is the essential one. Let's practice with this sentence:

▶ The guy with the mirrored sunglasses run in this park every morning.

The **COMPLETE SUBJECT** is *the guy with the mirrored sunglasses*, but who is it that does the running? It's the guy, and the fact that he has mirrored sunglasses is simply extra information. You could remove the phrase *with the mirrored sunglasses* and still have a complete sentence—it might not be very informative, but it's not incorrect.

To check for subject-verb agreement when a subject has more than one word, first locate the verb and then the complete subject. Then check each word in the subject until you find the one key word that determines the form of the verb. Since the **SIMPLE SUBJECT** here—*guy*—is in the third-person singular, and the verb is in the present tense, the verb should also be in the third-person singular:

▶ The guy with the mirrored sunglasses ~~run~~ $\overset{\text{runs}}{\wedge}$ in this park every morning.

Let's try one more problem sentence:

▶ The neighbor across the hall from the Fudds always sign for their packages.

First, find the verb: *sign*. The complete subject is *the neighbor across the hall from the Fudds*. What part of that subject indicates who does the signing? *Neighbor*. Everything else is extra. Since it's just one *neighbor*, the subject is singular, and since a third-person singular subject requires a present tense verb to have an -s ending, the edited sentence will be:

▶ The neighbor across the hall from the Fudds always ~~sign~~ $\overset{\text{signs}}{\wedge}$ for their packages.

> Edit

The sentence below has four subjects and four verbs. One (or more) of the subjects is singular, so its verb should have an -s ending. Edit and make any necessary changes.

All of the boxes need to be stacked neatly, and every box need to be labeled; the red box with the taped edges fit on top, and each of the boxes need its own lid.

In casual speech, you may not use the -s ending, or it may be hard to hear, so you may not be able to rely on your ear alone to edit this sentence. Think it through, and consult **S-5b** and **S-5f** to help you choose the appropriate verb forms.

》 **SEE S-5** for more on how to edit for subject-verb agreement. Go to **digital.wwnorton.com/littleseagull3** for additional practice.

E-3b Shifts in Tense

We live in the present moment; our ideas and our feelings are happening right now. Often, though, our present thoughts—and comments--are responses to things that happened in the past or that haven't happened yet. In conversation, we usually shift our verb tenses smoothly and automatically to account for actions that take place at different times, as in the following example of something you might hear or say:

▶ Flor *is* upset because Justin *informed* her that he *will not be able to come* to her graduation.

In writing, however, we need to take extra care to ensure that our tenses are clear, consistent, and appropriate to what we're describing. In contrast to face-to-face conversation—in which tone of voice, facial expressions, and hand gestures help create meaning—writing has to rely on carefully chosen words. Verb tenses work hard to put complex sequences of events into appropriate context. The previous example has three clauses, each in a different tense: Flor *is* upset (right now); because Justin *informed* her (in the past); that he *will not be able to come* (to an event in the future).

Checking for shifts in tense

In academic writing, you'll often need to discuss what other authors have written, and the different disciplines have different conventions and rules for doing that (see **R-4e**). In classes that require you to use **MLA** style, for example, you'll rely heavily on the simple present tense:

MLA   Morton argues that even though Allende's characters are not realistic, they're believable.

Notice how *argues*, *are not*, and *they're* all use the simple present tense even though Morton's article and Allende's novel were both written in the past. If you mention the date when something was written, however, the verb should be in the past tense. In contrast, disciplines that follow **APA** style require that references to published sources and research results be stated in the past tense or present perfect tense:

APA   Azele reported that 59% of the control group subjects showed high gamma levels.

Notice here that the two verbs in the sentence—*reported* and *showed*—are both in the past tense because both Azele's research and the report were done in the past. Be careful, though, because your sources may be writing about current or future conditions. If that's the case, be sure to preserve the tense of the original in your work, as the following example does.

APA   Donnerstag and Jueves predicted that another Jovian moon will soon be discovered.

Regardless of what class you're writing for, however, the most important thing about verb tenses is consistency—unless you have a reason to shift tense.

Editing confusing shifts in tense

Much of the editing that you do calls for sentence-by-sentence work, but checking for confusing shifts in tense often requires that you consider several sentences together.

Starting at the beginning, mark every MAIN VERB, along with any HELPING VERBS, in every sentence (remembering that there may be more than one clause in each sentence). Don't make any changes yet; just mark the verbs. Next, go back to the beginning and notice what tense you used each time. Examine each tense one by one, and when you notice a shift to a different tense, read carefully what you have written and look for a reason for the shift. If you can explain why the shift makes sense, leave it alone. Then move on to the next verb. Is it in the original tense or the new tense? Can you explain why? Continue all the way through your text, examining every verb tense and making sure that any shifts you find can be explained. Let's practice with two examples:

▶ Bates underestimated the public when she writes disparagingly about voters' intelligence.

First, we mark the verbs—*underestimated, writes*—and we notice that the first is in past tense while the second is in present. Is there a clear explanation for the shift? No, not really. If you are using **MLA** style, you'll want to put both verbs in the present: *underestimates* and *writes*. In **APA** style, past tense is more appropriate for both: *underestimated* and *wrote*. In any case, there is no reason to use two different tenses in the sentence. Here is another example, this time a little more complicated:

▶ All of the guests ate the stew, but only two showed symptoms of food poisoning.

It's true that the events (*ate, showed*) in both clauses of the example occurred in the past, but can we be certain that the symptoms were a result of eating the stew? Could the guests have had the symptoms already? The sentence isn't really clear.

▶ All of the guests ~~ate~~ ^had eaten^ the stew, but only two showed symptoms of food poisoning.

By changing the verb tense in the first clause to the **PAST PERFECT**, we show clearly that the stew was eaten before the food poisoning occurred. (We may never know what caused the illness, but at least we know the sequence of events.)

> **Edit**

Edit the following sentence to eliminate any confusing shifts in tense. Assume that the writing has to follow **APA** format for verb tenses.

> Levi (2013) notes that the trade deficit decreases from 2005 to 2015, but he warns that the improvement may be reversed because the new treaty will go into effect in 2020.

» **SEE S-4** and **S-9a** for more on how to edit confusing shifts in tense. Go to **digital.wwnorton.com/littleseagull3** for additional practice.

E-4 Editing Quotations

In academic writing, you are required not only to express your own ideas, but also to incorporate the ideas of other authors. In a way, you are engaging in a conversation with your sources, whether you draw from Aristotle, Toni Morrison, or a classmate. Your success as a writer has a lot to do with how well you weave your sources' ideas in with your own without your readers ever having to wonder who said what. Editing your work for citation and documentation issues therefore involves two main tasks:

- incorporating any words of others that you quote into your text so that everything flows smoothly

- making sure the punctuation, capitalization, and other such elements are correct

The conventions for citing and documenting sources in academic writing are very precise—every period, every comma, every quotation mark has its job to do, and they must be in exactly the right place.

E-4a Incorporating Quotations

Whenever we quote something someone else has said, we need to structure the sentences that contain the quoted material so that they read as smoothly as any other sentence. As writers, we need to master our use of language in much the same way that musicians have to master their instruments, and in both cases, it's not easy. Just as musicians playing together in an orchestra (or a garage band) have to coordinate with one another in tempo, key, and melody, you have to make sure that your words and those of others that you quote fit together smoothly.

Checking to see that quotations are incorporated smoothly

One good way to begin checking a draft to see how well any quotations have been incorporated is to read it aloud, or better yet, get someone else to read it aloud to you. If the reader (you or someone else) stumbles over a passage and has to go back and read the sentence again, you can be fairly certain that some changes are necessary. We can practice with some sentences that quote the following passage from a 2013 *Atlantic* article about fast food:

> Introduced in 1991, the McLean Deluxe was perhaps the boldest single effort the food industry has ever undertaken to shift the masses to healthier eating.
> —David Freedman, "How Junk Food Can End Obesity"

Assume that you might not want or need to quote the entire passage, so you incorporate just one part of Freedman's sentence into one of your sentences, as follows:

▶ Freedman refers to a failed McDonald's menu item "the McLean Deluxe was perhaps the food industry's boldest single effort to shift the masses to healthier eating."

If you read the sentence aloud, you should be able to notice that it is awkwardly structured and even hard to understand. Also, do you notice that the quoted section doesn't exactly match the author's words? Some of the words from the original are missing and some others have been added. Changing an author's words in a quoted section is only allowed if the original meaning is not altered in any way. Also, you need to indicate to your readers that you've modified the author's words. Let's see how we can go about fixing these things.

Editing sentences that include quotations

There are two ways of smoothly incorporating quoted material. One strategy is to adjust your own words to accommodate the quoted material; another is to lightly modify the quoted material to fit your sentence. Here's one way we might edit our sentence by adjusting our own words:

▶ ~~Freedman refers~~ to a failed McDonald's menu item, "the McLean Deluxe was perhaps the food industry's boldest single effort to shift the masses to healthier eating."

(*Referring* ... *Freedman notes that*)

Let's look at what we did. First, we changed the first two words. The meaning didn't change; only the structure did. Then, we added a **SIGNAL PHRASE** (*Freedman notes that*) to introduce the quoted words.

So far so good. But what about the places where we changed the author's words? If you modify an author's words, you need to signal to your readers what changes you've made, and there are precise conventions for doing that.

Enclose anything you add or change within the quotation itself in square brackets ([ ]), and insert ellipses (. . .) to show where any content from the original has been omitted.

▶ Referring to a failed McDonald's menu item, Freedman notes that "the McLean Deluxe was perhaps the [food industry's] boldest single effort . . . to shift the masses to healthier eating."

With minimal changes, the sentence now has all the necessary parts and reads smoothly. Note the two things we've done to modify the quotation. We've enclosed the words we added—*food industry's*—in square brackets, and we've inserted ellipses in place of the six words that were omitted from Freedman's sentence. It's worth repeating here that it is only permissible to add or delete words if the meaning of the quotation isn't substantially altered.

> Edit

Here is another sentence based on the Freedman passage:

> Freedman talks about an earlier effort the McLean Deluxe
> by McDonald's was perhaps the boldest try to shift the masses
> to healthier eating.

First, you'll have to make a few changes to help the sentence read smoothly. There are several ways to do that, but try to make as few changes as possible. Once the sentence reads smoothly, compare it with the original passage to see where you might need square brackets (for added material) or ellipses (to show where words have been removed). By the way, you don't have to put *McLean Deluxe* in quotation marks because it was not a term coined by Freedman.

>> **SEE E-4b**, **R-4**, and **P-4** for more on how to incorporate quotations. Go to **digital.wwnorton.com/littleseagull3** for additional practice.

E-4b Punctuating Quotations

Citation conventions exist to help us clearly distinguish our words from the words of our sources, and one way we do that is by punctuating quotations carefully. When you quote someone's exact words, you need to attend to four elements: quotation marks, capitalization, commas, and end punctuation. These elements let your readers know which words are yours and which are the words of someone else.

Checking to see how any quoted material is punctuated

Here is another sentence taken from the *Atlantic* article about fast food; let's use it in a variety of ways in order to show how to capitalize and punctuate sentences that quote from this passage.

> A slew of start-ups are trying to find ways of producing fresh,
> local, unprocessed meals quickly and at lower cost.
> > —David Freedman, "How Junk Food Can End Obesity"

You might write a sentence such as this one:

▶ It may one day be possible to get fast food that is healthy and affordable since a slew of start-ups are trying to find ways, according to David Freedman.

Structurally, the sentence is fine, but it includes a direct quotation from Freedman without letting readers know which words are his and which are yours. Even if you used Freedman's exact words accidentally, it would still be **PLAGIARISM**, which may carry a stiff penalty. The sentence needs to be edited.

Editing quotations to indicate who said what

There are numerous ways to edit the above sentence to make clear who said what. Here is one option:

▶ It may one day be possible to get fast food that is healthy and
affordable. ~~since~~ slew of start-ups are trying to find ways/.~~"according~~
According to David Freedman, "A
~~to Freedman.~~

What changed? First, we added quotation marks to enclose Freedman's exact words. Second, we broke the sentence into two and started the second one with the signal phrase *According to Freedman*, followed by a comma. Third, we capitalized the first letter of the quotation. Since A was capitalized in the original quotation, no brackets are necessary. Finally, notice the period. The sentence ends with the quoted material, so the period goes inside the quotation marks. Now let's look at how you might go about editing another sentence.

▶ Freedman asserts that many new businesses are working to develop fresh, local, unprocessed meals quickly and at lower cost.

Check your four elements. First, insert any necessary quotation marks; make sure they enclose Freedman's exact words. Second, is any additional capitalization necessary? If so, capitalize the appropriate word(s). Third, if there's a **SIGNAL PHRASE** before the quoted material, does it need to be followed by a comma? Finally, make sure any end punctuation is in the right place. Try editing the sentence yourself before you look at the revision below.

▶ Freedman asserts that many new businesses are working to develop
   "fresh, local, unprocessed meals quickly and at lower cost."
   ^   ^

The quoted portion is not a complete sentence, and we placed it in the middle of ours, so no capitalization was necessary. We didn't insert a comma because his words flow smoothly within the larger sentence. Since the sentence ends with the quoted material, we put the period inside the quotation marks.

Depending on the documentation style that you are using, you may need to provide parenthetical information at the end of any sentences that include quoted material. Some styles require that you name the author(s) if you haven't named them earlier in the sentence, along with the page number(s) where their words appeared. Here's how you would do so in MLA and APA style requirements.

MLA Freedman asserts that many new businesses are working to
develop "fresh, local, unprocessed meals quickly and at lower
cost" (82).

APA Freedman asserted that many new businesses are working to
develop "fresh, local, unprocessed meals quickly and at lower
cost" (2013, p. 82).

One more important point: notice that with parenthetical documentation, the final period of the sentence is no longer inside the quotation marks; it is after the parentheses. Consult the Chicago and CSE chapters to find out what kind of documentation each style requires.

> Edit

The following sentences cite the passage from Freedman's essay; they need to be formatted properly in order to read smoothly and also to show more clearly which words are the writer's and which are Freedman's. Remember the four elements: quotation marks, capitalization, commas, and end punctuation.

Healthy and affordable fast food may not be a reality yet, but we may not have too long to wait. As Freedman explains a slew of start-ups are trying to find ways to bring such meals to market.

It is possible to edit the sentence using only the four elements and not adding, subtracting, or changing any words. Try it.

>> **SEE P-1g, P-4, and P-8c** for more on how to edit documentation. Go to **digital.wwnorton.com/littleseagull3** for additional practice.

E-5 Editing Commas

Ideas are made out of words, right? So why should we care about commas? Well, here's why—they help those words make more sense. Nobody wants to have to read the same sentence two or three times in order to get it. Well-placed commas can make your sentence clear and easy to read—and can help keep the words (and ideas) correctly grouped together. Read this next sentence out loud:

▶ The boxer exhausted and pounded on wearily left the ring.

So. Did you start off expecting to read about the boxer's opponent who was getting "exhausted and pounded on"? Did you have to go back and start over? Bet you did. Well-placed commas would have immediately pointed us all in the right direction—like this:

▶ The boxer, exhausted and pounded on, wearily left the ring.

There are a lot of ways to err with commas. You might omit one that's necessary or place one where it doesn't belong. Even professional writers sometimes have trouble deciding where (and where not) to put a comma, and it's not always a big deal. This chapter won't make you a comma superstar, but it will show you how to edit your work for two of the comma problems that matter most to instructors and other readers: the commas that set off introductory information and the commas that distinguish between essential and nonessential information.

E-5a Introductory Information

English sentences generally begin with a SUBJECT. Without ever really thinking about it, those of us who read and write in English have an expectation that the first thing we read in a sentence will be its subject. Often, however (like right now), we begin a sentence in a different way. In academic writing especially, we might vary the structure of our sentences just to make our writing interesting. One way we vary our sentences is by starting some of them with introductory words, phrases, or even clauses. And usually we use a comma to set off those introductory words. That comma signals to readers that they haven't gotten to the subject yet; what they are seeing is additional information that is important enough to go first. For example:

▶ In Georgia, Lee's book jumped quickly to the top of the best-seller list.

Without the comma, readers might think the author's name was Georgia Lee, and they would get very lost in the sentence. Introductory words don't always cause so much confusion; in fact, some authors omit the comma if the introductory element is very short (one, two, or three words). Still, adding the comma after the introductory information is never wrong and demonstrates the care you take with your work.

Checking for commas after introductory information

▶ Initially the council proposed five miles of new bike paths; they later revised the proposal.

To check for introductory information, you should first identify the VERB—in this case, *proposed*. OK, now what's the subject? (In other words, who or what *proposed?*) The subject here is *the council*. Everything that goes before the subject is introductory information, so the comma goes between that information and the subject.

▶ Initially, the council proposed five miles of new bike paths; they later revised the proposal.

In the example above, the introductory element is only one word, and the comma could have been omitted, but its presence adds a little extra emphasis to the word *initially*, and in fact, that emphasis is probably why the author chose to put that word at the beginning, before the subject. The comma definitely helps. And sometimes, introductory elements can cause confusion:

▶ Tired and discouraged by the unsuccessful search for the fugitive Sgt. Drexler the detective and her squad returned to headquarters.

In this example, the introductory information is much longer, and without an appropriate comma, readers have no way of knowing if Sgt. Drexler is the name of the fugitive, the name of the detective, or someone else entirely. Let's imagine that Drexler is the fugitive. With one well-placed comma, the sentence is now perfectly clear.

▶ Tired and discouraged by the unsuccessful search for the fugitive Sgt. Drexler, the detective and her squad returned to headquarters.

Editing for commas after introductory information

Let's take a look at a few examples to see how we can figure out where to put commas with introductory elements. The following sentence needs a comma; where should it go?

▶ For the first three scoreless innings Clark struggled to stay awake.

How do you know where to put the comma? Let's follow the steps described in this chapter. First, identify the verb: *struggled*. Next, identify the subject—in other words, who or what struggled? The subject here is *Clark*, and everything that precedes it is introductory information.

▶ For the first three scoreless innings, Clark struggled to stay awake.

Here is one more example. Follow the same procedure to determine where to put the comma.

▶ In the chaotic final episode of season 2 the shocking plot twists left viewers breathless.

In this example, the comma should go after 2; the verb in the sentence is *left*, and the **COMPLETE SUBJECT** is *the shocking plot twists*. Everything that goes before the subject is introductory information, so the comma falls between that information and the subject:

▶ In the chaotic final episode of season 2, the shocking plot twists left
  viewers breathless.

> Edit

Try editing the following sentence by inserting a comma after the introductory information. Remember the technique: first, find the verb; second, find the subject. The comma goes before the subject because everything that precedes it is introductory information.

> Behind the parade marshal and the color guard the sponsors' convertible carrying the Founders' Day Queen will proceed along Cunningham Street.

≫ **SEE P-1b** for more on how to edit for commas after introductory information. Go to **digital.wwnorton.com/littleseagull3** for additional practice.

E-5b Essential and Nonessential Information

What do we mean by **ESSENTIAL** and **NONESSENTIAL** information? The simplest way to explain the difference is with examples.

▶ My sister Jamilah graduates on Saturday.

If the writer has more than one sister, the name *Jamilah* tells us which one; that's important to know because we don't want to congratulate the wrong sister. Therefore, her name is essential information. When the information is essential, it should not be set off with commas. But if the writer has only one sister, writing her name there is simply extra information; it's not essential. When the information is nonessential, we set it off with commas:

▶ My sister, Jamilah, graduates on Saturday.

Checking for essential and nonessential information

To check your work for these kinds of commas, read over what you've written and identify the **NOUNS**. When a noun—*stadium, achievement, amino acids,* whatever—is followed immediately by additional information about it, ask yourself if the information is essential: does it tell you which stadium, which achievement, which amino acids? If so, it shouldn't be set off with commas. If, however, the information is nonessential, and the sentence would still be fine without that information, it should be set off with a pair of commas. Let's examine two examples:

▶ The neighbors, who complained about parking, called a meeting to discuss the problem.

▶ The neighbors who complained about parking called a meeting to discuss the problem.

In these examples, the noun *neighbors* is followed by additional information. Which sentence talks about a situation where all of the neighbors complained? Which one describes a situation where only some of them did? Remember that the commas set off information that is extra and not essential. In the first sentence, the commas indicate that the information *who complained about parking* is extra, nonessential; it doesn't tell us which neighbors, so we can safely conclude that all of the neighbors complained. In the second sentence, the absence of commas lets us know that the information is essential; the clause *who complained about parking* tells us which neighbors called the meeting—only the ones who complained.

Editing commas with essential and nonessential information

Here is an example to practice with:

▶ Vitamins, such as B and C, are water-soluble and easily absorbed by the body; excess amounts are eliminated in the urine.

In order to edit the example, you will need to know if the phrase *such as B and C* is essential or if it's only additional information. In order to save you from looking it up, here it is: not all vitamins are water-soluble; some are fat-soluble and are stored in the body rather than quickly eliminated. Now, is the phrase *such as B and C* essential

information? And if it is, should this sentence have commas? Here
is the edited version:

▶ Vitamins⁄ such as B and C⁄ are water-soluble and easily absorbed by
the body; excess amounts are eliminated in the urine.

> Edit

The two sentences below are nearly identical; the difference is that
one has essential information about its subject, while the other one's
subject has extra information. Put commas in the appropriate places.

> Bette Midler who will perform in the opening act will do her sound
> check at 5:30.

> The backup singers who will perform in the opening act will do their
> sound check at 5:30.

SEE P-1d for more on how to edit for commas with essential and
nonessential information. Go to **digital.wwnorton.com
/littleseagull3** for additional practice.

E-6   Editing Words
That Are Often Confused

English has more than a million words, and any one of them could
be used appropriately—or inappropriately—in a variety of ways, so
no book could possibly help you edit all of the "wrong words" that
might turn up in your writing. A few basic strategies, however, can
help you with many of those problems. Chapter **L-4** lists some of
the words that are often confused, and this chapter offers tips for
identifying a few of those in your own work—and then editing as
need be. Although there are countless ways to get a word wrong,
many such problems can be traced back to two causes: words that

sound like other words (homophones) and apostrophes (which don't have any sound at all). Here's an example:

▶ Joe should of told them to buy there TV there because its cheaper and its screen is bigger.

Read that sentence out loud and it sounds exactly as the writer intended it; the meaning is perfectly clear. But your writing can't just "sound" right—it has to look right, too. In other words, the written words have to be correct. There are three wrong words in that sentence: *of*, *there*, and *its*. Let's look at each one.

Of/Have

The useful little word *of*, which is a **PREPOSITION**, sounds a lot like another very useful and common word, the verb *have*, especially in rapid or casual speech. The two are often confused when *have* is used as a **HELPING VERB** with the **MODALS** *can, could, may, might, must, should, will*, or *would*—especially in contractions, such as *could've* or *should've*. How do you know if the appropriate word is *of* or *have*? Try reframing your sentence as a question. That should tell you right away which one is the right choice.

▶ Should Joe of told them?

▶ Should Joe have told them?

You can probably tell right away that *have* is the better choice. When you're editing, develop the habit of noticing whenever you use a modal, and make sure the words that follow it are appropriate. *Have* can be written out in its full form or combined with the preceding word to form a contraction—*should've, would've*. Try it without the modal. *Have you told them?* That's good. *Of you told them?* Not so good. That's because *have* is a helping verb, and *of* is not.

There/Their/They're

There is a common and useful word that sounds exactly like another common word, *their*, and those two sound the same as a third common word, *they're*, the contracted form of *they are*. So not only do we have three homophones, but each of the three words is used very frequently in both speech and writing. That leads to a large number of wrong word problems. For example:

▶ For security screening, passengers must put all cell phones in the trays, and now *there* required to put *there* shoes *there*, too.

You'll notice three instances of *there* in the example, and two of them are "wrong words." The sentence should have one each of *they're*, *their*, and *there*, so let's take a closer look at each use of *there*.

THEY'RE Let's start with the first one. That part of the sentence is trying to say that the passengers—*they*—are required to do something, so the appropriate word would be the contraction of *they are*: *they're*. The word *they're* has only that one meaning, so using it is very simple. Just see if you can substitute "they are" for the word in question and still have the meaning you intended. If not, you'll need to make a change.

THEIR Now let's look at the second instance of *there*: *there shoes*. That part of the sentence is talking about the shoes that belong to the passengers, so the appropriate word would be a possessive: *their*. The word *their* has only that one uncomplicated meaning—it always indicates possession, as in the following examples:

▶ *Their* feet were swollen and *their* toes were numb, but the hikers were determined to reach Vogelsang before dark.

▶ The birds are squawking because the wind blew *their* nest down.

▶ Both of the radios still work, but *their* clocks are wrong.

When you're trying to decide if *their* is the right word, try asking if the word you are using is intended to show possession. In the examples above, *their* is correct because it indicates possession: Whose feet and toes? *Their* (the hikers') feet and toes. Whose nest? *Their* (the birds') nest. Whose clocks? *Their* (the radios') clocks.

THERE That leaves us with the final instance of *there* in our example sentence. That *there* is correct. Most of the time, as in our example, *there* simply indicates a place, telling *where* something is: Where's my phone? It's *there*, on the table. Sometimes, though, *there* is used as an **EXPLETIVE**, introducing information that's provided later in the sentence. For example:

▶ Whenever *there* was a big snowstorm, the neighbors all helped clear the street.

▶ *There* are three candidates in the race, but only one has the right experience.

That meaning of *there* simply indicates the existence of something—*a big snowstorm, three candidates*. Here's an example that uses both meanings:

▶ *There* is a coatrack behind the door; you can hang your jacket *there*.

To check whether *there* is the appropriate word, ask whether the word indicates either the existence of something or a place. If the word indicates either of those two things, *there* is the correct choice.

When editing your own work, check each instance of *there*, *their*, and *they're* to make sure that you've written the one you really mean. That may sound tedious, but here's a handy shortcut: use the Find function in your word processing program to search for each instance of *there*, *their*, and *they're*. That way, you won't miss any. Do your search one term at a time, in whatever order makes the most sense to you.

Now let's revise our original example sentence. Try it yourself before you look at the edited version below.

▶ For security screening, passengers must put all cell phones in the trays, and now ~~there~~ they're required to put ~~there~~ their shoes there, too.

It's / Its

How do you pronounce an apostrophe? You don't: apostrophes have no sound. So when there are two different words with only an apostrophe to distinguish them, they're going to sound alike. *It's* and *its* make for many "wrong word" problems. Although they're pronounced exactly the same, they really are two distinct words with distinct uses: *its* is the possessive form of *it*, and *it's* is a contraction of *it is*. That difference makes it easy to know which one is appropriate for your sentence. Let's look at one problematic sentence:

▶ When my phone fell, *its* screen shattered, but luckily, *its* still working.

There are two instances of its in the sentence, but one of them should really be it's. How can you tell which is which? Just check to see which one can be replaced by it *is*. Easy, right? The second one—it is still working. The one without the apostrophe, *its*, is the possessive form of *it*: the screen that belongs to it (the phone). So here's how you'd edit this sentence:

▶ When my phone fell, its screen shattered, but luckily, ~~its~~ still working.
                                                          it's
                                                           ^

Wait. Haven't you been told to use an apostrophe to indicate possessives, as in *the priest's robe, the frog's sticky tongue*? So how can it be that the version *without* the apostrophe is the possessive one? Isn't that confusing? Well, no. It is a **PRONOUN**, along with *he, I, she*, and *you*, for example. What are the possessive forms of those pronouns? *His. My. Her. Your.* Do you notice that those possessives don't have an apostrophe? Neither does *its*.

▶ Carmen used *her* binoculars to watch a hawk open *its* wings and glide on the wind.

If you know or suspect that you have problems confusing it's and its in your work, you can check for them using the Find function of your word processor. Search your text for each of the two words, and make sure that the possessive its has no apostrophe and that the contracted form of it is always appears as it's.

> Edit

Return now to the first problem sentence at the top of page 310, and try editing it using all of the techniques discussed above:

> Joe should of told them to buy there TV there because its cheaper and its screen is bigger.

» **SEE L-4** for more advice and examples on how to identify and edit wrong words. Go to **digital.wwnorton.com/littleseagull3** for additional practice.

S-1   Elements of a Sentence

In casual situations, we often use a kind of shorthand, because we know our audience will fill in the gaps. When we say "Coffee?" to a dinner guest, he knows we mean, "Would you like some coffee?" When we text "7 @ Starbucks?" to a friend, she'll understand that we're asking, "Should we meet at 7:00 at Starbucks?" In more formal writing or speaking situations, though, our audience may not share the same context; to be sure we're understood, we usually need to present our ideas in complete sentences. This chapter reviews the parts of a sentence.

S-1a Subjects and Predicates

A sentence contains a subject and a predicate. The subject, which usually includes a **NOUN** or **PRONOUN**, names the topic of the sentence; the predicate, which always includes a **VERB**, says what the subject is or does.

▶ Birds fly.

▶ Birds are feathered vertebrates.

Sometimes the subject and the predicate contain only one word. Usually, however, both contain more than one word.

▶ Birds of many kinds fly south in the fall.

▶ Flying in a V formation is characteristic of geese.

▶ One of the flock leads the others.

A sentence may contain more than one subject or verb.

▶ Birds and butterflies fly south in the fall.

314

► Birds fly south in the fall and return north in the spring.

At times, the subject comes after the verb.

► Here comes the sun.

► In the attic were old photographs and toys.

Expressing subjects explicitly

English requires an explicit subject in every CLAUSE, even if all of the clauses in a sentence are about the same subject.

► Although the dinner cost too much, ^it^ impressed my guests.

The only exception is commands, in which the subject is understood to be *you*.

► Eat smaller portions at each meal.

In informal conversation, speakers sometimes emphasize a noun subject by repeating it as a pronoun: *My friend Jing she changed her name to Jane.* In academic writing, though, don't repeat a subject this way.

► The visiting students ~~they~~ were detained at the airport.

Sentences beginning with *there* or *it*. In some cases where the subject comes after the verb, an EXPLETIVE—*there* or *it*—is required before the verb.

► ^There is^ ~~Is~~ no place like home.

► ^It is^ ~~Is~~ both instructive and rewarding to work with young children.

You can often rephrase the sentence to avoid using the expletive.

► ^Working with young children^ ~~It~~ is both instructive and rewarding. ~~to work with young children.~~

S-1b Clauses

A clause is a group of words containing a subject and a predicate. An independent clause can function alone as a sentence: *Birds fly*. A subordinate clause begins with a **SUBORDINATING WORD** such as *because, as,* or *which* and cannot stand alone as a sentence: *because birds fly*. (See p. 318 for a list of common subordinating words.)

```
┌─ INDEPENDENT CLAUSE ─┐ ┌──────── SUBORDINATE CLAUSE ────────┐
```
▶ My yard is now quiet because most of the birds flew south.

```
┌────────SUBORDINATE CLAUSE────────┐ ┌──────── INDEPENDENT CLAUSE ───────┐
```
▶ Although they travel really far, the birds always find their way back.

S-1c Phrases

A phrase is a word group that makes sense but lacks a subject, a verb, or both and thus cannot stand alone as a sentence. Some common ones are prepositional, appositive, participial, gerund, and infinitive phrases.

A prepositional phrase starts with a **PREPOSITION** such as *at, from, of,* or *in* and usually ends with a noun or pronoun: *at school, from home, in bed*. It usually functions as an adjective or adverb.

▶ The day *after the World Series* everyone *in San Francisco* celebrated.

An appositive phrase follows and gives additional information about a noun or pronoun. It functions as a noun.

▶ We all know that computers and their spawn, *the smartphone and cellphone,* have created a very different world from several decades ago.
                                                        —Alina Tugend,
                          "Multitasking Can Make You Lose . . . Um . . . Focus"

A participial phrase contains the **PRESENT PARTICIPLE** or **PAST PARTICIPLE** of a verb plus any **OBJECTS**, **MODIFIERS**, and **COMPLEMENTS**. It functions as an adjective.

▶ *Brimming with optimism,* I headed over to the neighborhood watering hole and waited.   —Hal Niedzviecki, "Facebook in a Crowd"

▶ A study from Princeton *issued at the same times as the Duke study* showed that women in the sciences reported less satisfaction in their jobs and less of a sense of belonging than their male counterparts.

—Anna Quindlen, "Still Needing the F Word"

A gerund phrase includes the -ing form of a verb plus any objects, modifiers, and complements. It functions as a noun.

▶ *Asking for candy on Halloween* was called trick-or-treating, but *asking for candy on November first* was called begging.

—David Sedaris, "Us and Them"

An infinitive phrase includes an infinitive (*to* plus the base form of a verb: *to read, to write*) and any objects, modifiers, and complements. It functions as a noun, an adjective, or an adverb.

▶ The plan *to commit more troops* requires top-level approval.

▶ The point of ribbon decals is *to signal that we support our troops*.

S-2   Sentence Fragments

Sentence fragments often show up in advertising: "Got milk?" "Good to the last drop." "Not bad for something that tastes good too." We use them in informal speech and text messages as well. In other kinds of writing, though, some readers consider fragments too informal, and in many academic writing situations, it's better to avoid them altogether. This chapter helps you identify and edit out fragments.

S-2a Identifying Fragments

A sentence fragment is a group of words that is capitalized and punctuated as a sentence but is not a sentence. A sentence needs at least one INDEPENDENT CLAUSE, which contains a SUBJECT and a VERB and does not start with a SUBORDINATING WORD.

NO SUBJECT	The catcher batted fifth. Fouled out, ending the inning. *Who fouled out?*
NO VERB	The first two batters walked. Manny Ramirez again. *What did Ramirez do again?*
SUBORDINATING WORD	Although the Yankees loaded the bases. *There is a subject (Yankees) and a verb (loaded), but although is a subordinating word. What happened after the Yankees loaded the bases?*

SOME SUBORDINATING WORDS

after	because	so that	until	while
although	before	that	when	who
as	if	though	where	which
as if	since	unless	whether	why

S-2b Editing Fragments

Since some readers regard fragments as errors, it's generally better to write complete sentences. Here are four ways to make fragments into sentences.

Add a subject

▶ The catcher batted fifth. ~~Fouled out,~~ He fouled out, ending the inning.

Add a verb

▶ The first two batters walked. Manny Ramirez *walked* again.

Sometimes, a fragment contains a verb form, such as a present participle or past participle, that cannot function as the main verb of a sentence. In these cases, you can either substitute an appropriate verb form or add a **HELPING VERB**.

▶ As the game went on, the fans started to lose interest. The pitcher's arm ~~weakening,~~ *weakened,* and the fielders ~~making~~ *made* a number of errors.

▶ The media influence the election process. Political commercials $\overset{are}{\wedge}$ appearing on television more frequently than in years past.

Remove the subordinating word

▶ I'm thinking about moving to a large city. ~~Because~~ I dislike the lack of privacy in my country town of three thousand residents.

Attach the fragment to a nearby sentence

▶ Some candidates spread nasty stories/ $\overset{about}{\wedge}$ ~~About~~ their opponents.

▶ These negative stories can deal with many topics/, $\overset{such}{\wedge}$ ~~Such~~ as marital infidelity, sources of campaign funds, and drug use.

▶ Put off by negative campaigning/, $\overset{some}{\wedge}$ ~~Some~~ people decide not to vote at all.

Note that using a semicolon to attach a fragment to a nearby sentence isn't a good solution. See **P–2** for tips on using semicolons.

S-2c Intentional Fragments

Writers sometimes use fragments intentionally.

FOR EMPHASIS   Throughout my elementary and middle school years, I was a strong student, always on the honor roll. I never had a GPA below 3.0. I was smart, and I knew it. *That is, until I got the results of the proficiency test.*
—Shannon Nichols, " 'Proficiency' "

TO BE INFORMAL   The SAT writing test predicts how successful a student will be in college. *Since when?*

TO LIST SEVERAL EXAMPLES   The small details stand out. *The bathrooms with green stalls and mirrors with painted Ducks slugging conference foes. The extra-large furniture tested to withstand 500 pounds. The elevators decorated with famous plays in Oregon football history, the actual plays, drawn up in Xs and Os by a coach. The room for professional scouts to watch footage of Oregon players. The ticker running sports scores.*
—Greg Bishop, "We Are the University of Nike."

Though fragments are common in informal contexts, they are often considered errors in academic writing.

S-3   Comma Splices, Fused Sentences

You'll sometimes see a comma splice in ads or literary works: "He dropped the bucket, the paint spilled on his feet." Or the comma may be omitted, forming a fused sentence: "He dropped the bucket the paint spilled on his feet." A comma splice or a fused sentence is generally regarded as an error in academic writing. This chapter shows how to recognize comma splices and fused sentences and edit them out of your writing.

S-3a Identifying Comma Splices and Fused Sentences

A comma splice occurs when two or more **INDEPENDENT CLAUSES** follow one another with only a comma between them.

COMMA   T. S. Eliot is best known for his poetry, he also wrote
SPLICE   several plays.

A fused sentence occurs when two or more independent clauses follow one another with no punctuation in between.

FUSED   The school board debated the issue for three days they
SENTENCE   were unable to reach an agreement.

S-3b Editing Comma Splices and Fused Sentences

There are several ways to edit out comma splices and fused sentences.

Make the clauses two sentences

▶ T. S. Eliot is best known for his poetry/. ^He^ also wrote several plays.

Use a comma and a COORDINATING CONJUNCTION

▶ The school board debated the issue for three days, ^but^ they were unable to reach an agreement.

Use a semicolon

If the relationship between the two clauses is clear without a coordinating conjunction, you can simply join them with a semicolon.

▶ Psychologists study individuals' behavior/; sociologists focus on group-level dynamics.

When clauses are linked by a **TRANSITION** such as *therefore* or *as a result*, the transition needs to be preceded by a semicolon and should generally be followed by a comma.

▶ The hill towns experienced heavy spring and summer rain/; therefore, the fall foliage fell far short of expectations.

Recast one clause as a subordinate clause

Add a **SUBORDINATING WORD** to clarify the relationship between the two clauses.

▶ ~~Initial~~ ^Although initial^ critical responses to *The Waste Land* were mixed, the poem has been extensively anthologized, read, and written about.

S-3c Intentional Comma Splices

Writers sometimes use only a comma between clauses that are very brief or closely parallel in structure, as in proverbs like *Marry in haste, repent at leisure*. In academic writing, though, such sentences may be seen as mistakes.

S-4 Verbs

Verbs are the engines of sentences, giving energy, action, and life to writing. "I Googled it" is much more vivid than "I found it on the Internet"—and the difference is the verb. Sometimes, however, our use of verbs can obscure our meaning, as when a politician avoids taking responsibility by saying, "Mistakes were made." Our choice of verbs shapes our writing in important ways, and this chapter reviews ways of using verbs appropriately and effectively.

S-4a Verb Tenses

To express time, English verbs have three simple tenses—present, past, and future. In addition, each of these verb tenses has perfect and progressive forms that indicate more complex time frames. The present perfect, for example, can be used to indicate an action that began in the past but is continuing into the present. The lists that follow show each of these tenses for the regular verb *talk* and the irregular verb *write*.

Simple tenses

PRESENT	PAST	FUTURE
I talk	I talked	I will talk
I write	I wrote	I will write

Use the simple present to indicate actions that take place in the present or that occur habitually. Use the simple past to indicate actions that were completed in the past. Use the simple future to indicate actions that will take place in the future.

▶ Most wealthy industrialized countries *operate* national health-insurance systems.

▶ In 2010, Congress *approved* the Affordable Care Act.

▶ Prohibiting English *will do* for the language what Prohibition *did* for liquor.   —Dennis Baron, "Don't Make English Official—Ban It Instead"

Use the present tense to express a scientific fact or a general truth even when the rest of the sentence is in the past tense.

▶ The security study showed that taxis and planes are the top places

where people l̶o̶s̶t̶ *lose* their phones.

In general, use the present tense to write about literature.

▶ In the first book of the series, Rowling *introduces* us to eleven-year-old Harry Potter; in the seventh and final volume, Harry *enters* full adulthood.

In **APA** style, use the past tense or the present perfect to report results of an experiment and the present tense to give your own insights into or conclusions about the results.

▶ The bulk of the data collected in this study *validated* the research of Neal Miller; the subjects *appeared* to undergo operant conditioning of their smooth muscles in order to relax their frontalis muscles and increase their skin temperatures. Subjects 3 and 6 each *failed* to do this in one session; subject 7 *failed* to do this several times. This finding *is* difficult to explain precisely.
　　　　　　　—Sarah Thomas, "The Effect of Biofeedback Training on Muscle Tension and Skin Temperature"

Perfect tenses

PRESENT PERFECT	PAST PERFECT	FUTURE PERFECT
I have talked	I had talked	I will have talked
I have written	I had written	I will have written

Use the present perfect to indicate actions that took place at unspecified times in the past or that began in the past and continue into the present (or have relevance in the present).

▶ Many teachers and parents *have resisted* the increasing pressure for more standardized testing of students.

Use the past perfect for an action that was completed before another past action began.

▶ By the time I was born, the Gulf War already end̶e̶d̶ *had* ended.
　The war ended before the writer was born.

Use the future perfect to indicate actions that will be completed at a specific time in the future.

► By this time next year, you *will have graduated*.

Progressive tenses

PRESENT PROGRESSIVE	PAST PROGRESSIVE	FUTURE PROGRESSIVE
I am talking	I was talking	I will be talking
I am writing	I was writing	I will be writing

PRESENT PERFECT PROGRESSIVE	PAST PERFECT PROGRESSIVE	FUTURE PERFECT PROGRESSIVE
I have been talking	I had been talking	I will have been talking
I have been writing	I had been writing	I will have been writing

Use progressive tenses to indicate continuing action.

► The Heat *are having* a great year, but the Spurs *are leading* the league.

► We *were watching* TV when the doorbell rang.

► During the World Cup, soccer fans around the world *will be watching* on TV or online.

► Willie joined the Grace Church Boy Choir when he was ten, and he *has been singing* ever since.

S-4b Verb Forms

There are four forms of a verb: the base form, the past, the past participle, and the present participle. Samples of each appear in the lists below. All of the various tenses are generated with these four forms.

The past tense and past participle of all regular verbs are formed by adding *-ed* or *-d* to the base form (*talked, lived*). Irregular verbs are not as predictable; see the list of some common ones below. The present participle consists of the base form plus *-ing* (*talking, living*).

BASE FORM   On Thursdays, we *visit* a museum.

PAST TENSE   Last week, we *visited* the Museum of Modern Art.

PAST PARTICIPLE	I have also *visited* the Metropolitan Museum, but I've not yet *been* to the Cloisters.
PRESENT PARTICIPLE	We will be *visiting* the Cooper-Hewitt Museum tomorrow to see the cutlery exhibit.

Some common irregular verbs

BASE FORM	PAST TENSE	PAST PARTICIPLE	PRESENT PARTICIPLE
be	was/were	been	being
bring	brought	brought	bringing
choose	chose	chosen	choosing
come	came	come	coming
do	did	done	doing
eat	ate	eaten	eating
find	found	found	finding
fly	flew	flown	flying
give	gave	given	giving
go	went	gone	going
hang (suspend)	hung	hung	hanging
have	had	had	having
know	knew	known	knowing
make	made	made	making
prove	proved	proved, proven	proving
rise	rose	risen	rising
set	set	set	setting
sit	sat	sat	sitting
teach	taught	taught	teaching
write	wrote	written	writing

It's easy to get confused about when to use the past tense and when to use a past participle. One simple guideline is to use the past tense if there is no helping verb and to use a past participle if there is one.

▶ For vacation last summer, my family ~~gone~~ went to the Outer Banks.

▶ After a week at the beach, we had ~~ate~~ eaten a lot of seafood.

Gerunds and infinitives

A gerund is a verb form ending in -ing that functions as a noun: *hopping*, *skipping*, *jumping*.

▶ Although many people like *driving*, some prefer *walking*.

An infinitive is a verb form made up of *to* plus the base form of a verb: *to hop, to skip, to jump*.

▶ Although many people like *to drive*, some prefer *to walk*.

In general, use infinitives to express intentions or desires, and use gerunds to express plain facts.

▶ I planned *to learn* Spanish, Japanese, and Arabic.

▶ I also wanted ~~studying~~ to study Russian.

▶ Unfortunately, I ended up *studying* only Spanish and Arabic—and *speaking* only Spanish.

▶ Just in time for Thanksgiving, the painters finished ~~to put~~ putting up the wallpaper.

Some verbs—*begin, continue, like, prefer*, and a few others—can be followed by either a gerund or an infinitive with little if any difference in meaning. But with several verbs—*forget, remember, stop*, and a few others—the choice of an infinitive or a gerund changes the meaning.

▶ I stopped *to eat* lunch.

In other words, I took a break so that I could eat lunch.

▶ I stopped *eating* lunch.

In other words, I no longer ate lunch.

Always use a gerund after a PREPOSITION.

▶ The water is too cold for ~~to swim.~~ swimming.

S-4c Helping Verbs

Do, have, be, and MODALS such as *can* and *may* all function as helping verbs that are used with MAIN VERBS to form certain TENSES and MOODS. *Do, have,* and *be* change form to indicate different tenses; modals do not.

FORMS OF *DO*	do, does, did
FORMS OF *HAVE*	have, has, had
FORMS OF *BE*	be, am, is, are, was, were, been
MODALS	can, could, may, might, must, shall, should, will, would, ought to

Do, does, and *did* require the base form of the main verb.

▶ That professor *did take* class participation into account when calculating grades.

▶ Sometimes even the smartest students *do* not *like* to answer questions out loud in class.

Have, has, and *had* require the past participle of the main verb.

▶ I *have applied* for insurance through one of the new exchanges.

▶ When all of the visitors *had gone*, the security guards locked the building for the night.

Forms of *be* are used with a present participle to express a continuing action or with a past participle to express the PASSIVE VOICE.

CONTINUING ACTION

▶ The university *is considering* a change in its policy on cell phone use.

▶ I *was studying* my notes from last week as I walked to class.

PASSIVE VOICE

▶ Six classes per semester *is considered* a heavy course load.

▶ Ancient Greek *was studied* by many university students in the early twentieth century, but it is not a popular major today.

Modals

Can, could, may, might, must, ought to, shall, should, will, and *would:* these are modals, a kind of helping verb used with the base form of a MAIN VERB to express whether an action is likely, possible, permitted, or various other conditions. Modals don't take the third-person –s or the –ed or –ing endings that ordinary verbs do.

Likelihood *will, could, ought to, may, might*

▶ The Spurs *will* win tomorrow. [*very certain*]

▶ The Lakers *could* defeat the Heat. [*somewhat certain*]

▶ It *ought to* be a very close series between the Warriors and the Cavaliers. [*moderately certain*]

▶ The Rockets *may* win their game tonight. [*less certain*]

▶ The Knicks *might* make the playoffs someday. [*much less certain*]

Assumption *must*

▶ The dog just started barking; he *must* hear our guests arriving.

Expectation *should, ought to*

▶ Two large onions *should* be enough for this recipe.

▶ The potatoes *ought to* be ready in twenty minutes.

Ability *can, could*

▶ Mick Jagger *can* still put on quite a performance, but years ago he *could* sing and throw himself around the stage more dramatically. How much longer *will* he *be able to* keep rocking?

Necessity or obligation *must, should, ought to*

▶ Travelers *must* have a passport for foreign travel.

▶ We *should* leave early tomorrow because of the holiday traffic.

▶ You *ought to* get to the airport at least two hours before your scheduled departure.

Permission and requests *may, can, could, would, will*

▶ People traveling with small children *may* board the plane first.

▶ The hotel's check-in time is 4:00 PM, but travelers *can* often check in earlier.

▶ *Would* someone help me put my suitcase in the overhead rack?

▶ *Will* you please turn off your phone?

Advice *should, ought to*

▶ You *should* never text while driving.

▶ You *ought to* be careful about using wi-fi networks in public places.

Intention *will, shall*

▶ Marianna *will* bring an apple pie for Thanksgiving dinner.

▶ We *shall* overcome.

S-4d Active and Passive Voice

Verbs can sometimes be active or passive. In the active voice, the subject performs the action of the verb (*Becky solved the problem*). In the passive voice, the subject receives the action (*the problem was solved by Becky*).

ACTIVE   One year ago, almost to the day, I *asked* my hairdresser to cut off 16 inches of my hair.
                                    —Suleika Jaouad, "Finding My Cancer Style"

PASSIVE   As a teenager I *was instructed* on how to behave as a proper señorita.   —Judith Ortiz Cofer, "The Myth of the Latin Woman"

Active verbs tend to be more direct and easier to understand, but the passive voice can be useful when you specifically want to emphasize the recipient of the action.

▶ In a sense, little girls *are urged* to please adults with a kind of coquettishness, while boys *are enjoined* to behave like monkeys toward each other.   —Paul Theroux, "Being a Man"

The passive voice is also appropriate in scientific writing when you want to emphasize the research itself, not the researchers.

▶ The treatment order was random for each subject, and it *was reversed* for his or her second treatment.
—Sarah Thomas, "The Effect of Biofeedback Training on Muscle Tension and Skin Temperature"

S-4e Mood

English verbs have three moods: indicative, imperative, and subjunctive. The indicative is used to state facts, opinions, or questions.

▶ Habitat for Humanity *has built* twelve houses in the region this year.

▶ What other volunteer opportunities *does* Habitat *offer*?

The imperative is used to give commands or directions.

▶ *Sit* up straight, and *do* your work.

The subjunctive is used to indicate unlikely or hypothetical conditions or to express wishes, requests, or requirements.

▶ We would be happier if we *had* less pressure at work.

▶ My mother wishes my brother *were* more responsible with his money.

▶ Most colleges require that each applicant *write* an essay.

The subjunctive has two types—one that is the same form as the past tense and one that is the same as the base form.

Conditional sentences

The subjunctive is used most often in conditional sentences, ones that include a clause beginning with *if* or another word that states a condition. Use the indicative in the *if* clause to show that you are confident the condition is posssible; use the subjunctive to show that it's doubtful or impossible.

If it's a fact or a possibility. When there's no doubt that the condition in the *if* clause is true or possible, use the indicative in both clauses.

▶ If an earthquake *strikes* that region, forecasters *expect* a tsunami.

▶ A century ago, if a hurricane *struck*, residents *had* very little warning.

▶ If you *follow* that diet for two weeks, you *will lose* about ten pounds.

If it's unlikely, impossible, or hypothetical. When the condition in the *if* clause is not likely or possible, use the subjunctive (same as the past form) in the *if* clause and *would* (or *could* or *might*) + the base form of a verb in the other clause. For *be*, use *were* in the *if* clause, not *was*.

▶ If I *won* the lottery, I *could pay off* my student loans.

▶ If Martin Luther King Jr. *were* alive, he *would acknowledge* progress in race relations, but he *would* also *ask* significant questions.

Because the subjunctive can sound rather formal, it's often not used in informal contexts. In formal and most academic writing, however, it's best to do so.

INFORMAL   I *wish* I *was* in Paris.

ACADEMIC   In *The Three Sisters,* Masha *wishes* she *were living* in Moscow.

When the *if* clause is about an event in the past that never happened, use the past perfect in the *if* clause and *would have* (or *could have* or *might have*) + a past participle in the other clause.

▶ If the police officer *had separated* the witnesses, their evidence *would have been* admissible in court.

Requests, recommendations, and demands

In *that* clauses following verbs such as *ask*, *insist*, or *suggest*, use the subjunctive to express a request, a recommendation, or a demand. Use the base form of the verb in the *that* clause.

▶ I recommended that Hannah *study* French as an undergraduate.

▶ The CEO will insist that you *be* at your desk before nine each morning.

S-4f Phrasal Verbs

Act up. Back down. Carry on. These are all phrasal verbs, composed of more than one word—usually a verb and a preposition. You know what *act* means. You know what *up* means. If English is not your primary language, however, you may need to check a dictionary to find out that *act up* means to "misbehave" (or to say that using another phrasal verb, you may need to *look it up*). With phrasal verbs, knowing the meaning of each part does not always help you to know what the phrasal verb itself means.

Phrasal verbs can be divided into two categories, separable and inseparable. With separable verbs, the parts can be separated by an OBJECT; with inseparable ones, the parts can never be separated.

SEPARABLE   I used to *look up* words in a dictionary; now I *look* them *up* on my phone.

INSEPARABLE   Jim and his family are *caring for* his elderly mother.

With separable phrasal verbs, you have a choice: you can put the object between the parts, or after the complete phrasal verb.

▶ With a hurricane forming nearby, NASA *called off* tomorrow's lunar launch.

▶ Darn! They *called* the launch *off?*

When the object is a long phrase, however, it almost always follows the complete verb.

▶ NASA engineers called ^off^ the launch of the lunar mission scheduled for tomorrow ~~off~~.

The personal pronouns *me, you, him, her, it, us,* and *them* are almost always placed between the parts.

▶ The launch was scheduled for yesterday, but NASA called off ^it^ ~~it~~ because of the weather.

Some phrasal verbs never take an object—for example, *come over* (meaning to "visit") and *catch on* (meaning to "become popular").

▶ Why don't you *come over* and see us sometime?

▶ Even the developers of *Pinterest* were astonished by how quickly it *caught on.*

With some phrasal verbs, the meaning changes depending on whether or not there is an object. To *look something up,* for instance, means to "find information"; without an object, to *look up* means to "get better."

▶ When in doubt, *look up* phrasal verbs in a dictionary.

▶ The sun's out and the roses are in bloom; things are *looking up!*

Go to **digital.wwnorton.com/littleseagull3** for a glossary of phrasal verbs.

Some common phrasal verbs

SEPARABLE

back up   means to "support": *Dodson's hypothesis is well stated, but the data do not back it up.*

break down   means to "divide into smaller parts": *Their analysis might be clearer if it broke the data down state by state.*

carry out   means to "fulfill" or "complete": *We plan to carry out a survey on what the students in our dorm are reading.*

find out   means to "learn" or "get information": *Some parents decide not to find out the gender before their baby is born because they want to be surprised; others just want to annoy relatives.*

point out   means to "call attention to": *The lizards blend in with the leaves so well that they were hard to see until the guide pointed them out.*

INSEPARABLE

call for   means to "require" or "deserve": *Our current economic situation calls for bold and innovative thinking.*

get over   means to "recover": *Grandma always insisted that the best way to get over a cold was to eat chicken soup.*

look into   means to "investigate": *GAO investigators are looking into allegations of fraud by some college recruiters.*

settle on   means to "decide on" or "choose": *We considered Elizabeth, Margaret, Jane, and many other names for our baby, but finally we settled on Susanna.*

touch on   means to "mention briefly": *The* Wall Street Journal *article focused on productivity and barely touched on issues of worker safety.*

DO NOT TAKE AN OBJECT

come about   means to "happen" or "occur": *How did the dispute come about in the first place?*

get by   means to "survive" or "manage," usually with few resources: *Many retired workers can't get by on just their pensions; they have to find part-time work as well.*

give in   means to "yield" or "agree": *After much discussion, members of the union voted not to give in to management's demands for a reduction in benefits.*

show up   means to "arrive": *Did everyone show up for the rehearsal?*

take off   means to "leave the ground": *The JetBlue flight took off an hour late because of thunderstorms in the Midwest.* It also means to "make great progress": *Sales of* Anna Karenina *took off in 2004, after it was recommended by Oprah Winfrey.*

S-5   Subject-Verb Agreement

Subjects and verbs should agree: if the subject is in the third-person singular, the verb should be in the third-person singular—"Dinner is on the table." Yet sometimes context affects subject-verb agreement, as when we say that "macaroni and cheese *make* a great combination" but that "macaroni and cheese *is* our family's favorite comfort food." This chapter focuses on subject-verb agreement.

S-5a Agreement in Number and Person

Subjects and verbs should agree with each other in number (singular or plural) and person (first, second, or third). To make a present-tense verb agree with a third-person singular subject, add *-s* or *-es* to the base form.

▶ A 1922 *ad* for Resinol soap *urges* women to "make that dream come true" by using Resinol.   —Doug Lantry, "'Stay Sweet as You Are'"

To make a present-tense verb agree with any other subject, simply use the base form without any ending.

▶ *I listen* to NPR every morning while *I brush* my teeth.

▶ *Drunk drivers cause* thousands of preventable deaths each year.

Be and *have* have irregular forms (shown on p. 325) and so do not follow the *-s / -es* rule.

▶ The test of all knowledge *is* experiment.
                —Richard Feynman, "Atoms in Motion"

▶ The scientist *has* a lot of experience with ignorance and doubt and uncertainty, and this experience *is* of great importance.
                —Richard Feynman, "The Value of Science"

In questions, a helping verb is often necessary. The subject, which generally goes between the helping verb and the main verb, should agree with the helping verb.

▶ How long *does an air filter last* on average?

▶ *Have the 10 ml pipettes arrived* yet?

S-5b Subjects and Verbs Separated

A verb should agree with its subject, not with another word that falls in between.

▶ In the backyard, the *leaves* of the apple tree *rattle* across the lawn.

—Gary Soto, "The Guardian Angel"

▶ The *price* of soybeans ~~fluctuate~~ fluctuates according to demand.

S-5c Compound Subjects

Two or more subjects joined by *and* are generally plural.

▶ Swiss cheese and shrimp *are* both high in vitamin B12.

However, if the parts of the subject form a single unit, they take a singular verb.

▶ Forty acres and a mule ~~are~~ is what General William T. Sherman promised each freed slave.

If the subjects are joined by *or* or *nor*, the verb should agree with the closer subject.

▶ Either you or she ~~are~~ is mistaken.

▶ Neither the teacher nor his students ~~was~~ were able to solve the equation.

S-5d Subjects That Follow the Verb

English verbs usually follow their subjects. Be sure the verb agrees with the subject even when the subject follows the verb, such as when the sentence begins with *there is* or *there are*.

▶ There ~~is~~ are too many unresolved problems for the project to begin.

▶ In the middle of the room ~~was~~ a desk and a floor lamp.

(were — inserted above "was")

S-5e Collective Nouns

Collective nouns such as *group, team, audience,* or *family* can take singular or plural verbs, depending on whether the noun refers to the group as a single unit or to the individual members of the group.

▶ The choir ~~sing~~ Handel's *Messiah* every Christmas.

(sings — inserted above "sing")

▶ Gregor's family *keep* reassuring themselves that things will be just fine
again.   —Scott Russell Sanders, "Under the Influence"
The word themselves *shows that* family *refers to its individual members.*

S-5f *Everyone* and Other Indefinite Pronouns

Most **INDEFINITE PRONOUNS**, such as *anyone, anything, each, either, everyone, everything, neither, nobody, no one, one, somebody, someone,* and *something,* take a singular verb, even if they seem plural or refer to plural nouns.

▶ Everyone in our dorm *has* already *signed* the petition.

▶ Each of the candidates ~~agree~~ with the president.

(agrees — inserted above "agree")

Both, few, many, others, and *several* are always plural.

▶ Although there are many great actors working today, few *are* as
versatile as Meryl Streep.

All, any, enough, more, most, none, and *some* are singular when they refer to a singular noun, but they are plural when they refer to a plural noun.

▶ Don't assume that all of the members of a family ~~votes~~ the same way.

(vote — inserted above "votes")

▶ Most of the music we heard last night ~~come~~ from the baroque period.

(comes — inserted above "come")

S-5g *Who, That, Which*

The **RELATIVE PRONOUNS** *who*, *that*, and *which* take a singular verb when they refer to a singular noun and a plural verb when they refer to a plural noun.

▶ In these songs, Lady Gaga draws on a tradition of camp that *extends* from drag queen cabaret to Broadway and disco.
—Jody Rosen, review of *Born This Way*

▶ Scott Karp, who *writes* a blog about online media, recently confessed that he has stopped reading books altogether.
—Nicholas Carr, "Is Google Making Us Stupid?"

One of the is always followed by a plural noun, and when the noun is followed by *who* or *that*, the verb should be plural.

▶ Jaime is one of the speakers who ~~asks~~ ask provocative questions.

Several speakers ask provocative questions. Jaime is one. Who refers to speakers, so the verb is plural.

If the phrase begins with *the only one*, however, the verb should be singular.

▶ Jaime is the only one of the speakers who ~~ask~~ asks provocative questions.

Only one speaker asks provocative questions: Jaime. Who thus refers to one, so the verb is singular.

S-5h Words Such as *News* and *Physics*

Words like *news*, *athletics*, and *physics* seem plural but are usually singular in meaning and take singular verb forms.

▶ The *news* of widespread layoffs *alarms* everyone in the company.

Some of these words, such as *economics*, *mathematics*, *politics*, and *statistics*, have plural meanings in some uses and take plural verbs.

▶ For my roommate, mathematics *is* an endlessly stimulating field.

▶ The complex mathematics involved in this proof *are* beyond the scope of this lecture.

S-5i Titles and Words Used as Words

Titles and words that are discussed as words are singular.

▶ *The Royal Tenenbaums* ~~depict~~ ^{depicts} three talented siblings who are loosely based on characters created by J. D. Salinger.

▶ *Man-caused disasters* ~~are~~ ^{is} a term favored by some political analysts as a substitute for the term *terrorist attacks.*

S-6 Pronouns

We use pronouns to take the place of nouns so that we don't have to write or say the same word or name over and over. Imagine how repetitive our writing would be without pronouns: *Little Miss Muffet sat on a tuffet eating Little Miss Muffet's curds and whey.* Luckily, we have pronouns, and this chapter demonstrates how to use them clearly.

S-6a Pronoun-Antecedent Agreement

Antecedents are the words that pronouns refer to. A pronoun must agree with its antecedent in gender and number.

IN GENDER   *Grandma* took *her* pie out of the oven.

IN NUMBER   *My grandparents* spent weekends at *their* cabin on White Bear Lake.

Generic nouns

Generic nouns refer to a type of person or thing (*a farmer, a soccer mom*). You'll often see or hear plural pronouns used to refer to singular generic nouns; in academic writing, however, most writers use pronouns that agree in number with their antecedents.

▶ Every lab technician should always wear goggles to protect ~~their~~ *his or her* eyes while working with chemicals.

▶ ~~Every lab technician~~ *Lab technicians* should always wear goggles to protect their eyes while working with chemicals.

Indefinite pronouns like everyone and each

INDEFINITE PRONOUNS such as *anyone, each, everyone,* and *someone* are singular even if they seem to be plural or refer to plural nouns.

▶ Everyone in the class did ~~their~~ *his or her* best.

If you find *his or her* awkward, you can rewrite the sentence to make the antecedents plural.

▶ ~~Everyone~~ *All of the students* in the class did their best.

In conversation and informal writing, *they* and other plural pronouns are often used to refer to indefinite pronouns or generic nouns that are grammatically singular; see page 341 for more on this usage.

▶ Somebody may beat me, but *they* are going to have to bleed to do it.
　　　　　　　　　　　　　　　　　　　　—Steve Prefontaine

Collective nouns like audience and team

Collective nouns such as *audience, committee,* or *team* take a singular pronoun when they refer to the group as a whole and a plural pronoun when they refer to members of the group as individuals.

▶ The winning team drew ~~their~~ *its* inspiration from the manager.

▶ The winning team threw ~~its~~ *their* gloves in the air.

He, his, *and other masculine pronouns*

To avoid SEXIST LANGUAGE, use *he*, *him*, *his*, or *himself* only when you know that the antecedent is male.

▶ Before meeting a new doctor, many people worry about not liking him/ or her.

Many writers have begun using *they*, *them*, and *their* to refer to a person whose gender is unknown or not relevant to the context.

▶ Someone in my building is selling *their* laptop; *they* put up a sign by the mailboxes.

Acceptance for this usage, known as SINGULAR THEY, is growing, and now includes the *Washington Post* and several other major publications. In addition, some people who challenge traditional binary genders prefer to use *they* rather than *he* or *she*. Ask your instructor if it's okay to use it in your class writing.

S-6b Pronoun Reference

A pronoun usually needs a clear antecedent, a specific word to which it refers.

▶ *My grandmother* spent a lot of time reading to me. *She* mostly read the standards, like *The Little Engine That Could.*

—Richard Bullock, "How I Learned about the Power of Writing"

Ambiguous reference

If there is more than one word that a pronoun could refer to, rewrite the sentence to clarify which one is the antecedent.

▶ After I plugged the printer into the computer, it sputtered and died.
the printer

What sputtered and died—the computer or the printer? The edit makes the reference clear.

Implied reference

If a pronoun does not refer clearly to a specific word, rewrite the sentence to omit the pronoun or insert an antecedent.

Unclear reference of *this*, *that*, and *which*. These three pronouns must refer to specific antecedents.

▶ Ultimately, the Justice Department did not insist on the breakup of
Microsoft, ~~which~~ set the tone for a liberal merger policy.
   <small>an oversight that</small>

Indefinite use of *they*, *it*, and *you*. Except in expressions like *it is raining* or *it seems that*, *they* and *it* should be used only to refer to people or things that have been specifically mentioned. *You* should be used only to address your reader.

▶ ~~In many~~ European countries/~~they~~ don't allow civilians to carry handguns.
   <small>Many</small>

▶ ~~On the~~ Weather Channel/~~it~~ said that storms would hit Key West today.
   <small>The</small>

▶ Many doctors argue that age should not be an impediment to
physical exercise ~~if you~~ have always been active.
   <small>for people who</small>

Both in conversation and in writing, antecedents are often left unstated if the audience will easily grasp the meaning. For academic writing, however, it's better not to use implied or indefinite antecedents.

S-6c Pronoun Case

Pronouns change case according to how they function in a sentence. There are three cases: subject, object, and possessive. Pronouns functioning as subjects or subject COMPLEMENTS are in the subject case; those functioning as OBJECTS are in the object case; those functioning as possessives are in the possessive case.

SUBJECT   *We* lived in a rented house three blocks from the school.

OBJECT   I went to my room and shut the door behind *me*.

POSSESSIVE   All *my* life chocolate has made me ill.

—David Sedaris, "Us and Them"

SUBJECT	OBJECT	POSSESSIVE
I	me	my / mine
we	us	our / ours
you	you	your / yours
he / she / it	him / her / it	his / her / hers / its
they	them	their / theirs
who / whoever	whom / whomever	whose

In subject complements

Use the subject case for pronouns that follow LINKING VERBS such as *be*, *seem*, *become*, and *feel*.

▶ In fact, Li was not the one who broke the code; it was ~~me~~. ^{I.}

If It was I *sounds awkward, revise the sentence further:* I broke it.

In compound structures

When a pronoun is part of a compound subject, it should be in the subject case. When it's part of a compound object, it should be in the object case.

▶ On our vacations, my grandfather and ~~me~~ went fishing together. ^I

▶ There were never any secrets between ~~he~~ and ~~I~~. *him   me.*

After *than* or *as*

Often comparisons with *than* or *as* leave some words out. When such comparisons include pronouns, your intended meaning determines the case of the pronoun.

▶ You trust John more than *me*.

This sentence means You trust John more than you trust me.

▶ You trust John more than *I*.

This sentence means You trust John more than I trust him.

Before or after infinitives

Pronouns that come before or after an INFINITIVE are usually in the object case.

▶ The professor asked Scott and ~~I~~ me to tell our classmates and ~~she~~ her about our project.

Before gerunds

Pronouns that come before a **GERUND** are usually in the possessive case.

▶ Savion's fans loved ~~him~~ his tap dancing to classical music.

With who *or* whom

There's strong evidence that *whom* is disappearing from use in both formal and informal contexts, but some instructors may expect you to use it. Use *who* (and *whoever*) where you would use *he* or *she*, and use *whom* (and *whomever*) where you would use *him* or *her*. These words appear most often in questions and in **SUBORDINATE CLAUSES**.

In questions. It can be confusing when one of these words begins a question. To figure out which case to use, try answering the question using *she* or *her*. If *she* works, use *who*; if *her* works, use *whom*.

▶ ~~Who~~ Whom do the critics admire most?

They admire her, *so change* who *to* whom.

▶ ~~Whom~~ Who will begin the discussion on this thorny topic?

She *will begin the discussion, so change* whom *to* who.

In subordinate clauses. To figure out whether to use *who* or *whom* in a subordinate clause, you need to determine how it functions in the clause. If it functions as a subject, use *who*; if it functions as an object, use *whom*.

▶ You may invite ~~whoever~~ whomever you like.

Whomever *is the object of* you like.

▶ I will invite ~~whomever~~ whoever is free that night.

Whoever *is the subject of* is free that night. *The clause* whoever is free that night *is the object of the whole sentence.*

When we or us precedes a noun

If you don't know whether to use *we* or *us* before a noun, choose the pronoun that you would use if the noun were omitted.

▶ *We* students object to the recent tuition increases.
  Without students, *you would say* We object, *not* Us object.

▶ The state is solving its budget shortfall by unfairly charging *us* students.
  Without students, *you would say* unfairly charging us, *not* unfairly charging we.

S-7   Parallelism

Been there, done that. Eat, drink, and be merry. For better or for worse. Out of sight, out of mind. All of these common sayings are parallel in structure, putting related words in the same grammatical form. Parallel structure emphasizes the connection between the elements and can make your writing rhythmic and easy to read. This chapter offers guidelines for maintaining parallelism in your writing.

S-7a In a Series or List

Use the same grammatical form for all items in a series or list—all nouns, all gerunds, all prepositional phrases, and so on.

▶ The seven deadly sins—*avarice, sloth, envy, lust, gluttony, pride,* and *wrath*—were all committed Sunday during the twice-annual bake sale at St. Mary's of the Immaculate Conception Church.   —*The Onion*

▶ After fifty years of running, biking, swimming, weight lifting, and playing tennis to stay in shape, Aunt Dorothy was unhappy to learn she needed knee surgery.

S-7b With Paired Ideas

One way to emphasize the connection between two ideas is to put them in identical grammatical forms. When you connect ideas with *and*, *but*, or another **COORDINATING CONJUNCTION** or with *either . . . or* or another **CORRELATIVE CONJUNCTION**, use the same grammatical structure for each idea.

▶ Many rural residents are voting on conservation issues and ~~agree~~ *agreeing* to pay higher taxes to keep community land undeveloped.

▶ General Electric paid millions of dollars to dredge the river and ~~for removing~~ *to remove* carcinogens from backyards.

▶ Sweet potatoes are highly nutritious, providing both dietary fiber and ~~as a good source of~~ vitamins A and C.

▶ Information on local cleanup efforts can be obtained not only from the town government but also ~~by going to~~ *at* the public library.

S-7c On Presentation Slides

PowerPoint and other presentation tools present most information in lists. Entries on these lists should be in parallel grammatical form.

During the 1946 presidential race, Truman
- Conducted a whistle-stop campaign
- Made hundreds of speeches
- Spoke energetically
- Connected personally with voters

S-7d On a Résumé

Entries on a résumé should be grammatically and typographically parallel. Each entry in the example below has the date on the left; the job title in bold followed by the company on the first line; the city and state on the second line; and the duties performed on the remaining lines, each starting with a verb.

2012–present   **INTERN**, Benedetto, Gartland, and Company
New York, NY
Assist in analyzing data for key accounts.
Design *PowerPoint* slides and presentations.

2011, summer   **SALES REPRESENTATIVE**, Vector Marketing Corporation
New York, NY
Sold high-quality cutlery, developing client base.

2010, summer   **TUTOR**, Grace Church Opportunity Project
New York, NY
Tutored children in math and reading.

S-7e In Headings

When you add headings to a piece of writing, put them in parallel form—all nouns, all prepositional phrases, and so on. Consider, for example, the following three headings in R-4 .

Acknowledging Sources
Avoiding Plagiarism
Understanding Documentation Styles

S-7f With All the Necessary Words

Be sure to include all the words necessary to make your meaning clear and your grammar parallel.

▶ Voting gained urgency in cities, ^in^ suburbs, and on farms.

▶ She loved her son more than ^she loved^ her husband.

The original sentence was ambiguous; it could also mean that she loved her son more than her husband did.

▶ A cat's skeleton is more flexible than ^that of^ a dog.

The original sentence compared one animal's skeleton to a whole animal rather than to another animal's skeleton.

S-8 Coordination, Subordination

When we combine two or more ideas in one sentence, we can use coordination to give equal weight to each idea or subordination to give more emphasis to one of the ideas. Assume, for example, that you're writing about your Aunt Irene. Aunt Irene made great strawberry jam. She did not win a blue ribbon at the Iowa State Fair.

COORDINATION   Aunt Irene made great strawberry jam, but she did not win a blue ribbon at the Iowa State Fair.

SUBORDINATION   Though Aunt Irene made great strawberry jam, she did not win a blue ribbon at the Iowa State Fair.

S-8a Linking Equal Ideas

To link ideas that you consider equal in importance, use a coordinating conjunction, a pair of correlative conjunctions, or a semicolon.

COORDINATING CONJUNCTIONS

and	or	so	yet
but	nor	for	

▶ The line in front of Preservation Hall was very long, *but* a good tenor sax player was wandering up and down the street, *so* I took my place at the end of the line.   —Fred Setterberg, "The Usual Story"

▶ New models of coursework may need to be developed, *and* instructors may need to be hired.
                —Megan Hopkins, "Training the Next Teachers for America"

Be careful not to overuse *and*. Try to use the coordinating conjunction that best expresses your meaning.

▶ Mosquitoes survived the high-tech zapping devices, ~~and~~ *but* bites were a small price for otherwise pleasant evenings in the country.

CORRELATIVE CONJUNCTIONS

either . . . or	not only . . . but also	whether . . . or
neither . . . nor	just as . . . so	

▶ *Just as* the summer saw endless rain, *so* the winter brought many snowstorms.

While a semicolon alone can signal equal importance, you might use a **TRANSITION** such as *therefore* or *in fact* to make the relationship between the ideas especially clear.

▶ Snowplows could not get through; trains stopped running.

▶ The 1996 film *Space Jam* stars Bugs Bunny and Michael Jordan, an unlikely pairing; *however,* the two are well matched in heroic status and mythic strengths.

S-8b Emphasizing One Idea over Others

To emphasize one idea over others, put the most important one in an **INDEPENDENT CLAUSE** and the less important ones in **SUBORDINATE CLAUSES** or **PHRASES**.

▶ ⌐————PHRASE————¬
Wanting to walk to work, LeShawn rented a somewhat expensive apartment downtown.

▶ ⌐————SUBORDINATE CLAUSE————¬
His monthly expenses were actually lower because he saved so much money in transportation costs.

S-9   Shifts

You're watching the news when your brother grabs the remote and changes the channel to a cartoon. The road you're driving on suddenly changes from asphalt to gravel. These shifts are jarring and sometimes disorienting. Similarly, shifts in writing—from one tense to another, for example—can confuse your readers. This chapter explains how to keep your writing consistent in verb tense, point of view, and number.

S-9a Shifts in Tense

Only when you want to emphasize that actions take place at different times should you shift verb **TENSE**.

▶ My plane *will arrive* in Albuquerque two hours after it *leaves* Portland.

Otherwise, keep tenses consistent.

▶ As the concert ended, several people ~~are~~ already on their way up the aisle, causing a distraction.
    [were]

In writing about literary works, use the present tense. Be careful not to shift to the past tense.

▶ The two fugitives start down the river together, Huck fleeing his abusive father and Jim running away from his owner. As they ~~traveled,~~ *[travel,]* they ~~met~~ *[meet]* with many colorful characters, including the Duke and King, two actors and con artists who involve Huck and Jim in their schemes.

S-9b Shifts in Point of View

Do not shift between first person (*I, we*), second person (*you*), and third person (*he, she, it, they, one*).

▶ When ~~one has~~ *[you have]* a cold, you should stay home to avoid infecting others.

S-9c Shifts in Number

Unnecessary shifts between singular and plural subjects can confuse readers.

▶ Because of late frosts, oranges have risen dramatically in price. But since ~~the orange is~~ *[oranges are]* such a staple, they continue to sell.

L-1   Appropriate Words

Cool. Sweet. Excellent. These three words can mean the same thing, but each has a different level of formality. We usually use informal language when we're talking with friends, and we use slang and abbreviations when we send text messages, but we choose words that are more formal for most of our academic and professional writing. Just as we wouldn't wear an old T-shirt to most job interviews, we wouldn't write in a college essay that *Beloved* is "an awesome book." This chapter offers you help in choosing words that are appropriate for different audiences and purposes.

L-1a Formal and Informal Words

Whether you use formal or informal language depends on your **PURPOSE** and **AUDIENCE**.

FORMAL   Four score and seven years ago our fathers brought forth on this continent, a new nation, conceived in Liberty, and dedicated to the proposition that all men are created equal.
               —Abraham Lincoln, Gettysburg Address

INFORMAL   Our family, like most, had its ups and downs.
               —Judy Davis, "Ours Was a Dad"

The first, more formal sentence was delivered in 1863 to twenty thousand people, including many officials and prominent citizens. The second, less formal sentence was spoken in 2004 to a small gathering of family and friends at a funeral.

Colloquial language (*What's up? No clue*) and slang (*A-list, S'up?*) are not appropriate for formal speech and most academic and professional writing.

>   Many   students
> ► ~~A lot of~~ high school ~~kids~~ have so little time for lunch that they end up
>   eating
> ~~gobbling down their food~~ as they race to class.

L-1b Pretentious Language

Long or complicated words might seem to lend authority to your writing, but often they make it sound pretentious and stuffy. Use such words sparingly and only when they best capture your meaning and suit your WRITING CONTEXT.

▶ ~~Subsequent to~~ adopting the new system, managers ~~averred~~ that their *After* ... *claimed* staff worked ~~synergistically~~ ~~in a way that exceeded parameters.~~ *together* *better than expected.*

L-1c Jargon

Jargon is a specialized vocabulary of a profession, trade, or field and should be used only when you know your audience will understand what you are saying. A computer enthusiast might easily understand the following paragraph, but most readers would not be familiar with terms like *HDMI*, *DVI*, and *1080p*.

▶ HDMI is the easiest and most convenient way to go about high-def. Why? Because you get [video] and sound in a single, USB-like cable, instead of a nest of component cables or the soundless garden hose of DVI. Also, unless you're trying to run 1080p over 100 feet or somesuch, stay away from premium brands. Any on-spec cheapie HDMI cable will be perfect for standard living room setups.
    —Rob Beschizza, "Which Is Better, HDMI or Component?"

When you are writing for an audience of nonspecialists, resist the temptation to use overly technical language.

▶ The ~~mini-sternotomy~~ at the lower end of the ~~sternum resulted in~~ *small incision* ... *breastbone preserved* her appearance. ~~satisfactory cosmesis.~~

L-1d Clichés

Steer clear of clichés, expressions so familiar that they have become trite (*white as snow, the grass is always greener*).

► The company needs a recruiter who thinks ~~outside the box.~~ unconventionally.

► After canoeing all day, we all slept ~~like logs.~~ soundly.

► Nita ~~is a team player,~~ collaborates well, so we hope she will be assigned to the project.

L-2   Precise Words

Serena Overpowers Sloane. Mariano Finishes Off the Sox. In each case, the writer could have simply used the word *beats*. But at least to sports fans, these newspaper headlines are a bit more precise and informative as a result of the words chosen. This chapter offers guidelines for editing your own writing to make it as precise as it needs to be.

L-2a *Be* and *Do*

Try not to rely too much on *be* or *do*. Check your writing to see where you can replace forms of these words with more precise verbs.

► David Sedaris's essay "Us and Them" ~~is about~~ focuses on his love/hate relationship with his family.

► Some doctors no longer believe that ~~doing~~ solving crossword puzzles can delay the onset of senility or Alzheimer's disease.

Sometimes using a form of *be* or *do* is the right choice, such as when you are describing something or someone.

▶ Most critics agree that *Citizen Kane, Casablanca,* and *The Shawshank Redemption are* some of the finest movies ever made.

L-2b Abstract and Concrete Words

Abstract words refer to general qualities or ideas (*truth, beauty*), whereas concrete words refer to specific things that can be perceived with our senses (*books, lipstick*). You'll often need to use words that are general or abstract, but remember that specific, concrete words can make your writing more precise and more vivid—and can make an abstract concept easier to understand.

▶ In Joan Didion's work, there has always been a fascination with what she once called "the unspeakable peril of the everyday"—the coyotes by the interstate, the snakes in the playpen, the fires and Santa Ana winds of California.

　　　　　　—Michiko Kakutani, "The End of Life as She Knew It"

The concrete words coyotes, snakes, fires, *and* winds *help explain the abstract* peril of the everyday.

L-2c Figurative Language

Figures of speech such as SIMILES and METAPHORS are words used imaginatively rather than literally. They can help readers understand an abstract point by comparing it to something they are familiar with or can easily imagine.

SIMILE　　His body is in almost constant motion—rolling those cigarettes, rubbing an elbow, reaching for a glass—but the rhythm is tranquil and fluid, *like a cat licking its paw.*
　　　　　　—Sean Smith, "Johnny Depp: Unlikely Superstar"

METAPHOR　And so, before the professor had even finished his little story, *I had become a furnace of rage.*
　　　　　　—Shelby Steele, "On Being Black and Middle Class"

L-3 Idioms

A piece of cake. Walking on air. Cute as a button. These are just three of the thousands of English idioms and idiomatic expressions that are used every day. Most idioms are phrases (and sometimes whole sentences) whose meaning cannot be understood by knowing the meanings of the individual words. We use idioms because they give a lot of information in few words and add color and texture to what we say or write. If you're learning English, a well-chosen idiom also demonstrates your fluency in the language. Some idioms appear more often in conversation than in formal writing, but many will be useful to you in your academic work.

L-3a Recognizing Idioms

When you read or hear a phrase that seems totally unrelated to the topic, you have probably encountered an idiom.

▶ Influencing Hollywood is a little *like herding cats.*
　　　　　　　　　　　　—Jane Alexander, *Command Performance*

　Cats are notoriously independent and indifferent to following directions; thus a difficult, maybe impossible task is said to be "like herding cats."

▶ As the economy contracts, we Americans are likely to find that we have been living too *high on the hog.*   —*Los Angeles Times*

　Ham, ribs, bacon, and other meats that are considered the most tasty and desirable are from the upper parts of the hog. People who live extravagantly or luxuriously are sometimes said to be living "high on the hog."

▶ This internship is not just about class credit. This is about really getting *a leg up* for when you graduate.
　　　　　　　　　　　　—Morgan to Chelsea, *Days of Our Lives*

　When a rider is mounting a horse, another person often supports the rider's left leg while the right one swings over the horse's back. Having "a leg up" means you've been given extra help or certain advantages.

▶ I love to see a young girl go out and *grab* the world *by the lapels.*
—Maya Angelou

Grabbing the front of a jacket, or "grabbing someone by the lapels," is a firm and aggressive move that aims to take charge of a situation.

L-3b Understanding Idioms

Idioms may seem peculiar or even nonsensical if you think about their literal meanings, but knowing where they originated can help you figure out what they mean. Many idioms, for example, originate in sports, music, and animal contexts, where their meanings are literal. Used in other contexts, their meanings are similar, if not exactly literal.

▶ When the senator introduced the bill, she thought passage would be a *slam dunk* since public opinion was strongly favorable.

In basketball, a player scores a "slam dunk" by shoving the ball through the basket in a dramatic way. As an idiom, a "slam dunk" refers to a victory gained easily or emphatically.

▶ George Saunders' commencement speech really *struck a chord* with the Syracuse graduates.

A chord is a group of musical notes that harmonize; to "strike a chord" with an audience means to make a connection by bringing up something interesting or relevant to them.

▶ Some members of Congress think that limiting food stamps will get more Americans back to work; I think they're *barking up the wrong tree.*

This idiom refers to a dog in pursuit of an animal that has disappeared into a group of trees; the dog is barking at one tree, but its prey has climbed up another. To "bark up the wrong tree" means to pursue the wrong course of action.

You can sometimes figure out the meaning of an idiom based on its context; but if you're not sure what it means or how to use it properly, look it up online—go to **digital.wwnorton.com/littleseagull3** for links to some good sources. The *Cambridge Dictionary of American Idioms* is a good print source.

L-3c Common Idiomatic Expressions in Academic and Professional Writing

Idiomatic expressions are words that go together like peanut butter and jelly—you often find them together. You've probably encountered expressions such as *with respect to, insofar as,* or *as a matter of fact* in academic or professional writing. Many of these expressions function as TRANSITIONS, helping readers follow your reasoning and understand how your ideas relate to one another. You're expected to signal the connections among your ideas explicitly in academic writing, and the following idiomatic expressions can help you do so.

To shift to a narrower focus

with respect to, with regard to   indicate the precise topic you are addressing: *The global economic situation is much more complicated with respect to certain nations' high levels of debt.*

insofar as   sets a limit or scope for a statement: *Despite her short stature, Bates is the team leader insofar as direction and determination are concerned.*

in particular   points to something especially true within a generalization: *Cosmetic surgery procedures for men have increased tremendously in the last decade; liposuction and eyelid surgery, in particular, showed dramatic increases.*

To give examples

a case in point   frames an example that illustrates a point: *Recent business activity shows a clear trend toward consolidation. The merger of two airlines last year is a case in point.*

for instance   indicates an example that illustrates an idea: *Green vegetables are highly nutritious; one serving of kale, for instance, provides the full daily recommended value of vitamins A and C.*

To add information

in addition   introduces a new but related point: *Locally grown tomatoes are available nearly everywhere; in addition, they are rich in vitamin C.*

along the same lines   connects two similar ideas: *Many cities are developing parking meter plans along the same lines as the system in Chicago.*

by the same token   signals a point that follows the logic of the previous point: *Insider trading has damaged the reputation of the financial industry in general; by the same token, high-profile embezzlers like Bernie Madoff have eroded the public's confidence in many investment advisers.*

as a matter of fact, in fact   signal a statement that explains or contrasts with a previous point: *Wind power is an increasingly common energy source; as a matter of fact, wind energy generation quadrupled between 2000 and 2006.*

To emphasize something

of course   emphasizes a point that is (or should be) obvious: *Fresh foods are preferable to processed foods, of course, but fresh foods are not always available.*

in any case, in any event   introduce something that is true regardless of other conditions: *The city has introduced new precautions to ensure the election goes smoothly; the results will be closely scrutinized in any event.*

To signal alternatives or conflicting ideas

on the one hand . . . on the other hand   introduces contrasting ideas or conditions: *On the one hand, some critics have loudly rejected reality television; on the other hand, unscripted shows are often received well by the public.*

up to a point   signals acceptance of part but not all of an argument or idea: *The senator's statement is correct up to a point, but her conclusions are misguided.*

have it both ways   to benefit from two conflicting positions: *Tech companies want to have it both ways, asking the government to be more transparent about its use of user data while not disclosing that they are using these data for their own commercial purposes.*

of two minds   signals ambivalence, validates conflicting ideas: *On the question of whether organic food is worth the extra cost, I am of two minds: I like knowing that the food is grown without chemicals, but some studies suggest that the health benefits are questionable.*

in contrast signals a change in direction or a different idea on the same subject: *Large birds such as crows can live for more than ten years; in contrast, tiny hummingbirds generally live less than three years.*

on the contrary signals an opposite idea or opposing position: *Some bankers claim that the proposed mortgage regulations would harm the economy; on the contrary, the new rules would be the most effective means of reinvigorating it.*

in fact, as a matter of fact signal a statement that challenges or refutes a previous statement: *Nicholas Carr suggests that Google is making us stupid; in fact, some argue that by giving us access to more information, it's making us better informed.*

To summarize or restate something

in brief, in short introduce a short summary of points already established: *In brief, the accident was caused by a combination of carelessness and high winds.*

in other words signals a restatement or explanation of the preceding idea: *Our opposition to the proposal is firm and unequivocal; in other words, we emphatically decline.*

in conclusion, in sum signal the final statement or section of a text: *In conclusion, the evidence points to a clear and simple solution to the problem.*

Sports idioms in business writing. You'll encounter and use many idioms in business writing, especially ones that come from sports—probably because the competitiveness of the business world makes it easily comparable to sports. Following are some idioms that often come up in business contexts.

a team player someone who acts in the interest of a whole team or group rather than for individual gain: *The best managers are team players, making sure that the credit for a success is shared among everyone who contributed to the effort.*

to cover all the bases an expression that comes from baseball, where the fielders must protect all four bases against the other team's runners; as an idiom, it means to be thorough—to deal with all aspects of a situation and consider all possibilities: *Her report was well executed; it covered all the bases and anticipated all possible counterproposals.*

across the board   a large board at a racetrack displays the names of all the horses in a race; to place an equal bet on every horse is to bet "across the board," so the idiom refers to something affecting all items in a group equally: *Proponents of the new health-care policy insist that it will reduce costs across the board, from doctor visits to medical procedures to prescription medicines.*

Considering context. Many idiomatic expressions are quite informal. These can be used effectively in casual conversation or social media, but they are rarely if ever appropriate in academic or professional writing. As with all writing, you need to consider your AUDI-ENCE and PURPOSE when you use idiomatic expressions.

In a conversation with a friend or family member,   you might say *let's cut to the chase*; with a business colleague, however, it may be more appropriate to suggest that you *get right to the point,* or *focus on what's most important.*

In an email to a friend,   you might say something sounds *like a piece of cake*; with your boss, it would be more appropriate to say it sounds *doable* or *easy to do.*

On Facebook,   you might describe an improv show as *over the top*; in a review for a class, it would be more appropriate to say it was *excessive* or *outrageous.*

L-4 Words Often Confused

When you're tired, do you *lay* down or *lie* down? After dinner, do you eat *desert* or *dessert*? This chapter's dual purpose is to alert you to everyday words that can trip you up and to help you understand the differences between certain words that people tend to confuse.

accept, except *Accept* means "to receive willingly": *accept an award.* *Except* as a preposition means "excluding": *all languages except English.*

adapt, adopt *Adapt* means "to adjust": *adapt the recipe to be dairy free.* *Adopt* means "to take as one's own": *adopt a pet from a shelter.*

advice, advise *Advice* means "recommendation": *a lawyer's advice.* *Advise* means "to give advice": *We advise you to learn your rights.*

affect, effect *Affect* is usually a verb that means "to produce a change in": *Stress can affect health. Effect* is a noun that means "result": *The effects of smoking are well known.* As a verb, it means "to cause": *A mediator works to effect a compromise.*

all right, alright *All right* is the preferred spelling.

allusion, illusion *Allusion* means "indirect reference": *an allusion to Beowulf. Illusion* means "false appearance": *an optical illusion.*

a lot Always two words, *a lot* means "a large number or amount" or "to a great extent": *a lot of voters; he misses her a lot.* The phrase is too informal for most academic writing.

among, between Use *among* for three or more items: *among the fifty states.* Use *between* for two items: *between you and me.*

amount, number Use *amount* for things you can measure but not count: *a large amount of water.* Use *number* for things you can count: *a number of books.*

as, as if, like *Like* introduces a noun or **NOUN PHRASE**: *It feels like silk.* To begin a subordinate clause, use *as* or *as if*: *Do as I say, not as I do; It seemed as if he had not prepared at all for the briefing.*

bad, badly   Use *bad* as an adjective following a linking verb: *I feel bad.* Use *badly* as an adverb following an action verb: *I play piano badly.*

capital, capitol   A *capital* is a city where the government of a state, province, or country is located: *Kingston was the first state capital of New York.* A *capitol* is a government building: *the dome of the capitol.*

cite, sight, site   *Cite* means "to give information from a source by quoting, paraphrasing, or summarizing": *Cite your sources. Sight* is the act of seeing or something that is seen: *an appalling sight.* A *site* is a place: *the site of a famous battle.*

compose, comprise   The parts *compose* the whole: *Fifty states compose the Union.* The whole *comprises* the parts: *The Union comprises fifty states.*

could of   In writing, use *could have* (*could've*).

council, counsel   *Council* refers to a body of people: *the council's vote. Counsel* means "advice" or "to advise": *her wise counsel; she counseled victims of domestic abuse.*

criteria, criterion   *Criteria* is the plural of *criterion* and takes a plural verb: *Certain criteria have been established.*

data   *Data,* the plural of *datum,* technically should take a plural verb (*The data arrive from many sources*), but some writers treat it as singular (*The data is persuasive*).

desert, dessert   *Desert* as a noun means "arid region": *Mojave Desert.* As a verb it means "to abandon": *He deserted his post. Dessert* is a sweet served toward the end of a meal.

disinterested, uninterested   *Disinterested* means "fair" or "unbiased": *a disinterested jury. Uninterested* means "bored" or "indifferent": *uninterested in election results.*

emigrate (from), immigrate (to)   *Emigrate* means "to leave one's country": *emigrate from Slovakia. Immigrate* means "to move to another country": *immigrate to Canada.*

etc.   The abbreviation *etc.* is short for the Latin *et cetera,* "and other things." *Etc.* is fine in notes and bibliographies, but avoid using it in your writing in general. Substitute *and so on* if necessary.

everyday, every day   Everyday is an adjective meaning "ordinary": *After the holidays, we go back to our everyday routine.* Every day means "on a daily basis": *Eat three or more servings of fruit every day.*

fewer, less   Use *fewer* when you refer to things that can be counted: *fewer calories.* Use *less* when you refer to an amount of something that cannot be counted: *less fat.*

good, well   Good is an adjective: *She looks good in that color; a good book.* Well can be an adjective indicating physical health after a linking verb *(She looks well despite her recent surgery)* or an adverb following an action verb *(He speaks Spanish well).*

hopefully   In academic writing, avoid *hopefully* to mean "it is hoped that"; use it only to mean "with hope": *to make a wish hopefully.*

imply, infer   Imply means "to suggest": *What do you mean to imply? Infer* means "to conclude": *We infer that you did not enjoy the trip.*

its, it's   Its is a possessive pronoun: *The movie is rated R because of its language.* It's is a contraction of "it is" or "it has": *It's an action film.*

lay, lie   Lay, meaning "to put" or "to place," always takes a direct object: *She lays the blanket down.* Lie, meaning "to recline" or "to be positioned," never takes a direct object: *She lies on the blanket.*

lead, led   The verb *lead* (rhymes with *bead*) means "to guide": *I will lead the way.* Led is the past tense and past participle of *lead: Yesterday I led the way.* The noun *lead* (rhymes with *head*) is a type of metal: *Use copper pipes instead of lead pipes.*

literally   Use *literally* only when you want to stress that you don't mean *figuratively: While sitting in the grass, he realized that he literally had ants in his pants.*

loose, lose   Loose means "not fastened securely" or "not fitting tightly": *a pair of loose pants.* Lose means "to misplace" or "to not win": *lose an earring; lose the race.*

man, mankind   Use *people, humans, humanity,* or *humankind* instead.

many, much   Use *many* when you refer to things that can be counted: *many books.* Use *much* to refer to something that cannot be counted: *much knowledge.*

may of, might of, must of   In writing, use *may have*, *might have*, or *must have*.

media   *Media*, a plural noun, takes a plural verb: *Many political scientists believe that the media have a huge effect on voting behavior.* The singular form is *medium*: *TV is a popular medium for advertising.*

percent, percentage   Use *percent* after a number: *80 percent*. Use *percentage* after an adjective or article: *an impressive percentage; the percentage was impressive.*

principal, principle   As a noun, *principal* means "a chief official" or "a sum of money": *in the principal's office; raising the principal for a down payment.* As an adjective, it means "most important": *the principal cause of death.* *Principle* means "a rule by which one lives" or "a basic truth or doctrine": *Lying is against her principles; the principles of life, liberty, and the pursuit of happiness.*

raise, rise   Meaning "to grow" or "to cause to move upward," *raise* always takes a direct object: *He raised his hand.* Meaning "to get up," *rise* never takes a direct object: *The sun rises at dawn.*

the reason . . . is because   Use *because* or *the reason . . . is (that)*, but not both: *The reason for the price increase was a poor growing season* or *prices increased because of a poor growing season.*

reason why   Instead of this redundant phrase, use *the reason* or *the reason that*: *Psychologists debate the reasons that some people develop depression and others do not.*

respectfully, respectively   *Respectfully* means "in a way that shows respect": *Speak to your elders respectfully.* *Respectively* means "in the order given": *George H. W. Bush and George W. Bush were the forty-first president and the forty-third president, respectively.*

sensual, sensuous   *Sensual* suggests sexuality: *a sensual caress.* *Sensuous* involves pleasing the senses through art, music, and nature: *the violin's sensuous solo.*

set, sit   *Set*, meaning "to put" or "to place," takes a direct object: *Please set the vase on the table.* *Sit*, meaning "to take a seat," does not take a direct object: *She sits on the bench.*

should of   In writing, use *should have* (*should've*).

stationary, stationery   *Stationary* means "staying put": *a stationary lab table*. *Stationery* means "writing paper": *the college's official stationery*.

than, then   *Than* is a conjunction used for comparing: *She is taller than her mother*. *Then* is an adverb used to indicate a sequence: *Finish your work, and then reward yourself*.

that, which   Use *that* to add information that is essential for identifying something: *The wild horses that live on this island are endangered*. Use *which* to give additional but nonessential information: *Abaco Barb horses, which live on an island in the Bahamas, are endangered*.

their, there, they're   *Their* signifies possession: *their canoe*. *There* tells where: *Put it there*. *They're* is a contraction of "they are": *They're busy*.

to, too, two   *To* is either a preposition that tells direction (*Give it to me*) or part of an infinitive (*To err is human*). *Too* means "also" or "excessively": *The younger children wanted to help, too*; *It's too cold to sit outside*. *Two* is a number: *tea for two*.

unique   Because *unique* suggests that something is the only one of its kind, avoid adding comparatives or superlatives (*more, most, less, least*), intensifiers (such as *very*), or qualifiers (such as *somewhat*).

weather, whether   *Weather* refers to atmospheric conditions: *dreary weather*. *Whether* refers to a choice between options: *whether to stay home or go out*.

who's, whose   *Who's* is a contraction for "who is" or "who has": *Who's the best candidate for the job? Who's already eaten? Whose* refers to ownership: *Whose keys are these? Tom, whose keys were on the table, had left*.

would of   In writing, use *would have* (*would've*).

your, you're   *Your* signifies possession: *your diploma*. *You're* is a contraction for "you are": *You're welcome*.

L-5   Prepositions

A great session with your favorite video game. You've finally reached the cave of the dying wise man who will tell you the location of the key that you need. He points a long, bony finger toward a table and struggles to rasp out one word, "jar." You're down to your last life. You only have one chance. Is the key *in* the jar? *under* it? *behind* it? Oh, that one little preposition makes all the difference!

Real life is seldom this dramatic, but correct prepositions do make a difference. Prepositions are words like *at, from, in,* and *with* that describe relationships, often in time and space: *at work, in an hour, with your mom.* English has a large number of prepositions compared to other languages, and sometimes it's difficult to choose the right one.

Prepositions are always followed by noun or pronoun **OBJECTS**. (You can't just "write about"; you have to write about something.) Together a preposition and its object form a prepositional phrase. In the following examples, the prepositions are underlined and the prepositional phrases are italicized.

▶ This is a book *about writing.*

▶ We're *in the midst of a literacy revolution.* —Andrea Lunsford

▶ Research is formalized curiosity. It is poking and prying *with a purpose.*
—Zora Neale Hurston

▶ *In the years between 1969 and 1978,* I lived, worked, and played *with the children and their families in Roadville and Trackton.*
—Shirley Brice Heath

The table and lists on the following page summarize the basic differences in the ways to use three common prepositions—*at, on,* and *in.*

AT	a specific point	●	at home at the gym at noon
ON	a line	——————	on the avenue on the table on a specific day
IN	a shape or enclosure	⬭	in a container in the park in two hours

Prepositions of place

AT   *a specific address or business:* at 33 Parkwood Street, at McDonald's
     a public building or unnamed business: at the library, at the gym
     a general place: at home, at work

ON   *a surface:* on the floor, on the grass, on the wall
     a street: on Ninth Street, on Western Avenue
     an electronic medium: on the radio, on the web
     public transportation: on the bus, on an airplane

IN   *a container, room, or area:* in the jar, in my office, in the woods
     a geographic location: in San Diego, in the Midwest
     a printed work: in the newspaper, in Chapter 3

Prepositions of time

AT   *a specific time:* at 4:30 PM, at sunset, at lunchtime

ON   *a day of the week:* on Friday
     an exact date: on September 12
     a holiday: on Thanksgiving, on Veteran's Day

IN   *a defined time period:* in an hour, in three years
     a month, season, or year: in June, in the fall, in 2011
     a part of the day: in the morning, in the evening

L-6 Unnecessary Words

At this point in time. Really unique. In a manner of speaking. Each of these phrases includes words that are unnecessary or says something that could be expressed more concisely. This chapter shows you how to edit your own writing to make every word count.

L-6a *Really, Very,* and Other Empty Words

Intensifiers such as *really* and *very* are used to strengthen what we say. Qualifiers such as *apparently, possibly, seem,* or *tend to* are a way to soften what we say. It's fine to use words like these when they are necessary. Sometimes, however, they are not. You shouldn't say that something is "very unique," because things either are unique or they're not; there's no need to add the intensifier. And why say that someone is "really smart" when you could say that he or she is "brilliant"?

▶ Accepted by five colleges, Jackson ~~seems to be facing an apparently very~~ difficult decision. *is facing a*

L-6b *There Is, It Is*

<small>EXPLETIVE</small> constructions like *there is* and *it is* can be useful ways to introduce and emphasize an idea, but sometimes they only add unnecessary words. Eliminating them in such cases can make the sentence more concise and also make its verb stronger.

▶ ~~It is necessary for~~ Americans today ~~to~~ learn to speak more than one language. *must*

▶ ~~There are four~~ large moons and more than thirty small ones ~~that~~ orbit Jupiter. *Four*

In certain contexts, however, expletives can be the best choices. Imagine the ending of *The Wizard of Oz* if Dorothy had said "No place is like home" instead of the more emphatic—and sentimental—"There's no place like home."

L-6c Wordy Phrases

Many common phrases use several words when a single word will do. Editing out such wordy phrases will make your writing more concise and easier to read.

WORDY	CONCISE
as far as . . . is concerned	concerning
at the time that	when
at this point in time	now
in spite of the fact that	although, though
in the event that	if
in view of the fact that	because, since

▶ ~~Due to the fact that~~ ^{Because} Professor Lee retired, the animal sciences department now lacks a neurology specialist.

L-6d Redundancies

Eliminate words and phrases that are unnecessary for your meaning.

▶ Painting the house purple ~~in color~~ will make it stand out from the many white houses in town.

▶ Dashing ~~quickly~~ into the street to retrieve the ball, the young girl was almost hit by a car.

▶ Campers should know how much wood is ~~sufficient~~ enough for a fire to burn all night.

L-7   Adjectives and Adverbs

Adjectives and adverbs are words that describe other words, adding important information and detail. When Dave Barry writes that the Beatles "were the *coolest* thing you had ever seen" and that "they were *smart*; they were *funny*; they didn't take themselves *seriously*," the adjectives and adverbs (italicized here) make clear why he "wanted *desperately* to be a Beatle." This chapter will help you use adjectives and adverbs in your own writing.

L-7a Choosing between Adjectives and Adverbs

Adjectives are words used to modify **NOUNS** and **PRONOUNS**. They usually answer one of these questions: Which? What kind? How many?

▶ *Two* rows of *ancient oak* trees lined the *narrow* driveway.

▶ *Many* years of testing will be needed to determine whether the *newest* theories are *correct*.

▶ If you are craving something *sweet,* have a piece of fruit.

Adverbs are words used to modify **VERBS**, adjectives, and other adverbs. They usually answer one of these questions: How? When? Where? Why? Under what conditions? To what degree? Although many adverbs end in -ly (*tentatively, immediately*), many do not (*now, so, soon, then, very*).

▶ Emergency personnel must respond *quickly* when an ambulance arrives.

▶ Environmentalists are *increasingly* worried about Americans' consumption of fossil fuels.

▶ If the senator had known that the news cameras were on, she would not have responded *so angrily.*

Well *and* good

Use *well* as an adjective to describe physical health; use *good* to describe emotional health or appearance.

▶ Some herbs can keep you feeling ~~good~~ *well* when everyone else has the flu.

▶ Staying healthy can make you feel *good* about yourself.

Good should not be used as an adverb; use *well*.

▶ Because both Williams sisters play tennis so ~~good,~~ *well,* they've frequently competed against each other in major tournaments.

Bad *and* badly

Use the adjective *bad* after a **LINKING VERB** to describe an emotional state or feeling. In such cases, the adjective describes the subject.

▶ Arguing with your parents can make you feel *bad*.

Use the adverb *badly* to describe an **ACTION VERB**.

▶ Arguing with your parents late at night can make you sleep *badly*.

L-7b Using Comparatives and Superlatives

Most adjectives and adverbs have three forms: the positive, the comparative, and the superlative. The comparative is used to compare two things, and the superlative is used to compare three or more things.

COMPARATIVE   Who's the *better* quarterback, Eli Manning or his brother?

SUPERLATIVE   Many Colts fans still consider Peyton Manning to be the *best* quarterback ever.

The comparative and superlative of most adjectives are formed by adding the endings *-er* and *-est*: *slow, slower, slowest*. Longer adjectives and most adverbs use *more* and *most* (or *less* and *least*): *clearly, more clearly, most clearly*. If you add *-er* or *-est* to an adjective or adverb, do not also use *more* or *most* (or *less* and *least*).

▶ The ~~most~~ lowest point in the United States is in Death Valley.

A few adjectives and adverbs have irregular comparatives and super-latives.

	COMPARATIVE	SUPERLATIVE
good, well	better	best
bad, badly	worse	worst
far (distance)	farther	farthest
far (time or amount)	further	furthest
little (amount)	less	least
many, much, some	more	most

L-7c Placing Modifiers Carefully

Place adjectives, adverbs, and other MODIFIERS so that readers clearly understand which words they modify.

▶ The doctor explained advances in cancer treatment to the families of patients. ~~at the seminar.~~ *at the seminar*

The doctor, not the patients, is at the seminar.

▶ ~~The~~ surgeons assured the patient that they intended to make only two small incisions. ~~before the anesthesiologist arrived.~~ *Before the anesthesiologist arrived, the*

The original sentence suggests that the incisions will be made without anesthesia, surely not the case.

To avoid ambiguity, position limiting modifiers such as *almost*, *even*, *just*, *merely*, and *only* next to the word or phrase they modify—and be careful that your meaning is clear. See how the placement of *only* can result in two completely different meanings.

▶ A triple-threat athlete, Martha ~~only~~ played soccer *only* in college.

▶ A triple-threat athlete, Martha ~~only~~ played *only* soccer in college.

Be careful that your placement of *not* doesn't result in a meaning you don't intend.

▶ When I attended college, every student was ~~not~~ using a laptop.
^{not}

Dangling modifiers

Modifiers are said to be dangling when they do not clearly modify any particular word in the sentence. You can usually fix a dangling modifier by adding a **SUBJECT** that the modifier clearly refers to, either in the rest of the sentence or in the modifier itself.

▶ Speaking simply and respectfully, many people ~~felt comforted by the doctor's~~ presentation.
^{the doctor comforted}
^{with his}

The doctor was speaking, not the other people.

▶ While running to catch the bus, the shoulder strap on my bag broke.
^{I was}

Split infinitives

When you place a modifier between *to* and the base form of the verb in an **INFINITIVE**, you create a split infinitive. *to deliberately avoid.* When a split infinitive is awkward or makes a sentence difficult to follow, put the modifier elsewhere in the sentence.

▶ Professional soccer players are expected to ~~rigorously~~ train every day.
^{rigorously}

Sometimes, however, a split infinitive is easier to follow.

▶ One famous split infinitive appears in the opening sequence of *Star Trek*: "to boldly go where no man has gone before."

L-8   Articles

A, an, and *the* are articles, words used before a noun to indicate whether something is general or specific. Use *a* or *an* with nouns whose specific identity is not known to your audience: *I'm reading a great book.* Use *the* with nouns whose specific identity is known to your audience, whether the noun describes something specific: *the new book by Dave Eggers*—or is something you've mentioned: *Beverly is almost finished writing her book. The book will be published next year.* Sometimes no article is needed: *Books are now available in print and online.*

L-8a When to Use *A* or *An*

Use *a* or *an* before singular count nouns referring to something that's not specific or that you're mentioning to your audience for the first time. Count nouns name things that can be counted: *one book, two books.* Use *a* before consonant sounds: *a tangerine, a university;* use *an* before vowel sounds: *an orange, an hour.*

▶ *An apartment* near campus might be rather expensive.

   Any apartment near campus would be expensive, not just a specific one.

▶ I put *a carrot,* some tomatoes, and a little parsley in the salad.

   This carrot is being mentioned for the first time.

Do not use *a* or *an* before a noncount noun. Noncount nouns name abstract items (*respect, curiosity*) and liquids and masses that cannot be measured with numbers (*milk, sand, rice*).

▶ Our team could use *some encouragement* from the coach

▶ The last thing Portland needs this week is *more rain.*

L-8b When to Use *The*

Use *the* before any nouns whose identity is clear to your audience and before superlatives.

▶ Mando ordered a cheeseburger and french fries and asked for *the burger* to be well done.

   The article the is used because it refers to a cheeseburger that's already been mentioned: the one that Mando ordered.

▶ His friends had raved about *the fries* at this restaurant.

The specific fries are identified: they are the ones at this restaurant.

▶ His friends were right; these were *the best fries* he'd ever eaten.

The is used before a superlative: these were the best fries ever.

Use *the* with most plural **PROPER NOUNS** (*the Adirondack Mountains, the Philippines, the Dallas Cowboys*) and with singular proper nouns in the following categories.

LARGER BODIES OF WATER the Arctic Ocean, the Mississippi River

GOVERNMENT BODIES the US Congress, the Canadian Parliament

HISTORICAL PERIODS the Renaissance, the Tang Dynasty

LANDMARKS the Empire State Building, the Taj Mahal

REGIONS the East Coast, the Middle East, the Mojave Desert

RELIGIOUS ENTITIES, TEXTS, AND LEADERS the Roman Catholic Church, the Qur'an, the Dalai Lama

L-8c When No Article Is Needed

No article is needed before noncount nouns (*salt, imagination, happiness*) and plural count nouns (*ideas, puppies*) when they refer to something "in general."

▶ *Milk* and *eggs* are on sale this week.

▶ *Information* wants to be free.   —Stewart Brand, *Whole Earth Review*

▶ Be less curious about people and more curious about *ideas*.

—Marie Curie

Brand and Curie refer to information and ideas in general, not a specific kind of information or specific ideas.

No article is needed with most singular **PROPER NOUNS**: *Barack Obama, Lake Titicaca, Yosemite.*

L-9 Words for Building Common Ground

A secretary objects to being called one of "the girls." The head of the English department finds the title "chairman" offensive. Why? The secretary is male, the department head is a woman, and those terms don't include them. We can build common ground with others—or not—through the words we choose, by including others or leaving them out. This chapter offers tips for using language that is positive and inclusive and that will build common ground with those we wish to reach.

L-9a Avoiding Stereotypes

Stereotypes are generalizations about groups of people and as such can offend because they presume that all members of a group are the same. The writer Geeta Kothari explains how she reacts to a seemingly neutral assumption about Indians: "Indians eat lentils. I understand this as an absolute, a decree from an unidentifiable authority that watches and judges me."

We're all familiar with stereotypes based on sex or race, but stereotypes exist about other characteristics as well: age, body type, education, income, occupation, physical ability, political affiliation, region, religion, sexual orientation, and more. Be careful not to make any broad generalizations about any group—even neutral or positive ones (that Asian students work especially hard, for example, or that Republicans are particularly patriotic).

Also be careful not to call attention to a person's group affiliation if that information is not relevant.

▶ The ~~gay~~ physical therapist who worked the morning shift knew when to let patients rest and when to push them.

L-9b Using Preferred Terms

When you are writing about a group of people, try to use terms that members of that group use themselves. This advice is sometimes easier said than done, because language changes—and words that were commonly used ten years ago may not be in wide use today. Americans of African ancestry, for example, were referred to many years ago as "colored" or "Negro" and then as "black"; today, the preferred terminology is "African American."

When you are referring to ethnicities, especially of individuals, it's usually best to be as specific as possible. Instead of saying that someone is Latina, Latino, or Hispanic, for instance, say that he or she is Puerto Rican or Dominican or Cuban, as appropriate. The same is true of religions; specify a denomination or branch of religion when you can (a Sunni Muslim, an Episcopalian, an Orthodox Jew). And while "Native American" and "American Indian" are both acceptable as general terms, it's often better to refer to a particular tribal nation (Dakota, Chippewa).

It is becoming more common for people to specify (or ask one another about) their preferred pronouns, a trend that is in response to increasing flexibility about gender identity. It may not be accurate to automatically refer to someone as *he* or *she* on the basis of their appearance. Some individuals opt to be referred to as *they*, a usage that transforms *they* from its conventional usage as plural to a singular pronoun of unspecified gender. See **S-6a** for more information about preferred pronouns.

L-9c Editing Out Sexist Language

Sexist language is language that stereotypes or ignores women or men—or that unnecessarily calls attention to someone's gender. Try to eliminate such language from your writing. In particular, avoid nouns that include *man* when you're referring to people who may be either men or women.

INSTEAD OF	USE
man, mankind	humankind, humanity, humans, people
salesman	salesperson
fireman	firefighter
congressman	representative, member of Congress
male nurse	nurse
woman truck driver	truck driver

He, she, they

Writers once used *he, him,* and other masculine pronouns as a default to refer to people whose sex was unknown to them. Today such usage is not widely accepted—and it is no way to build common ground. Here are some alternatives.

Use *he or she* or other masculine and feminine pronouns joined by *or*. (Note, however, that using this option repeatedly may become awkward.)

▶ Before anyone can leave the country, he _or she_ must have a passport or some other official documentation.

Replace a singular noun or pronoun with a plural noun

▶ Before ~~anyone~~ _travelers_ can leave the country, ~~he~~ _they_ must have a passport or some other official documentation.

Eliminate the pronoun altogether

▶ Before ~~anyone can leave~~ _leaving_ the country, ~~he~~ _a traveler_ must have a passport or some other official documentation.

Increasingly, *they* is being used to refer to a person whose gender is unknown or not relevant to the context. This usage may not be acceptable in academic writing; check with your instructor about whether it's appropriate in your writing.

▶ Someone left *their* clothes in the washing machine overnight.

L-10   Englishes

"English? Who needs that? I'm never going to England," declares Homer in an early episode of *The Simpsons*. Sorry, Homer. Anyone using this book does need English. In fact, most of us need a variety of Englishes—the "standard" English we're expected to use at school, the specialized English we use in particular academic and professional fields, and the colloquial English we use in various other communities we belong to. This chapter offers some guidance in using these many varieties of English effectively and appropriately in academic writing.

L-10a Standard Edited English

This is the variety used—and expected—in most academic and professional contexts, and one you need to be able to use comfortably and competently. "Standard" means that it is nearly uniform throughout the English-speaking world. Despite some minor differences—in England and Canada, for example, *labor* is *labour* and an *elevator* is a *lift*—the uniformity means that your writing has the potential to be understood by millions of people. "Edited" means that it is carefully written and polished. And "English"—well, you already know what that is.

L-10b Formal and Informal English

Some of the variation in English comes from levels of formality. Academic writing is usually formal. The tone is crisp and serious; information is stated directly. These characteristics display your competence and authority. The most informal language, on the other hand, tends to be found in the ways we talk with our close friends and relatives; those conversations are full of IDIOMS and slang.

Words with the same basic meaning can convey very different messages when they have different levels of formality—and so the words you choose should always be guided by what's appropriate to your AUDIENCE, TOPIC, and the larger context.

See, for example, two headlines that appeared in two different newspapers on the day that Pope Benedict XVI announced his resignation:

▶ Pope Resigns in Historic Move   *—Wall Street Journal*

▶ I'M OUTTA HERE, GUYS: Pope Gives God 2 Weeks' Notice
                                                    —New York Post

The first headline is from the *Wall Street Journal,* a newspaper dedicated to business news, with an audience of corporate and government executives. Its tone is professional and businesslike, and its English is formal. The second is from the *New York Post,* a daily tabloid newspaper known for its sensationalist headlines; its English is informal, going for laughs and marking a sharp contrast with the pomp and majesty of the papal office.

In the cartoon below the adult understands quite well what the child is saying; she's merely suggesting a more formal and polite—and appropriate—way to express his judgment of the painting.

"Instead of 'It sucks' you could say, 'It doesn't speak to me.'"

Mixing formal and informal

Occasionally mixing in an informal element—a playful image, an unexpected bit of slang—can enliven formal writing. For example, in a book about the alimentary canal, science writer Mary Roach gives detailed, well-researched descriptions of all aspects of digestion, including the anatomy of the digestive system. Although her topic is serious, she stirs in some irreverent METAPHORS and surprising comparisons along the way, as this description of the esophagus shows.

▶ The esophagus is a thin, pink stretchable membrane, a biological bubble gum. —Mary Roach, *Gulp: Adventures on the Alimentary Canal*

Such everyday imagery makes a potentially dry subject come to life. What's more, the information is easier to remember. Quick: what color is your esophagus? You remembered, didn't you?

L-10c English across Fields

If you've ever listened in on a group of nurses, software designers, lawyers, or taxi drivers, you probably heard words you didn't understand, jokes you didn't think were funny. All professional fields have their own specialized language.

Restaurant staff, for example, have a shorthand for relaying food orders and seating information. In this example from an essay about blue-collar work, UCLA professor Mike Rose describes a restaurant where his mother was a waitress:

▶ *Fry four on two*, my mother would say as she clipped a check onto the metal wheel. Her tables were *deuces, four-tops*, or *six-tops* according to their size; seating areas also were nicknamed. The *racetrack*, for instance, was the fast-turnover front section. Lingo conferred authority and signaled know-how.   —Mike Rose, "Blue Collar Brilliance"

You might not know what *deuces* or *four-tops* are (or maybe you do), but it's language Rose's mother knows her colleagues will understand. On the one hand, specialized language allows professionals to do their work with greater ease and efficiency; on the other hand, it marks and helps construct a community around a certain field of work.

L-10d English across Regions

Have you ever wished that British TV shows had subtitles? The characters are definitely speaking English, but you may have a hard time understanding them. Every region has its own accent, of course, but there may also be words and expressions that are unfamiliar or mean something different to those who don't live there. In Australia (and parts of Wisconsin), for example, a *bubbler* is a drinking fountain. In India, the *hall* is the part of the house known in the United States as the living room.

In the US South, *y'all* is the way many folks say *you all*. Country singer Miranda Lambert, a native of Texas, uses *y'all* frequently in her *Twitter* feed, such as in this tweet thanking a North Dakota audience after a performance:

▶ Thanks New Town ND! Y'all were so fun! And LOUD! Came to party
and did it right!   —Miranda Lambert, @mirandalambert, June 8, 2013

In choosing to use *y'all* rather than the more standard *you*, Lambert emphasizes her southern heritage and establishes a friendly, down home tone.

Other regions as well have their own forms of the second person plural. In Chicago and New York you might hear *youse*, and in Pittsburgh it's *yinz*. Such local language is widely understood in the regions where it is used, though it may sound strange to people from other places. Using regional language in your writing can be a good way to evoke a place—and, like Lambert, can demonstrate pride in your own regional roots.

L-10e Englishes across Cultures and Communities

Some varieties of English are associated with a particular social, ethnic, or other community. African American English is perhaps the best-known of these Englishes. Not all African Americans use it, and those who do may not use it exclusively. Not all of its users are African Americans themselves. All of its users, however, follow the conventions and rules that make this variety of English consistent and recognizable.

Linguist Geneva Smitherman has written extensively on this variety of English, often using the language itself to support her points. See how she shifts from standard edited English into African American English to establish her authority as an insider and drive home her point with a stylistic punch.

▶ Think of black speech as having two dimensions: language and style. . . .
Consider [this example]. Nina Simone sing: "It bees dat way sometime."
Here the language aspect is the use of the verb *be* to indicate a
recurrent event or habitual condition, rather than a one-time-only
occurrence. But the total expression— "It bees dat way sometime" —also
reflects Black English style, for the statement suggests a point of view,
a way of looking at life, and a method of adapting to life's realities. To
live by the philosophy of "It bees dat way sometime" is to come to grips
with the changes that life bees puttin us through, and to accept the
changes and bad times as a constant, ever-present reality.

　　　　　　　　　　　　　—Geneva Smitherman, *Talkin and Testifyin:*
　　　　　　　　　　　　　　　　　The Language of Black America

Many other communities develop their own Englishes as well. Ethnic communities often use an English that includes words from another language. Men and women often speak differently, as Deborah Tannen and other linguists have shown. Even young people use an English that might sound very strange coming from a gray-haired elder (imagine your grandfather greeting you with "Dude!").

The differences can be subtle but sometimes a single word can make someone sound young, or old, or Texan, or Canadian—and can establish credibility with an audience. See how a simple "OMG" is enough to establish hipness with young readers of a newspaper article about a fashion show for puppies:

▶ If your pup has been good this year, it deserves a treat from Ware
of the Dog, a line of luxury knits from the designer Tom Scott and
his friend Jackie Rosenthal. The collection includes OMG-cute alpaca
sweaters, cable-knit turtlenecks, hoodies and a geometric-pattern
merino jacquard pullover.　　—"Shopping Snapshots," *New York Times*

Speaking to the article's young audience, the phrase *OMG-cute* not only shows off knowledge of youth culture but also puts a little zest into an otherwise lifeless list of items.

L-10f Mixing Englishes

As a writer, you can use different varieties of English or even different languages for various purposes. Here are some examples and suggestions for doing so effectively and appropriately.

To evoke a person or represent speech

When you are describing people, you may want to quote their words, to let readers "hear" them talk—and to let them speak for themselves. Some multilingual authors flavor their English writing with words or phrases from another language to give readers an authentic sense of someone's words or thoughts. Even if some readers don't understand the non-English words, they usually add more flavor than meaning. See, for example, how Sandra Cisneros mixes English and Spanish in relating an exchange between her parents as they bicker about a trip to visit relatives. Using two languages in the dialogue adds flavor and realism, and the context makes the meaning clear even for readers who don't speak Spanish.

> ▶ "Zoila, why do you insist on being so stubborn?" Father shouts into the mirror, clouding the glass. "*Ya verás*. You'll see, *vieja*, it'll be fun." "And stop calling me *vieja*," Mother shouts back. "I hate that word! Your mother's old; I'm not old."   —Sandra Cisneros, *Caramelo*

When writing dialogue, you may sometimes want to use nonstandard spelling to mimic dialect or sound, as Flannery O'Connor does with the speech of a young boy questioning an outlaw.

> ▶ "What you got that gun for?" John Wesley asked. "Whatcha gonna do with that gun?"   —Flannery O'Connor, "A Good Man Is Hard to Find"

To evoke a place or an event

In certain settings or situations—sports, auctions, math class—you will hear language you wouldn't hear anywhere else. In some cases, the topics require specialized words. There's no way to talk about golf without mentioning *par* or *putting* or *a hole in one*, or to teach math without words like *variable* or *function*. In other cases, people tend to use a certain kind of language. Think about the conversations you'd hear in a board meeting, or the ones you'd hear in a sports bar.

Such language can be used to evoke a place or an event, as in this recap of a 2013 NBA playoff game between the Los Angeles Lakers and the Dallas Mavericks.

▶ The Mavericks played Bryant aggressively, trapping him out of the pick and roll and forcing him into tough shots. He had his moments, he made his share of shots despite great defensive strategy, and ended the night right. Bryant picked up his tenth rebound to seal his triple-double and put up a beautiful hook shot to cap it off and send it home.   —Drew Garrison, *Silver Screen and Roll*

The writer can assume that his readers are familiar with the language he uses; in fact, many readers probably watched the game and just read the recap in order to relive it. His use of basketball **JARGON** helps put them back in the action. But for an audience unfamiliar with basketball, he'd need to explain terms like *pick and roll* and *triple double*.

To build common ground with an audience

Language is one good way to establish credibility and build common ground with readers. For example, in a feature article about how letters to the editor are chosen for publication in the daily newspaper of a city in Minnesota, the writer included the word *uff-da*, a purely local touch:

▶ We don't publish mass produced letters. There are people in these United States who like to send letters to every newspaper in the country on a weekly basis. *Uff-da!* These are easy to catch. There are also some lobbying organizations who provide forms for supporters where writers don't actually pen their own thoughts.
—Tim Engstrom, *Albert Lea Tribune*

Uff-da is a Norwegian expression that is widely used in the region. It means *wow!, whew!, no kidding!,* or even *OMG!* depending on the situation. The writer doesn't need it to convey his meaning, but using it demonstrates a sense of local knowledge and pride—and helps build common ground with his readers.

Think carefully, however, before using words from a language or variety of language that you don't speak yourself; you may offend some readers. And if by chance you use words incorrectly, you could even damage your credibility.

P-1 Commas

Commas matter. Consider the title of the best-selling book *Eats, Shoots & Leaves*. The cover shows two pandas, one with a gun in its paw, one whitewashing the comma. Is the book about a panda that dines, then fires a gun and exits? Or about the panda's customary diet? In fact, it's a book about punctuation; the ambiguity of its title illustrates how commas affect meaning. This chapter shows when and where to use commas in your writing.

P-1a To Join Independent Clauses with *And, But,* and Other Coordinating Conjunctions

Put a comma before the COORDINATING CONJUNCTIONS *and, but, for, nor, or, so,* and *yet* when they connect two INDEPENDENT CLAUSES. The comma signals that one idea is ending and another is beginning.

▶ I do not love Shakespeare, but I still have those books.
　　　　　　　　　　　　—Rick Bragg, "All Over But the Shoutin'"

▶ Most people think the avocado is a vegetable, yet it is actually a fruit.

▶ The blue ribbon went to Susanna, and Sarah got the red ribbon.

　Without the comma, readers might first think both girls got blue ribbons.

Although some writers omit the comma, especially with short independent clauses, you'll never be wrong to include it.

▶ I was smart, and I knew it.　　　—Shannon Nichols, "'Proficiency'"

No comma is needed between the verbs when a single subject performs two actions.

▶ Many fast-food restaurants now give calorie counts on menus and offer a variety of healthy meal options.

▶ Augustine wrote extensively about his mother,/ but mentioned his father only briefly.

P-1b To Set Off Introductory Words

Use a comma after an introductory word, PHRASE, or CLAUSE to mark the end of the introduction and the start of the main part of the sentence.

▶ Typically, a girl has a best friend with whom she sits and talks, frequently telling secrets.
                —Deborah Tannen, "Gender in the Classroom"

▶ In terms of wealth rather than income, the top 1 percent control 40 percent.   —Joseph E. Stiglitz, "Of the 1%, by the 1%, for the 1%"

▶ Even ignoring the extreme poles of the economic spectrum, we find enormous class differences in the life-styles among the haves, the have-nots, and the have-littles.
                —Gregory Mantsios, "Class in America—2003"

▶ When Miss Emily Grierson died, our whole town went to her funeral.
                —William Faulkner, "A Rose for Emily"

Some writers don't use a comma after a short introductory word, phrase, or clause, but it's never wrong to include one.

P-1c To Separate Items in a Series

Use a comma to separate the items in a series. The items may be words, PHRASES, or CLAUSES.

▶ I spend a great deal of time thinking about the power of language —the way it can evoke an emotion, a visual image, a complex idea, or a simple truth.   —Amy Tan, "Mother Tongue"

Though some writers leave out the comma between the final two items in a series, this omission can confuse readers. It's never wrong to include the final comma.

▶ Nadia held a large platter of sandwiches—egg salad, peanut butter, ham, and cheese.

Without the last comma, it's not clear whether there are three or four kinds of sandwiches on the platter.

P-1d To Set Off Nonessential Elements

A nonessential (or nonrestrictive) element is one that could be deleted without changing the basic meaning of the sentence; it should be set off with commas. An essential (or restrictive) element is one that is needed to understand the sentence; therefore, it should not be set off with commas.

NONESSENTIAL

▶ Spanish, which is a Romance language, is one of six official languages at the United Nations.

The detail about being a Romance language adds information, but it is not essential to the meaning of the sentence and so is set off with commas.

ESSENTIAL

▶ Navajo is the Athabaskan language that is spoken in the Southwest by the Navajo people.

The detail about where Navajo is spoken is essential: Navajo is not the only Athabaskan language; it is the Athabaskan language that is spoken in the Southwest.

Note that the meaning of a sentence can change depending on whether or not an element is set off with commas.

▶ My sister, Mary, just published her first novel.

The writer has only one sister.

▶ My sister Mary just published her first novel.

The writer has more than one sister; the one named Mary just published a novel.

Essential and nonessential elements can be clauses, phrases, or words.

CLAUSES

▶ He always drove Chryslers, which are made in America.

▶ He always drove cars that were made in America.

PHRASES

▶ I fumble in the dark, trying to open the mosquito netting around my bed.

▶ I see my mother clutching my baby sister.
                    —Chanrithy Him, "When Broken Glass Floats"

WORDS

▶ At 8:59, Flight 175 passenger Brian David Sweeney tried to call his wife, Julie.

▶ At 9:00, Lee Hanson received a second call from his son Peter.
                    —The 9/11 Commission, "The Hijacking of United 175"

Sweeney had only one wife, so her name provides extra but nonessential information. Hanson presumably had more than one son, so it is essential to specify which son called.

P-1e To Set Off Parenthetical Information

Information that interrupts the flow of a sentence needs to be set off with commas.

▶ Bob's conduct, most of us will immediately respond, was gravely wrong.   —Peter Singer, "The Singer Solution to World Poverty"

▶ With as little as two servings of vegetables a day, it seems to me, you can improve your eating habits.

P-1f To Set Off Transitional Expressions

TRANSITIONS such as *thus, nevertheless, for example,* and *in fact* help connect sentences or parts of sentences. They are usually set off with commas.

▶ The real world, *however,* is run by money.
                    —Joanna MacKay, "Organ Sales Will Save Lives"

When a transition connects two INDEPENDENT CLAUSES in the same sentence, it is preceded by a semicolon and is followed by a comma.

▶ There are few among the poor who speak of themselves as lower class; *instead*, they refer to their race, ethnic group, or geographic location.
—Gregory Mantsios, "Class in America—2003"

P-1g To Set Off Direct Quotations

Use commas to set off quoted words from the speaker or source.

▶ Pa shouts back, "I just want to know where the gunfire is coming from."   —Chanrithy Him, "When Broken Glass Floats"

▶ "You put a slick and a con man together," she said, "and you have predatory lenders."
—Peter Boyer, "Eviction: The Day They Came for Addie Polk's House"

▶ "Death and life are in the power of the tongue," says the proverb.

P-1h To Set Off Direct Address, *Yes* or *No*, Interjections, and Tag Questions

DIRECT ADDRESS	"Yes, Virginia, there really is a Santa Claus."
YES OR *NO*	No, you cannot replace the battery on your iPhone.
INTERJECTION	Oh, a PS4. How long did you have to wait to get it?
TAG QUESTION	That wasn't so hard, was it?

P-1i With Addresses, Place Names, and Dates

▶ Send contributions to Human Rights Campaign, 1640 Rhode Island Ave., Washington, DC 20036.

▶ Athens, Georgia, is famous for its thriving music scene.

▶ Amelia Earhart disappeared over the Pacific Ocean on July 2, 1937, while trying to make the first round-the-world flight at the equator.

Omit the commas, however, if you invert the date (on 2 July 1937) or if you give only the month and year (in July 1937).

P-1j Checking for Unnecessary Commas

Commas have so many uses that it's easy to add them unnecessarily. Here are some situations when you should not use a comma.

Between a subject and a verb

▶ What the organizers of the 1969 Woodstock concert did not anticipate/was the turnout.

▶ The event's promoters/turned down John Lennon's offer to play with his Plastic Ono Band.

Between a verb and its object or complement

▶ Pollsters wondered/how they had so poorly predicted the winner of the 1948 presidential election.

▶ Virtually every prediction indicated/that Thomas Dewey would defeat Harry Truman.

▶ The *Chicago Tribune*'s famous wrong headline was/an embarassment to the newspaper.

After a coordinating conjunction

▶ The College Board reported a decline in SAT scores and/attributed the decline to changes in "student test-taking patterns."

▶ The SAT was created to provide an objective measure of academic potential, but/studies in the 1980s found racial and socioeconomic biases in some test questions.

After *like* or *such as*

▶ Many American-born authors, such as/Henry James, Ezra Pound, and F. Scott Fitzgerald, lived as expatriates in Europe.

After a question mark or an exclamation point

▶ Why would any nation have a monarch in an era of democracy?/you might ask yourself.

▶ "O, be some other name!/" exclaims Juliet.

P-2   Semicolons

Semicolons offer one way to connect two closely related thoughts. Look, for example, at Martha Stewart's advice about how to tell if fruit is ripe: "A perfectly ripened fruit exudes a subtle but sweet fragrance from the stem end, appears plump, and has deeply colored skin; avoid those that have wrinkles, bruises, or tan spots." Stewart could have used a period, but the semicolon shows the connection between what to look for and what to avoid when buying peaches or plums.

P-2a Between Independent Clauses

Closely related independent clauses are most often joined with a comma plus *and* or another COORDINATING CONJUNCTION. If the two clauses are closely related and don't need a conjunction to signal the relationship, they may be linked with a semicolon.

▶ The silence deepened; the room chilled.
> —Wayson Choy, "The Ten Thousand Things"

▶ The life had not flowed out of her; it had been seized.
> —Valerie Steiker, "Our Mother's Face"

A period would work in either of the examples above, but the semicolon suggests a stronger connection between the two independent clauses.

Another option is to use a semicolon with a TRANSITION that clarifies the relationship between the two independent clauses. Put a comma after the transition.

▶ There are no secret economies that nourish the poor; on the contrary, there are a host of special costs.   —Barbara Ehrenreich, *Nickel and Dimed: On (Not) Getting By in America*

P-2b In a Series with Commas

Use semicolons to separate items in a series when one or more of the items contain commas.

▶ There are images of a few students: Erwin Petschaur, a muscular German boy with a strong accent; Dave Sanchez, who was good at math; and Sheila Wilkes, everyone's curly-haired heartthrob.
                    —Mike Rose, "Potato Chips and Stars"

P-2c Checking for Mistakes with Semicolons

Use a comma, not a semicolon, to set off an introductory clause.

▶ When the sun finally sets̸, everyone gathers at the lake to watch the fireworks.

Use a colon, not a semicolon, to introduce a list.

▶ Every American high school student should know that the US Constitution contains three sections̸: preamble, articles, and amendments.

P-3 End Punctuation

She married him. She married him? She married him! In each of these three sentences, the words are the same, but the end punctuation completely changes the meaning—from a simple statement to a bemused question to an emphatic exclamation. This chapter will help you use periods, question marks, and exclamation points in your writing.

P-3a Periods

Use a period to end a sentence that makes a statement.

▶ Rose Emily Meraglio came to the United States from southern Italy as a little girl in the early 1920s and settled with her family in Altoona, Pennsylvania.   —Mike Rose, "The Working Life of a Waitress"

An indirect question, which reports something that someone else has asked, ends with a period, not a question mark.

▶ Presidential candidates are often asked how they will expand the economy and create jobs?.
                                                          ^

When a sentence ends with an abbreviation that has its own period, do not add another period.

▶ The Rat Pack included Frank Sinatra and Sammy Davis Jr./

See **P-10** for more on periods with abbreviations.

P-3b Question Marks

Use a question mark to end a direct question.

▶ Did I think that because I was a minority student jobs would just come looking for me? What was I thinking?
                                           —Richard Rodriguez, "None of This Is Fair"

Use a period rather than a question mark to end an indirect question.

▶ Aunt Vivian often asked what Jesus would do?.
                                                 ^

P-3c Exclamation Points

Use an exclamation point to express strong emotion or add emphasis to a statement or command. Exclamation points should be used sparingly, however, or they may undercut your credibility.

▶ "Keith," we shrieked as the car drove away, "Keith, we love you!"
                                           —Susan Jane Gilman, "Mick Jagger Wants Me"

When the words themselves are emotional, an exclamation point is often unnecessary, and a period is sufficient.

▶ It was so close, so low, so huge and fast, so intent on its target that I swear to you, I swear to you, I felt the vengeance and rage emanating from the plane.   —Debra Fontaine, "Witnessing"

P-4 Quotation Marks

"Girls Just Want to Have Fun" "Two thumbs up!" "Frankly, my dear, I don't give a damn." These are just some of the ways that quotation marks are used—to indicate a song title, to cite praise for a movie, to set off dialogue. In college writing, you will use quotation marks frequently to acknowledge when you've taken words from others. This chapter will show you how to use quotation marks correctly and appropriately.

P-4a Direct Quotations

Use quotation marks to enclose words spoken or written by others.

▶ "Nothing against Tom, but Johnny may be the bigger star now," says director John Waters. —Sean Smith, "Johnny Depp: Unlikely Superstar"

▶ Newt Gringrich and Jesse Jackson have both pounded nails and raised funds for Habitat for Humanity. This is what Millard Fuller calls the "theology of the hammer."
                    —Diana George, "Changing the Face of Poverty"

When you introduce quoted words with *he said*, *she claimed*, or another such **SIGNAL PHRASE**, put a comma after the verb and capitalize the first word of the quote if it's a complete sentence. When you follow a quote with such an expression, use a comma before the closing quotation mark (unless the quote is a question or an exclamation).

▶ When my mother reported that Mr. Tomkey did not believe in television, my father said, "Well, good for him. I don't know that I believe in it either."

"That's exactly how I feel," my mother said, and then my parents watched the news, and whatever came on after the news.

—David Sedaris, "Us and Them"

You do not need any punctuation between *that* and a quotation, nor do you need to capitalize the first word of the quote.

▶ We were assigned to write one essay agreeing or disagreeing with George Orwell's statement that/"the slovenliness of our language makes it easier for us to have foolish thoughts."

In dialogue, insert a new paragraph and a new pair of quotation marks to signal each change of speaker.

▶   "What's this?" the hospital janitor said to me as he stumbled over my right shoe.
"My shoes," I said.
"That's not a shoe, brother," he replied, holding it to the light.
"That's a brick."   —Henry Louis Gates Jr., "A Giant Step"

See **P–8c** for help with capitalization in a direct quotation.

P-4b Long Quotations

Long quotations should be set off without quotation marks as **BLOCK QUOTATIONS**. Each documentation style has distinct guidelines for the length and formatting of block quotations; you'll find more on long quotations in **MLA-d**, **APA-d**, **CMS-c**, and **CSE-c**. The following example uses MLA style, which calls for setting off quotations of five or more typed lines of prose by indenting them five spaces (or half an inch) from the left margin. Note that in the following example, the period precedes the parenthetical documentation.

Biographer David McCullough describes Truman's railroad campaign as follows:

No president in history had ever gone so far in quest of support from the people, or with less cause for the effort, to judge by informed opinion. . . . As a test of his skills and judgment as a professional politician, not to say his stamina and disposition at age sixty-four, it would be like no other experience in his long, often difficult career, as he himself understood perfectly. (655)

P-4c Titles of Short Works

Use quotation marks to enclose the titles of articles, chapters, essays, short stories, poems, songs, and episodes of television series. Titles of books, films, newspapers, and other longer works should be in italics (or underlined) rather than enclosed in quotation marks.

▶ In "Unfriendly Skies Are No Match for El Al," Vivienne Walt, a writer for *USA Today,* describes her experience flying with this airline.
—Andie McDonie, "Airport Security"

Note that the title of the newspaper is italicized, whereas the newspaper article title takes quotation marks.

▶ With every page of Edgar Allan Poe's story "The Tell-Tale Heart," my own heart beat faster.

▶ Rita Dove's poem "Dawn Revisited" contains vivid images that appeal to the senses of sight, sound, smell, and taste.

P-4d Single Quotation Marks

When you quote a passage that already contains quotation marks, whether they enclose a quotation or a title, change the inner ones to single quotation marks.

▶ Debra Johnson notes that according to Marilyn J. Adams, "effective reading instruction is based on 'direct instruction in phonics, focusing on the orthographic regularities of English.' "

▶ Certain essays are so good (or so popular) that they are included in almost every anthology. *The Norton Reader* notes, "Some essays—Martin Luther King Jr.'s 'Letter from Birmingham Jail' and Jonathan Swift's 'Modest Proposal,' for example—are constant favorites" (xxiii).

P-4e With Other Punctuation

When other punctuation follows material in quotation marks, it should go inside the closing quotation mark in some cases and outside in others. The following guidelines are those that are conventional in the United States; they differ from those in many other countries.

Commas and periods

Put commas and periods inside closing quotation marks.

▶ "On the newsstand, the cover is acting as a poster, an ad for what's inside," she said. "The loyal reader is looking for what makes the magazine exceptional."
                    —Katharine Q. Seelye, "Lurid Numbers on Glossy Pages!"

Semicolons and colons

Put semicolons and colons outside closing quotation marks.

▶ No elder stands behind our young to say, "Folks have fought and died for your right to pierce your face, so do it right"; no community exists that can model for a young person the responsible use of the "right"; for the right, even if called self-expression, comes from no source other than desire.   —Stephen L. Carter, "Just Be Nice"

▶ According to James Garbarino, author of *Lost Boys: Why Our Sons Turn Violent and How We Can Save Them*, it makes no sense to talk about violent media as a direct cause of youth violence. Rather, he says, "it depends": Media violence is a risk factor that, working in concert with others, can exacerbate bad behavior.
                    —Maggie Cutler, "Whodunit—The Media?"

Question marks and exclamation points

Put question marks and exclamation points inside closing quotation marks if they are part of the quotation but outside if they apply to the whole sentence.

▶ Then she began to talk more loudly. "What he want, I come to New York tell him front of his boss, you cheating me?"
                    —Amy Tan, "Mother Tongue"

▶ How many people know the words to "Louie, Louie"?

P-4f With Parenthetical Documentation

When you provide parenthetical DOCUMENTATION for a quotation, put it after the closing quotation mark, and put any end punctuation that's part of your sentence after the parentheses.

▶ An avid baseball fan, Tallulah Bankhead once said, "There have been only two geniuses in the world: Willie Mays and Willie Shakespeare" (183).

P-4g Checking for Mistakes with Quotation Marks

Avoid using quotation marks to identify slang or to emphasize a word. Remove the quotation marks, or substitute a better word.

SLANG   Appearing /hip/ is important to many parents in New York.

EMPHASIS   The woman explained that she is /only/ the manager, not the owner, of the health club.

Do not put quotation marks around indirect quotations, those that do not quote someone's exact words.

▶ Grandmother always said that /meat that was any good didn't need seasoning./

P-5   Apostrophes

McDonald's: "I'm *lovin'* it" proclaims an ad, demonstrating two common uses of the apostrophe: to show ownership (*McDonald's*) and to mark missing letters (*I'm, lovin'*). This chapter offers guidelines on these and other common uses for apostrophes.

P-5a Possessives

Use an apostrophe to make a word possessive: *Daniel Craig's eyes, someone else's problem, the children's playground.*

Singular nouns

To make most singular nouns possessive, add an apostrophe and -s.

▶ The challenge now will be filling the park**'s** seats.
　　　　　—Michael Kimmelman, "A Ballpark Louder Than Its Fans"

▶ In Plato**'s** *Phaedrus*, Socrates bemoaned the development of writing.
　　　　　—Nicholas Carr, "Is Google Making Us Stupid?"

▶ Bill Gates**'s** philanthropic efforts focus on health care and education.

If adding -'s makes pronunciation awkward, some writers use only an apostrophe with singular nouns that end in -s: *Euripedes', George Saunders'*.

Plural nouns

To form the possessive of a plural noun not ending in -s, add an apostrophe and -s. For plural nouns that end in -s, add only an apostrophe.

▶ Are women**'s** minds different from men**'s** minds?
　　　　　—Evelyn Fox Keller, "Women in Science"

▶ The neighbors**'** complaints about noise led the club owner to install soundproof insulation.

▶ Did you hear that Laurence Strauss is getting married? The reception will be at the Strausses**'** home.

Personal pronouns

Personal pronouns such as *we, she,* and *you* have their own possessive forms, which never take an apostrophe. See **S-6c** for a complete list.

▶ The graduates let out a cheer as they tossed *their* hats in the air—and later got a good chuckle when the valedictorian accidentally stepped on *hers*.

Something, everyone, *and other indefinite pronouns*

To form the possessive of an INDEFINITE PRONOUN, add an apostrophe and -s.

▶ Clarabelle was everyone's favorite clown.

Joint possession

To show that two or more individuals possess something together, use the possessive form for the last noun only.

▶ Carlson and Ventura's book is an introduction to Latino writers for English-speaking adolescents.

To show individual possession, make each noun possessive.

▶ Jan's and Al's heart transplants inspired me to become an organ donor.

Compound nouns

For nouns made up of more than one word, make the last word possessive.

▶ The surgeon general's report persuaded many people to stop smoking.

P-5b Contractions

An apostrophe in a contraction indicates where letters have been omitted.

▶ I've learned that sometimes friends and business don't mix.
—Iliana Roman, "First Job"

I've *is a contraction of* I have; don't *is a contraction of* do not.

P-5c Plurals

You'll often see apostrophes used to pluralize numbers, letters, abbreviations, and words discussed as words: 7's, A's, NGO's, *thank you*'s. Usage is changing, however, and in the case of numbers, abbreviations, and words discussed as words, you should leave out the apostrophe in your own writing.

Plural of numbers

▶ The winning hand had three 8**s**.

▶ We were astonished to hear Grandma Eleanor say she loved the 1950**s**.

Plural of abbreviations and words discussed as words

▶ How many TV**s** does the average American family have in its home?

▶ The resolution passed when there were more *ayes* than *nays*.

   See that words discussed as words are italicized but the -s ending is not.

Plural of letters

Italicize the letter but not the -s ending: *ABCs*. To avoid confusion, use an apostrophe with lowercase letters and uppercase *A* and *I*.

▶ Mrs. Duchovny always reminded us to dot our *i*'**s** and cross our *t*'**s**.

▶ The admissions officers spoke enthusiastically about the college's no-grades option—and then said we'd need mostly *A*'**s** to get in.

P-5d Checking for Mistakes with Apostrophes

Do not use an apostrophe in the following situations.

With plural nouns that are not possessive

▶ Both ~~cellist's~~ played encores.
  cellists

With his, hers, ours, yours, *and* theirs

▶ Look at all the lettuce. ~~Our's~~ is organic. Is ~~your's?~~
  Ours _yours?_

With the possessive its

▶ It's an unusual building; ~~it's~~ style has been described as postmodern, but it fits beautifully with the Gothic buildings on our campus.
  its

   It's is a contraction meaning "it is" or "it has"; its is the possessive form of it.

P-6   Other Punctuation

Some carpenters can do their jobs using only a hammer and a saw, but most rely on additional tools. The same is true of writers: you can get along with just a few punctuation marks, but having some others in your toolbox—colons, dashes, parentheses, brackets, ellipses, and slashes—can help you say what you want to more precisely—and can help readers follow what you write more easily. This chapter can help you use these other punctuation marks effectively.

P-6a Colons

Colons are used to direct attention to words that follow the colon: an explanation or elaboration, a list, a quotation, and so on.

▶ What I remember best, strangely enough, are the two things I couldn't understand and over the years grew to hate: grammar lessons and mathematics.   —Mike Rose, "Potato Chips and Stars"

▶ I sized him up as fast as possible: tight black velvet pants pulled over his boots, black jacket, a red-green-yellow scarf slashed around his neck.   —Susan Jane Gilman, "Mick Jagger Wants Me"

▶ She also voices some common concerns: "The product should be safe, it should be easily accessible, and it should be low-priced."
                    —Dara Mayers, "Our Bodies, Our Lives"

▶ Fifteen years after the release of the Carnegie report, College Board surveys reveal data are no different: test scores still correlate strongly with family income.   —Gregory Mantsios, "Class in America—2003"

Colons are also used after the salutation in a business letter, in ratios, between titles and subtitles, between city and publisher in bibliographies, between chapter and verse in biblical references, and between numbers that indicate hours, minutes, and seconds.

- ► Dear President Michaels:
- ► For best results, add water to the powder in a 3:1 ratio.
- ► *The Last Campaign: How Harry Truman Won the 1948 Election*
- ► New York: Norton, 2014.
- ► "Death and life are in the power of the tongue" (Proverbs 18:21).
- ► The morning shuttle departs at 6:52 AM.

P-6b Dashes

You can create a dash by typing two hyphens (--) with no spaces before or after or by selecting the em dash from the symbol menu of your word-processing program.

Use dashes to set off material you want to emphasize. Unlike colons, dashes can appear not only after an independent clause but also at other points in a sentence. To set off material at the end of a sentence, place a dash before it; to set off material in the middle of the sentence, place a dash before and after the words you want to emphasize.

- ► After that, the roller coaster rises and falls, slowing down and speeding up—all on its own.
  —Cathi Eastman and Becky Burrell, "The Science of Screams"
- ► It did not occur to me—possibly because I am an American—that there could be people anywhere who had never seen a Negro.
  —James Baldwin, "Stranger in the Village"

Dashes are often used to signal a shift in tone or thought.

- ► The best way to keep children home is to make the home atmosphere pleasant—and let the air out of the tires.   —Dorothy Parker

Keep in mind that dashes are most effective if they are used only when material needs particular emphasis. Too many dashes can interfere with the flow and clarity of your writing.

P-6c Parentheses

Use parentheses to enclose supplemental details and digressions.

▶ When I was a child, attending grade school in Washington, DC, we took classroom time to study manners. Not only the magic words "please" and "thank you" but more complicated etiquette questions, like how to answer the telephone ("Carter residence, Stephen speaking") and how to set the table (we were quizzed on whether knife blades point in or out).   —Stephen L. Carter, "Just Be Nice"

▶ In their apartments they have the material possessions that indicate success (a VCR, a color television), even if it means that they do without necessities and plunge into debt to buy these items.
                    —Diana George, "Changing the Face of Poverty"

▶ Before participating in the trials, Seeta and Ratna (not their real names) knew nothing about H.I.V.
                         —Dara Mayers, "Our Bodies, Our Lives"

P-6d Brackets

Put brackets around words that you insert in a QUOTATION.

▶ As Senator Reid explained, "She [Nancy Pelosi] realizes that you cannot make everyone happy."

If you are quoting a source that contains an error, put the Latin word *sic* in brackets after the error to indicate that the mistake is in the original source.

▶ Warehouse has been around for 30 years and has 263 stores, suggesting a large fan base. The chain sums up its appeal thus: "styley [*sic*], confident, sexy, glamorous, edgy, clean and individual, with it's [*sic*] finger on the fashion pulse."
                    —Anne Ashworth, "Chain Reaction: Warehouse"

P-6e Ellipses

Ellipses are three spaced dots that indicate an omission or a pause. Use ellipses to show that you have omitted words within a QUOTATION.

If you omit a complete sentence or more in the middle of a quoted passage, add the three dots after the period.

ORIGINAL

▶ The Lux ad's visual content, like Resinol's, supports its verbal message. Several demure views of Irene Dunne emphasize her "pearly-smooth skin," the top one framed by a large heart shape. In all the photos, Dunne wears a feathery, feminine collar, giving her a birdlike appearance: she is a bird of paradise or an ornament. At the bottom of the ad, we see a happy Dunne being cuddled and admired by a man.

　　　　　　　　　　　—Doug Lantry, " 'Stay Sweet as You Are' "

WITH ELLIPSES

▶ The Lux ad's visual content . . . supports its verbal message. Several demure views of Irene Dunne emphasize her "pearly-smooth skin," the top one framed by a large heart shape. . . . At the bottom of the ad, we see a happy Dunne being cuddled and admired by a man.

If you use parenthetical documentation after quoted material, place ellipses *before* the parentheses to indicate the deletion of words, but put the end punctuation *after* the parentheses.

▶ According to Kathleen Welch, "One can turn one's gaze away from television, but one cannot turn one's ears from it without leaving the area . . . " (102).

P-6f Slashes

When you quote two or three lines of poetry and run them in with the rest of your text, use slashes to show where one line ends and the next begins. Put a space before and after each slash.

▶ In the opening lines of the poem, he warns the reader to "Lift not the painted veil which those who live / Call Life" (1-2).

　　　　　—Stephanie Huff, "Metaphor and Society in Shelley's 'Sonnet'"

P-7   Hyphens

If your mother gives you much needed advice, has she given you a great deal of advice that you needed, or advice that you needed badly? What about a psychiatry experiment that used thirty five year old subjects? Were there thirty-five subjects who were a year old? thirty subjects who were five years old? or an unspecified number of thirty-five-year-old subjects? Hyphens could clear up the confusion. This chapter provides tips for when to use hyphens and when to omit them.

P-7a Compound Words

Compound words can be two words (*ground zero*), a hyphenated word (*self-esteem*), or one word (*outsource*). Check a dictionary, and if a compound is not there, assume that it is two words.

Compound adjectives

A compound adjective is made up of two or more words. Most compound adjectives take a hyphen before a noun.

▶ a little-known trombonist

▶ a foul-smelling river

Do not use a hyphen to connect an -ly adverb and an adjective.

▶ a carefully executed plan

A compound adjective after a noun is usually easy to read without a hyphen; add a hyphen only if the compound is unclear without it.

▶ The river has become foul smelling in recent years.

Prefixes and suffixes

A hyphen usually isn't needed after a prefix or before a suffix (*preschool, antislavery, counterattack, catlike, citywide*). However, hyphens are necessary in the following situations.

WITH *GREAT-, SELF-, -ELECT*   great-aunt, self-hatred, president-elect

WITH CAPITAL LETTERS   anti-American, post-Soviet literature

WITH NUMBERS   post-9/11, the mid-1960s

TO AVOID DOUBLE AND TRIPLE LETTERS   anti-intellectualism, ball-like

FOR CLARITY   re-cover (cover again) *but* recover (get well)

Numbers

Hyphenate fractions and compound numbers from twenty-one to ninety-nine.

▶ three-quarters of their income

▶ thirty-five subjects

P-7b At the End of a Line

Use a hyphen to divide a multisyllabic word that does not fit on one line. (A one-syllable word is never hyphenated.) Divide words between syllables as shown in a dictionary, after a prefix, or before a suffix. Divide compound words between the parts of the compound, if possible. Do not leave only one letter at the end or the beginning of a line.

   op-er-a-tion   knot-ty   main-stream

Dividing internet addresses

Do not insert a hyphen in a URL or DOI that you break at the end of a line. It's standard practice to break URLs or DOIs that won't fit on a line after a double slash or before any other punctuation mark. See the chapters on APA, Chicago, MLA, and CSE for more specific advice on how to divide internet addresses in each of those styles.

P-8   Capitalization

Capital letters are an important signal, either that a new sentence is beginning or that a specific person, place, or brand is being discussed. Capitalize *Carol*, and it's clear that you're referring to a person; write *carol*, and readers will know you're writing about a song sung at Christmas. This chapter offers guidelines to help you know what to capitalize and when.

P-8a Proper Nouns and Common Nouns

Capitalize proper nouns, those naming specific people, places, and things. All other nouns are common nouns and should not be capitalized.

PROPER NOUNS	COMMON NOUNS
Sanjay Gupta	a doctor
Senator Feinstein	a senator
Uncle Daniel	my uncle
France	a republic
the Mississippi River	a river
the West Coast	a coast
Christianity	a religion
Allah	a god
the Torah	a sacred text
Central Intelligence Agency	an agency
US Congress	the US government
Kansas State University	a university
Composition 101	a writing course
World War II	a war
July	summer
the Middle Ages	the fourteenth century
Kleenex	tissues

Adjectives derived from proper nouns, especially the names of people and places, are usually capitalized: *Shakespearean, Swedish, Chicagoan.* There are exceptions to this rule, however, such as *french fries, roman numeral,* and *congressional.* Consult your dictionary if you are unsure whether an adjective should be capitalized.

Many dictionaries capitalize the terms *Internet, Net,* and *World Wide Web,* but you'll see variations such as *Website* and *website.* Whether you capitalize or not, be consistent throughout a paper.

P-8b Titles before a Person's Name

A professional title is capitalized when it appears immediately before a person's name but not when it appears after a proper noun or alone.

Senator (*or* Sen.) Elizabeth Warren   Elizabeth Warren, the senator

P-8c The First Word of a Sentence

Capitalize the first word of a sentence. The first word of a quoted sentence should be capitalized, but not the first word of a quoted phrase.

▶ Speaking about acting, Clint Eastwood notes, "You can show a lot with a look.... It's punctuation."

▶ Sherry Turkle argues that we're living in "techno-enthusiastic times" and that we're inclined "to celebrate our gadgets."

Interrupted quotations

Capitalize the second part of an interrupted quotation only if it begins a new sentence.

▶ "It was just as nice," she sobbed, "as I hoped and dreamed it would be."   —Joan Didion, "Marrying Absurd"

▶ "On the newsstand, the cover is acting as a poster, an ad for what's inside," she said. "The loyal reader is looking for what makes the magazine exceptional."
                    —Katharine Q. Seelye, "Lurid Numbers on Glossy Pages!"

P-8d Titles and Subtitles

Capitalize the first and last words and all other important words of a title and subtitle. Do not capitalize less important words such as ARTICLES, COORDINATING CONJUNCTIONS, and PREPOSITIONS.

"Give Peace a Chance"
Pride and Prejudice
The Shallows: What the Internet Is Doing to Our Brains

Each documentation style has guidelines for formatting titles in notes and bibliographies. You'll find more on titles and subtitles in MLA-c, APA-c, CMS-b, and CSE-b.

P-9 Italics

Italic type tells us to read words a certain way. Think of the difference between the office and *The Office*, or between time and *Time*. In each case, the italicized version tells us it's a specific television show or magazine. This chapter provides guidelines on using italics in your writing.

P-9a Titles of Long Works

Titles and subtitles of long works should appear in italics (or underlined). Notable exceptions are sacred writing such as the Qur'an or the Old Testament and historical documents such as the Declaration of Independence.

BOOKS   *War and Peace; The Hobbit; The Brief Wondrous Life of Oscar Wao*

PERIODICALS   *The Atlantic; Teen Vogue; College English*

NEWSPAPERS   *Los Angeles Times*

PLAYS   *Medea; Six Degrees of Separation*

LONG POEMS   *The Odyssey; Paradise Lost*

FILMS AND VIDEOS   *Selma; Inside Out; The Wizard of Oz*

MUSICAL WORKS OR ALBUMS   *The Four Seasons; Rubber Soul*

RADIO AND TV SERIES   *Fresh Air; Modern Family; Game of Thrones*

PAINTINGS, SCULPTURES   the *Mona Lisa*; Michelangelo's *David*

DANCES BY A CHOREOGRAPHER   Mark Morris's *Gloria*

SOFTWARE   *Adobe Acrobat XI Standard*

SHIPS, SPACECRAFT   *Queen Mary; Challenger*

WEBSITES   *Salon; Etsy; IMDb*

A short work, such as a short story, an article, an episode of a series, or a song, takes quotation marks.

P-9b Words Discussed as Words

Italicize a word you are discussing as a word. The same practice applies to numbers, letters, and symbols.

▶ In those 236 words, you will hear the word *dedicate* five times.
                                    —William Safire, "A Spirit Reborn"

▶ Most American dictionaries call for one *t* in the word *benefited*.

▶ All computer codes consist of some combination of *0*s and *1*s.

Some writers use quotation marks rather than italics to signal words discussed as words.

▶ I would learn, when I asked some people who didn't show up the next day, that "definitely attending" on Facebook means "maybe" and "maybe attending" means "likely not."
                                    —Hal Niedzviecki, "Facebook in a Crowd"

P-9c Non-English Words

Use italics for an unfamiliar word or phrase in a language other than English. Do not italicize proper nouns.

▶ *Verstehen*, a concept often associated with Max Weber, is the sociologist's attempt to understand human actions from the actor's point of view.

If the word or phrase has become part of everyday English or has an entry in English-language dictionaries, it does not need italics.

▶ An ad hoc committee should be formed to assess the university's use of fossil fuels and ways to incorporate alternative energy sources.

▶ The plot of *Jane Eyre* follows the conventions of a bildungsroman, or a coming-of-age story.

P-9d For Emphasis

You can use italics occasionally to lend emphasis to a word or phrase, but do not overuse them.

▶ It is, perhaps, as much what Shakespeare did *not* write as what he did that seems to indicate something seriously wrong with his marriage.
　　　　　—Stephen Greenblatt, "Shakespeare on Marriage"

▶ Despite a physical beauty that had . . . hordes of teenage girls (and a few boys) dreaming of touching his hair *just once*, Depp escaped from the Hollywood star machine.
　　　　　—Sean Smith, "Johnny Depp: Unlikely Superstar"

P-10   Abbreviations

MTV. USA. OC. DNA. *fwiw.* DIY. These are some common abbreviations, shortcuts to longer words and phrases. You can use common abbreviations if you are sure your readers will recognize them. If not, spell out the full term with the abbreviation in parentheses the first time it appears. After that, you can use the abbreviation alone.

▶ In a recent press release, officials from the international organization Médecins Sans Frontières (MSF) stressed the need for more effective tuberculosis drugs.

Periods are generally used in abbreviations of personal titles that precede a name and in Latin abbreviations such as *e.g.* or *etc.* They are not needed for state abbreviations such as *CA*, *NY*, or *TX*, or for most abbreviations made up of initials, like *AP* or *YMCA*. In some cases, periods are optional (*BCE* or *B.C.E.*). Be sure to use them or omit them consistently. If you're not sure about periods for a particular abbreviation, check a dictionary.

P-10a With Names

Most titles are abbreviated when they come before or after a name.

Mr. Ed Stanford	Ed Stanford Jr.
Dr. Ralph Lopez	Ralph Lopez, MD
Prof. Susan Miller	Susan Miller, PhD

Do not abbreviate job titles that are not attached to a name.

      nurse
▶ The ~~RN~~ who worked with trauma victims specialized in cardiac care.
      ^

P-10b With Numbers

The following abbreviations can be used with numbers.

632 BC ("before Christ")
344 BCE ("before the common era")
AD 800 (*"anno Domini"*)
800 CE ("common era")
10:30 AM (*or* a.m.)
7:00 PM (*or* p.m.)

Notice that BC, BCE, and CE follow the date, while AD precedes the date. Remember that the abbreviations in the list cannot be used without a date or time.

▶ By early ~~p.m.,~~ *afternoon,* all prospective subjects for the experiment had checked in.

P-10c In Notes and Documentation

With only a few exceptions, the names of months, days of the week, colleges and universities, cities, states, and countries should not be abbreviated in the body of a paper. But they often are abbreviated in footnotes and bibliographies; follow the rules of whichever documentation system you are using.

The same applies to Latin abbreviations like *ibid., op. cit.,* and *et al.:* while you may use them in notes and documentation, they're not appropriate in the body of your text. Use equivalent English expressions (such as "and others" for *et al.*) instead.

▶ Being left-handed presents some challenges for writers—~~e.g.,~~ *for example,* it hurts to write in spiral notebooks, and ink smears across the page and the side of your hand.

P-11 Numbers

Numbers may be written with numerals (*97*) or words (*ninety-seven*). Spell out numbers and fractions that you can write in one or two words (*thirteen, thirty-seven, thirty thousand, two-thirds*). Use numerals otherwise (*578; 5,788*). Spell out any number that begins a sentence. Be aware, however, that the conventions for writing numbers vary across disciplines.

In the humanities, **MLA** and Chicago recommend spelling out all numbers up to a hundred (*twenty-five*) and all round numbers (*fifty thousand*) and using numerals for specific numbers above one hundred (101).

▶ In a survey of *two hundred* students, 135 said they spent more than two hours each day writing.

In the social sciences, **APA** recommends spelling out numbers one through nine and using numerals for all the rest.

▶ *Nine 40*-minute interviews of subjects in *three* categories were conducted for this study.

In the sciences, **CSE** recommends using numerals in almost any situation, but spelling out zero and one to avoid confusion with l and O.

▶ The physician recommended one dose of 200 mg per day for 8 days.

In most business writing, spell out numbers one through ten and use numerals for all numbers over ten (*ten goals, 11 strategies*).

▶ We received *35* applications and identified *five* strong candidates, who we'll interview this week.

For very large numbers that include a fraction or decimal, use a combination of numerals and words.

▶ One retailer sold more than 4.5 million of its basic T-shirts last year.

In addition, numerals are generally used in the following situations.

ADDRESSES   500 Broadway; 107 175th Street

DATES   December 26, 2012; 632 BCE; the 1990s

MONEY IN EXACT AMOUNTS $3.75; $375,000; a deficit of $3.75 trillion

PARTS OF WRITTEN WORKS   volume 2; Chapter 5; page 82; act 3, scene 3

PERCENTAGES   66 percent (*or* 66%)

RATIOS   16:1 (*or* 16 to 1)

STATISTICS   a median age of 32

TIMES OF DAY   6:20 AM (*or* a.m.)

WHOLE NUMBERS WITH DECIMALS OR FRACTIONS   66.7; 66 2/3; 59½

Credits

Glossary / Index

A

a, an, 373–74
abbreviations, 413–15
    names with, 414

abstract, 79–82 A writing GENRE that summarizes a book, an article, or a paper, usually in words. Authors in some academic fields must provide, at the top of a report submitted for publication, an abstract of its content. The abstract may then appear in a journal of abstracts, such as *Psychological Abstracts*. An *informative abstract* summarizes a complete report; a briefer *descriptive abstract* provides only a brief overview; a *proposal abstract* (also called a TOPIC PROPOSAL) requests permission to conduct research, write on a topic, or present a report at a scholarly conference. Key Features: SUMMARY of basic information • objective description • brevity
    formatting guidelines
        APA style, 201, 205
        CSE style, 261
    key elements, 80
    tips for writing, 81–82

Note: This glossary/index defines key terms and directs you to pages in the book where you can find specific information on these and other topics. Words set in SMALL CAPITAL LETTERS are themselves defined in the glossary/index.

abstract words
    precise writing and, 354
    signal verbs and, 114
academic contexts, 6–8
Academic Search Complete, 98
academic searches, 99

academic writing, 6–8 Writing done in an academic or scholarly context, such as for course assignments. Key Features: evidence that you've carefully considered the SUBJECT • clear, appropriately qualified THESIS • response to what others have said • good reasons supported by evidence • acknowledgment of multiple perspectives • carefully documented sources • confident, authoritative STANCE • indication of why your topic matters • careful attention to correctness

a case in point, 357
accept, except, 361
access dates, documenting
    Chicago style, 226
    MLA style, 132
acknowledging sources, 116–17
across the board, 360
action, calls to, 29

action verb, 371 A VERB that expresses a physical or mental action (*jump, consider*).

active voice, 329–30 When a VERB is in the active voice, the SUBJECT performs the action: *He sent a gift.*

AD (*"anno domini"*), 414–15

ad hominem argument   A logical FAL-LACY that attacks someone's charac-ter rather than addresses the issues. (*Ad hominem* is Latin for "to the man.")

adapt, adopt, 361
addresses, 390, 416

adjective, 370–73   A MODIFIER that describes a NOUN or PRONOUN (a *challenging* task, a *cloudless blue* sky).
    choosing vs. adverb, 370–73
    comparatives and superlatives,
        371–72, 456–57
    compound, 407
    placement of, proper, 372–73

adverb, 370–73   A MODIFIER that tells more about a VERB (speak *loudly*), an ADJECTIVE (*very* loud), another ad-verb (*very* loudly), or a whole CLAUSE (*Sometimes* speaking loudly is coun-terproductive).
    choosing vs. adjective, 370–73
    comparatives and superlatives,
        371–72
    placement of, proper, 372–73

advertisements, documenting
    APA style, 199–200
    MLA style, 153
advice, advise, 361
affect, effect, 361
African American English, 382
after, as subordinating word, 318
afterwords, documenting
    Chicago style, 217
    MLA style, 148

agreement, 285–89, 334–41   The cor-respondence between a SUBJECT and VERB in person and number (*the <u>dog</u> <u>chases</u> the children down the street*) or between a PRONOUN and its ANTECED-ENT in gender and number (*the <u>cat</u> nursed <u>her</u> kittens; the <u>children</u> flee be-cause <u>they</u> are afraid*).
    pronoun-antecedent, 339–41
        collective nouns, 340–41
        editing, 285–89
        in gender, 341
        generic nouns, 340
        indefinite pronouns, 340
        singular *they,* 288, 341
        why it matters, 285
    subject-verb, 292–95, 334–39
        agreement in number and
            person, 335
        collective nouns, 337
        compound subjects, 336
        editing, 292–95
        indefinite pronouns, 337
        news, physics, etc., 338–39
        relative pronouns, 338
        subjects and verbs separated, 336
        subjects following verbs, 336–37
        titles and words used as words, 339
        who, that, which, 338
        why it matters, 292
all, 337
all right, alright, 361
allusion, illusion, 361
almanacs, 97
along the same lines, 358
a lot, 361
although, as subordinating word, 318
am. See be
American Psychological Association
        (APA) style. *See* APA style

among, between, 361
amount, number, 361
an, 373–74

analogy, 22 A STRATEGY for COMPARISON that explains something unfamiliar in terms of something familiar.

analysis, 49–53, 62–65 A writing GENRE that methodically examines something by breaking it into its parts and noting how they work in relation to one another. *See also* literary analysis; rhetorical analysis

AND (Boolean operator), 96–97

anecdote, 46 A brief NARRATIVE used to illustrate a point.
in opening paragraphs, 29
in presentations, 38

annotated bibliography, 74–78 A writing GENRE that gives an overview of published research and scholarship on a topic. Each entry includes complete publication information and a SUMMARY or an ABSTRACT. A *descriptive annotation* summarizes the content of a source without commenting on its value; an *evaluative annotation* gives an opinion about the source along with a description of it. Key Features: statement of the scope • complete bibliographic information • relevant commentary • consistent presentation
creating, 76–77
descriptive vs. evaluative, 74–76
key elements, 75–76

annotating, 84

antecedent, 339–42 The NOUN or PRONOUN to which a pronoun refers. In *Maya* lost *her* wallet, *Maya* is the antecedent of *her*.
pronoun-antecedent agreement, 339–40
pronoun reference, 341–42

anthologies, documenting
Chicago style, 216
MLA style, 126, 145–46
any, 337
anyone, 340
anyone, 337
anything, 337

APA style, 170–207 A system of DOCUMENTATION used in the social sciences. APA stands for the American Psychological Association.
abstracts and, 205
directory (table of contents), 170–73
formatting guidelines, 200–203
in-text documentation, 173–78
notes, 178–79
quotations and paraphrases, 173–74, 201–2
reference list, 179–200, 202, 207
books (print), 179–84
miscellaneous sources, 195–200
online sources, 187–95, 197, 200
periodical articles, 184–87, 190–93
sources not covered by APA, 195–200
sample pages, 203–7
title pages, 200, 204

APA *style (cont.)*
  writing style, 201
    spelling out of numbers, 416
    verb tenses in signal phrases,
      115, 323

apostrophes, 309–13, 399–402
  with contractions, 401
  mistakes with, 402
  with plurals, 401–2
  with possessives, 400–401

appendix   A section at the end of a
written work for supplementary material that would be distracting in the
main part of the text.

application letter   A letter written to
apply for a job or other position. Key
Features: succinct indication of qual-
ifications • reasonable and pleasing
tone • conventional, businesslike
form

appositive phrases, 316
appropriateness
  of language, 351–53, 380, 446–47
  of sources, 76–77, 92–96
archives, digital, 99
are. *See* be

argument, 43–48   A writing GENRE
and STRATEGY that uses REASONS and
EVIDENCE to support a CLAIM or POSI-
TION and, sometimes, to persuade an
AUDIENCE to accept that position. Key
Features: clear and arguable position
• necessary background • good reasons • convincing support for each
reason • appeal to readers' values •

trustworthy TONE • careful consideration of other positions
  analyzing, 86
  evaluating, 102–5
  writing
    key elements, 43–45
    organizing, 47, 48
    tips for writing, 45–48

art, documenting MLA style, 133, 153–55

article, 373–75   The word *a*, *an*, or *the*,
used to indicate that a NOUN is indefinite (*a* writer, *an* author) or definite
(*the* author).
  capitalizing, in titles, 411
  when to use, 374

articles, periodical. See periodical articles
Artstor, 100
as, 343
  vs. *as if* and *like*, 361
  pronoun case and, 341
  as subordinating word, 318
as a matter of fact, 358, 359
at, 366–67
atlases, 97

audience, 2–3   Those to whom a text
is directed—the people who read, listen to, or view the text.
  for annotated bibliographies, 76
  appealing to readers' values, 44
  appropriate language and, 380
  arguments and, 46
  building common ground, 385
  idioms and, 360
  reading strategy, 84
  research sources and, 103, 105
  rhetorical context and, 8

audio material
    online collections of, 100
    in presentations, 39
audio sources, documenting
    APA style, 196–200
    MLA style, 153–58

authorities People or texts that are cited as support for an ARGUMENT. A structural engineer may be quoted as an authority on bridge construction, for example. *Authority* also refers to a quality conveyed by writers who are knowledgeable about their subject.

authors, documenting
    APA style, 173–77, 179–83,
        186–87
    Chicago style, 211–13, 215, 217,
        226, 254
    CSE style, 249, 252
    MLA style, 130–31, 134–36

B

bad, badly, 362, 371
balance
    argument and, 86
    as a design element, 31

bandwagon appeal A logical FAL-LACY that argues for thinking or acting in a certain way just because others do.

bar graphs, 35

base form, 324 The simplest form of a verb: *eat, have, be, buy.* The base form doesn't indicate tense (*ate, had*)

or third person in the present (*is, buys*).

BC ("before Christ"), 414–15
BCE ("before the common era"), 414–15
be
    conditional sentences with, 330
    as helping verb, 327
    overuse of, 353
because, as subordinating word, 318
been. See be
before, 318

begging the question A logical FAL-LACY that argues in a circle, assuming as a given what the writer is trying to prove.

believing and doubting game, 84
between, among, 361

bibliography, 210–38 At the end of a researched text prepared in CHI-CAGO STYLE, a list with full publication information for all the sources cited in the text. *See also* annotated bibliography; reference list; works-cited list

    abbreviations in, 415
    annotated, 74–78
    bibliographic information, 76
    formatting, 240
        APA style (reference list),
            179–200, 202, 207
        Chicago style, 210–38, 240, 244
        CSE style (reference list), 248–62,
            265
        MLA style (works cited), 129–58
    sample, 244
    working, 91

block quotation, 108–9   In a written work, a long quotation that is set off and usually indented from the main text and presented without quotation marks. Each STYLE specifies its own guidelines for the minimum amount of text to put into a block quotation.
    formatting guidelines
        APA style, 201
        Chicago style, 239
        CSE style, 261
        MLA style, 159
    punctuation with, 396

blog entries, documenting
    APA style, 194
    Chicago style, 232
    CSE style, 259–60
    MLA style, 151
book in a series, documenting
    Chicago style, 220
    MLA style, 146
book reviews. *See* reviews
books, documenting
    APA style
        electronic, 193–94
        print, 179–84
    Chicago style
        electronic, 229–31
        print, 211–20
    CSE style
        electronic, 255
        print, 248–52
    MLA style
        electronic, 145–49
        print, 130–38, 144
books, library catalog searches for, 98
Boolean operators, 96–97
both, 337

brackets, 405   Square parentheses ([ ]) used to indicate words inserted in a quotation.
    quoting and, 108
    uses of, 405

brainstorming, 9   A process for GENERATING IDEAS AND TEXT by writing down everything that comes to mind about a topic, then looking for patterns or connections among the ideas.
    as a reading strategy, 83
    reflections and, 71

building common ground. *See* common ground
by the same token, 358

C

can, as a modal verb, 328, 329
capital, capitol, 362
capitalization, 409–11
    of personal titles, 410
    of proper nouns, 409–10
    of quotations, 410
    of titles and subtitles of works, 410
captions, 36
cartoons, documenting MLA style, 154

case, 289–91, 322–44   The different forms some PRONOUNS can take to indicate how they function in a sentence, for example, as the SUBJECT or OBJECT. *I* and *me* refer to the same person, but they are not interchangeable in a sentence: *Joanne offered me one of the puppies, but I am allergic to dogs.*

case studies, 46

cause and effect, 19–20 A STRATEGY for analyzing why something occurred or speculating about what its consequences will be. Cause and effect can serve as the organizing principle for a paragraph or a whole text.

CE ("common era"), 414–15
chapters in edited collections and
 books, documenting
  Chicago style, 216
  CSE style, 251
charts
 as design element, 35
 reading, 87–88

***Chicago* style, 208–44** A system of DOCUMENTATION for papers in history and some subject areas in the humanities. *Chicago* is short for *The Chicago Manual of Style*, which is published by the University of Chicago Press.
 bibliography elements, 210–38, 244
  books, 211–20
  miscellaneous sources, 235–38
  online sources, 226–35
  periodical articles, 221–25
  sources not covered by *Chicago*,
   235–38
 directory (table of contents),
  208–9
 documenting with notes and
  bibliography, 210–38, 243
 formatting guidelines, 238–40, 242
 in-text documentation, 210
 quotations in, 108, 239, 242
 sample pages, 240–44
 title pages, 241

writing style
 spelling out of numbers, 415
 verb tenses in signal phrases,
  115

chronological order, 60 A way of organizing text that proceeds from the beginning of an event to the end. Reverse chronological order proceeds in the other direction, from the end to the beginning.

citation, 107–265 In a text, the act of giving information from a source. A citation and its corresponding parenthetical DOCUMENTATION, footnote, or endnote provide minimal information about the source; complete bibliographic information appears in a list of WORKS CITED or REFERENCES at the end of the text. *See also* APA style; *Chicago* style; CSE style; MLA style

cite, sight, site, 362

claim, 43 A statement that asserts a belief or position. In an ARGUMENT, a claim needs to be stated in a THESIS or clearly implied, and it requires support by REASONS and EVIDENCE.
 arguments and, 43, 46
 revising, 13
 tentative thesis and, 10

classification and division, 20 A STRATEGY that either groups (classifies) numerous individual items by their similarities (for example, classifying cereal, bread, butter, chicken, cheese, cream, eggs, and oil as carbohydrates, proteins, and fats) or

classification and division (cont.)
breaks (divides) one large category into small categories (for example, dividing food into carbohydrates, proteins, and fats). Classification and/or division can serve as the organizing principle for a paragraph or a whole text.

clause, 269, 316 A group of words that consists of at least a SUBJECT and a PREDICATE; a clause may be either INDEPENDENT or SUBORDINATE.
    commas and, 308–9
    comma splices and, 272–75, 320–21
    emphasizing ideas and, 349
    essential (restrictive), 388–89
    explicit subjects needed in, 315
    fragments and, 270–72, 317–20
    independent, 316, 320, 386, 392
    nonessential (nonrestrictive),
        388–89
    subordinate, 316, 321, 344, 349

cliché, 352–53 An expression used so frequently that it is no longer fresh: *busy as a bee*.
    avoiding, 15

close reading, 64

clustering, 9 A process for GENERATING IDEAS AND TEXT in which a writer visually connects thoughts by jotting them down and drawing lines between related items.

CMS style. *See Chicago* style

coherence, 25–28 The quality that enables an AUDIENCE to follow a text and to see the connections among ideas, sentences, and paragraphs. Elements that can help to achieve coherence include the title, a clearly stated or implied THESIS, TOPIC SENTENCES, an easy-to-follow organization with clear TRANSITIONS, and PARALLELISM among comparable ideas.

collaboration, 16 The process of working with others.

collective noun, 340–41 A NOUN— such as *committee, crowd, family, herd,* or *team*—that refers to a group.

colloquial language, 351
colons, 398, 403–4
commas, 386–92
    comma splices and, 320–21
    coordinating conjunctions and, 386
    editing, 304–7
    introductory words and, 387
    quotations and, 370
    setting off text with
        addresses and place names, 390
        direct address, *yes/no*, interjec-
           tions, tag questions, 390
        nonessential elements, 388–89
        parenthetical information, 389
        transitional expressions, 389–90
    unnecessary, 391–92
    why they matter, 304–5

comma splice, 320–21 Two or more INDEPENDENT CLAUSES joined with only a comma: *I came, I saw, I conquered.*
    editing, 272–75
    identifying, 320
    intentional, 321

comments online, documenting
APA style, 191–92
MLA style, 143

common ground, 376–78   Shared values. Writers build common ground with AUDIENCES by acknowledging others' POINTS OF VIEW, seeking areas of compromise, and using language that includes, rather than excludes, those they aim to reach.
language and, 376–78
mixing Englishes and, 385

common knowledge, 116
common nouns, 409–10
comparatives, 371–72

comparison and contrast, 21–22   A STRATEGY that highlights the similarities and differences between items. Using the *block method* of comparison-contrast, a writer discusses all the points about one item and then all the same points about the other item; using the *point-by-point method*, a writer discusses one point for both items before going on to discuss the next point for both items, and so on. Sometimes comparison and/or contrast serves as the organizing principle for a paragraph or a whole text.
block method, 57
point-by-point method, 57

complement, 316   A NOUN, noun phrase, PRONOUN, or ADJECTIVE that modifies either the SUBJECT or the direct OBJECT of a sentence. A subject complement follows a LINKING VERB and tells more about the subject: *She is a good speaker. She is eloquent.* An object complement describes or renames the direct object: *Critics called the movie a masterpiece. We found the movie enjoyable.*
as element of a sentence, 342
pronoun case and, 316–17
unnecessary commas and, 391

complete subject, 293–94   The SIMPLE SUBJECT plus any MODIFIERS. The complete subject can be one word (*I enjoy carrots*), two words (*The girls went to the grocery store*), or many words: *The old farmer with the multi-colored carrots has a booth at the market.*

compose, comprise, 362
compound adjectives, 407
compound nouns, 401
compound structures, 343
computer software, documenting
APA style, 197
conciseness, 368–69

conclusion, 29   The way a text ends, a chance to leave an AUDIENCE thinking about what's been said. Five ways of concluding a college essay: reiterating your point, discussing the implications of your ARGUMENT, asking a question, referring back to your OPENING, or proposing some kind of action.
closing paragraphs, 29
editing, 14
getting responses on, 12
of presentations, 39
signaling, 27

concrete words, 354
conditional sentences,
    330–31
conference proceedings,
    documenting
  APA style, 196
  CSE style, 251–52
  MLA style, 148
conflicting ideas, signaling,
    358–59
conjunctions
  coordinating, 346, 348, 386, 391,
    392
  correlative, 346, 349
consistency
  in abbreviations, 414
  as a design principle, 30
  in phrasing of headings, 33
  in verb tense, 350
context
  academic, 6–8
  considering, as reading strategy,
    84, 85
  for research, 90
  rhetorical analysis and,
    49, 51
  writing, 2–5
contractions, 401
contrast. *See* comparison and
    contrast
contrast (design), 31

coordinating conjunction, 348–49 One of these words—*and, but, or, nor, so, for,* or *yet*—used to join two elements in a way that gives equal weight to each one (*bacon and eggs; pay up or get out*).

commas and, 386, 391–92
comma splices and, 321

fused sentences, 277, 321
linking equal ideas, 348–49

coordination and subordination,
    348–49
corporations as authors,
    documenting
  Chicago style, 212–13
  CSE style, 249–50
correctness, attention to, 8

correlative conjunction A pair of words used to connect two equal elements: *either . . . or, neither . . . nor, not only . . . but also, just as . . . so,* and *whether . . . or.*

linking equal ideas, 348–49
with paired ideas, 346

could, as a modal verb, 328, 329
could of, 362
council, counsel, 362
Council of Science Editors (CSE)
    style. *See* CSE style

counterargument, 44–45, 47 In ARGUMENT, an alternative POSITION or an objection to the writer's position. The writer of an argument should not only acknowledge counterarguments but also, if at all possible, accept, accommodate, or refute each one.

annotated bibliographies and, 77
evaluating, in rhetorical analyses,
    52
identifying, as reading strategy, 86

count noun, 293, 374 A word that names something that can be counted: *one book, two books.*

court cases, documenting MLA style, 154

cover all the bases, 359–60

credibility   The sense of trustworthiness that a writer conveys through text.
  annotated bibliographies and, 77
  evaluating sources and, 114
  signal verbs and, 104

criteria   In EVALUATION, the standards against which something is judged

criteria, criterion, 362

CSE style, 245–65   A system of DOC-UMENTATION used in the physical sciences, life sciences, and mathematics. CSE is short for Council of Science Editors.
  directory (table of contents), 245–46
  formatting guidelines, 260–62
  in-text documentation, 246–47
  quotations in, 108, 261
  reference lists, 248–62, 265
    books (electronic), 255–56
    books (print), 248–52
    citation-name format, 248
    citation-sequence format, 247, 248
    name-year format, 247
    periodical articles (electronic), 256–58
    periodical articles (print), 252–54
    sources not covered by CSE style, 256
  sample pages, 262–65

writing style
  spelling out of numbers, 416
  verb tenses in signal phrases, 115

cubing   A process for GENERATING IDEAS AND TEXT in which a writer looks at a topic in six ways—to DESCRIBE it, to COMPARE it to something else, to associate it with other things or CLASSIFY it, to ANALYZE it, to apply it, and to ARGUE for or against it.

D

dangling modifiers, 373
dashes, 404
data, 362
databases
  documenting articles
    APA style, 191–93
    Chicago style, 228–30
    CSE style, 255–57
    MLA style, 140, 141, 144
  searching, 98–99
dates, commas with, 416
decimals, 416

definition, 22–23   A STRATEGY that says what something is. *Formal definitions* identify the category that something belongs to and tell what distinguishes it from other things in that category: a worm as an invertebrate (a category) with a long, rounded body and no appendages (distinguishing features); *extended definitions* go into more detail: a paragraph or even an essay explaining why a

definition (cont.)
character in a story is tragic; *stipulative definitions* give a writer's own use of a term, one not found in a dictionary. Definition can serve as the organizing principle for a paragraph or a whole text.

definitions, in reports, 55
degrees, abbreviations of, 414

description, 23 A STRATEGY that tells how something looks, sounds, smells, feels, or tastes. Effective description creates a clear DOMINANT IMPRESSION built from specific details. Description can be *objective, subjective,* or both. Description can serve as the organizing principle for a paragraph or a whole text.
    in personal narratives, 58, 59
    in reflections, 71–72
    in rhetorical analysis, 51

descriptive abstracts, 79–80
descriptive annotations, 74, 77
desert, dessert, 362

design, 30–36 The way a text is arranged and presented visually. Elements of design include font, color, illustration, layout, and white space.
    elements
        fonts, 31–32
        headings, 33
        layout, 32
    italics, 32
    layout and, 32
    lists and, 32
    paragraphs and, 32

principles of, 30–31
of reports, 55
visuals, 33–36
diagrams, 35

dialogue, 58 A STRATEGY for adding people's own words to a text. *See also* quotation

dictionaries, documenting
    Chicago style, 219
    MLA style, 126
did. See do
digital archives, 99
direct address, 390
direct object. *See* object
directories, web, 99, 100
direct questions, 394
direct quotations, 390, 395–96
discussions, online. *See* online
        forums, documenting
disinterested, uninterested, 362
dissertations, documenting
    APA style, 198
    MLA style, 149
division. *See* classification and
        division
do
    as helping verb, 327
    overuse of, 353

documentation, 107–265 Publication information about the sources cited in a text. The documentation usually appears in an abbreviated form in parentheses at the point of CITATION or in an endnote or a footnote. Complete documentation usually appears as a BIBLIOGRAPHY, list of WORKS CITED, or REFERENCES at the end of the text. Styles vary by discipline. *See also*

APA style; *Chicago* style; CSE style; MLA style
  academic writing, 7
  avoiding plagiarism
    paraphrases, 112
    summaries, 113
    quotations, 108–9
    understanding documentation
      styles, 118
    visuals, 36

document numbers, documenting
  CSE style, 255, 257
document URLs, 99
does. See do
Dogpile, 99

DOI, 130 A digital object identifier, a stable number identifying the location of a source accessed through a database.
  documenting
    APA style, 187–88, 190, 194
    Chicago style, 226, 231
    MLA style, 130, 133, 141
    CSE style, 231

dominant impression The overall effect created through specific details when a writer DESCRIBES something.

draft, 11–12 To put words on paper or screen. Writers often write several drafts, REVISING each until they achieve their goal and submit a finished final draft.

drawings, documenting 35
DVDs, documenting
  APA style, 196
  Chicago style, 237
  MLA style, 157

E

each
  singular pronoun with, 337
  singular verb with, 340
ebooks, documenting
  APA style, 193–94
  Chicago style, 229, 231
  CSE style, 255
  MLA style, 145
EBSCOhost, 98
-ed form of verbs, 324

edit, 13–15 To fine-tune a text by examining each word, PHRASE, sentence, and paragraph to be sure that the text is correct and precise and says exactly what the writer intends. *See also* editing errors that matter

editing errors that matter, 268–313
  commas, 304–9
  comma splices, 272–75
  fragments, 270–72
  fused sentences, 275–78
  mixed constructions, 278–81
  pronouns, 281–91
  quotations, 298–304
  sentences, 269–81
  shifts in tense, 295–98
  subject-verb agreement, 292–95
  verbs, 291–98
  words often confused, 309–13
effect, affect, 361
e.g., 415
either, 337, 340
either . . . or, 349

either-or argument A logical FALLACY, also known as a false dilemma, that oversimplifies to suggest that

either-or argument (cont.)
only two possible POSITIONS exist on a complex issue.

electronic books. *See* ebooks

ellipses, 405–6 Three spaced dots (. . .) that indicate an omission or a pause.

emails, documenting
APA style, 195
Chicago style, 235
MLA style, 151–52
emigrate (from), immigrate, 362

emotional appeal, 44 In ARGUMENT, an appeal to readers' feelings. Emotional appeals should be used carefully in academic writing, where arguments are often expected to emphasize logical reasons and evidence more than emotion.

emphasis
idioms indicating, 357
italics for, 413
of one idea over others, 349
encyclopedia entries, documenting
Chicago style, 219
MLA style, 126
end punctuation, 393–95

Englishes, 379–85 The plural form recognizes that there are many legitimate varieties of English.
across cultures and communities, 382–83
across fields, 381–82
across regions, 382
formal and informal, 379–81
mixing, 384–85
overview, 379
standard edited English, 379

enough, 337
ERIC, 99

essential element, 388–89 A word, PHRASE, or CLAUSE with information that is necessary for understanding the meaning of a sentence: *French is the only language <u>that I can speak</u>.*

et al., 415
etc., 362

ethical appeal In ARGUMENT, a way a writer establishes credibility with readers, such as by demonstrating knowledge of the topic; pointing out common ground between the writer's values and those of readers; or incorporating the views of others, including opposing views, into the argument.

ethnic designations, 377
evaluating sources, 92–96, 102–5

evaluation A writing GENRE that makes a judgment about something— a source, poem, film, restaurant, whatever—based on certain CRITERIA. Key Features: description of the subject • clearly defined criteria • knowledgeable discussion of the subject • balanced and fair assessment

evaluative annotations, 74–75, 77
evaluative thesis statements, 64

events, writing about, 57
every day, *everyday*, 363
everyone, 337, 340, 401
everything, 337

evidence, 44, 46 In ARGUMENT, the data you present to support your REASONS. Such data may include statistics, calculations, examples, ANECDOTES, QUOTATIONS, case studies, or anything else that will convince your reader that your reasons are compelling. Evidence should be sufficient (enough to show that the reasons have merit) and relevant (appropriate to the argument you're making).

in academic writing, 7
analyzing evidence, 12, 52, 86
in arguments, 44, 47
kinds of evidence, 47, 50
in literary analysis, 64

examples
as development pattern, 25
idioms indicating, 357
transitions, 27
except, *accept*, 361
exclamation points
commas and, 392
quotation marks and, 398
use of, 394–95

explanation of a process, 24 A STRATEGY for telling how something is done or how to do something. An explanation of a process can serve as the organizing principle for a paragraph or a whole text.

expletive A word such as *it* and *there* used to introduce information provided later in a sentence: *It was difficult to drive on the icy road.* *There is plenty of food in the refrigerator.*

there, *there is*, *it is*, 312, 368–69

F

Facebook, documenting
  APA style, 196
  MLA style, 152
facts
  citing, 115
  as evidence, 47
  in opening paragraphs, 29

fallacy, 86 Faulty reasoning that can mislead an AUDIENCE. Fallacies include AD HOMINEM, BANDWAGON APPEAL, BEGGING THE QUESTION, EITHER-OR ARGUMENT (also called false dilemma), FALSE ANALOGY, FAULTY CAUSALITY (also called *post hoc, ergo propter hoc*), HASTY GENERALIZATION, and SLIPPERY SLOPE.

arguments and, 52, 86
evaluating, in rhetorical analysis, 52
identifying when reading, 86

false analogy A FALLACY comparing things that resemble each other but are not alike in the most important respects.

faulty causality A FALLACY, also called *post hoc, ergo propter hoc* (Latin for "after this, therefore because of

faulty causality (cont.)
this"), that mistakenly assumes the
first of two events causes the second.

feedback, getting, 12
few, 337
fewer, less, 363

field research The collection of firsthand data through observation, interviews, and questionnaires or surveys.
    conducting, 101–2
    for reports, 54

field tags (databases), 97
figurative language, 354

figure, 33–36 A photo, graph, chart,
diagram, or drawing. Used by writers to help make a point in ways that
words alone cannot. *See also* visual

films, documenting
    APA style, 196
    MLA style, 154–55
filtering search results, 87
flipcharts, 39
flow. *See* coherence
flowcharts, 35

font, 31–32 A typeface, such as
Calibri or Times New Roman.
    as design element, 31–32
    formatting guidelines
        APA style, 200–201
        MLA style, 158–59
    in presentation software, 40
    serif vs. sans serif, 31–32, 40

for, 348, 386

foreign words, italics for, 413
forewords, documenting
    Chicago style, 217
    MLA style, 148
for instance, 357

formal writing Writing intended to
be evaluated by someone such as an
instructor or read by an AUDIENCE expecting academic or businesslike argument and presentation. Formal writing
should be carefully REVISED, EDITED, and
PROOFREAD. *See also* informal writing

formal and informal language
    appropriate words and, 351
    in presentations, 38
    varieties of English and, 379–81
formatting guidelines, 30–36
    APA style, 200–203
    Chicago style, 238–40
    CSE style, 260–62
    MLA style, 158–60
forums, online. *See* online forums,
        documenting
fragments. *See* sentence fragments

freewriting, 9 A process for GENER-
ATING IDEAS AND TEXT by writing con-
tinuously for several minutes without
pausing to read what has been written.

fused sentence, 320–21 Two or more
INDEPENDENT CLAUSES with no punctuation between them: *I came I saw I
conquered.*
    editing, 275–78, 320–21
    identifying, 320–21
    why they matter, 275

future tenses, 322–23
  future perfect, 323–24
  future perfect progressive, 324
  future progressive, 324

G

gender, and pronoun agreement, 341

generating ideas and text, 9–10 A set of processes that help writers develop a topic, examples, REASONS, EVIDENCE, and other parts of a text.
  for abstracts, 81
  for annotated bibliographies, 76–77
  for arguments, 45–47
  for literary analysis, 63–64
  for personal narratives, 59–60
  for proposals, 67–68
  for reflections, 71–72
  for reports, 55–56
  for rhetorical analysis, 50–51

generic nouns, 340

genre, 3–4 A kind of writing marked by and expected to have certain key features and to follow certain conventions of style and presentation. In literary texts, readers recognize such genres as the short story and the novel and the poem; in academic and workplace settings, readers and writers focus on such genres as AB-STRACTS, ANNOTATED BIBLIOGRAPHIES, APPLICATION LETTERS, ARGUMENTS, EVALUATIONS, LAB REPORTS, PERSONAL NARRATIVES, LITERARY ANALYSES, PRO-FILES, PROPOSALS, REFLECTIONS, RÉSUMÉS, REPORTS, and RHETORICAL ANALYSES.
  and contexts, 2–4, 18
  and purposes, 2
  and reading, 84
  specific genres
    abstracts, 79–82
    annotated bibliographies, 74–78
    arguments, 43–48
    literary analyses, 62–65
    personal narratives, 58–61
    proposals, 66–69
    reflections, 70–73
    reports, 54

gerund, 326 A VERB form ending in -*ing* that functions as a NOUN: *Swimming improves muscle tone and circulation. See also* present participles
  vs. infinitives, 326
  and pronouns, 344

good, well, 363, 371
Google, search and sites, 99, 100
government documents, documenting
  APA style, 197
  Chicago style, 237–38
government sites, 99
graphic narratives, documenting
  MLA style, 147
graphs, 35
  documenting APA style, 199
  reading, 87–88
group writing projects, 16

H

had. See have
handouts, 39, 41
has. See have

hashtag, 99 A number sign (#) in front of a word or unspaced phrase (#BlackLivesMatter), used in social media to mark posts by KEYWORD or theme and make them searchable by these tags. Also used to add commentary on a web text outside from elsewhere on the web.

hasty generalization A FALLACY that reaches a conclusion based on insufficient or inappropriately qualified EVIDENCE.

have, as a helping verb, 310, 327
he, him, his, etc., 341, 378
he, she, they, 378
headings
  as design element, 33
  formatting guidelines
    APA style, 201
    CSE style, 261
  parallelism in, 347

helping verb, 327–29 A VERB that works with a main verb to express a TENSE and MOOD. Helping verbs include *do, have, be,* and MODALS: *Elvis has left the building. Pigs can fly.*
  modals, 328–29
  sentence fragments and, 318–19
  shifts in tense and, 297

homophones, 309–13
hopefully, 363
Humanities International Index, 99
hyphens, 407–8
  with compound words, 407
  at end of a line, 408
  with numbers, 408
  with prefixes and suffixes, 407–8

I

idiom, 355–60, A PHRASE or group of words that means something different from the literal meaning of each word separately. For example, *a piece of cake* means anything very easy to accomplish; when used as an idiom, it has nothing to do with actual cake.
  common academic and professional idioms, 357–60
  formal and informal English and, 379
  recognizing, 355–56
  sports idioms, 359–60
  understanding, 356

i.e., 415
if, in conditional sentences, 318
illusion, allusion, 361
illustrations, formatting
  APA style, 202–3
  Chicago style, 239–40
  CSE style, 261–62
  MLA style, 160
image collections, 100
images, documenting CSE style, 258–59
images in presentations, 38–41
immigrate (to), emigrate (from), 362
imperative mood, 330
implied pronoun reference, 341
imply, infer, 363
in
  with idioms, 357–59
  vs. *at, on*, 366–67

indefinite pronoun, 292, 293 A PRONOUN—such as *all, anyone, anything, everyone, everything, few, many, nobody, nothing, one, some,* and *some-*

thing—that does not refer to a specific person or thing.
> possessive forms, 401
> pronoun-antecedent agreement and, 340
> subject-verb agreement and, 337

indents
> APA style, 200–201, 206
> *Chicago* style, 240
> CSE style, 261
> general guidelines, 32
> MLA style, 158–59

independent clause, 316 A CLAUSE containing a SUBJECT and a VERB that can stand alone as a sentence: *She sang. The world-famous soprano sang several popular arias.*
> editing
>> comma splices, 320
>> emphasizing ideas, 349
>> punctuation
>>> commas, 386
>>> semicolons, 392–93
>>> sentence structure and, 316

indexes, periodical, 98–99
indicative mood, 330
indirect quotations, 399
indirect questions, 394
infer, imply, 363

infinitive, 343 *To* plus the base form of the verb: *to come, to go.* An infinitive can function as a NOUN (*He likes to run first thing in the morning*); an ADJECTIVE (*She needs a campaign to run*); or an ADVERB (*He registered to run in the marathon*).

vs. gerunds, 326
infinitive phrases, 316–17
pronoun case before or after, 343–44
split, 373

infographics, documenting CSE style, 258–59
informal language. *See* formal and informal language

informal writing Writing not intended to be evaluated, sometimes not even to be read by others. Informal writing is produced primarily to explore ideas or to communicate casually with friends and acquaintances. *See also* formal writing

informative abstracts, 81
InfoTrac, 98
-ing form of verbs, 326

inquiry, writing as A process for investigating a topic by posing questions, searching for multiple answers, and keeping an open mind.

integrating sources, 107–15
> paraphrasing, 110–12
> quoting, 108–10
> summarizing, 112–13
> using signal phrases, 113–14
> verb tenses, 114–15

interjection, 390 A word expressing surprise, resignation, agreement, and other emotions. It can be attached to a sentence or stand on its own: *Well, if you insist. Ouch!*

internet addresses, dividing, 408. *See also* URLs
internet research, 96–97, 99–100

interpretation The act of making sense of something or explaining what one thinks it means. Interpretation is one goal of writing a LITERARY ANALYSIS or RHETORICAL ANALYSIS.
    literary analysis and, 63
    rhetorical analysis and, 49–50

interrupted quotations, 410
interviews
    conducting, 101
    documenting
      APA style, 185
      Chicago style, 235–36
      MLA style, 155
in-text documentation
    APA style, 173–78
    Chicago style, 210
    CSE style, 246–47
    MLA style, 122–28
    with other punctuation, 399
introduction. *See* opening paragraphs
introductory words
    commas and, 387

irregular verb, 325 A VERB that does not form its past TENSE and PAST PARTICIPLE by adding -ed or -d to the base form (as in *eat, ate, eaten*).

is. See be
it, indefinite use, 342
italics, 32, 411–13
    for emphasis, 413
    non-English words, 413

titles of long works, 411–12
    APA style, 179, 211
    Chicago style, 185
    MLA style, 131
words as words, 412
it is, there is, 14, 368–69
it's, its, 15, 312–13, 363

J

jargon, 352, 385 A specialized vocabulary of a profession, trade, or field that should be used only when you know your AUDIENCE will understand what you are saying.

journal articles, documenting
    APA style
      electronic, 190, 191–93
      print, 185–87
    Chicago style
      electronic, 227–29
      print, 221–25
    CSE style
      electronic, 255–58
      print, 252–54
    MLA style
      accessed via database, 140
      electronic, 138, 140, 141
      print, 136, 137, 138
journals, keeping, 10
Jr., 414
JSTOR, 98
just as . . . so, 349

K

keyword A term that a researcher inputs when searching for information electronically.
    guidelines for, 96–97
    in library catalogs, 98

in periodical databases, 99
on the web, 99

L

lab report A writing GENRE that covers the process of conducting an experiment in a controlled setting. Key Features: explicit title • ABSTRACT • PURPOSE • methods • results and discussion • REFERENCES • APPENDIX • appropriate format

language
    abstract, 354
    appropriate, 351–53
    be and *do*, 353
    building common ground, 376–78, 385
    clichés, 352–53
    colloquial, 351
    concrete, 354
    Englishes, 379–85
    figurative, 354
    formal and informal, 5, 351, 379–81
    idioms, 355–60
    jargon, 352
    precise, 353–54
    pretentious, 352
    sexist, 377–78
    standard edited English, 79
    stereotypes, 376
    unnecessary words, 368–69
    varieties of (see Englishes)

lay, lie, 363

layout, 32 The way text is arranged on a page or screen—for example, in paragraphs, in lists, on charts, with headings.

lead, led, 363
less, fewer, 363
letters, documenting
    APA style, 187, 195
    Chicago style, 219
    MLA style, 142, 148
LexisNexis Academic Universe, 98
library catalogs, searching, 98
Library of Congress, 100
lie, lay, 363
like
    no comma after, 391
    vs. *as* and *as if*, 361
line graphs, 35
line spacing, 32
    APA style, 200
    Chicago style, 238
    CSE style, 261
    MLA style, 158–59
linking equal ideas, 348–49

linking verb, 343 A VERB that expresses a state of being: *appear, be, feel, seem.*

listing, 72 A process for GENERATING IDEAS AND TEXT by making lists while thinking about a topic, finding relationships among the notes, and arranging the notes as an OUTLINE.

lists
    layout and, 32
    parallelism in, 14

literacy portfolio An organized collection of materials showing examples of one writer's progress as a reader and/or writer

literally, 363

literary analysis, 62–65 A writing GENRE that examines a literary text (most often fiction, poetry, or drama) and argues for a particular INTERPRETATION of the text. Key Features: arguable THESIS • careful attention to the language of the text • attention to patterns or themes • clear interpretation • MLA style
  key elements, 62–63
  MLA style, 63
  organization, 65
  tips for writing, 63–65
  verb tenses, 64–65

literary present, 350
literary works, documenting MLA
     style

literature Literary works—including fiction, poetry, drama, and some nonfiction; also, the body of written work produced in given field.

logical appeal In ARGUMENT, an appeal to readers based on the use of logical reasoning and of EVIDENCE such as facts, statistics, authorities on the subject, and so on.

long quotations, 108–9, 396
  formatting guidelines
    APA style, 201
    Chicago style, 239
    CSE style, 261
    MLA style, 159

looping, 9 A process for GENERATING IDEAS AND TEXT in which a writer writes about a topic quickly for several minutes and then reads the results and writes a one-sentence summary of the most important or interesting idea, which becomes the beginning of another round of writing and summarizing, and so on, until the writer finds a tentative focus for writing.

loose, lose, 363
a lot, 361

M

magazine articles, documenting
  APA style
    electronic, 191
    print, 186
  Chicago style
    electronic, 227
    print, 222, 225
  CSE style
    print, 254
  MLA style
    electronic, 138, 139
    print, 139
main ideas, 11
main points
  identifying, as a reading strategy, 86
  in presentations, 38
  strategies for developing, 19–25
    cause and effect, 19–20
    classification and division, 20
    comparison and contrast, 21–22
    definition, 22–23
    description, 23
    examples, 25
    narration, 24–25
    process explanation, 24
    topic sentences, 18–19

main verb The verb form that presents the action or state. It can stand alone or be combined with one or more HELPING VERB. *My dog might have buried your keys. Leslie Jones is a comedian. Alexa was wearing a gown by Milly. The agent didn't appear old enough to drive.*

man, mankind, 363
many, 337, 363
maps, documenting
    APA style, 199
    MLA style, 155–56
margins
    as design element, 32
    formatting guidelines
        APA style, 200–201, 206, 242
        Chicago style, 238
        CSE style, 261, 264
        MLA style, 158–59, 161
may, as modal, 327
may of, may have, 364
MD, 414
media, medium, 364

medium, 5 A way that a text is delivered—for example, in print, with speech, or online.

memoir A GENRE that focuses on something significant from the writer's past. Key Features: good story • vivid details • clear significance

metaphor, 354 A figure of speech that makes a comparison without using the word *like* or *as:* "All the world's a stage / And all the men and women merely players" (Shakespeare, *As You Like It*).

metasearches, 99
might, as modal verb, 328
might of, might have, 364
misplaced modifiers, 372–73

mixed construction, 278 A sentence that starts out with one structure and ends up with another one: *Although bears can be deadly is not a good reason to avoid camping altogether.*

    ways of editing, 278

MLA style, 119–53 A system of DOCUMENTATION used in the humanities. MLA stands for the Modern Language Association.

    annotated bibliographies and, 74, 76
    design and, 30
    directory (table of contents), 119–22
    formatting, 158–60
    in-text documentation, 122–28
    notes, 129
    quotations in, 108–9
    sample research paper, 160–69
    works-cited list, 129–58, 160, 169
        articles, 137–43
        audio, visual, and other sources, 153–58
        books, 130–37, 144–49
        core elements, 129–34
        personal communication and social media, 151–52
        short works, 137, 139, 141–43
    writing style
        spelling out of numbers, 415
        verb tenses for signal phrases and, 114–15

modal, 327–29 A helping VERB—such as *can, could, may, might, must,*

modal (cont.)
ought to, should, will, or *would*—used with the base form of a verb to express whether an action is likely, possible, permitted, or various other conditions.

Modern Language Association (MLA) style. *See* MLA style

modifier, 316 A word, PHRASE, or CLAUSE that describes or specifies something about another word, phrase, or clause (*a long, informative speech; the actors spoke in unison; the man who would be king*). *See also* adjective; adverb; participial phrase
careful placement of, 372
dangling, 373

mood, 330–31 A characteristic of VERBS that indicates a writer's attitude about whether a statement is possible or unlikely. The *indicative mood* is used to state fact or opinion: *I'm waiting to buy tickets.* The *imperative mood* is used to give commands or directions: *Sit down, and take off your shoes.* The *subjunctive mood* is used to express wishes or requests or to indicate unlikely conditions: *I wish the ticket line were shorter.*
helping verbs and, 327

more, most, 337
much, many, 363

multimedia Using more than one medium of delivery, such as print,

speech, or electronic. Often used interchangeably with MULTIMODAL.

multimodal Using more than one mode of expression, such as words, images, sound, links, and so on. Often used interchangeably with MULTIMEDIA.

multiple authors, documenting
APA style, 175, 181–82
Chicago style, 214
CSE style, 249
MLA style, 123–24, 134–35
musical scores, documenting MLA style, 156
music recordings, documenting APA style, 196
must, as modal verb, 328
must of, must have, 364

N

narration, 24–25 A STRATEGY for presenting information as a story, for telling "what happened." It is a pattern most often associated with fiction, but it shows up in all kinds of writing. When used in an essay, a REPORT, or another academic GENRE, narration is used to support a point—not merely to tell an interesting story for its own sake. It must also present events in some kind of sequence and include only pertinent detail. Narration can serve as the organizing principle for a paragraph or a whole text.

narratives. *See* personal narratives

narrowing
  a thesis, 10
  a topic, 56, 90–91
National Archives, 100
Naxos Music Library, 100
neither (singular), 337, 340
neither . . . nor, 349
news, physics, etc., 338–39
newspaper articles, documenting
  APA style
    electronic, 191
    print, 185, 186
  Chicago style
    electronic, 228
    print 221, 222–23
  CSE style
    print, 254
    electronic, 256
  MLA style
    electronic, 141
    print, 139, 141, 142
news sites, web, 99
no, yes, commas with, 390
nobody (singular), 337

noncount noun, 375 A word that names an abstract item (*happiness, curiosity*) and liquids and masses (*milk, sand, salt*) that cannot be measured with numbers.

none (singular or plural), 337

nonessential element, 388–89 A word, PHRASE, or CLAUSE that gives additional information but that is not necessary for understanding the basic meaning of a sentence. *I learned French, which is a Romance lan-* *guage, online.* Nonessential elements should be set off with commas.

nonrestrictive element. *See*
    nonessential element
no one (singular), 337
nor, 348, 386
NOT (Boolean operator), 96–97
notes
  abbreviations in, 415
  APA style, 178–79
  Chicago style, 210–38, 240, 243
  first citation, 210
  MLA style, 129
not only . . . but also, 349

noun, 314–15 A word that names a person, place, thing, or idea (*teacher, Zadie Smith, forest, surgeon general, Amazon River, notebook, democracy*). *See also* proper noun; subject-verb agreement
  collective, 340–41
  common, 409–10
  compound, 401
  count, 374
  generic, 340
  noncount, 293
  possessive forms of, 400–401
  proper, 409–10

noun phrase, 361 A NOUN or PRO-NOUN plus any MODIFIERS: *My little sister would wear that tattered old hooded sweatshirt every day if we let her.*

number, amount, 361
number and person
  shifts in, 350
  subject-verb agreement, 335

numbers, 415–16
  with abbreviations, 414–15
  with hyphens, 408
  MLA style, numbers in, 131

O

object, A word or phrase that follows a PREPOSITION or that receives the action of a VERB. In the sentence *I handed him the mail that was on the table, him* is an indirect object and *mail* is a direct object of the verb *handed; table* is an object of the preposition *on.*

  in participial phrases,
      316–17
  with phrasal verbs, 332–34
  with prepositions, 366
  pronoun case and, 342–43

object case, 342–43
observation, field research,
      101–2
of, have, 310
on, vs. *at, in,* 366–67
one (singular), 337
online forums, documenting
  APA style, 195
  Chicago style, 235
  MLA style, 152
online reviews, documenting MLA
      style, 143
online sources, documenting
  APA style, 187–95, 197, 200
  Chicago style, 226–35
  CSE style, 254–60
  MLA style, 143, 149–51,
      153–58

opening The way a text begins, which plays an important role in drawing an AUDIENCE in. Some ways of opening a college essay: with a dramatic statement, a vivid image, a provocative question, an ANECDOTE, or a startling CLAIM.

  editing, 14
  opening paragraphs, 28–29

or, 348
OR (Boolean operator), 96–97
organization. *See also* patterns of
      development
  of paragraphs, 19–27
  revising to improve, 13
  thematic, 53
  types of works
      abstracts, 81–82
      annotated bibliographies, 78
      arguments, 47–48
      literary analysis, 65
      personal narratives, 81–82
      proposals, 68–69
      reflections, 72–73
      reports, 56–57
      rhetorical analysis, 53
organizing a draft, 11
others (plural), 337
ought to, as modal verb, 328, 329

outlining, 11 A process for GENERAT-ING IDEAS AND TEXT or for organizing or examining a text. An *informal outline* simply lists ideas and then numbers them in the order that they will appear; a *working outline* distinguishes supporting from main ideas by indenting the former; a *formal outline* is arranged as a series of headings and indented subheadings, each on a separate line, with letters and numerals indicating relative levels of importance.

P

page numbers
    APA style, 173–77, 200, 206
        Chicago style, 226, 238, 242
        CSE style, 260, 264
        MLA style, 130, 158, 161
paired ideas, parallelism with, 346

paragraph, 17–29. A group of sentences that focuses on one main idea, which is often stated in a TOPIC SENTENCE.

paragraphs, developing, 17–29
    focusing on the main point, 17–18
        sticking to the main point, 19
        topic sentences and, 18–19
    making paragraphs flow, 25–28
        parallel structures, 26
        repetition, 25–26
        transitions, 26–27
    opening and closing paragraphs, 28–29
    strategies for developing, 19–25
        cause and effect, 19–20
        classification and division, 20
        comparison and contrast, 21–22
        definition, 22–23
        description, 23
        examples, 25
        narration, 24–25
        process explanation, 24
    transitions, 26–27
    when to start a new, 28

parallelism, 345–50 A writing technique that puts similar items into the same grammatical structure. For example, every item on a to-do list might begin with a command: *clean, wash, buy;* or a discussion of favorite hobbies might name each as a GERUND: *running, playing basketball, writing poetry.*
    with all necessary words, 347
    editing for, 14, 245–50
    in headings, 347
    making paragraphs flow and, 26
    with paired ideas, 346
    in paragraphs, 26
    in presentations, 38
    on presentation slides, 346
    on résumés, 346–47

paraphrase, 108, 110–12 To reword someone else's text using about the same number of words but not the phrasing or sentence structure of the original. Paraphrasing is generally called for when a writer wants to include the details of a passage but does not need to quote it word for word. Like a QUOTATION or SUMMARY, a paraphrase requires DOCUMENTATION.
    general guidelines, 110–12
    integrating sources
        APA style, 173, 174
        Chicago style, 210
        MLA style, 122
    in responses, 7

parentheses, 405
parenthetical documentation. *See* in-text documentation
participial phrases, 316

passive voice, 329–30 When a VERB is in the passive voice, the subject is acted upon: *A gift was given to José.*
  helping verbs and, 327

past participle, 324–25 A VERB form used with a HELPING VERB to create perfect tenses (*have walked*) or used alone as an ADJECTIVE (*processed* food). The past participle of most verbs is formed by adding -*ed* or -*d* to the base form; some past participles, though, are irregular (*the written word*).

past perfect, 297, 323 The VERB tense used to indicate that an action was completed before another action in the past began.

past perfect progressive, 324
past progressive, 324
past tenses, 115, 297, 322–23, 324

patchwriting, 112 PARAPHRASES that lean too heavily on the words or sentence structure of the source, adding or deleting some words, replacing words with synonyms, altering the syntax slightly—in other words, not restating the passage in fresh language and structure.

patterns, identifying
  in literary analyses, 62–63, 105–6
  as reading strategy, 85
  synthesizing ideas and, 105–6
patterns of development, 19–25
  cause and effect, 19–20
  classification and division, 20
  comparison and contrast, 21–22
  definition, 22–23

  description, 23
  examples, 25
  narration, 24–25
  process explanation, 24
percent, percentage, 364
percentages, with numbers, 416
perfect tenses, 323–24
periodical articles, documenting
  APA style, 185–87, 190–93
  Chicago style, 221–25, 227–29
  CSE style, 252–54, 255–58
  MLA style, 136–43
periodical articles, researching, 98–99
periods, 394, 398
  uses of, 394
  quotations marks and, 398

permalink, 99, 130 A URL that permanently links to a specific web page or blog post.

permission, to use visuals, 36
person and number
  and subject-verb agreement, 335
  shifts in, 350
personal interviews. *See* interviews
personal names, abbreviations with, 414

personal narrative, 58–61 A writing GENRE that tells a story about a writer's personal experience. Memoir and autobiography are two common types of personal narratives. Key Features: well-told story • vivid detail • indication of the narrative's significance
  key elements, 58–61
  organization, 61–62
  tips for writing, 59–60

PhD, 414
photographs, 34

phrasal verb, 332–34 A verb composed of more than one word—usually a verb and a preposition: *call off, carry out, back down.*

phrase, 316–17 A group of words that lacks a SUBJECT, a VERB, or both.
  essential (restrictive), 388–89
  nonessential (nonrestrictive), 388–89

pie charts, 34
place names, commas with, 390

plagiarism, 117–18 The use of another person's words, ideas, or even sentence structures without appropriate credit and DOCUMENTATION. Plagiarism is a serious breach of ethics. *See also* sources

plays, documenting MLA style, 125
plurals, 401–2
podcasts, documenting
  APA style, 195
  Chicago style, 234–35
  CSE style, 259
  MLA style, 156
poems
  documenting MLA style, 125–26
  quoting MLA style, 125–26

point of view, 350 The choice a writer makes of whether to use the first person (*I, we*), the second person (*you*), or the third *person* (*he, she, it, they, a student, the students*).

popular vs. scholarly sources, 93–96

position, 43 A statement that asserts a belief or CLAIM. In an ARGUMENT, a position is usually stated in a THESIS or clearly implied, and it requires support with REASONS and EVIDENCE.

possessive forms
  apostrophes with, 400–401
  of pronouns, 342
precise words, 353–54

predicate, 314–15 In a sentence or CLAUSE, the VERB and the words that tell more about the verb—MODIFIERS, COMPLEMENTS, and OBJECTS. In the sentence *Mario forcefully stated his opinion*, the predicate is *forcefully stated his opinion.*

prefaces, documenting
  Chicago style, 217
  MLA style, 148
preferred terms, using, 377
prefixes, hyphens with, 407–8

preposition, 366–67 A word or group of words that tells about the relationship of a NOUN or PRONOUN to another word in the sentence. Some common prepositions are *after, at, before, behind, between, by, for, from, in, of, on, to, under, until, with,* and *without.*
  at, in, on, 367
  with gerunds, 326
  in phrasal verbs, 332
  in prepositional phrases, 316

presentations
  delivering, 41–42
  handouts, 41
  key elements, 37–38
  practicing, 41
  repetition and, 38
  signpost language, 37
  tips for composing, 38–41
  using gestures, 42
  visuals, 38, 39, 40–41, 346
presentation software, 39–41

present participle, 324–25 A VERB form used with a HELPING VERB to create progressive TENSES (*is writing*) or used alone as an ADJECTIVE (*a living organism*). The present participle of a verb always ends in *-ing*.
  forming, 324–25
  helping verbs and, 324
  participial phrases and, 316
  pronoun case and, 344
  sentence fragments and, 318

present perfect, 323 A TENSE used to indicate actions that took place at no specific time in the past or that began in the past and continue into the present: *I have often wondered how I can make my love of language into a career. He has cried every day since his companion of fifty years died.*
  APA style, 115, 296, 323
  forming, 322
  signal phrases and, 115

present perfect progressive, 324
present progressive, 324
present tenses, 114–15, 322–23
pretentious language, 352

primary source, 93 A source such as a literary work, historical document, work of art, or performance that a researcher examines firsthand. Primary sources also include experiments and FIELD RESEARCH. In writing about the Revolutionary War, a researcher would likely consider the Declaration of Independence a primary source and a textbook's description of how the document was written a SECONDARY SOURCE.

principal, principle, 364
Prof., 414

profile, 101 A GENRE that presents an engaging portrait of a person, place, or event based on firsthand FIELD RESEARCH. Key Features: interesting subject • necessary background • interesting angle • firsthand account • engaging details

progressive tenses, 324

pronoun, 339–45 A word that takes the place of a NOUN, such as *she, anyone, whoever.*
  editing, 281–91
  he, she, they, 288, 341, 378
  indefinite, 292, 293, 337, 340, 401
  pronoun-antecedent agreement, 282, 285–89, 339–41
  pronoun case, 282, 289–91, 342–45
  pronoun reference, 341–42
  relative, 338
  why pronouns matter, 281–91

pronoun reference, 282–85, 341–42 The way in which a PRONOUN indi-

cates its ANTECEDENT. Pronoun reference must be clear and unambiguous in order not to confuse readers.
   editing, 282
   why it matters, 282–83

proofread, 15 To check for correct spelling and punctuation as well as for page order, missing text, and consistent use of FONTS.

proper noun, 409–10 A NOUN that names a specific person, place, or thing: *Uncle Bob, France, World War II*.
   capitalization of, 409–10
   use of *the* with, 375

proposal, 66–69 A GENRE that argues for a solution to a problem or suggests some action. Key Features: well-defined problem • recommended solution • answers to anticipated questions • call to action • appropriate TONE
   key elements, 66–67
   organizing, 68–69
   tips for writing, 67–68
ProQuest, 98
PsychINFO, 99
Publication Manual of the American
      Psychological Association, 170

pull quote, 31 A brief excerpt set off within a text in order to highlight certain information. Pull quotes are often set in a different FONT or color.

punctuating quotations, 301–4, 405–6
punctuation, 386–406
   apostrophes, 309–13, 399–402

brackets, 109, 405
colons, 398, 403–4
commas, 304–9, 386–92, 398
dashes, 404
ellipses, 108, 405–6
exclamation points, 392, 394–95, 398
hyphens, 407–8
MLA style, 133–34
parentheses, 405
periods, 394, 398
punctuating quotations, 301–4
question marks, 392, 394, 398
quotation marks, 395–99
semicolons, 392–93, 398
slashes, 406

purpose, 2 A writer's goal: to explore ideas; to express oneself; to entertain; to demonstrate learning; to inform; to persuade; and so on. Purpose is one element of the RHETORICAL SITUATION.

Q

qualifiers, 365, 368
qualifying thesis statement, 10, 46

qualifying word, 6, 10, 46 A word such as *frequently, often, generally, sometimes,* or *rarely* that limits a CLAIM in some way.

questioning, 9 A process of GENERATING IDEAS AND TEXT about a topic—asking, for example, *What? Who? When? Where? How?* and *Why?* or other questions. *See also* questions

question marks, 392, 394, 398

questions
in closing paragraphs, 29
direct, 394
for generating ideas, 9, 59
indirect, 394
in opening paragraphs, 29
research questions, 91–92
tag questions, 390
with *who* or *whom*, 344

quotation, 107–10 The use of someone else's words exactly as they were
spoken or written. Quoting is most
effective when wording is worth
repeating or makes a point so well
that no rewording will do it justice.
Quotations need to be acknowledged
with DOCUMENTATION.
block style, 108–9
brackets in, 109, 405
capitalization of interrupted, 410
changes to, 109
commas with, 390
direct, 395–96
editing, 298–304
ellipses in, 108, 405–6
formatting long quotations
APA style, 201–2
Chicago style, 239
CSE style, 261
MLA style, 159
incorporating, 108–10
indirect, 399
short, 108
vs. paraphrase and summary,
107–13
punctuating, 390, 398

quotation marks, 395–99
common mistakes, 399
with direct quotations, 395–96

with other punctuation, 397–98
with parenthetical documentation,
399
single, 397
with titles of short works, 397

R

raise, rise, 364
ratios, 416
*The Reader's Guide to Periodical
Literature*, 98
reading
analyzing an argument, 52, 86
annotating, 84
believing and doubting game,
84
close reading of literature, 64
evaluating sources, 102–5
previewing the text, 83
reading critically, 83–86,
104–5
reading for patterns and connections, 85, 105–6
reading visual texts, 86–88
really, 368

reason, 43–44, 46 Support for a
CLAIM or POSITION. A reason, in turn,
requires its own support in the form
of EVIDENCE.
in academic writing, 7
in arguments, 43–44, 46
evidence, 46
in rhetorical analysis, 52
in sources, 104

the reason . . . is because, 364
reason why, 364
recommendations, 331
redundancies, 369

references, 179–200, 248–62 The list of sources at the end of a text prepared in APA STYLE or CSE STYLE.
APA style, 179–200, 202, 207
CSE style, 248–62, 265

reference works, 97
documenting
APA style, 192
Chicago style, 219
MLA style, 141–42

reflection, 70–73 A GENRE of writing that presents a writer's thoughtful, personal exploration of a subject. Key Features: topic intriguing to the writer • some kind of structure • specific details • speculative TONE
generating ideas and text for, 71–72
key elements, 70–71
organizing, 72–73
tips for writing, 71–72

relative pronoun, 338 A PRONOUN such as *that, which, who, whoever, whom,* or *whomever* that introduces a SUBORDINATE CLAUSE: *The professor who gave the lecture is my adviser.*

repetition
making paragraphs flow, 25–26
in presentations, 38

report, 54–57 A writing GENRE that presents information to readers on a subject. Key Features: tightly focused TOPIC • accurate, well-researched information • various writing STRATEGIES • clear DEFINITIONS • appropriate DESIGN

key elements, 54–55
organizing, 56–57
tips for writing, 54–57

research
acknowledging sources, 116
avoiding plagiarism, 117–18
choosing a topic, 90–91
evaluating sources, 102–5
field research, 101–2
finding sources, 92–96
incorporating words and ideas of others, 107–18
internet, 99–100
posing research questions, 91–92
reading sources critically, 104–5
searching electronically, 96–97
synthesizing ideas, 105–7
types of sources
internet, 96–97, 99–100
library catalogs, 98
databases and indexes, 98–99
reference works, 97
research questions, 91–92
respectfully, respectively, 364
response to and from others, 6–7, 15
restrictive element. *See* essential element

résumé, 346–47 A GENRE that summarizes someone's academic and employment history, generally written to submit to potential employers. DESIGN and word choice depend on whether a résumé is submitted as a print document or in an electronic or scannable form. Key Features: organization that suits goals and experience • succinctness • design that highlights key information (for print) or that uses only one typeface (for scannable)

revision, 13 The process of making substantive changes, including additions and cuts, to a DRAFT so that it contains all the necessary content and presents it in an appropriate organization. During revision, writers generally move from whole-text issues to details with the goals of sharpening their focus and strengthening their position.

rhetorical analysis, 49–53 A writing GENRE in which a writer looks at what a text says and how it says it. Key Features: SUMMARY of the text • attention to context • clear INTERPRETATION or judgment • reasonable support for conclusions
  key elements, 49–50
  tips for writing, 50–53

rhetorical situation. *See* writing context
rise, raise, 364
run-on sentence. *See* fused sentence

S

sacred texts, documenting
  Chicago style, 220
  MLA style, 127, 147
sample paper/pages
  APA style, 203–7
  Chicago style, 240–44
  CSE style, 262–65
  MLA style, 160–69
scholarly vs. popular sources, 93–96

secondary source, 93 An ANALYSIS or INTERPRETATION of a PRIMARY SOURCE. In writing about the Revolutionary War, a researcher would likely consider the Declaration of Independence a primary source and a textbook's description of how the document was written a secondary source.

second person. *See* person and number
seem, 343
semicolons, 392–93
  comma splices and, 321
  with correlative conjunctions, 349
  with independent clauses, 392–93
  mistakes with, 393
  quotation marks with, 398
  in series, 393
sensual, sensuous, 364
sentence elements
  clauses, 315
  phrases, 316–17
  predicates, 314–15
  subjects, 314–15

sentence fragment, 317–20 A group of words that is capitalized and punctuated as a sentence but is not one, either because it lacks a SUBJECT, a VERB, or both, or because it begins with a word that makes it a SUBORDINATE CLAUSE.
  editing, 270–72, 318–19
  identifying, 317–18
  intentional, 319–20

sentences
  comma splices, 272–75
  declarative, 8
  editing, 14–15, 269–81
  elements of, 314–17
  fragments, 270–72
  fused sentences, 275–78, 299
  mixed constructions, 278–81

series
  comma, 387
  parallelism in, 14, 345
set, sit, 364
several, 337

sexist language, 377–78 Language that stereotypes or ignores women or men or needlessly calls attention to gender.
  editing out, 15, 377–78
  singular *they,* 288, 341, 378

shall, as modal verb, 328, 329
shifts, 349–50
  in number, 350
  in point of view, 350
  in tense, 295–98, 350
    editing, 295–98
short works, documenting MLA
      style, 137–43
should, as modal verb, 328, 329
should of, should have, 365
sight, site, cite, 362

signal phrase, 113–15 A phrase used to attribute quoted, paraphrased, or summarized material to a source, as in *she said* or *he claimed.*
  acknowledging sources, 116
  credibility and, 114
  general guidelines, 113–15
  integrating sources
    APA style, 173
    MLA style, 122–23
  signal verbs, 113–14
  stance and, 113
  verb tenses and, 114–15

significance, indicating, 58–59,
      60

simile, 354 A figure of speech that uses *like* or *as* to compare two items: "Still we live meanly, like ants" (Thoreau, *Walden*), "The Wind begun to knead the Grass— / As Women do a Dough—" (Dickinson).

simple subject, 293–94 The word that determines the form of the VERB: *The young farmer from Ten Barn Farm has the best tomatoes at the market.* The simple subject is *farmer,* a singular NOUN; for that reason, the verb *has* is singular. *See also* complete subject

simple tense, 322–23
simplicity, 30
since, as subordinating word,
      318

singular they, 288, 341, 378 The use of *they, them,* and *their* to refer to a person whose gender is unknown or not relevant to the context. Traditionally, *they* has referred only to plural items, but the use of singular *they* is now becoming more accepted.

singular vs. plural. See agreement
sit, set, 364
site, sight, cite, 362
slashes, 406
slides, 38, 39, 40–41

slippery slope A FALLACY that asserts, without EVIDENCE, that one event will lead to a series of other events that will end in disaster.

so, 348, 386
social media
 documenting
  APA style, 187–95, 196
  CSE style, 20
  MLA style, 151–52
 searches on, 99
software, documenting APA style, 195
some (singular or plural), 337
somebody, someone, always singular,
  337, 340
something (singular), 337, 340
so that, as subordinating word, 318
sources
 acknowledging, 90–91, 116–17
 avoiding plagiarism, 117–18
 deciding when to quote,
  paraphrase, or summarize,
  107–8
 documenting, 7, 36, 112, 116
 evaluating, 76, 78, 102–5
 integrating, 107–18
 paraphrasing, 110–12, 122
 popular, 93, 95
 primary and secondary, 76, 93
 quoting, 107–10, 112
 researching, 77, 96–97
 scholarly, 93, 94, 96
 summarizing, 77, 112–13, 122
 synthesizing, 106–7
spacing
 APA style, 200–201, 206
 Chicago style, 238, 242
 CSE style, 261, 264
 MLA style, 158–59, 161
specialized language, 352
spelling checkers, computer, 15
split infinitives, 373
spoken texts. *See* presentations
sports idioms, 359–60
stable URLs, 99

stance, 4–5 A writer's attitude toward his or her subject—for example, reasonable, neutral, angry,
curious. Stance is conveyed through
TONE and word choice.
 authoritative, as an element of
  academic writing, 7–8
 entering the conversation and, 107
 evaluating sources and, 105, 107
 research and, 90, 105, 107
 rhetorical context and, 8
 signal phrases and, 113
 writing purpose and, 2

statement of scope, 76
stationary, stationery, 365
statistics, 46, 115, 416
stereotyping language, 15, 376

strategy, 19–25 A pattern for orga-
nizing text to ANALYZE CAUSE AND EF-
FECT, CLASSIFY AND DIVIDE, COMPARE
AND CONTRAST, DEFINE, DESCRIBE, EX-
PLAIN A PROCESS, give EXAMPLES, and
NARRATE.

style In writing, the arrangement of
sentences, CLAUSES, PHRASES, words,
and punctuation to achieve a desired
effect; also, the rules of capitalization, punctuation, and so on for DOC-
UMENTATION of a source.
 literary analyses and, 64–65

subject, 314–15 The NOUN or PRO-
NOUN plus any MODIFIERS that tell
who or what a sentence or CLAUSE
is about. A simple subject is a single
noun or pronoun. A complete subject
is the simple subject plus any modifiers. In the sentence *Ten commuters*

waited for the late bus, the complete subject is *Ten commuters* and the simple subject is *commuters*. *See also* subject-verb agreement
  complete subjects, 294
  editing sentences and, 14
  expressing explicitly, 315–16
  sentence fragments and, 318
  simple subjects, 293, 294

subject case, 342

subject complement, 343 A word that follows a LINKING VERB and modifies the SUBJECT of a sentence. A subject complement tells more about the subject: *The tennis players are disappointed about losing the tournament last week.*

subject directories, 100

subject-verb agreement, 334–39 The agreement in number (singular or plural) and person (first, second, or third) of a SUBJECT and its VERB: *Danny rides his bike to school; his brothers ride the bus.*
  agreement in number and person, 335
  collective nouns, 337
  compound subjects, 336
  editing, 292–95
  indefinite pronouns and, 337
  relative pronouns and, 338
  subjects and verbs separated, 336
  subjects following verbs, 336–37
  titles and words used as words, 339
  who, that, which, 338
  words such as *news* and *physics*, 338–39

subjunctive mood, 330–32

subordinate clause A clause that begins with a SUBORDINATING WORD and therefore cannot stand alone as a sentence: *She feels good when she exercises. My roommate, who was a physics major, tutors students in science.*
  editing comma splices, 321
  emphasizing idea, 349
  who, whom, 344

subordinating word, 31 A word such as a RELATIVE PRONOUN or a subordinating conjunction that introduces a SUBORDINATE CLAUSE: *The ice sculpture melted because the ballroom was too hot.* Common subordinating words include *although, as, because, if, since, that, which*, and *why*.
  editing comma splices, 274–75, 321
  editing fused sentences, 277
  sentence fragments and, 318

subordination and coordination, 348–49
subtitles, capitalizing, 410
such as, comma with, 391
suffixes, hyphens with, 407–8

summary, 107–8, 112–13 The use of one's own words and sentence structure to condense someone else's text into a briefer version that gives the main ideas of the original. As with PARAPHRASING and QUOTATION, summarizing requires DOCUMENTATION.
  in conclusions, 29
  documenting, 113
  integrating sources
    APA style, 173, 174
    Chicago style, 210

summary (cont.)
general guidelines, 112–13
as reading strategy, 85
specific types of text
abstracts, 81
annotated bibliographies, 74, 78
rhetorical analysis, 49, 51
topic and, 109
transitions to signal, 27
superlatives
forming and using, 371–72
the with, 374
surveys, 102

synthesis, 105–7 A process of bringing together ideas and information from multiple sources in order to discover patterns and gain new insights and perspectives.

T

tables, 34, 202–3
tag questions, 390
television programs, documenting
APA style, 197
MLA style, 157–58
templates, 31

tense, 322–24 A characteristic of VERBS that indicates the time when action occurs or expresses a state of being. The three main tenses are the present (*I play*), the past (*I played*), and the future (*I will play*). Each tense has perfect (*I have played*), progressive (*I am playing*), and perfect progressive (*I have been playing*) forms. *See also* verb *and specific tenses*

editing, 295–98
literary analysis and, 64–65
modals, 328–29
regular and irregular forms, 324–26
shifts in, 295–98
signal phrases in APA, *Chicago*, CSE, and MLA styles, 114–15
why it matters, 295

testimony, 46
text messages, documenting
APA style, 195
MLA style, 152
textual analysis. *See* rhetorical analyses
textual evidence, 46
than and pronoun case, 343
than, then, 365
that
specific antecedent for, 342
subject-verb agreement and, 338
as subordinating word, 318
vs. *which*, 365
the, 373–75
when to capitalize in titles, 410
then, than, 365
there, their, they're, 310–12, 365
there is, it is, 310–12, 365, 368–69
therefore, as transition, 349

thesis, 46 A statement that identifies the TOPIC and main point of a piece of writing, giving readers an idea of what the text will cover.

in academic writing, 6
evaluative, 64
for specific types of writing
abstracts, 81
arguments, 52, 86
literary analysis, 62, 64
reflections, 72
reports, 56
rhetorical analyses, 52
tentative, 10–11

they
  indefinite use, 342
  singular, 288, 341, 378
they're, their, there, 310–12, 365
third person. *See* person and number
this, specific antecedent for, 342
though, as subordinating word, 318
time, 414–15, 416
title pages, formatting
  APA style, 200, 204
  Chicago style, 238, 241
  CSE style, 260, 263
  MLA style, 158, 161
titles, personal, 410, 414
titles of works
  capitalizing, 411
  italics, 411–12
  quotation marks, 397
  in specific styles
    APA style, 179
    Chicago style, 211
    CSE style, 248
    MLA style, 131
to, too, two, 365

tone, 4–5 The way a writer's or speaker's STANCE toward the readers and subject is reflected in the text.
  academic writing and, 7–8
  formal and informal, 37–38
  trustworthy, 44

topic, 4 The specific subject written about in a text. A topic should be narrow enough to cover, not too broad or general. A topic needs to be developed appropriately for its AUDIENCE and PURPOSE.
  appropriate language and, 380
  for arguments, 45
  choosing, 45, 59, 90–91
  indicating why it matters, 8

  narrowing, 56, 90–91
  of personal narratives, 59
  of reports, 54, 55
  research and, 90–91
  of rhetorical analysis, 50

topic proposal A statement of intent to examine a topic; also called a proposal ABSTRACT. Some instructors require a topic proposal in order to assess the feasibility of the writing project that a student has in mind. Key Features: concise discussion of the subject • clear statement of the intended focus • rationale for choosing the subject • mention of resources

topic sentence, 18–19 A sentence, often at the beginning of a paragraph, that states the paragraph's main point. The details in the rest of the paragraph should support the topic sentence.

transition, 26–28 A word or PHRASE that helps to connect sentences and paragraphs and to guide readers through a text. Transitions can help to show comparisons (*also, similarly*); contrasts (*but, instead*); examples (*for instance, in fact*); sequence (*finally, next*); time (*at first, meanwhile*); and more.

  with commas, 389
  common academic, 357–59
  editing paragraphs, 14
  list of, 26–28
  in presentations, 37
  with semicolons, 321, 392

translations, documenting
  APA style, 183
  Chicago style, 217–18
  MLA style, 135

trustworthiness, 44. *See also* credibility

Turabian, Kate L., *A Manual for Writers or Research Papers, Theses, and Dissertations*, 208, 240

tweets, documenting
  APA style, 196
  MLA style, 152

Twitter searches, 99

U

uninterested, disinterested, 362

unique, 365

University of Chicago Press style. *See Chicago* style

unknown authors, documenting
  APA style, 176, 183, 186
  Chicago style, 217
  MLA style, 125, 135

unless, as subordinating word, 318

unnecessary words, 368–69

until, as subordinating word, 318

URLs
  accessing through databases, 96
  dividing, 408
  documenting
    APA style, 177, 187–88
    Chicago style, 226, 231
    CSE style, 255
    MLA style, 130, 133
  relevance of sources and, 103–4
  stable, 99

us, we, 345

V

vagueness, avoiding, 15

values, appealing to readers, 44

vantage point The physical position from which a writer DESCRIBES something.

verb, 322–34 A word that expresses an action (*dance, talk*) or a state of being (*be, seem*). A verb is an essential element of a sentence or CLAUSE. Verbs have four forms: base form (*smile*), past tense (*smiled*), PAST PARTICIPLE (*smiled*), and PRESENT PARTICIPLE (*smiling*). *See also* base form
  active and passive, 329–30
  base form, 324
  conditional, 330–31
  gerunds, 326
  editing, 291–98
  helping, 327–29
  infinitives, 326
  irregular, 325
  main (*see* main verb)
  modals (*can, should*, etc.), 328–29
  phrasal, 332–34
  regular, 324–25
  signal verbs, 113–14
  subject-verb agreement, 292–25, 334–39
  tense, 322–24 (*see also* tense)

verse plays, documenting MLA style, 125

versions, documenting MLA style, 131

video collections, 100

video games, documenting
  APA style, 198–99
  MLA style, 158

videos, documenting
  APA style, 194, 195, 196
  Chicago style, 234, 237
  CSE style, 259
  MLA style, 156

visual, 33–36 A photograph, chart, graph, table, video, or similar item used as part of a writer's text.

captions, 36
  obtaining permission for, 36
  in presentations, 39
  reading, 86–88
  tips for using, 36
  types of, 34–35
    bar graphs, 35
    diagrams, 35
    flowcharts, 35
    line graphs, 35
    pie charts, 34
    photographs, 34
    tables, 34

visual sources, documenting
  APA style, 196–200
  MLA style, 153–58
visual texts, reading, 86–88
The Voice of the Shuttle, 100

W

was. See be
we, us, 345
weather, whether, 365
web searching. *See* internet research
websites, documenting
  APA style, 188–89, 193
  Chicago style, 231–33
  CSE style, 256, 258
  MLA style, 149–51
well, good, 363, 371
when, as subordinating word, 318
where, as subordinating word, 318
whether, as subordinating word, 318
whether, weather, 365
whether . . . or, 349
which
  specific antecedent for, 342
  subject-verb agreement and, 338
  as subordinating word, 318
  vs. *that*, 365

while, as subordinating word, 318
whiteboards, 39
white space, 32
who
  subject-verb agreement and, 338
  as subordinating word, 318
  vs. *whom*, 344
whom, who, 344
who's, whose, 365
why, as subordinating word, 318
wiki entries, documenting
  APA style, 194
  MLA style, 151
will, 328, 329
words
  abstract, 354
  appropriateness of, 351–53
  clichés, 352–53
  concrete, 354
  empty, 368
  Englishes, 379–85
  formal and informal, 351, 381
  jargon, 352
  non-English, 413
  precise, 353–54
  pretentious language, 352
  qualifying, 6, 10
  sexist language, 377–78
  that build common ground,
    376–78, 385
  unnecessary, 368–69
words as words, italics for, 412
words often confused, 361–65
  editing, 309–13
wordy phrases, 369

working bibliography, 91 A record of all sources consulted during research. Each entry provides all the bibliographic information necessary for correct DOCUMENTATION of each source, including author, title, and

working bibliography (cont.)
publication information. A working bibliography is a useful tool for recording and keeping track of sources.

works-cited list, 129–58 A list at the end of a researched text prepared in MLA STYLE or CHICAGO STYLE that contains full bibliographic information for all the sources cited in the text.
  core elements, 129–34
    authors and other contributors, 130–31
    dates, 132
    location, 132–33
    numbers, 131
    publishers, 132
    punctuation, 133–34
    titles, 131
    versions, 131
  MLA documentation style, 129–58

works in an anthology, documenting
  APA style, 183
  MLA style, 145–46
work without page numbers, documenting
  APA style, 177
  MLA style, 128
would, as modal verb, 328, 329
would of, would have, 365

writing context, 2–5 The rhetorical situation in which writing or other communication takes place, including PURPOSE, AUDIENCE, GENRE, TOPIC, STANCE, TONE, MEDIUM, and DESIGN.
  academic contexts, 6–8
  audience, 8

  design, 8, 30
  genre, 8
  media, 8
  purpose, 8

writing portfolio A collection of writing selected by a writer to show his or her work, including a statement assessing the work and explaining what it demonstrates.

writing process, 9–16 In writing, a series of actions that may include GENERATING IDEAS AND TEXT, DRAFTING, REVISING, EDITING, and PROOFREADING.
  brainstorming, 9
  clustering, 9
  collaborating, 16
  drafting, 11–12
  editing, 13–15
  freewriting, 9
  generating ideas, 9–10
  looping, 9
  proofreading, 15
  questioning, 9
  revising, 13

WWW Virtual Library, 100

Y

yes, no, commas with, 390
yet, linking ideas with, 348, 386
you, specific antecedent for, 342
your, you're, 365

Revision Symbols

abbr	abbreviation **413**	^	insert
adj	adjective **370**	*i/p*	interesting point
adv	adverb **370**	*ital*	italics **411**
agr	agreement **334, 339**	*jarg*	jargon **352**
⌄	apostrophe **399**	*lc*	lowercase letter **409**
no ⌄	unnecessary apostrophe **402**	*mm*	misplaced modifier **372**
art	article **373**	*nice*	well done!
awk	awkward*	*num*	number **415**
cap	capitalization **409**	¶	new paragraph
case	pronoun case **342**	//	parallelism **345**
cite	citation needed **107–118**	*pass*	passive voice **329**
cliché	cliché **352**	*ref*	pronoun reference **341**
⌣	close up space	*run-on*	comma splice or fused sentence **320**
^	comma needed **386**	*sexist*	sexist language **377**
no ^	unnecessary comma **391**	*shift*	confusing shift **349**
cs	comma splice **320**	*sl*	slang **351**
def	define **22**	#	insert space
~	delete	*sp*	spelling
dm	dangling modifier **373**	*trans*	transition **25**
doc	documentation **119–265**	~	transpose
emph	emphasis **349**	*vb*	verb **322**
frag	sentence fragment **317**	*wrdy*	wordy **368**
fs	fused sentence **320**	*ww*	wrong word **361**
hyph	hyphen **407**		

*__Awk__ usually indicates a problem with phrasing that cannot be easily described in a brief marginal comment. If you can't figure out the problem, ask your instructor for clarification.

MLA Documentation Directory

IN-TEXT DOCUMENTATION 122
NOTES 129
LIST OF WORKS CITED 129
Core Elements 129
Authors and Other Contributors 134
1. One author *134*
2. Two authors *134*
3. Three or more authors *134*
4. Two or more works
by the same author *135*
5. Author and editor
or translator *135*
6. No author or editor *135*
7. Organization or government
as author *136*

Articles and Other Short Works 136
Documentation Maps 137, 138, 140
8. Article in a journal *136*
9. Article in a magazine *139*
10. Article in a newspaper *139*
11. Article from a database *141*
12. Entry in a reference work *141*
13. Editorial *142*
14. Letter to the editor *142*
15. Review *143*
16. Comment on online article *143*

Books and Parts of Books 144
Documentation Map 145
17. Basic entries for a book *144*
18. Anthology *144*
19. Work in an anthology *144*
20. Multivolume work *146*
21. Book in a series *146*
22. Graphic narrative *147*
23. Sacred text *147*
24. Edition other than the first *147*

25. Republished work *147*
26. Foreword, introduction, preface,
or afterword *148*
27. Published letter *148*
28. Paper at a conference *148*
29. Dissertation *149*

Websites 149
Documentation Map 150
30. Entire website *149*
31. Work on a website *151*
32. Blog entry *151*
33. Wiki *151*

Personal Communication
and Social Media 151
34. Personal letter *151*
35. Email *151*
36. Text message *152*
37. Post to an online forum *152*
38. Post to social media 152

Audio, Visual, and Other Sources 153
39. Advertisement *153*
40. Art *153*
41. Cartoon *154*
42. Court case *154*
43. Film *154*
44. Interview *155*
45. Map *155*
46. Musical score *156*
47. Online video *156*
48. Oral presentation *156*
49. Podcast *156*
50. Radio program *157*
51. Sound recording *157*
52. TV show *157*
53. Video game *158*

APA Documentation Directory

IN-TEXT DOCUMENTATION 173
NOTES 178
REFERENCE LIST 179
Print Books 179
Documentation Map 180
1. One author 181
2. Two or more works by the same author 181
3. Two or more authors 181
4. Organization or government as author 182
5. Author and editor 182
6. Edited collection 182
7. Work in an edited collection 183
8. Unknown author 183
9. Edition other than the first 183
10. Translation 183
11. Multivolume work 184
12. Article in a reference book 184

Print Periodicals 184
13. Article in a journal paginated by volume 185
14. Article in a journal paginated by issue 185
15. Article in a magazine 186
16. Article in a newspaper 186
17. Interview in a periodical 186
18. Article by unknown author 186
19. Book review 187
20. Letter to the editor 187

Online Sources 187
Documentation Maps 189, 190, 194
21. Work from a nonperiodical website 188

22. Article in an online periodical 191
23. Comment on an online article 191
24. Article from a database 192
25. Article or chapter from the web or an online reference work 192
26. Electronic book 192
27. Wiki entry 193
28. Blog entry 193
29. Online video 193
30. Podcast 195
31. Episode from a TV show or other series found online 195

Personal Communication and Social Media 195
32. Personal letter, email, text message, or conversation 195
33. Post to an online forum 195
34. Post to social media 196

Audio, Visual, Multimedia, and Other Sources 196
35. Film, video, or DVD 196
36. Music recording 196
37. Proceedings of a conference 196
38. Television program 197
39. Computer software 197
40. Government document 197
41. Dissertation 198
42. Technical or research report 198
43. Video game 198
44. Data set or graph 199
45. Map 199
46. Advertisement 199

Chicago Documentation Directory

Print Books 211

Documentation Map 213

1. One author *212*
2. Multiple authors *214*
3. Organization or corporation as author *214*
4. Author and editor *215*
5. Editor only *215*
6. Part of a book *216*
7. Unknown author *217*
8. Translation *217*
9. Edition other than the first *218*
10. Multivolume work *218*
11. Dictionary or encyclopedia entry *219*
12. Published letter *219*
13. Book in a series *220*
14. Sacred text *220*
15. Source quoted in another source *220*

Print Periodicals 221

Documentation Maps 224, 225

16. Article in a journal *221*
17. Article in a magazine *222*
18. Article in a newspaper *222*
19. Unsigned article *222*
20. Book review *223*

Online Sources 226

Documentation Maps 230, 233

21. Article in an online journal *227*
22. Article in an online magazine *227*
23. Online newspaper article *228*
24. Article from a database *228*
25. Ebook *229*
26. Website *231*
27. Blog entry *232*
28. Video *234*
29. Podcast *234*
30. Email or online posting *235*

Other Kinds of Sources 235

31. Broadcast interview *235*
32. Sound recording *236*
33. Video or DVD *237*
34. Government publication *237*

CSE Documentation Directory

Print Books   248

Documentation Map   250

1. One author   *249*
2. Multiple authors   *249*
3. Organization or corporation as author   *249*
4. Editor   *251*
5. Work in an edited collection   *251*
6. Chapter of a book   *251*
7. Paper or abstract from conference proceedings   *251*
8. Edition other than the first   *252*

Print Periodicals   252

Documentation Map   253

9. Article in a journal   *252*
10. Article in a magazine   *254*
11. Article in a newspaper   *254*

Online Sources   254

Documentation Map   257

12. Online book   *255*
13. Article accessed through a database   *255*
14. Article in an online journal   *256*
15. Article in an online newspaper   *256*
16. Website   *256*
17. Part of a website   *258*
18. Image or infographic   *258*
19. Podcast or webcast   *259*
20. Video   *259*
21. Blog entry   *259*
22. Social media post   *260*